ORDER IN DISORDER

ORDER IN DISORDER

Intratextual Symmetry in Montaigne's "Essais"

Randolph Paul Runyon

THE OHIO STATE UNIVERSITY PRESS | COLUMBUS

Copyright © 2013 by The Ohio State University.
All rights reserved.

Library of Congress Cataloging-in-Publication Data
Runyon, Randolph, 1947–
Order in disorder : intratextual symmetry in Montaigne's Essais / Randolph Paul Runyon.
p. cm.
Includes bibliographical references and index.
ISBN-13: 978-0-8142-1240-0 (cloth : alk. paper)
ISBN-10: 0-8142-1240-9 (cloth : alk. paper)
ISBN-13: 978-0-8142-9342-3 (cd-rom)
ISBN-10: 0-8142-9342-5 (cd-rom)
Montaigne, Michel de, 1533–1592. Essais—Criticism and interpretation. 2. Symmetry in literature. I. Title.
PQ1645.R86 2013
844'.3—dc23
                                                    2013012565

Cover design by Laurence J. Nozik
Text design by Juliet Williams
Type set in Adobe Garamond Pro
Printed by Thomson-Shore, Inc.

♾ The paper used in this publication meets the minimum requirements of the American National Standard for Information Sciences—Permanence of Paper for Printed Library Materials. ANSI Z39.48–1992.

9 8 7 6 5 4 3 2 1

CONTENTS

Acknowledgments	ix
INTRODUCTION: Marginal Symmetry	1
I. BOOK ONE	26
1. Of Means and Ends: I: 1 and I: 57	26
2. The Less Said: I: 2 and I: 56	31
3. Something to Hide: I: 3 and I: 55	36
4. Frivolous and Vain: I: 4 and I: 54	41
5. In or Out: I: 5 and I: 53	49
6. Trouble Back Home: I: 6 and I: 52	52
7. Words, in Effect: I: 7 and I: 51	55
8. Of Idleness and Horses: I: 8 and I: 50	58
9. Lying, After a Fashion: I: 9 and I: 49	63
10. Excess Baggage: I: 10 and I: 48	66
11. Enough Already: I: 11 and I: 47	70
12. Anagrams: I: 12 and I: 46	72
13. A Waiting Game: I: 13 and I: 45	74
14. More Than One Port in a Storm: I: 14 and I: 44	75
15. Custom and Princely Grandeur: I: 15 and I: 43	78
16. Judging Julian Judging: I: 16 and I: 42	80
17. Glory, Given and Taken: I: 17 and I: 41	82
18. Empty Signs: I: 18 and I: 40	84

19. Prolonging Life: I: 19 and I: 39 — 88
20. Unmasking Masks: I: 20 and I: 38 — 90
21. Powers of Attraction: I: 21 and I: 37 — 92
22. Complementarities and Buried Allusions: I: 22 and I: 36 — 95
23. Here and There: I: 23 and I: 35 — 96
24. How to Paint a Dog: I: 24 and I: 34 — 98
25. Well-Nourished Daughters: I: 25 and I: 33 — 102
26. God's Wrath and the Weather: I: 26 and I: 32 — 106
27. Things to Come: I: 27 and I: 31 — 109
28. Of Immoderation: I: 28 and I: 30 — 112

II. BOOK TWO — 119

1. Sorting Out the Pieces: II: 1 and II: 37 — 119
2. Slipping It In: II: 2 and II: 36 — 121
3. Suicide Is Painless: II: 3 and II: 35 — 125
4. Caesar the Procrastinator: II: 4 and II: 34 — 130
5. Suffering Innocence: II: 5 and II: 33 — 132
6. Parallel Deaths: II: 6 and II: 32 — 136
7. Rewards and Punishments: II: 7 and II: 31 — 141
8. Hidden Monsters: II: 8 and II: 30 — 143
9. Only When You Need It: II: 9 and II: 29 — 149
10. Act Your Age: II: 10 and II: 28 — 151
11. Doubly Cruel: II: 11 and II: 27 — 155
12. Opposable Thumbs: II: 12 and II: 26 — 159
13. Eyes Wide Shut: II: 13 and II: 25 — 167
14. Equivalent Equivalents: II: 14 and II: 24 — 172
15. Civil War vs. Civil War: II: 15 and II: 23 — 176
16. Spreading the News: II: 16 and II: 22 — 179
17. Spitting Images: II: 17 and II: 21 — 182
18. Consubstantial Consubstantiality: II: 18 and II: 20 — 187

III. BOOK THREE — 190

1. Distant Harmonies: III: 1 and III: 13 — 190
2. Distant Theft: III: 2 and III: 12 — 197
3. Intercourse with the Lame: III: 3 and III: 11 — 203
4. The Little Things: III: 4 and III: 10 — 209
5. Sexual Vanity, Vain Sex: III: 5 and III: 9 — 213
6. Borrowed Wealth: III: 6 and III: 8 — 217

IV. JOURNEY TO THE CENTER OF THE BOOK   225
   I: 29, II: 19, and III: 7   225

EPILOGUE: The Playful Text   253

Appendix   257
Works Cited   265
Index of Names   273
Index to the *Essays*   275

ACKNOWLEDGMENTS

My fascination with Montaigne was ignited many years ago by Professor Jean Paris in an inspiring seminar he taught at Johns Hopkins University. With his generous encouragement I began what became a lifelong journey to the center of the *Essays*. He enabled early publication of some initial findings in 1973 in the Parisian journal *Change* and persuaded the organizers of a Renaissance Symposium held at SUNY-Albany in October 1975 to invite me to speak in his place. I continued to develop my readings of the *Essays'* symmetries at conferences held by the Modern Language Association, the Sixteenth-Century Society, the Groupe de Recherche sur le Recueil, the University of Massachusetts at Amherst, and the University of Cincinnati. Earlier versions of my argument appeared in two volumes edited by Daniel Martin, *The Order of Montaigne's "Essays"* (Hestia Press, 1989) and *Montaigne and the Gods* (Hestia Press, 1993); in *Essays in European Literature for Walter Strauss*, edited by Alice N. Benston and Marshall C. Olds (Studies in Twentieth-Century Literature, 1990); in *Le Recueil littéraire: Pratiques et théorie d'une forme*, edited by Irène Langlet (Presses Universitaires de Rennes, 2003); and in *Freedom Over Servitude: Montaigne, La Boétie, and "On Voluntary Servitude,"* edited by David Lewis Schaefer (Greenwood Press, 1998).

I am grateful to the students of my graduate seminars at Miami University for allowing me to test out and clarify these readings of the *Essays*. I am indebted to the manuscript's readers at The Ohio State University Press for helping me to improve it and avoid a number of errors, though of course they are not responsible for those it may still contain. Heartfelt thanks are due to the Press's Eugene O'Connor for his eagle eye and most especially to Senior Editor Sandy Crooms for her unflagging and resourceful support.

Most of all, thanks go to Elizabeth, who for years has patiently listened as I enthused over the *Essays* and told me what worked and what didn't.

My translation of La Boétie's 29 sonnets, the original middle of Book One of the *Essays,* together with some additional discussion of the connections between chapters 5 and 8 in Book Three, may be found in an online appendix at the following url: https://ohiostatepress.org/Books/Book%20Pages/Runyon%20Order.html

INTRODUCTION
Marginal Symmetry

MONTAIGNE BEGINS "De l'amitié" [Of friendship] (I: 28), the chapter[1] that comes just before the middle of the first book of the *Essays,* by talking about a middle that corresponds to that one and hinting at the way his book may be arranged:

> Considerant la conduicte de la besoingne d'un peintre que j'ay, il m'a pris envie de l'ensuivre. Il choisit le plus noble endroit & milieu de chasque paroy, pour y loger un tableau elabouré de toute sa suffisance, & le vuide tout au tour il le remplit de crotesques, qui sont peintures fantasques, n'ayants grace qu'en la varieté & estrangeté. Que sont-ce icy aussi à la verité que crotesques & corps monstrueux, rappiecez de divers membres, sans certaine figure, n'ayants ordre, suite ny proportion que fortuite? Desinit in pescem mulier formosa superne.

---

1. I follow André Tournon in referring to the constituent parts of the *Essays* as chapters instead of essays: "the term *essay* being reserved, in line with Montaigne's usage, for the operation that takes place throughout the text" (*Route par ailleurs: Le « nouveau langage » des* Essais [Paris: Honoré Champion, 2006], 12). Patrick Henry argues that "It can never be overstressed . . . that the word 'essais,' as employed by Montaigne, refers to his entire work, not to the one hundred and seven individual segments which he calls 'chapitres.' The latter term obviously suggests a unified work, parts of a whole, not independent pieces" (p. 859 of "Reading Montaigne Contextually: 'De l'incommodité de la grandeur' (III, 7)" (*The French Review* 61.6 [May 1988]: 859–65).

[As I was considering the way a painter I employ went about his work, I was taken with the desire to imitate him. He chooses the noblest place, the middle of each wall, to place a picture labored over with all his skill, and the empty space all around it he fills with grotesques, which are fantastic paintings whose only charm lies in their variety and strangeness. What are these here too, in truth, but grotesques and monstrous bodies, pieced together of divers members, with no definite shape, having no order, sequence, or proportion other than by chance? "A lovely woman tapers off into a fish."] (I: 28, 183a, DM 252–53; 135*)[2]

When he asks "Que sont-ce icy" [What are these here] he means the *Essays*, as he is preparing the reader for the next chapter, the numerically central one of the fifty-seven of which Book One is composed, and thus "le plus noble endroit & milieu" [the noblest place, the middle] in which he will put a text borrowed from his late friend Etienne de La Boétie.

But what does he mean by "crotesques"? The word comes from the Italian *grotto*, a cave. In the late fifteenth century, a young Roman fell through a crevice on a hill and found himself in what he thought was a subterranean cavern. It was actually the ruins of Nero's *Domus Aurea*, an extensive complex the emperor had built as a residence after the fire of 64 C.E. After his death, the Romans covered it in with earth, erected new constructions above it, and Nero's pleasure palace eventually faded from memory. When it was rediscovered in the Renaissance, the wall paintings that came to be known as grotesques were a revelation that sent shock waves through the world of art. Raphael and other artists visited these rooms to study the decorations and translate them into their own work. The "crotesques" to which Montaigne likens his *Essays* are essentially symmetrical, as Emmanuel Naya explains, "combining leafy interlacings with a profusion of fantastical subjects, hybrid beings proliferating in such a way as to suggest, beneath the symmetry of the arrangements, an impression of disorder."[3] This form of decoration was not

---

2. Where possible I quote from the 1580 edition for Books One and Two, and the 1588 edition for Book Three, citing them as DM, using Daniel Martin's photographic reproduction (Geneva: Slatkine, 1976 and 1988). I modernize the spelling only to the extent of incorporating the letters *j* and *v* and an accented *à* where appropriate. I do not italicize Montaigne's Latin quotations, as he did, so that I may reserve italics for certain key words not italicized in the original; all italics, therefore, are mine. Other passages are quoted from Pierre Villey's edition (Paris: Presses Universitaires de France, 1964). I give page numbers in Villey in any case, followed by those in the first edition (indicated by DM); the number after the semicolon indicates the page in Donald Frame's translation (*The Complete Essays of Montaigne*, tr. Donald M. Frame [Stanford: Stanford University Press, 1965]); an asterisk indicates that I have altered that translation. I provide my own translations of other texts originally in French.

3. Montaigne, *Essais I*, ed. Emmanuel Naya, Delphine Reguig-Naya, and Alexandre Tarrête (Paris: Gallimard Folio Classique, 2009), 645.

new when Nero built his palace, going back to at least 100 B.C.E. Yet it was new to the Renaissance. Geoffrey Harpham writes that it was characterized by

> symmetrical anatomical impossibilities, small beasts, human heads, and delicate, indeterminate vegetables, all presented as ornament with a faintly mythological character imparted by representations of fauns, nymphs, satyrs, and centaurs. . . . In them the eye is continually soothed by the balance and proportion of the figures, and continually reassured that nothing means or coheres, nothing signifies. All is lively and symmetrical.[4]

These symmetries often appeared, especially in their Renaissance reincarnations, in vertical chains on either side of a central axis—as they do on the title page of the 1588 edition of the *Essays* themselves. When Montaigne says of his own "grotesques" that they have no "ordre, suite ny proportion que fortuite" [order, sequence, or proportion other than by chance] he is alluding to this Roman style, of which Vitruvius complained that it depicted

> monsters rather than definite representations taken from definite things. Instead of columns there rise up stalks; instead of gables, striped panels with curled leaves and volutes. Candelabra uphold pictured shrines and above the summits of these, clusters of thin stalks rise from their roots in tendrils with little figures seated upon them at random. Again, slender stalks with heads of men and animals attached to half the body. Such things neither are, nor can be, nor have been. . . . For how can a reed actually sustain a roof . . . or a soft and slender stalk a seated statue, or how can flowers and half-statues rise alternatively from roots and stalks?[5]

As Naya puts it—"beneath the symmetry of the arrangements, an impression of disorder"—it combines order and chaos. The order arises from the horizontal symmetry, the disorder from the vertical chain that suggests but immediately contradicts a cause-and-effect relationship between weak reeds and the statues they supposedly support (Montaigne alludes to those impos-

---

4. Geoffrey Harpham, *On the Grotesque: Strategies of Contradiction in Art and Literature* (Princeton: Princeton University Press, 1982), 26, 30. See also Nicole Dacos, *La découverte de la Domus Aurea et la formation des grotesques à la Renaissance* (London: The Warburg Institute, 1969), who writes that Renaissance artists inspired by the Nero's palace created systems "composed of repeated elements that alternated or were divided symmetrically on either side of an axis. . . . These decorative types are at the origin of almost all grotesques, whether they extended vertically or horizontally" (52).

5. Vitruvius, *De Architectura*, quoted in Harpham, 26. Vitruvius was writing at an earlier time, but describing the same style.

sibilities here in quoting Horace about what begins as a woman but ends as a fish).[6] The *Essays* are similarly a combination of order and disorder, of planning and chance.

My thesis is that Montaigne was being very specific, and truthful, in describing his book in this way. The chapters of his *Essays* are indeed grotesques, a combination on the one hand of illogical disorder, when read in sequence from one chapter to the next (and, as many readers have realized, within many a chapter), and on the other persistent symmetry, when read with attention to the way he arranged them around the center of each of his three books: I: 29, II: 19, and III: 7. Every chapter to the left of those centers has a symmetrical companion to the right with which it shares rarely-occurring words and phrases in addition to parallel situations; the three central chapters are linked to each other in the same way. In Appendix A I list 165 of those symmetrical lexical links, of which 76 (46%) feature words or phrases, some of which are combined with situational similarities, that either appear nowhere else in the *Essays* at all (there are 57 such occurrences) or appear nowhere else in their Book (there are 19 instances) save in symmetrically arranged chapters. Each of the 52 chapter pairs (28 in Book One, 18 in Book Two, 6 in Book Three) provides at least one lexical link; 47 (90%) give two or more; 23 of them give three or more. Of the 52 chapter pairs, 37 (71%) offer lexical links unique either to their Book or to the *Essays* as a whole. The rarity of these lexical connections is attested by Roy E. Leake's *Concordance* to the *Essays*.[7]

The situational similarities that link each of the chapters are not the amorphous thematic parallels Michel Butor suggested in *Essais sur les Essais*, though it was reading his book in 1969 that prompted me to seek out the symmetries I eventually found.[8] Butor had the merit of calling our attention to the supreme significance of the mysterious chapter I: 29, which is easy to miss in most editions today because it either isn't there (since Montaigne removed it in his plans for an edition he did not live to complete) or is

---

6. Where did Montaigne see this painter of his create such a work? Some tantalizing traces remain of paintings on the walls of the "cabinet" in Montaigne's chateau, but Alain Legros finds that although "the rare vestiges certainly show 'variété' around the central paintings," there can be found "no 'peinture fantasque,' no trace of 'corps monstrueux, rappiecez de divers membres'" (Alain Legros, *Essais sur poutres: Peintures et inscriptions chez Montaigne* [Paris: Klincksieck, 2000], 126). He wonders if they might have been painted on a wall that had been redone later, or in a room on the floor below, or somewhere else in the chateau. Later he comments that Montaigne's "intention was less to describe the work of his painter *in this room* . . . than his own writing practice, his original *dispositio* . . . more enchanting than laboriously-wrought paintings and well-made books" (169).

7. Roy E. Leake, *Concordance des Essais de Montaigne* (Geneva: Droz, 1981).

8. Michel Butor, *Essais sur les Essais* (Paris: Gallimard, 1968).

relegated to an appendix at the end. But the few symmetries Butor proposes, in addition to not really being based on I: 29 as the absolute center of Book One but on an alleged "double center" composed of I: 28 and I: 29, are not compelling:

> Thus chapter 30, "Of moderation," continues the discouraging comments on marriage of chapter 28; chapter 32, "That we should meddle soberly with judging divine ordinances," responds to 27, "It is folly to measure the true and false by our own competence"; chapter 34, "Fortune is often met in the path of reason," pursues what is said about fortune in 24, "Various outcomes from the same plan." One can then see that the chapter on clothing, I: 36, responds to that on the imagination, I: 21, and naturally the one on Cato the Younger, I: 37, to I: 20, "That to philosophize is to learn to die." (*Essais sur les Essais*, 73)

With I: 29 as the center, Butor's pairings of I: 27 with I: 32, I: 21 with I: 36, and I: 20 with I: 37 disappear; what he says of the continuities linking I: 28 with I: 30 and I: 24 with I: 34 is true, but hardly scratches the surface of the wealth of connections that are actually there. He rightly gives II: 19 a place of honor as the center of Book Two and notes that the symmetrically aligned chapters II: 11 and II: 27 both allude to cruelty in their titles, but it is highly unusual that a pair of chapters should advertise their symmetrical connection on the surface. Obviously most do not, for if they did there would not be much disagreement about the *Essays*' symmetrical structure. A theme as broad as cruelty can be found in many places in the *Essays:* the word *cruauté* appears in 24 chapters other than II: 11 and II: 27; *fortune*, which Butor thought connected I: 24 and I: 34, appears in 33 other chapters within Book One alone. André Tournon cites Butor's pairings and then comments:

> To these one could add the theme of imperturbability in chapters I: 12 and I: 44, inane predictions in I: 11 and I: 47, illusions of language in I: 9 and I: 51, and those of thought in I: 4 and I: 53. Someone who would be satisfied by more strained connections might uncover other correspondences, for instance between I: 22 and I: 33 on social competition and cooperation. The text lends itself to these "vain subtleties," and it matters little that the numerical center of these perceived couplings is only approximate. For it is not a question of arithmetic but of disposition, and as we know the decorative motifs of "grotesques" always involve slight distortions in the balancing pattern: the corresponding figures are similar, but different, and even the foliage that at first glance gives an impression of perfect symmetry is

not strictly identical from left to right. The point of these figures is to present the appearance of a proliferation that is almost orderly, of almost controlled aberration, where the threat of chaos is diverted into artistic caprice. Is this to say that in comparing his book to those "grotesques" Montaigne admits to having adopted a resolutely ludic and ornamental agenda? This is hardly likely.[9]

It would be pointless indeed to look for a pattern in the placement of themes like cruelty and fortune (Butor) or imperturbability and inane predictions (Tournon), for precisely because they are among Montaigne's major concerns they will tend to appear in more places than two. The components of the symmetrical connections I will reveal are so much more specific, subtle, and elaborate that it is surprising that they could even appear more than once, and all the more surprising that these sorts of complex repetitions keep appearing in symmetrically corresponding chapters. In other words, I am not at all concerned with the placement of themes, major or minor, but instead with symmetrically placed lexemes and situational parallels.

Besides, if we want to figure out what Montaigne meant by saying that his surrounding chapters are equivalent to surrounding grotesques there is no point in looking for major themes, because what appear in the mirroring grotesques, for example in the engraving by Nicoletto da Modena that Tournon reproduces to accompany the passage I quoted above, are nothing like major themes. In that engraving the major themes, the Judgment of Paris and Orpheus playing his violin for an audience of animals, are presented in the central axis. The grotesques on either side are crescent moons with human faces, warriors, Cupids, birds, enchained captives, and monsters: motifs, not themes, not allusions to specific narratives.

Tournon remarks that it does not much matter that "the numerical center of these perceived couplings is only approximate." But the only reason it is approximate in the first place is that both his and Butor's examples are not equidistant from any constant center. That they decided to take that tack hardly rules out the possibility of a constant center, the basis for my analysis. Butor's theory of a double center comprising I: 28–29, which Tournon adopts only for the sake of debunking Butor, gives us 27 chapters on one side but 28 on the other, which could hardly be an accurate analogy to Renaissance grotesques, for the latter typically display the same number of figures on either side (as for example in the Nicoletto da Modena engraving

---

9. André Tournon, "Configuration du premier livre," in *Essais de Michel de Montaigne*, Livre I. Edited by André Tournon (Paris: Imprimerie Nationale, 1998), 35–36.

Tournon provides). But if we were to try to make sense of Tournon's couplings, or Butor's (I: 27 and I: 32, for instance), we would find that some are not even centered around I: 28–29.

The slight differences between one grotesque and its symmetical counterpart to which Tounon calls our attention are real, but hardly a justification for rejecting the analogy Montaigne proposes between his chapters and the artist's grotesques. The opposite is in fact the case, for those subtle differences, particularly in the work of Nicolleto da Modena,[10] are analogous to those we will find in the *Essays*' symmetrical doublings. In the engraving Tournon includes, we see the front of one cupid but the back of its symmetrical counterpart; of two seated female nudes both with their back to the central axis, one faces the viewer while the other's face appears in profile. The same artist in another engraving (plate 156 in Dacos) follows a similar procedure for three other pairs of figures, and in addition depicts a pair of seated, winged females who are writing, one having finished writing the letter A, the other still engaged in writing a B. This kind of subtle difference, sometimes with precise oppositions (such as that between a completed letter and one still being written), happens throughout the *Essays*. Take the case of II: 11 and II: 27, a symmetrical pairing to which Butor briefly alludes, "De la cruauté" [Of cruelty] and "Couardise mere de la cruauté" [Cowardice, the mother of cruelty]. Such a similarity of title, as I have said, is hardly typical of the *Essays*. More typical, as I will show, and at the same time more striking is the parallelism of the following two passages, one from each of these two chapters: "tout ce qui est au dela de la mort simple me semble pure cruauté" [all that is beyond plain death seems to me pure cruelty] (II: 11, 431a, DM 144; 314) and "Tout ce qui est au dela de la mort simple, me semble pure cruauté" [All that is beyond plain death seems to me pure cruelty] (II: 27, 700a, DM 511; 530).[11] Although *cruauté* appears many other times elewhere in the *Essays*, only in these two instances do the other echoing words appear with it. In this case, however, Montaigne is saying the same thing in both passages; quite often in such mirroring passages he will say the opposite. Elsewhere in these two chapters the association of *cruauté* with another

---

10. See, in addition to the example Tournon reproduces, plates 156 and 157 in Dacos, as well as the grotesques created for the Vatican Loggia by Raphael and Jean d'Udine (especially plate 174 in Dacos) and the work of Pinturicchio (Dacos, plates 86–88).

11. Géralde Nakam notes the striking recurrence of this sentence (*Le Dernier Montaigne* [Paris: Honoré Champion, 2002], 198, and *Montaigne: La Manière et la Matière* [Paris: Honoré Champion, 2006], 125), but does not speak of any other symmetrical echoes. Drawing on just this this one instance (II: 11 and II: 27), she concludes that the symmetry of Book Two is more striking than that of Book One, in fact, that "the symmetry is only striking in Book Two" (*Le Dernier Montaigne*, 198), as if it were otherwise absent from Book One, and present in Book Two only in this instance.

term, *mollesse* [softness], reveals a subtle opposition like that between the two writing women (and that, together with two other lexemes, *ouïr* and *gémir*, appears only in these two chapters): in II: 11, Montaigne says he has an *aversion* to cruelty because of his own "mollesse" [softness] (429a; 313), but in II: 27 he says that men characterized by "mollesse" have a *propensity* to cruelty (693b; 523). One passage contradicts the other. As he would later confess, "je me contredits bien à l'adventure" [I indeed contradict myself sometimes] (III: 2, 805b; 611*).

More recently, in his entry "Organisation des *Essais*" in the *Dictionnaire de Montaigne,* Tournon continues to argue against any intentional arrangement: "The ingeniousness of modern critics has tried . . . to weave subtle connections between contiguous or distant chapters"—the latter, in my case, through their symmetrical cross-references. "Such investigations can reveal partial arrangements that are potentially meaningful . . . but they are not convincing with regard to the whole collection because they cannot prevail against the express declarations of the writer."[12] Only fragments of the total arrangement have been brought to light until now[13]; perhaps the fuller picture presented here has a chance of carrying more conviction. What I am proposing is a hypothesis. The only way to determine its validity is to try it out. I propose trying it out with every single pair of symmetrically related chapters, and we will see if it works.

As for Montaigne's express declarations, they are no more free of contradiction nor more absolute than any other statement in his book. As Yves Delègue writes, "Le risque d'erreur est minime en effet pour qui parle des *Essais:* tout y est dit, et son contraire" [The risk of error is minimal for anyone who speaks of the *Essays:* everything is said there, and its contrary].[14] Montaigne not only makes contradictory statements, but describes his own discourse as at times "menteur" [lying]:

> Non seulement le vent des accidens me remue selon son inclination, mais en outre je me remue et trouble moy mesme par l'instabilité de ma posture. . . . Toutes les contrarietez s'y trouvent selon quelque tour et en quelque façon. Honteux, insolent; . . . *menteur,* veritable. . . .

---

12. *Dictionnaire de Michel de Montaigne,* ed. Philippe Desan (Paris: Honoré Champion, 2007), 847–51.

13. In articles of mine (listed in Works Cited) dating back to 1973 that I would not presume Tournon has all read. As far as I know, Butor (and Nakam, following in his footsteps) is the only other to have explored the symmetrical hypothesis.

14. *Montaigne et la mauvaise foi: L'écriture de la vérité* (Paris: Honoré Champion, 1998), 8.

[Not only does the wind of accident move me at will, but, besides, I am moved and disturbed as a result merely of my own unstable posture. . . . All contradictions may be found in me by some twist and in some fashion. Bashful, insolent; . . . *lying*, truthful. . . .] (II: 1, 335b; 242)

The *Essays* are a work of fiction told by an unreliable narrator.[15] Montaigne freely admits that he is inconsistent, whether it be because he has the right to change his mind—

Je pourray tantost changer, non de fortune seulement, mais aussi d'intention. C'est un contrerolle de divers et muables accidens et d'imaginations irresoluës et, quand il y eschet, contraires: soit que je sois autre moy-mesme, soit que je saisisse les subjects par autres circonstances et considerations.

[I may presently change, not only by chance, but also by intention. This is a record of various and changeable occurrences, and of irresolute and, when it so befalls, contradictory ideas: whether I am different myself or whether I take hold of my subjects in different circumstances and aspects.] (III: 2, 805b; 611)

—or because he has forgotten what he wrote or what he had in mind when he wrote it:

J'aurai elancé quelque subtilité en escrivant. (J'enten bien: mornée pour un autre, affilé pour moy. Laissons toutes ces honnestetez. Cela se dit par chacun selon sa force); et je l'ay si bien perdu que je ne sçay ce que j'ay voulu dire: et l'a l'estanger descouverte par fois avant moy.

[I will have tossed off some subtle remark as I write. (I mean, of course, dull for anyone else, sharp for me. But let's leave aside all these amenities. Each man states this kind of thing according to his powers.) Later I have lost the point so thoroughly that I do not know what I meant; and sometimes a stranger has discovered it before I do.] (I: 10, 40c; 27)

Et suis si excellent en l'oubliance que mes esrits mesmes et compositions, je ne les oublie pas moins que le reste. On m'allegue tous les coups à moy-mesme sans que je le sente.

---

15. As Patrick Henry notes, "The most pervasive tendency in modern Montaigne criticism is to envision the *Essais* as fiction rather than history" ("Reading Montaigne Contextually," 859).

[I am so good at forgetting that I forget even my own writings and compositions no less than the rest. People are all the time quoting me to myself without my knowing it.] (II: 17, 651b; 494)

When we read the chapters in symmetrical pairs yet another kind of self-contradiction emerges, of which an example is Montaigne's seeing civil wars in a positive light in II: 15 but in a negative one in II: 23.[16] Those parallel chapters, like the others, have so many other cross-references between them that it is clear that Montaigne had one of them in mind—indeed, before his eyes—when he was writing or rewriting the other, even if he may have begun them at different times. Consequently those two contradictory views of civil strife must at some point have also been in his mind at the same time. This apparent self-contradiction can be attributed neither to his having changed his mind nor to his having forgotten when he wrote one chapter what he had written in the other. There are many instances, however, of oppositions between symmetrically linked chapters, many of which do not at first glance present themselves as opposing opinions on Montaigne's part but are nevertheless intriguingly opposed. For example, each of the first pair of chapters is about diverse means to a same end (as one's title indicates) but the ends are exactly opposite: not dying in I: 1, dying in I: 57. In the second pair, a visible "contenance" [countenance] in I: 56 denotes a failure to communicate while an invisible "contenance" in I: 2 communicates what could not be communicated if it were visible.

Tournon insists that no such arrangement is possible (certainly no symmetrical one, though he does cites several instances of sequential links) because Montaigne tells us he leaves everything to chance: "Je n'ay point d'autre sergent de bande à ranger mes pieces que la fortune. A mesme que mes resveries se presentent, je les entasse" [I have no other marshal but chance to arrange my pieces. As my fancies present themselves, I pile them up] (II: 10, 409a, DM 100-1; 297*). But as Alfred Glauser remarks, "What Montaigne calls fortune is a controlled fate [un sort dirigé]," and the essayist's statements about chance are just another of his paradoxes: "Paradox is the leaven of the work. . . . Chance is controlled."[17] And Montaigne's assertion that he records his "resveries" at the moment they present themselves is undercut by his writing elsewhere of "mes contes prenans place selon leur

---

16. Jean-Yves Pouilloux delights in listing such contradictions in *Lire les « Essais » de Montaigne* (Paris: Maspero, 1969), 29–38. "Adding up these contrary meanings produces a net result of zero. . . . Montaigne does not produce coherent opinions, but on the contrary divergent ones on a given subject; it is never certain that Montaigne is really speaking of what he seems to be talking about" (35).

17. Alfred Glauser, *Montaigne paradoxal* (Paris: Nizet, 1972), 11.

opportunité, non tousjours selon leur aage" [my stories finding their place not always by their chronology but by their opportuneness] (III: 9, 964c; 736*). The admission that he places his anecdotes by their opportuneness is consistent with what we will find here, that often a story in one chapter will show opportune connections with a passage in that chapter's symmetrical partner.

Although the story is undoubtedly apocryphal, it is tempting to compare the medieval scholars who, arguing over what Aristotle said concerning how many teeth a horse should have, rejected out of hand an outsider's suggestion that someone just go and count them, to scholars of the *Essays* who argue back and forth over whether Montaigne says his book is the product of chance or of order (a question his contradictory statements give them plenty of reason to argue). Why not just go count the teeth?

The book trumps the author; what can be found in the book trumps whatever "express declarations" its narrator may have made, as that narrator himself declares: The *Essays* "peut sçavoir assez de choses que je ne sçay plus, et tenir de moy ce que je n'ay point retenu et qu'il faudroit que, tout ainsi qu'un estranger, j'empruntasse de luy, si besoin m'en venoit. Il est plus riche que moy, si je suis plus sage que luy" [may know a good many things that I no longer know and hold from me what I have not retained and what, just like a stranger, I should have to borrow from it if I came to need it. If I am wiser than it, it is richer than I] (II: 8, 402c; 293).

Tournon himself counted one of the teeth without realizing it when he discovered in the margins of the Bordeaux Copy that a post-1588 addition to III: 9 was originally a post-1588 addition to III: 5 (*Route par ailleurs*, 347).[18] In other words, that symmetrical pair of chapters are so attuned to each other, indeed so much the same text, that the passage could have appeared in either one.

Both Sayce (*The Essays of Montaigne*, 260–62) and Frédéric Brahami[19] remind us that Montaigne also declares "Mon humeur est de regarder autant à la forme qu'à la substance" [My humor is to consider the form as much as the substance] (III: 8, 928b; 708) and "Qu'on ne s'attende pas aux matieres, mais à la façon que j'y donne" [Do not linger over the matter but over my fashioning of it] (II: 10, 408a; 296*). He may seem to denigrate his book by saying that "ce n'est qu'une marqueterie mal jointe" [it is only a badly joined marquetry] (III: 9, 964c; 736*), but as Brahami points out, "In vain does Montaigne claim his right to disorder, for . . . the badly joined

---

18. See my discussion of this floating passage in the section on III: 5 and III: 9.
19. "Ordre," in *Dictionnaire de Montaigne*, 840–42.

marquetry is nevertheless a marquetry, in the same way that the 'monstrous' grotesques that provide the artistic model for Book One are not pure chaos" (841).

A similar statement on Montaigne's part, that his *Essays* are a "ce fagotage de tant de diverses pieces" [this bundle of so many disparate pieces] (II: 37, 758a, DM 599; 574*) should be read in light of what he says elsewhere in the same chapter (the last in Book Two and thus the concluding chapter in the 1580 edition) about assembling pieces: "[il] faut que toutes ces pieces, il les sçache proportionner & rapporter l'une à l'autre, pour en engendrer une parfaicte symmetrie" [he must know how to proportion all these pieces and relate them to one another to engender a perfect symmetry] (II: 37, 773a, DM 627; 587). He is not talking about his book in this passage. But these words may well have a secondary relevance to the book because of what he says in the symmetrically matching chapter (the first in Book Two): "Il est impossible de renger les pieces, à qui n'a une forme du tout en sa teste" [A man who does not have in his head a picture of the whole cannot possibly arrange the pieces] (II: 1, 337a, DM 9; 243*). In other words, he writes of arranging pieces to form a symmetry at a moment when he is arranging certain "pieces" (these parallel passages) to form a symmetry. And he does this in the same book he calls a mere "fagotage" of disparate pieces.

Montaigne's statement in "De l'oysiveté" [Of idleness] (I: 8) that his book is the record of the chimera and monsters to which his idle mind gave birth in a manner "sans ordre, & sans propos" [without order and without purpose] (I: 8, 33a; DM 32; 21*) could leave the impression that that record itself, the act of "les mettre en rolle" [writing them down], was similarly lacking in order. But when he writes again, in a post-1588 addition to "Du démentir" [Of giving the lie] (II: 18), of his wild reveries and keeping a record of them it turns out that there is some order involved after all: "Aux fins de renger ma fantasie à resver mesme *par quelque ordre et projet,* et la garder de se perdre et extravaguer au vent, il n'est que de donner corps et mettre en registre tant de menues pensées qui se presentent à elle. J'escoute à mes resveries par ce que j'ay à les enroller" [In order to train my fancy even to dream *with some order and purpose,* and in order to keep it from losing its way and roving with the wind, there is nothing like embodying and registering all the little thoughts that come to it. I listen to my reveries because I have to record them] (II: 18, 665c; 504). Gisèle Mathieu-Castellani takes note of the contradiction: "From the chapter 'De l'oiseveté' to the chapter 'Du démentir,'" we find "the same network of images of extravagance, the same project of *enrollement* . . . but henceforth the record keeping" is justified by "the awareness of a rigorous obligation of order and conservation."[20] That Montaigne may have succeeded in bringing some order to his reveries is suggested by the way the chapter "Democritus et Heraclitus" [On Democritus and Heraclitus] (I: 50), symmetrically paired with "De l'oysiveté," brings a symmetrical ordering to the assertion of the absence of order. The "sans ordre, & sans propos" of I: 8 finds an echo in the way Montaigne in I: 50 describes his writing process as proceeding "sans dessein et sans promesse": "Semant icy un mot, icy un autre, eschantillons despris de leur piece, escartez, *sans dessein et sans promesse*" [Sowing a word here, there another, samples separated from their context, dispersed, *without a plan and without a promise*] (I: 50, 302c; 219). Even André Tournon, who rejects any ordering principle, though without referring to this echo, finds that these two chapters have enough in common that I: 50 is "perhaps placed in a symmetrical position with chapter I: 8" (in his edition of the *Essais,* I, 631).

That this is not just a self-referential but a metafictional phenomenon becomes apparent if we grant that the *Essays* are a work of fiction—a book about a man writing about various topics, some more philosophical than others, in a miscellany of "diverses pieces" not forming an organized whole. That would indeed be a fiction if it should turn out that they *did* form an organized whole. The metafiction emerges when Montaigne subtly alludes through the symmetrical echoes themselves to the fact that they are symmetrical echoes. As he says of freaks of nature in "D'un enfant monstrueux" [Of a monstrous child] (II: 30), that is of unnatural monsters like those that appear in the symmetrical grotesques, which often depict human heads on animal torsos, that are the visual equivalent of his book, "cette figure qui nous estonne, se rapporte et tient à quelque autre figure de mesme genre inconnu à l'homme . . . mais nous n'en voyons pas l'assortiment et la relation" [this figure that astonishes us is related and linked to some other figure of the same kind unknown to man . . . but we do not see their arrangement and relation] (II: 30, 713c; 539*). My task is to make apparent that "assortiment" and "relation."

This approach to Montaigne reveals a hidden dimension to every chapter, which is especially interesting in the case of some of the very brief ones in Book One of which Pierre Villey complained that "All one can say about most of these chapters is that there is nothing to say"[21]—the ones only one or two pages long that seem to be just a bunch of anecdotes thrown

---

20. Gisèle Mathieu-Castellani, *Montaigne ou la vérité du mensonge* (Geneva: Droz, 2000), 68.
21. Pierre Villey, *Les sources et l'évolution des "Essais" de Montaigne*. 2 vols. (Paris: Hachette, 1908), vol. 2, 44.

together, that on their own really do not constitute a well-wrought text. For we have only been reading half of what Montaigne intended, as he may be suggesting when in the course of writing about dividing his book into chapters he remarks, "à l'adventure ay-je quelque obligation particuliere à ne dire qu'*à demy*" [perhaps I have some personal obligation to speak only *by halves*] (III: 9, 995–96c; 762). Those brief and scanty chapters will make much more sense when we read their other half. Antoine Compagnon once asked, "How are we to read the *Essays?* Simply put, what is their unity? The book, the chapter, the sentence? All these answers have been suggested, yet none has proved satisfactory."[22] (By "the book" he means Book One, Two, or Three considered separately.) Perhaps even to look for a "unity" short of the entire collection is to miss the total unity Montaigne gave it, but I propose that one of the unities we should consider is that formed by each symmetrical pair.

Although Montaigne's characterization of his chapters as grotesques is a direct allusion to the style of decoration inspired by the Roman grotesques discovered in the Domus Aurea, and a way of hinting at their symmetrical arrangement, he is hardly alone in creating a literary work based on symmetry. There were antecedents among the classical texts he knew so well. Ring-composition, in which lexical and situational parallels and oppositions are arranged in the form of symmetrical echoes, is now recognized as a feature of the *Iliad* and the *Odyssey*. According to Glenn W. Most,

> In recent years, a consensus has begun to emerge among scholars that the Homeric epics indeed bear the signs of such large-scale narrative organization [as] ring-composition and recurrence, parallelism and opposition. . . . To be sure, such devices as ring-composition are ultimately anchored in the mechanics of oral composition: they function, like Ariadne's thread, to bring a poet out of a story by the same path on which he entered it and to return him to the mainline of action. But already in Homer, and of course all the more in later Greek poets, such mechanical devices are functionalized and thematized: rather than simply aiding the poet, they contribute to his poem's meaning.[23]

Cedric W. Whitman, an early proponent of this theory, argued that the *Iliad*

---

22. P. 24 of Antoine Compagnon, "A Long Short Story: Montaigne's Brevity," *Yale French Studies* 64 (1983): 24–50.

23. Pp. 20–21 and 20n–21n of Glenn W. Most, "The Structure and Function of Odysseus' Apologoi," *Transactions of the American Philological Association* 119 (1989): 15–30.

as a whole forms one large concentric pattern, within which a vast system of smaller ones, sometimes distinct and sometimes interlocking, gives shape to the separate parts. It has been suggested that such "onion skin" design arose from a device originally mnemonic. . . . But . . . such a purpose is clearly superseded when it becomes the structural basis of a fifteen-thousand-line poem such as the *Iliad*. It has become an artistic principle. . . . It is commonplace in ancient art for technical devices which are functional in one medium to be transferred to another medium where they are purely ornamental.[24]

In a remarkable study Paul Claes focuses primarily on the sequential linkages uniting Catullus's *Carmina,* but in addition to these he discerns three symmetrical clusters, poems 1–36, 76–92, and 92–107.[25] The central poem of each differs from the rest: 17 because it is the only poem in the collection in Priapean meter, 84 and 99 because they are longer than the others in the cluster.[26] Claes bases his argument on both repeating lexemes and thematic parallels. For example, to take just a small section of one of these:

80: Quid . . . Gelli / 88: Quid . . . Gelli
81: Nemone . . . tanto potuit . . . homo / 87: Nulla potest mulier tantum
82: Quinti / 86: Quintia
83: sentis / 85: sentio

80: perverse sex by day / 88: perverse sex by night
81: friend more loved than any man / 87: mistress more loved than any woman
82: Catullus' rival Quintius / 86: Lesbia's rival Quintia
83: Lesbia's contradictory feelings / 85: Catulus' contradictory feelings (122–23)

Building on the insights of Paul Maury, Otto Skutsch argues that Virgil's *Eclogues* are arranged in a symmetry linking 1 with 9, 2 with 8, 3 with 7, and 4 with 6, with the center of that symmetry, 5, linked to the concluding 10.[27] 1 and 9 are both about land expropriations and both feature omens of

---

24. Cedric W. Whitman, *Homer and the Homeric Tradition* (Cambridge: Harvard University Press, 1957), 97–98.
25. Paul Claes, *Concatenatio Catulliana: A New Reading of the Carmina* (Amsterdam: J. C. Gieben, 2002), 120–26.
26. This would be true of 84 if he limited the cluster to 77–91, as 76 is longer.
27. Otto Skutsch, "Symmetry and Sense in the *Eclogues*," *Harvard Studies in Classical Philology* 73 (1969): 153–69.

disaster[28]; complaints of frustrated love comprise 2 and 8; both 3 and 7 are composed of singing matches between two shepherds; 4 and 6 both "provide supernatural revelations. The first comes from the Sibyl . . . presenting the glorious future, and the second from Silenus . . . interpreting the terrible past."[29] *Eclogues* 5 and 10, as James R. G. Wright observes, are united in their allusions to Theocritus's first *Idyll*. "*Eclogue* 5 begins where *Idyll* 1 leaves off, with the death of Daphnis. . . . *Eclogue* 10 presents the historical figure Gallus"—a poet friend of Virgil's—"but predicates of him much of what is said by Theocritus about Daphnis."[30] Specifically, in *Eclogue* 10 Gallus, dying of unhappy love, is visited by gods (Apollo, Silvanus, and Pan) who ask him why he is letting himself suffer so; in *Idyll* 1 Daphnis, dying of unhappy love, is visited by gods (Hermes, Priapus, and Aphrodite) who interrogate him similarly.

In Matthew S. Santirocco's reading, the first three books of Horace's *Odes,* published together in 23 B.C.E., likewise show a high degree of organization, primarily through links between neighboring poems, but as Claes found in Catullus, some symmetrical arrangements emerge as well: "Just as the midpoint of each book is marked by a poem to Maecenas, so the collection as a whole is also anchored at its center." That center is composed of the first 12 poems of Book 2, whose

> alternation of Horace's two most important meters and . . . thematic comprehensiveness . . . establish their status as a group. Placed in the exact center of the collection, with thirty-eight odes preceding them and thirty-eight following, they serve not only to open the second book but also to stabilize the entire ensemble. If there is centerpinning, there is also framing. Just as the ends of Book I are individually linked by poems that balance each other, so the collection as a whole is surrounded by rings that link 1.1–7 respectively with 3.30–24.[31]

---

28. Charles Segal spells out some additional connections between 1 and 9. There are two characters in both, one of whom complains to the other about being kicked off his land. "Both involve exile from a peaceful, familiar world; and both develop a contrast . . . between a shepherd facing exile and one who is still at rest within the pastoral world." In addition to the omen in both that Skutsch mentions Segal cites among "[s]ome deliberate verbal echoes" the following: "Insere, Daphni, piros" [Graft your pear-trees, Daphnis] in 9 and "Insere nunc, Meliboee, piros" [Now, Meliboeus, graft your pear-trees] in 1 (p. 173 of Charles Segal, "*Tamen Cantabitis, Arcades*—Exile and Arcadia in *Eclogues* 1 and 9," in *Virgil: Critical Assessments of Classical Authors, volume 1: General Articles and the Eclogues.* Ed. Philip Hardie (New York: Routledge, 1999), 172–202.

29. I am quoting a paraphrase of Maury's argument found on p. 103 of Niall Rudd, "Architecture. Theories about Virgil's *Eclogues,*" in Hardie, 91–115.

30. P. 138 of James R. G. Wright, "Virgil's Pastoral Programme: Theocritus, Callimachus and *Eclogue* 1," in Hardie, 116–71.

31. Matthew S. Santirocco, *Unity and Design in Horace's Odes* (Chapel Hill: University of North

More important than the symmetry is the fact that these texts—particularly Catullus' *Carmina* and Horace's *Odes*—are organized in some way, despite such diversity from one poem to the next that they may seem at first reading (like Montaigne's *Essays*) to be arranged in a haphazard manner. A closer examination, one that both Claes and Santirocco argue was available to and practiced by some contemporary readers, would reveal a hidden network of cross-references. As Claes writes, "The unexpected order was meant to astonish the connoisseur and to test his acumen" (24). "The combination of juxtaposition and contrast seems to aim at *concordia discors* 'harmony in discord,' which is an essential feature of [the] Hellenistic aesthetics" that inspired Catullus (28). We will find the same esthetic in the *Essays*. Whether it be through symmetry or concatenation, in Montaigne as in Catullus and Horace two texts at a time (two chapters, two poems) are brought together in confrontation by the structure of the collection in which they appear, and the "suffisant lecteur" [able reader] (I: 24, 127a; 93) is challenged to find the paradox of their connection. Thus a "giron" [lap] in "De la tristesse" (I: 2) denoting sexual orgasm is matched by in "Des prieres" (I: 56) by the "giron" of God Himself, very much as Catullus's elegy for his brother in *Carmina* 101

> is clearly linked with the previous satirical attack (poem 100) by repetition of *frater* and *fraternus*. The incongruous juxtaposition of a sexual and a sepulchral poem seems rather tasteless, but should be interpreted as a typical example of Hellenistic variation, especially as a mixture of gravity and humour, i.e. *spoudaiogeloion*. In such cases lexical concatenation connects and disjoins at the same time. (Claes, 51)

The contrast and connections between Horace's odes 1.27 and 1.28 are similarly surprising. In the former, "As a party in progress rapidly degenerates into a brawl, the poet urges moderation and restraint (1–8). A question at line 9 indicates that he too (*me quoque*) has been urged to join in the merriment." 1.28 begins with the narrator lecturing "Archytas on the inevitability of death.... At line 21, however, the speaker includes himself (*me quoque*) among the dead, thereby revealing that he is not Horace, as we had assumed" and as he had been in the preceding poem. In both poems, "the speaker introduces himself into the situation by means of the phrase, *me quoque*" (Santirocco, 63–64), which turns out to be "surprisingly rare in the *Odes*," occurring in only one other poem (Santirocco, 196n). This is far from the only connection between the poems, but is a particularly interesting one

---

Carolina Press, 1986), 150.

since the same phenomenon of rarely-occurring phrases is what consistently unites the chapters in the *Essays*.

While Montaigne knew those texts well, we do not know if he was aware of their symmetries and concatenations. I am not arguing that they influenced him in that direction but that such intratextual structures and such doubling effects are so widespread and such a naturally occurring phenomenon in literary collections that Montaigne did not need to be influenced to do it. Among examples from his own time one could cite the symmetrical and concatenting structure of the emblems in Maurice Scève's *Délie* (1544),[32] the symmetrical structures Doranne Fenoaltea sees in Ronsard's *Odes*,[33] and Edwin Duval's revelations about Rabelais, particularly his *Tiers Livre* and *Quart Livre*.[34]

In *Thinking in Circles: An Essay on Ring Composition*, Mary Douglas discusses symmetrical composition in the Bible, Homer, Herodotus, Thucydides, and in folk traditions of many unrelated cultures. As I will do here, Douglas looks for "key phrases . . . that are repeated in the matched sections" and "cannot be found anywhere else in the book."[35] My proposal that we read symmetrically associated chapters together parallels Douglas's observation concerning poetic collections that "the poems once regarded as separate units can now be read as connected sequences" (7). Those chapter pairs form an *intratext* constituted by the intratextuality of its component parts. That is, by contrast to intertextuality, where foreign texts take up residence in a text (as do Montaigne's borrowed quotations and anecdotes), in intratextuality it is textual fragments from elsewhere in the text that do so. As Douglas further observes, "the matching of sections often contains surprises; items are put into concordance that had not previously been seen to be similar. Parallelism gives the artist opportunities of taking the text to deeper levels of analogy" (36). Montaigne certainly seizes that opportunity, for the stories he tells "portent souvent, hors de mon propos, la semence

---

32. As I argue in "'continuelz discors': The Silent Discourse of *Délie*'s Emblems," *L'Esprit Créateur* 28.2 (1988): 58–67.

33. Doranne Fenoaltea, *Du palais au jardin: L'architecture des* Odes *de Ronsard* (Geneva: Droz, 1990).

34. Edwin M. Duval, *The Design of Rabelais's* Tiers Livre de Pantagruel (Geneva: Droz, 1997) and *The Design of Rabelais's* Quart Livre de Pantagruel (Geneva: Droz, 1998). At the numerical midpoint of the *Tiers Livre* he finds two meaningful words (Duval, *Tiers Livre*, 126); at the numerical midpoint of Book One of the *Essays* we will likewise find two significant words (one of them—*rien* [nothing]—prophesying the fate of that middle]), as well as a surprising pair of numerical coincidences. There is a religious component in Duval's reading of Rabelais, however, which is absent from my reading of Montaigne.

35. Mary Douglas, *Thinking in Circles: An Essay on Ring Composition* (New Haven: Yale University Press, 2007), 54. Here she is discussing the symmetrical structure of the book of Numbers.

d'une matiere plus riche et plus hardie, et sonnent à gauche un ton plus delicat, et pour moy qui n'en veux exprimer d'avantage, et pour ceux qui rencontreront mon air" [often bear, outside of my subject, the seeds of a richer and bolder material, and sound off to the side a subtler note, both for myself, who do not wish to express anything more, and for those who get my drift] (I: 40, 251c; 185). They function in a larger context, in other words, than their immediate one.

Many of the texts Douglas and other investigators of ring composition examine are narratives, often long narratives composed of smaller ones. The *Essays*, though they contain hundreds of brief narratives, are not themselves one. Rabelais's *Tiers Livre* resembles them in this way, composed of discrete episodes and lacking the overarching narrative of a *Gargantua* or *Pantagruel*, as well as having a hidden symmetrical design. Montaigne may claim that his work is a haphazard collection, in the passages Tournon cites, but so did Rabelais. That did not deter Duval from finding a design beneath its surface:

> [C]ontrary to its own emblematic self-representations in the prologue and in chapter 24, it is neither a haphazard assemblage of incompatible parts nor an aimless shaggy dog story. Its two most conspicuous, self-avowed defects—the incongruity of its parts and the absence of a telos at the end—are in fact complementary aspects of a single, perfectly coherent design of a higher order. (Duval, *The Design of Rabelais's* Tiers Livre, 132).

Ring composition is a subset of the literary parallelism that so fascinated Roman Jakobson, who quoted with approval Gerard Manley Hopkins's observation that

> The artificial part of poetry, perhaps we shall be right to say all artifice, reduces itself to the principle of parallelism. The structure of poetry is that of continuous parallelism, ranging from the technical so-called Parallelisms of Hebrew poetry and the antiphons of Church music to the intricacy of Greek or Italian or English verse.[36]

Commenting on this, Jakobson finds the etymology of *prose* and *verse* suggestive: from *proversa* as "speech turned straightforward" and *versus* as "return."

---

36. Quoted in "Grammatical Parallelism and Its Russian Facet," in Roman Jakobson, *Language in Literature* (Cambridge: Harvard University Press, 1987), 145. Jakobson in an interview said, "there has been no other subject during my entire scholarly life that has captured me as persistently as have the questions of parallelism" (Roman Jakobson and Krystyna Pomorska, *Dialogues* [Cambridge: MIT Press, 1988], 100).

So that "on every level of language the essence of poetic artifice consists in recurrent returns" (*Language and Literature,* 145). This does not mean that parallelism cannot also occur in prose. "A number of types of literary prose are constructed according to a strict principle of parallelism," he said in reply to the question of whether he still believed in a sharp distinction "between *versus* and *proversa,* particularly in light of your theory of prose as a structure based on the principle of contiguity and poetry as a structure founded on the principle of similarity?" He added that parallelism in prose can appear when parallel structures

> deviate maximally from total submission to the elementary principle of succession in time. Nonetheless, there is a notable hierarchical difference between the parallelism of verse and that of prose. In poetry, it is the verse itself that dictates the structure of parallelism. The prosodic structure of the verse as a whole, the melodic unity and the repetition of the line and of its metrical constituents determine the parallel distribution of elements of grammatical and lexical semantics. . . . Inversely, in prose semantic units differing in extent play the primary role in organizing parallel structures. In this case, the parallelism of units connected by similarity, contrast, or contiguity actively influences the composition of the plot, the characterization of the subjects and objects of the action, and the sequence of themes in the narrative. (*Dialogues,* 106–7)

The only kind of prose Jakobson is thinking of here is prose narrative, which Montaigne's book is not. But unlike a prose narrative, the *Essays* have a structural equivalent to the prosodic structure in verse where Jakobson finds the potential for parallelism, whether that be line positions in successive stanzas, or rhymes, or other repeating structures. It is that the *Essays* are divided into chapters. We can look for parallels in sequential chapters—as Tournon in at least one instance has done, despite claiming that there is no order to the *Essays'* overall structure—or in symmetrical ones. He does a good job of revealing subtle ties linking "Consideration sur Ciceron" (I: 40) and "De ne communiquer sa gloire" (I: 41), thereby showing, as he points out, how misguided Gallimard was to have adopted Marie de Gournay's rearrangement of the *Essais* for the 2007 Pléiade edition, which moves chapter 14 of the First Book to lodge it precisely between those two chapters, I: 40 and I: 41.[37]

---

37. *Les Essais.* Ed. Jean Balsamo, Michel Magnien and Catherine Magnien-Simonin (Paris: Gallimard / Pléiade, 2007). André Tournon, "Du bon usage de l'édition posthume des *Essais,*" *Bulletin de la Société des Amis de Montaigne* 7: 29–30 (January–June 2003): 77–91.

There is absolutely no evidence Montaigne intended such a change. From my symmetrical reading I will produce even more evidence (a lot more in fact, since it involves all the chapter pairs between I: 14 and I: 40) to show what an "énorme bévue" [enormous blunder], as Tournon puts it ("Du bon usage," 87), that editorial decision was. Marie de Gournay is hardly a trustworthy source, basing her edition as she claims on a possibly mythical copy that is contradicted in myriad ways by Montaigne's marginal notes on the Bordeaux Copy, which was not discovered until 1777 and thus unavailable to scholars when her succeeding editions held sway throughout the seventeenth and eighteenth centuries. She inserted praise of herself at the end of II: 17 that has no equivalent in the Bordeaux Copy. As Claude Blum points out, she kept modifying that passage throughout her successive editions from 1595 to 1635.[38] If she was being scrupulously faithful to Montaigne's text, as she claimed, then why did the text in her possession keep changing? On top of that, in 1624 she fraudulently claimed that she had uncovered a manuscript of poems by Pierre de Ronsard (Blum, 65–69). But even if evidence were to surface that Montaigne at some later moment wanted the order of the chapters changed, my analyses of the chapter pairs in each instance focus first on the texts of the original 1580 edition of Books One and Two and the original 1588 edition of Book Three, and only then do they consider the alterations Montaigne made, which in many instances add symmetrical connections.

The 1580 edition is worth studying on its own, as I will do here. Pierre Coste, who edited Montaigne in 1725, argued that the first version has its virtues:

> One has but to compare the first editions of the *Essais* with the subsequent ones to see that those frequent additions threw a lot of disorder and confusion into the arguments that were originally very clear and logical. Montaigne's style . . . could be compared to a necklace of pearls that had first been composed of perfectly round ones of equal size and among which were added others not so perfectly round but much bigger. The latter in increasing the necklace's price made it lose a good part of its beauty. It is the same with most of the thoughts that Montaigne inserted from time to time in his book. . . . Because Montaigne could easily see what connected his first thoughts despite what he inserted between them, he counted on an attentive reader to see it as well as he. But sometimes what remains of

---

38. Claude Blum, "La Pléiade en habits de Gournay," *Nouveau Bulletin de la Société Internationale des Amis de Montaigne* 3 (1er semestre 2008): 55–70.

those connections is so faint that it is impossible to see it without consulting the earlier editions.[39]

In *Intratextual Baudelaire* I likewise began with the first edition (1857) of the *Fleurs du mal,* and then considered the changes the poet made for the second (1861), revealing a host of textual alterations (both between the poems' 1857 and 1861 versions and in the case of poems new to the second edition between their version there and their prior separate publication) that enhance the sequential structure. These changes reveal authorial intent. So too do the additions and subtractions by which La Fontaine departed from the sources for his *Fables* and *Contes*. Though we may live in the age of the death of the author, reports of that death, as Mark Twain said of his own, are greatly exaggerated.

"Intratextuality" is a fairly recent term, susceptible to varying definitions. According to Helen Morales in 2000,

> In its weakest formulation the term intratextuality merely indicates the property whereby one part of a text refers to or relates to another part of the same text. . . . The stronger formulation of the term understands intratextuality to be a property of texts where the internal design, structure, and partition of the text are particularly paraded.[40]

I offered an even stronger formulation in 1992 in a book on Raymond Carver's short story collections, defining it as "what can happen when the texts in a text (poems or stories in an intelligently assembled sequence) begin to refer to each other in ways that seems to refer to their doing so" (*Reading Raymond Carver,* 9). Carver's stories (like Baudelaire's poems, Montesquieu's *Persian Letters,* and La Fontaine's *Fables* and *Contes*) refer to each other through their sequential structure. They are metafictional but their metafictionality arises from their intratextuality—that is, they are self-referential (and hence metafictional) through their sequential structure.

The intratextuality of collections is a different thing from the intratextuality of an ostensibly unified work. Internal partition is more obvious in collections like Catullus' *Carmina* or Montaigne's *Essays* or Baudelaire's *Fleurs*

---

39. Quoted by Claude Blum on pp. 10–11 of "L'édition des *Essais* à travers les âges: histoire d'un sinistre," in *Éditer les* Essais *de Montaigne: Actes du Colloque tenu à l'Université Paris IV-Sorbonne les 27 et 28 janvier 1995,* ed. Claude Blum and André Tournon (Paris: Honoré Champion, 1997), 5–19.

40. P. 326 of Helen Morales, "Endtext" in *Intratextuality: Greek and Roman Textual Relations,* edited by Helen Morales and Alison Sharrock (Oxford: Oxford University Press, 2000), 325–29. "Endtext" in *Intratextuality: Greek and Roman Textual Relations,* edited by Helen Morales and Alison Sharrock (Oxford: Oxford University Press, 2000), 325–29.

du mal than it is in the *Aeneid,* a play, or a novel, because in collections individual chapters or poems are presented as if they were self-sufficient and independent texts while the books of the *Aeneid,* like chapters in a novel or acts of a play, together tell the same overarching story. We do not know at the outset whether a collection as a whole is a work of art comprising inter-relating parts; some are, some not. Of Morales's two formulations, the second seems more applicable to collections of ostensibly independent texts because in them the partitions are particularly "paraded." Yet it is not clear that she was thinking of such collections at all because her essay comes at the end of a volume of articles on classical texts she co-edited none of which focuses on a collection to ask whether its parts cohere (even the one on Catullus deals with just one poem).

Kip Wheeler's definition of "intratextual meaning" does concern itself uniquely with collections: "Meaning that originates not within a work itself, but that originates in a related work in the same collection." He cites William Blake's *Songs of Innocence* and *Songs of Experience,* and *"The Canterbury Tales,* in which the various pilgrims' tales seem to 'bounce off' each other, echoing the themes, phrasing, concerns, and ideas of previous storytellers. . . . The overall meaning originates not in one single pilgrim's pronouncement, but rather *between* or *amongst* the various statements made by other pilgrims."[41] But though this definition may be adequate for intratextuality generally, it does not take into account structural elements of a collection that often contribute to intratextuality: sequence (Catullus, Horace, La Fontaine, Montesquieu, Baudelaire) and symmetry (Virgil, Montaigne). Long before the term was invented, Cleanth Brooks gave a beautifully intratextual reading (though without using that term) of a compound text both symmetrical and sequential (since there are only two parts to it), Milton's "L'Allegro–Il Penseroso." According to Brooks the two poems are "twin halves of *one* poem," elements in one finding echoes in the other. "The cheerful man's day is balanced by the pensive man's day at every point." Moving beyond the fairly obvious opposing elements that "everyone knows," Brooks finds for example that the "high lonely Tower" where the pensive man meditates at midnight migrates to the other poem. Although "'high' and 'lonely' seem inevitably associated with the tower, and the tower itself, the inevitable symbol of the meditative, ascetic life, one remembers that towers are to be found all through 'L'Allegro'—yet they're associated with anything but lonely solitude," from the tower where sings the lark to the pleasing "Towered Cities" where the

---

41. Kip Wheeler, "Literary Terms and Definitions," at http://web.cn.edu/kwheeler/lit_terms_I.html.

cheerful man enjoys his ramble. Like the recurring words in the *Essays'* symmetrical chapters, towers appear in both poems but in quite different contexts. They travel from one chapter to its distant double, but leave their thematic baggage behind (or in Milton's case, pick up the opposite kind of baggage at their destination).[42]

I am not the first to allude to the *Essays'* intratextuality. Jules Brody has written of their "intratextual" dimension, of how they invite the reader "to pursue and compare observed lexical recurrences, synonymies or on occasion even sizeable passages which continue to impinge on one another even at several pages' distance," of "the absolutely uncanny way in which Montaigne's words respond to one another, in the Baudelairean sense, across the pages of the essay."[43] He stays within the limits of a chapter at a time, but there is no reason his insightful word-centered ("philological") approach could not be applied to the *Essays* as a whole, and in particular to the intratext formed by each symmetrical pair. Michel Beaujour has writtten of what he terms the *Essays'* "intratextual memory," a "system of cross-references, amplifications, and palinodes."[44] This intratextual memory is "a text that refers to itself as it imitates the mechanisms of involuntary memory and free invention" and "eventuates in the production of a text that . . . that tends more and more to refer only to its own past in passing again over the traces already written"—that is, to its own text in prior versions—"and that tends always more toward its own self-sufficiency, even though it never quite succeeds, and for good reason, in folding back and closing completely upon itself."[45] Beaujour of course is not referring to any structural elements but to the intratextuality of the *Essays* as a whole.

The thematic equential connections traced by R. A. Sayce and Marianne Meijer do not conflict with, far less contravene, the symmetrical ones I will present here.[46] Few sequential links have so far been brought to light. While

---

42. Cleanth Brooks, *The Well Wrought Urn* (New York: Harcourt Brace, 1947; 1975), 50–66.

43. Pp. 269–70 of Jules Brody, "'Du repentir' (III: 2): A Philological Reading," *Yale French Studies* 64 (1983): 238–72.

44. Michel Beaujour, *Poetics of the Literary Self-Portrait*, translated by Yara Milos (New York: New York University Press, 1991), 20.

45. P. 45 of Michel Beaujour, "Les *Essais:* Une mémoire intratextuelle," in *Textes et Intertextes: Études sur le XVIe siècle pour Alfred Glauser,* ed. Floyd Gray and Marcel Tetel (Paris: Nizet, 1979): 29–45.

46. For Sayce, see pages 264–65 of *The Essays of Montaigne: A Critical Exploration* (London: Weidenfeld and Nicolson, 1972), and "L'ordre des *Essais* de Montaigne" (*Bibliothèque d'Humanisme et de Renaissance* 18 [1956]: 7–22). Marianne S. Meijer pursues the same hypothesis in "L'ordre des « Essais » dans les deux premiers volumes" (in *Montaigne et les Essais: 1580–1980,* ed. Pierre Michel [Paris: Champion, 1983], 17–27), and "Guesswork or Facts: Connections between Montaigne's Last Three Chapters (III: 11, 12, and 13)" (*Yale French Studies* 64 [1983]: 167–79). Patrick Henry in "Reading

I feel that Montaigne's comparing his *Essays* to grotesques in I: 28 probably means that there is no more sequential order to his chapters than there is to the vertical chains on either side of the decorative art to which he alludes, nevertheless both ordering systems, symmetrical and sequential, could coexist. As far as my chapters are concerned, you are welcome to read them in any order. There are a few cross-references between successive ones, but not many. This book is not a continuous narrative nor a gradually unfolding argument, but a commentary that gives serious consideration to every chapter, the neglected with the famous. Begin where you will; omit what you wish. It is my hope that you will be pleasantly surprised by the new perspective that can be gained by reading any chapter in the company of its hidden other half.

Montaigne Contextually: 'De l'incommodité de la grandeur' (III, 7)" brings to light sequential connections between III: 6, 7, and 8.

I

BOOK ONE

1. Of Means and Ends

"Par divers moyens on arrive à pareille fin" [By diverse means one arrives at the same end] (I: 1) and *"De l'aage"* [Of age] (I: 57)

The time has long passed since Pierre Villey's disparagement of Book One's early chapters—"All one can say about most of these chapters is that there is nothing to say"—held sway.[1] There has recently been more and more to say, especially about the first. Celso Martins Azar Filho reports that the first chapter "is today considered a kind of introduction" to the *Essays* because it presents "ideas Montaigne judged fundamental and indispensable to understanding his work. . . . In fact, this text could be compared to the overture to an opera, in which most of the elements or themes to be developed are already present."[2] Lawrence D. Kritzman writes of this chapter that because "each of its stories possesses its own language that contradicts the meaning of another story" it serves "as a nuclear thematic model for the *Essais*."[3] For

---

1. Pierre Villey, *Les sources et l'évolution des "Essais" de Montaigne*, vol. 2: 44.
2. P. 15 of Celso Martins Azar Filho, "Le premier chapitre des *Essais*," *Bulletin de la Société des Amis de Montaigne* 8. 37–38 (January–June 2005): 15–30.
3. Lawrence D. Kritzman, *Destruction/Découverte: Le Fonctionnement de la Rhétorique dans les*

Frieda S. Brown, it justifies its liminal position as "the gateway," even if it cannot be said to possess "the rich development and fullness of later and better known essays."[4] Hugo Friedrich writes that its content justifies its position as the first chapter, for it "sets up the predominant moral theme of the *Essais*, namely the question of whether one can come to an understanding of concrete changeable man with general, rigid maxims."[5] Edwin M. Duval writes, "One could hardly imagine a better introduction to the *Essays*. I say 'introduction' in the strong sense of the term, for the logical path of the chapter seems made to *lead* us . . . from the active world of wars to the contemplative world of the *Essays*, from *exercitus* to the exercise of our natural faculties."[6]

I am particularly taken with Duval's formulation, because the kind of reading in which I invite you to engage is indeed such an exercise in contemplation, where there is at each juncture a puzzle to be solved—that of discovering how does one chapter respond to its symmetrically-linked partner—and where each chapter, by virtue of its place in Montaigne's overall scheme, has a claim on our attention. Wars and cruelty and begging for mercy are important (so much so that David Quint described his book *Montaigne and the Quality of Mercy* as "an extended commentary on Montaigne's first essay"[7]), but to the degree to which the *Essays* are not just the reflection of the writer's thought and not merely historically conditioned by their times the last chapter of Book One should merit as careful a reading as the first. "De l'aage" (1: 57) is much less studied than "Par divers moyens" because its apparent subject is much less compelling. Why should we care as much about natural life expectancy and compulsory retirement from public service as we would about how to escape from the wrath of a vengeful captor?

But if we are interested in why Montaigne ordered the chapters the way he did, if we can catch enough clues to begin to overhear one chapter conversing with another, and if we can tune in to the ways the *Essays* turn their topics into allusions to their own arrangement, then we can understand what Montaigne found interesting about tenure of office and the unnaturalness of natural deaths. This first symmetrical pair provides a good introduction

---

"Essais" de Montaigne (Lexington, KY: French Forum Publishers, 1980), 29, 21.

4. Pp. 144, 138–39 of Frieda S. Brown, "'By Diverse Means We Arrive at the Same End': Gateway to the *Essays*," In *Approaches to Teaching Montaigne's Essays*, ed. Patrick Henry (New York: Modern Language Association of America, 1994), 138–45.

5. Hugo Friedrich, *Montaigne*, translated by Dawn Eng (Berkeley: University of California Press, 1991), 145.

6. P. 900 of Edwin M. Duval, "Le début des 'Essais' et la fin d'un livre," *Revue d'Histoire Littéraire de la France* 99. 5 (1988): 896–907. Among other readings of I: 1 Steven Rendall's is particularly useful (*Distinguo: Reading Montaigne Differently* [Oxford: Clarendon Press, 1992], 15–21).

7. David Quint, *Montaigne and the Quality of Mercy: Ethical and Political Themes in the Essais* (Princeton: Princeton University Press, 1998), xi.

to the others, for it will be characteristic of those as it is of this pair that the chapters speak not only of the same things but of opposite things. As we will see in this instance, the "pareille fin" to which "divers moyens" lead is life in the first chapter but in the last, death.

"La plus commune façon" [The commonest way]—the *Essays'* first chapter began in 1580—"d'amollir les coeurs, de ceus qu'on a offensez, lors qu'ayant vengeance en main, ils nous tiennent à leur mercy, c'est de les émouuoir à commiseration & a pitié: toutes fois la braverie, la constance, & la resolution, moyens tous contraires ont quelque fois servi a ce mesme effet" [of softening the hearts of those we have offended, when with vengeance in hand they hold us at their mercy, is to move them to commiseration and pity; however, audacity, steadfastness, and resolution—entirely opposite means—have sometimes served to produce this same effect] (I: 1, 7a, DM 1; 3*). Thus the "divers moyens" to which the chapter's title refers turn out to number only two, of which one is most commonly used while the other has only "sometimes" [quelque fois] worked. But from the evidence Montaigne goes on to cite, despite the minority status the first sentence gives it, the second method appears the better choice. Of the seven anecdotes related in 1580, to which an eighth was added in 1588 and two more after 1588, in only one is the first method successful—and then just barely. The citizens of Thebes, having brought their military captains to trial for having stayed in command past their allotted term, absolved "à toutes peines" [just barely] Pelopidas, who yielded under the weight of their accusations and made "supplications" to escape the penalty. On the other hand, Epamnondas proudly recounted his mighty deeds and reproached the Thebans for accusing him. He was let off as well, the citizens barely having the heart to cast their ballots, and walking away from the assembly singing his praises (I: 1, 8a, DM 5–6; 4*).

In all the other cases Montaigne cites, the second means is resorted to. In the 1580 edition, in five out of six cases where the second is tried it is successful; in the three added in subsequent editions it is not, but in none of those three is the first means even attempted. In three out of the five instances in 1580 in which the second method succeeds the first method had been first tried but proved fruitless.

It would appear that although the first method is the most commonly attempted (a conclusion to which we might have arrived anyway in presuming that most people lack the courage to try the other), the cumulative effect of the examples cited is to suggest that the second is the better choice. In this way, the chapter finds a parallel in "De l'aage," where a certain common opinion is also shown to be wrong: "Je ne puis recevoir la *façon* dequoy nous establissons la durée de nostre vie. Je voy que les sages l'accoursissent bien fort au pris de la *commune* opinion" [I cannot accept the *way* in which we establish the duration of our life. I see that the sages, as compared with the *common* opinion, make it a great deal shorter] (I: 57, 326a, DM 490; 236*). I have italicized *façon* and *commune* in this quotation from the first two sentences of I: 57 because they recall the first words of the first sentence of I: 1: "La plus *commune façon* d'amollir les coeurs, de ceus qu'on a offensez, lors qu'ayant vengeance en main. . . ." Thus Book One begins by setting up a verbal echo, and begins its conclusion by completing it.

Montaigne's point is that an average human lifespan is shorter than we think, and that the common opinion is wrong as well that holds that most of us can expect to die of old age: "c'est la *façon* de mort la plus rare de toutes, & la moins en usage. Nous l'appelons seule naturelle, comme si c'estoit contre nature de voir un homme se rompre le col d'une cheute, s'estoufer d'un naufrage, se laisser surprendre à la peste ou à un pleuresi . . . on doit à l'aventure appeller plus tost naturel ce qui est general, *commun,* & universel" [it is the rarest *way* of dying of all, and the least in use. We call it alone natural, as if it were unnatural to see a man break his neck in a fall, drown in a shipwreck, fall victim to the plague or pleurisy. . . . One should perhaps instead call natural that which is general, *common,* and universal] (I: 57, 326a; DM 491–92; 236–37*). The first words of the other chapter—"La plus *commune façon*"—are echoed again here, where another *façon,* being rare, is not *commun[e].*[8]

Other verbal echoes will lead us to see just how deeply these two chapters parallel each other. In the first one's title, by diverse means "on *arrive* à pareille fin," while the end of which Montaigne writes in the other is an end at which one likewise *arrives:* Cato the Younger thought that his age of 48 years was "bien meur & bien auancé, considerant combien peu d'hommes y *arrivent*" [very ripe and advanced, considering how few men *arrive* there] (I: 57, 326a, DM 491; 236*); the essayist goes on to declare, "mon opinion est de regarder que l'aage auquel nous sommes *arrivez,* c'est un aage auquel peu de gens *arrivent*" [my opinion is to consider that the age at which we have *arrived* is an age at which people few *arrive*] (I: 57, 326a, DM 493; 237*). Furthermore, death is an end at which we all arrive by *diverse* means: of a broken neck, of drowning, of pleurisy and the plague, and once in two or three hundred years, of old age.

In both chapters one arrives at one's end by diverse means. In the chapter whose title makes a point of the diversity of those means, there is a choice of two such means, though the one commonly attempted, the evidence shows,

---

8. Old age was a "*façon* de mort" in 1580 and 1588; in 1595 it became an "espèce."

is only rarely a genuine means to the end in question. In the other chapter, the means are genuinely diverse (ironically so, given that it is the other chapter's title, not this one's, that speaks of their diversity), though the one commonly thought to be common is, the evidence shows, rare.

Of all the cases cited in I: 1, only one illustrates the title's assertion by a contrasting diversity of means leading to the same end. In all the other cases, either the first means is tried unsuccessfully and then the second leads to the desired end, or only the second is attempted, and not always with success. Only in the case of Pelopidas and Epaminondas do both means lead to a "pareille fin."[9] And only in that case is the end really the same, that of avoiding death at the hands of the same avenger for the same reason. It is, indeed, a special case. By coincidence (or maybe not) it is also features the rarest of echoes with "De l'aage." Pelopidas and Epaminondas were brought before the bar of justice and obliged to defend their lives "pour avoir continué leur charge *outre* le temps qui leur avoit esté *prescript* & preordonné" [for having continued their mandate *beyond* the time that had been *prescribed* and foreordained for them] (I: 1, 81, DM 5; 4*). In 1: 57 a death from old age is "la borne, au dela de laquelle nous n'yrons pas, & que la loy de nature a *prescript* pour n'estre point *outre*-passée" [the limit beyond which we will not go, and that the law of nature has *prescribed* not to be passed *beyond*] (I: 57, 326a, DM 492; 237*). Nowhere else in Book One do *outre* (either alone or as a prefix) and *prescrit* (whether masculine or feminine, singular or plural) appear in the same sentence. Both the law of nature and the law of Thebes prescribe a length of time that one cannot pass beyond.

Pelopidas and Epaminondas as military men who retire too late from their assigned duty find an inverse parallel in "De l'aage" when Montaigne takes up the case of soldiers retiring too soon. Servius Tullius let his knights retire from service at age 47; Augustus at 45. Montaigne thinks that is too young an age, preferring 55 or 60. In fact, "Je serois d'advis qu'on estan-

---

9. Epaminondas occupies a special place in Montaigne's esteem, with Homer and Alexander one of the three greatest men of history in the chapter "Des plus excellens hommes [On the most excellent men] (II: 36)—in fact, of the three, "le plus excellent, à mon gré" [the most excellent, to my mind] (II: 36, 756a; 572). He is in Montaigne's personal mythology the heroic equivalent of Plutarch, his most esteemed writer. Part of his fascination for Epaminondas is tied up with his fascination for Plutarch, that is for a part of Plutarch that will remain forever inaccessible to Montaigne, the Life of Epaminondas Plutarch wrote (together with the parallel Life of Scipio Aemilianus) that is missing from his *Parallel Lives*. "O quel desplaisir le temps m'a faict d'oster de nos yeux . . . la couple de vies justement la plus noble qui fust en Plutarque" [Oh, what pain time has given me by removing from our eyes . . . the most noble couple of lives that were in Plutarch] (II: 36, 757c; 573*). Epaminondas' contemporary equivalent in Montaigne's estimation is surely Étienne de La Boétie, whose text (the twenty-nine sonnets Montaigne made the centerpiece of Book One) likewise disappeared, in the passage of time, from the text of these *Essays* that, as I will try to show, have much in common with the *Parallel Lives* (a parallel that Marcel Tetel has suggested (*Montaigne: Updated Edition*. [Boston: G. K. Hall / Twayne's World Authors Series, 1990], 87).

dit nostre vacation et occupation autant qu'on pourroit pour la commodité publique" [I should be of the opinion that our employment and occupation should be extended as far as possible, for the public welfare] (I: 57, 327a, DM 494; 237). Montaigne has it both ways, setting up a parallel between the time limit imposed by Theban law on Pelopidas and Epaminondas and the time limit imposed by nature's law on the human lifespan, a parallel he underlines by his choice of echoing words, but also setting up a parallel between Pelopidas and Epaminondas' desire to stay in office longer than is legal and his own assertion that employment in public service should be extended as long as possible. It is as if he were taking up Pelopidas and Epaminondas' defense—but doing so in the symmetrically-related chapter.

Up this point everything I have discussed comes from the 1580 edition (the genuine 1580 text that Daniel Martin's reproduction provides, and not just the "A" passages from modern editions, which are not totally reliable). So it is apparent that Montaigne was engaged in these secret symmetries from the beginning. But we will see that in subsequent editions he added even more connections. An instance of that may be the curious B (that is, 1580) addition to I: 57 consisting entirely of "Si l'espine nou *pique* quand nai, / A pene que *pique* jamai, disent-ils en Dauphiné" [If the thorn doesn't *prick* at birth / It will hardly ever *prick,* they say in Dauphiné] (I: 57, 327b; 237*), which may have been placed there in connection with the B addition to I: 1 concerning Alexander the Great, who, "tout *piqué* d'une si chère victoire, car entre autres dommages, il avoit receu deux fresches blessures sur sa personne" [*pricked* by such a dearly won victory, for among other damage he had received two fresh wounds on his person] (I: 1, 9b; 5*) was uncharacteristically merciless to Betis. The point of the Dauphinois proverb is that if a trait isn't apparent in youth (by the age of twenty, as Montaigne says) it is unlikely ever to appear. But Alexander's pique and its consequence are at odds, as Montaigne notes, with his being normally "si gratieux aux vaincus" [so gracious to the vanquished] (I: 1, 9b; 5*). Even though it is in contradiction with the rest of what he says about Alexander it does fit well with the addition of the passage with "pique" to the corresponding chapter.

2. The Less Said

"De la tristesse" [Of sadness] (I: 2) and "Des prieres" [Of prayers] (1: 56)

In "Des prieres" Montaigne argues against praying any prayer but the Lord's Prayer, which he finds suitable for all occasions: before and after meals, upon rising and going to bed; indeed "à toutes actions particulieres, ausquelles on a accoustumé de mesler des prieres, je voudroy que ce fut le seul patenostre que les Chrestiens y emploiassent" [on all particular actions with which we are accustomed to associate prayers, I should like it to be the Lord's Prayer alone that Christians employ] (I: 56, 318a, DM 482; 230*).[10] Not only is it true that it "dit tout ce qui nous sert" [says all that serves us] (I: 56, DM 483; 230*),[11] but no other prayer is going to do any good anyway, for God "nous favorise selon la raison de sa justice, non selon nos inclinations & volontez" [favors us according to the reason of his justice, not according to our inclinations and desires] (I: 56, 318a, DM 483; 230*).[12] Montaigne's position against putting religious thoughts into any words other than those God has prescribed extends to his approval of the Church's forbidding "l'usage promiscue, temeraire & indiscret" [the promiscuous, reckless, and indiscreet use] of the Psalms. "Cette voix est trop divine. pour n'avoir autre usage que d'exercer les poulmons et plaire à nos oreilles. C'est de la conscience qu'elle doit estre produite, & non pas de la langue" [This voice is too divine to have no other use than to exercise our lungs and please our ears; it is from the conscience that it should be produced, and not from the tongue] (I: 56, 320a, DM 484–85; 232*). The prayers men make are too often not worth making, and betray unchristian thoughts. "L'avaricieux le prie pour la conservation vaine et superflue de ses tresors" [The miser prays to him for the vain and superfluous conservation of his treasures] (I: 56, 324a, DM 486; 235); the thief, the murderer, and the adulterer pray for success in their enterprises.

What could this drastic limitation of what ought to be said in prayer have to do with sadness, the ostensible subject of I: 2, "De la tristesse"? We can arrive at the answer once we realize that I: 2 is actually about emotions, of which sadness is but one example, that are so great that they cannot be expressed.[13] Psammenitus, for example, said not a word when his daughter was taken prisoner and his son put to death, but began to beat his head in

---

10. In post-1588 editions, "seul" is replaced by "sinon seulement, au moins toujours" [if not only, at least always] (I: 56, 318c).

11. Altered after 1588 to "tout ce qu'il nous faut" [all we need], incorrectly attributed by Villey (p. 318) and by Rat (p. 303) to the "A" stratum.

12. Altered after 1588 to "et nous favorise selon la raison d'icelle, non selon nos demandes" [et favors us according to its reasons, not acording to our demands].

13. Fausta Garavini likewise notes that "the title 'Of sadness' is far from embracing all the content of the chapter." After the beginning, "it all has very little to do with sadness, except that what underlies these successive displacements—from sadness to love to joy to shame—the leveling similarity that welds these examples together is the excessive character of passion, whose effects are fatal." Pp. 131–32 of her article "Le Fantasme de la mort muette (à propos de I, 2, 'De la tristesse')," *Bulletin de la Société des Amis de Montaigne,* 7th series, no. 13–16 (July–December 1988, January–June 1989): 127–39. The effect of such passion is not just death but also silence.

grief when he saw one of his servants among the captives: "c'est, respondit-il, que ce seul dernier desplaisir se peut signifier par larmes, les deux premiers surpassans de bien loin tout moyen de se pouvoir exprimer" ["it is," he said, "because this last grief alone can be signified by tears; the first two far surpass any power of expression"] (I: 2,12a, DM 8; 6). Montaigne cites the case of the painter who could depict the grief of the onlookers at Iphigenia's sacrifice but "quand se vint au pere de la fille, il le peignit le visage couvert, comme si nulle contenance ne pouvoit representer ce degré de deuil" [when he came to the girl's father portrayed him with his face covered, as if no countenance could represent that degree of grief] (I: 2, 12a, DM 9; 6). Likewise, poets depict Niobe as mute as stone at the news of her children's death. As Petrarch wrote, speaking of love, not sadness, "Chi puo dir, com' egli arde é in picciol fuoco" [He who can say how he burns, burns little] (I: 2, 13a, DM 10; 7); similarly, Seneca: "Curae leves loquuntur, ingentes stupent" [Light cares can speak, but heavy ones are mute] (I: 2, 13a, DM 11; 8). That this chapter, despite its title, is not about sadness but rather the impossibility of expressing, and in some cases even surviving, extremely strong emotions really becomes apparent when Montaigne leaves sadness behind to move on to instances of lust and unexpected pleasure, and then to examples of persons dying from joy: a mother who saw her son return from battle alive, Sophocles, Dionysius the tyrant, Talva, and Pope Leo X. He concludes with a curious case of death from shame, that of Diodorus the dialectician, who collapsed and died "pour en son eschole & en public ne se pouvoir desveloper d'un argument qu'on luy avoit faict" [because in his own school and in public he could not refute an argument that had been put to him] (I: 2, 14a, DM 12; 8*).

The discussion in "De la tristesse" turns not only away from its own title but towards the discussion in "Des prieres" of what Montaigne there says of what "doit estre produit" [should be produced] "de la conscience . . . & non pas de la langue" [from the conscience . . . and not from the tongue] (I: 56, 320a, DM 484–85; 232*). In I: 2 a passion that can be expressed is not worth expressing ("Chi puo dir, com' egli arde é in picciol fuoco"), while in I: 56 a prayer of human invention, as opposed to the Lord's Prayer, is not worth expressing, either because God knows our needs anyway and will dispense them according to his justice with no regard for our desire or because such prayers are selfish and criminal. What is genuine and heartfelt—be it grief or piety—cannot be expressed. In I: 2 it cannot be expressed at all; in 1: 56 it cannot be humanly expressed, only divinely expressed in the words God gave us to say in the Lord's Prayer.

Yet another instance of the general rule that the deepest passion cannot find expression is "la défaillance fortuite, qui surprent les amoureus si hors de saison, cete glace qui les saisit par la force d'une ardeur extreme *au giron mesme de la joüyssance*" [the accidental failing that surprises lovers so unseasonably, this freezing that seizes them by the force of extreme ardor *in the very lap of enjoyment*] (I: 2, 13ab, DM 11; 7). Montaigne added the words I have italicized in 1588. The sexual context of this *giron*[14] clashes intriguingly with the devotional context of an answering *giron* in "Des prières": "la loi divine . . . nous appelle à soy, ainsi fautier et detestables comme nous sommes: elle nous tend les bras et nous reçoit en son *giron*, pour vilains, ords et bourbeux que nous soyons" [divine law . . . calls us to herself, sinful and detestable as we are; she stretches out her arms and receives us in her *lap*, no matter how vile, filthy, and besmirched we are] (I: 56, 325a, DM 489; 236*). Instead of praying even memorized prayers insincerely with "l'ame pleine de concupiscence, non toucheé de repentance" [our soul full of lust, untouched by repentance] (I: 56, 325a, DM 489; 236), we should simply crawl into that lap, and be suitably grateful that God pardons us. God as a mother with outstretched arms and a waiting lap is now (beginning in 1588) paralleled by a mistress with an equally welcoming lap, though it waits in vain.

In 1582 Montaigne made an addition to the beginning of I: 56: "Je propose icy des fantasies informes & irresolues, comme font ceux qui *publient* des questions doubteuses à debattre aux *escoles*" [I put forward formless and unresolved notions, as do those who *publish* doubtful questions to debate in the *schools*] (I: 56, 317a'; 229).[15] He doubtless inserted these introductory remarks (which continue beyond the passage quoted here) to mollify the Papal censor, who had objected to what he had written in this chapter about the inefficacy of any prayer other than the Lord's Prayer. Yet now the beginning of this chapter also echoes the end of I: 2, with its account of Diodorus the dialectician who died of shame "pour en son *eschole* & en *public* ne se pouvoir desveloper d'un argument qu'on luy avoit faict" [in his own *school* and in *public* not being able to refute an argument that had been put to him] (I: 2, 14a, DM 12; 8).

We have seen that the two chapters talk about the same thing; do they also talk about it in opposite ways, as do I: 1 and I: 57? Indeed, and by repeating a certain word. In the first example in "De la tristesse" of an emotion too great to be expressed, Psammenitus remained motionless and mute

---

14. And of this *jouissance;* elsewhere in the *Essays, jouir* can mean to have an orgasm: "Amasis, Roy d'Egypte, espousa Laodice tresbelle fille Grecque: et luy . . . se trouva court à jouir d'elle, et menaça de la tuer, estimant que ce fust quelque sorcerie" [Amasis, king of Egypt, married Laodice, a very beautiful Greek girl; and he . . . fell short when it came to enjoying her, and threatened to kill her, thinking it was some sort of sorcery] (I: 21, 101c; 71).

15. *Essais. Reproduction photographique de la deuxième édition (Bordeaux 1582)* (Paris: Société des Textes Français Modernes, 2005), 296.

when his daughter was led away, and when his son was taken out to be killed, "se maintint en cete mesme *contenance*" [he maintained the same *countenance*] (I: 2, 11a, DM 7; 6*), which is to say that his countenance communicated nothing at all. And a painter chose to represent Iphigenia's father with his face covered, "comme si nulle *contenance* ne pouvoit representer ce degré de deuil" [as if no *countenance* could represent that degree of grief] (I: 2,12a, DM 9; 6). In both instances, the countenance does not communicate, whether from taciturnity or invisibility. In "Des prieres," a countenance is likewise associated with a failure to communicate: "Nous prions par usage et par coustume: ou, pour mieus dire, nous lisons ou prononçons nos prieres: ce n'est en fin, que *contenance*" [We pray out of habit and custom, or to speak more correctly, we read or pronounce our prayers. It is, in the end, but *countenance*] (I: 56, 319a, DM 484; 230–31*). Prayer is communication with God, but here merely reading or pronouncing prayers is said to be mere countenance, undertaken by someone only pretending to pray and therefore not really communicating. It is all appearance, and is thus the opposite of Agamemnon's countenance because his was entirely invisible, and communicated his grief all the better for that reason.

In a post-1588 alteration *contenance* in the I: 56 passage just quoted became *mine* ["outward show" or "facial expression"]. But in the meantime, two other *contenances* had appeared in I: 56, as Montaigne kept tinkering with the text. The first to be added, in 1588,[16] appears in a passage whose sense parallels that of the passage just quoted about prayers spoken from habit which are nothing more than countenance: "Il semble à la verité, que nous nous servons de nos prieres, comme ceux qui emploient les paroles sainctes & divines à des sorceleries & effectz magiciens, & que nous facions nostre conte que ce soit de la contexture, ou son, ou suite des motz, ou de nostre *contenance,* que depende leur effect" [It seems, in truth, that we use our prayers like those who use holy and divine words for sorceries and magical effects; and that we count on their effect depending on the texture, sound, or sequence of the words, or on our *countenance*] (I: 56, 325ab, DM 489; 236*). The words "ou de nostre *contenance*" are those added in 1588. This passage is fascinating for the way it seems to allude to the phenomenon of which it is an instance, the repetition of words from one chapter to another—the common *contexture* linking chapters like these through the repetition of the word itself *contenance.* Montaigne's zeal for using the same prayer (the Lord's Prayer) on all sorts of different occasions and contexts now seems self-referential too, for that is what he does with particular words and

---

16. Villey incorrectly dates it from 1580.

"suite[s] des mots," from *outre* and *prescript* in the previous pair of chapters to *countenance* here.

A third *contenance* appears in the following 1588 passage, concerning the proper use of the Psalms: "et y apporter le corps mesme disposé en *contenance* qui tesmoigne une particuliere attention et reverence" [and always bring even the body disposed in a *countenance* that bears witness to a particular attentiveness and reverence] (I: 56, 321b; 232*). In opposition to the uncommunicative countenances of Psammenitus and Agamemnon, this one does communicate; in contrast to the other two in "Des prieres," it is sincere.

To sum up, to the presence in I: 2 of a missing *contenance* (in the depiction of Agamemnon's grief) I: 56 responds with a complicated series of textual changes in which *contenances* gradually appear and disappear, and whose expressive power is, ironically, problematic.

3. Something to Hide

"Nos affections s'emportent au dela de nous" [Our feelings carry themselves beyond us] (I: 3) and "Des senteurs" [Of smells] (I: 55)

In I: 3 Montaigne writes of posthumous concerns such as the belief that celestial favors "nous accompaignent au tombeau, & continuent à nos reliques" [accompany us to the tomb, and continue with our remains] (I: 3, 18a, DM 13; 10*). He cites, in 1580 (adding more later), the cases of: the defeated defenders of a besieged fortress being obliged to carry out the keys of the city on the body of the deceased commander of the siege; an argument over whether it was seemly to ask for safe conduct through enemy territory to carry the body of the Venetian commander to Venice, since in life he would never have been afraid of his enemies; King Edward I of England requesting that after his death his bones be carried onto the battlefield "comme si la destinée avoit fatalement ataché la victoire à ses membres" [as if destiny had fatally attached victory to his limbs] (I: 3, 18a, DM 14; 11); and Captain Bayard, who when mortally wounded had his steward set him at the base of a tree facing the enemy. Montaigne then provides (and in the 1580 edition concludes the chapter with) an "exemple aussi remerquable pour cete consideration, que nul des precedens" [example as remarkable for the present consideration as any of the preceding ones], that of the Emperor Maximilian, who had many great qualities, including physical beauty. But unlike most kings, who are not averse to conducting official business while seated on the toilet, he would let no one see him in that situation. He would even urinate in private, "aussi religieux qu'une fille à ne *descouvrir* ny à medecin ny à qui que ce fut les parties qu'on a accoustumé de tenir cachées : & jusques à telle superstition, qu'il ordonna par parolles expresses de son testament, qu'on luy attachat des calessons quand il seroit mort" [as scrupulous as a virgin not *to uncover*, either to a doctor or to anyone else whatever, the parts that are customarily kept hidden: and to such a point of superstition that he ordered in so many words in his will that they should put underdrawers on him when he was dead] (I: 3, 18–19a, DM 16; 11*).

This piquant anecdote finds lexical and situational parallels in the following passage from "Des senteurs" (comprising a fourth of the fewer than two hundred words that made up that chapter in 1580): "La plus parfaicte senteur d'une femme c'est ne sentir à rien. Et les bonnes senteurs estrangieres, on a raison de les tenir pour suspectes à ceus qui s'en servent, & d'estimer qu'elles soient emploiées pour *couvrir* quelque defaut naturel de ce costé là" [The most perfect smell for a woman is to smell of nothing. And perfumes are rightly considered suspicious in those who use them, and thought to be used *to cover up* some natural defect in that quarter] (I: 55, 314a, DM 481; 228). Some "défaut naturel" is what one could reasonably conclude Maximilian to have had and to have wanted to conceal. In that light, what the emperor refused to *descouvrir* parallels what perfumes are used to *couvrir*.

"Des senteurs" closed with the following Latin quotation in 1580 (and continued to include it in subsequent editions): "*Posthume* non bene olet, qui bene semper olet" [*Postumus,* one does not smell good who always smells good] (I: 55, 314a, DM 481; 228*). Considering that chapter I: 3 is about what happens after death, it is an interesting coincidence that Martial, the poet whose line Montaigne is citing, was addressing someone who happened to be named Postumus, the superlative of the adverb *post* in Latin, meaning a last-born male child. Martial (ca. 38–104 C.E.) spelled it without the h; Montaigne in quoting him spells it with.[17] The word was "in late Latin written *posthumus* through erroneous attribution to *humus* the earth or (as explained by Servius [ca. 420 C.E.]) *humare* to bury" (*Oxford English*

---

17. Here is Martial's epigram, whose fourth line Montaigne quotes: Esse quid hoc dicam, quod olent tua basia murram / Quodque tibi est numquam non alienus odor? / Hoc mihi suspectum est, quod oles bene, Postume, semper: / Postume, non bene olet qui bene semper olet [What am I to understand from the circumstance, that your kisses always smell of myrrh, and that you never have about you an odor other than unnatural? That you always smell so agreeably, Postumus, makes me suspect that you have something to conceal. He does not smell pleasantly, Postumus, who always smells pleasantly] (Martial, Epigrams. Book 2. *Bohn's Classical Library* (1897) at http://www.tertullian.org/fathers/martial_epigrams_book02.htm).

Dictionary). *Humare* becomes in French *inhumer*, a verb that appears twice in I: 3, and nowhere else: (1) in a 1588 addition: "par les loix Grecques, celuy qui demandoit à l'ennemy un corps pour l'*inhumer*, renonçait à la victoire" [by Greek laws he who asked the enemy for a body *to bury* it renounced the victory] (I: 3, 17b; 10); (2) in a post-1588 addition: the Athenians executed their captains because after a naval victory they pursued the enemy rather than "recueillir et *inhumer* leurs morts" [gather up and *bury* their dead] (I: 3, 20c; 13). These occurrences of the verb intimately connected to the h in "Posthume" as Montaigne spells it are part of the fabric of intratextual connections that he continued to create between his symmetrically paired chapters in successive editions. The last line of "Des senteurs" in the first edition uncannily combines the posthumous nature of those affections that "s'emportent au dela de nous," in other words the entire argument of I: 3, with the argument and theme of I: 55. This is true even though the contexts—posthumous effects and smells—would seem at first glance to have nothing at all to do with each other.

The posthumous concerns listed in I: 3 are presented as absurdities, particularly as they culminate in Maximilian's insistence on being buried in underpants. Montaigne remarks that the latter should have added a codicil to his will, that whoever attach them to his corpse be blindfolded. The idea that celestial favors accompany us to the tomb and continue with our remains is in Montaigne's estimation wrong. Such favor may have existed in life for some but they do not persist beyond it, and are not, as Edward I seemed to have thought, destined to remain attached to our bones. "Des senteurs," however, offers a concrete, material case of something that originates in a body yet does persist beyond it: *senteurs*. The 1588 edition develops this opposition between a persistence that isn't (in I: 3) and a persistence that is (in I: 55) and a post-1588 addition develops it still more. A 1588 addition to I: 55 enriches the comparison by creating verbal echoes with the other chapter: "Quelque odeur que ce soit, c'est merveille combien elle *s'attache* à moy, et combien j'ay la peau propre à s'en abreuver. Celuy qui se plaint de nature, desquoy elle a laissé l'homme sans instrument à *porter* les senteurs aux nez, a tort, car elles *se portent* elles mesmes" [Whatever the odor is, it is a marvel how it *attaches itself* to me and how apt my skin is to imbibe it. He who complains of nature that she has left man without an instrument to *carry* smells to his nose is wrong, for they *carry themselves*] (I: 55, 315b; 228*). That smells "*se portent* elles mesmes" [*carry themselves*] places them in parallel with the affections that in I: 3's title "*s'emportent*" [*carry themselves* away]. That Montaigne in this passage should focus on the portability of smells is a direct invitation to read this chapter in tandem with I: 3, for in the instances he cites there that verb keeps insisting:

1. The defeated citizens of Rancon were obliged to "*porter* les clefs de la place sur le corps" [*carry* the keys to the city on the body] (I: 3, 17a, DM 12; 10*) of their dead enemy.
2. A fellow officer was opposed to asking the enemy's permission to "*raporter*" [*carry back*] the body of Bartolomeo Alviano through enemy territory to Venice (I: 3, 17a, DM 12; 10).
3. Edward I gave instructions to "*porter*" [*carry*] his bones into every battle against the Scots (I: 3, 18a, DM 14; 10–11).

To these from 1580 Montaigne added two more in 1588:

4. John Vischa wanted his followers to make a drum out of his skin to "*porter*" [*carry*] into battle (I: 3, 18b; 11).
5. There were Indians who "*portoient*" [*carried*] one of their captains' bones into combat against the Spaniards (I: 3, 18b; 11).

In the first sentence of the passage quoted above I italicize "*s'atache*" [attaches itself] as well. Here's why: when Montaigne writes of King Edward I of England requesting that after his death his bones be carried onto the battlefield he adds this remark: "comme si la destinée avoit fatalement *ataché* la victoire à ses membres" [as if destiny had fatally *attached* victory to his limbs] (I: 3, 18a, DM 14; 11). Odors are not only, as some believe posthumous powers to be, portable; like them, they are attachable as well.

The word play extends to the other instance of attaching in I: 3, Maximilian's demand "qu'on luy *attachat* des calessons quand il seroit mort" [that one *attach* underdrawers on him when he died] (I: 3, 19a, DM 16; 11*). The connection is to the covering role those attachable drawers would play, for smells can cover too, as we have seen: "les bonnes senteurs estrangieres, on a raison de les tenir pour suspectes a ceus qui s'en servent, & d'estimer qu'elles soient emploiées pour *couvrir* quelque defaut naturel de ce costé la" [perfumes are rightly considered suspicious in those who use them, and thought to be used to *cover up* some natural defect in that quarter] (I: 55, 314a, DM 481; 314).

Montaigne made a distinction between his first two examples in I: 3 (the surrender of Rancon and Bartolomeo Alviano) and his third (Edward I, who wanted his bones carried onto future battlefields): "Les premiers ne reservent au tombeau, que la reputation acquise par leurs actions passées: mais cetuy cy y veut encore trainer la puissance d'*agir*" [The first examples reserve for the tomb only the reputation acquired by their past actions; but the latter wants to include as well the power to *act*] (I: 3, 18a, DM 14; 11*). In the passage added to I: 55 in 1588 in which he shows that odors have the same portability divine favor is claimed to have in I: 3 he goes on to explain how, like the victory attached to Edward I's bones, it has the power to *act:* "Les medecins pourroient, croi-je, tirer des odeurs plus d'usage qu'ils ne font: car j'ay souvent aperçeu qu'elles me changent, et *agissent* en mes esprits selon qu'elles sont" [The doctors might, I believe, derive more use from odors than they do; for I have often noticed that they change me and *act* upon my spirits according to their properties] (I: 55, 315b; 229*). He cites incense in churches, which has the power to awaken and purify the senses, leading us to contemplation.

It is as if the parallel chapters were engaged over the years and through successive editions in a continuing conversation, as additions in one reply to things said in the other. We already saw instances of this in the previous pairing, I: 2 and I: 56, finding alterations that added still more instances of *contenance* to I: 56 as if in response to those in I: 2. So far we have seen this happen in the case of *porter, s'attacher,* and *agir* (with I: 3 even appearing to respond with two more instances of *porter* to I: 55's reply to its first three instances). It happens again in a post-1588 addition to I: 3 that appears to echo two other words from the I: 55 passage just quoted, *changer* and *selon:* "nature nous faict voir, que plusieurs choses mortes ont encore des relations occultes à la vie. Le vin s'altere aux caves, selon aucunes mutations des saisons de sa vigne. Et la chair de venaison *change* d'estat aux saloirs et de goust, *selon* les loix de la chair vive, à ce qu'on dit" [nature shows us that many dead things still have occult relations to life. Wine alters in the cellars according to certain seasonal changes in its vine. And venison *changes* its condition and flavor in the salting tubs *according to* the laws of the live flesh, so they say] (I: 3, 21c; 13). Though both the preposition *selon* and the verb *changer* are so common that one or the other of them can be found in almost any chapter, they appear in the same sentence only here, in this late addition to I: 3, and in the passage in I: 55 where Montaigne says that odors "me *changent,* et agissent en mes esprits *selon* qu'elles sont" [*change* me and act upon my spirits *according to* their properties] (I: 55, 315b; 229*). The conversation continues, as well as the metafiction: like the dead and living venison chapters 3 and 55 have an occult relation to each other, each *changing* according to [*selon*] *changes* that occur in the other.

4. Frivolous and Vain

"Comme l'ame descharge ses passions sur des objects faux, quand les vrais luy defaillent" [How the soul discharges its passions on false objects when the true are lacking] (I: 4) and *"Des vaines subtilitez"* [Of vain subtleties] (I: 54)

As Michel Butor points out (*Essais sur les Essais,* 164), "Des vaines subtilitez" (I: 54) is the central chapter of the *Essays'* 107 (57 + 37 + 13), even though the last 13 chapters, comprising Book Three, would not appear until 1588. Yet Montaigne could have already envisioned that there would be 13 more chapters to complete the 94 in the first two books. In fact, there is evidence that he was aware in writing I: 54 that it would become the numerical center of the whole:

1. The last sentence of the chapter places the *Essays* themselves in a middle position, suggesting that the chapter itself could be a microcosm of the whole: "si ces essais estoient dignes qu'on en jugeat, il en pourroit advenir à mon advis, qu'ilz ne plairoient guiere aus espritz grossiers & ignorans, ny guiere aus delicatz & savans. Ceux la ny entendroint pas assez, ceux cy y entendroient trop, ils trouveroient place entre ces deux extremitez" [if these essays were worthy of being judged, it seems to me that they would hardly please gross and ignorant minds nor delicate and scholarly ones either. The former would not understand enough; the latter would understand too much. They would find a place between these two extremities] (I: 54, 313a, DM 480; 227*).[18] Montaigne made two successive changes to the very last words, each of which intensified this centering effect. The first change was to add the phrase "ils trouveroient place entre ces deux extremités," which did not appear on page 480 of the 1580 but among the errata in the front of the book ("Les plus insignes fautes survenues en l'impression du premier livre" [The most egregious errors arising in the printing of the first book]). Of all the *fautes* it is by the far the most substantial, the other twenty-nine concerning only commas, periods, or the addition or alteration of at most one or two words at a time. The only erratum that is an entire sentence, it looks less like a printer's error than an author's afterthought. In any case, he apparently wanted to make sure these last words, which so curiously seem to allude to the chapter itself, would not get left out of his text. He had

---

18. In 1582 Montaigne replaced "aus espritz grossiers & ignorans, ny guiere aus delicatz & savans" by "aux espritz communs & vulgaires, ni guiere aux singuliers & excellens" [common and vulgar minds, nor singular and excellent ones] (DM 480n).

another afterthought in 1582, when he changed these words to "Ils pourroient vivoter en la moyenne region" [They might be able to get by in the middle region]. Of these two changes the first ("ils trouveroient place entre ces deux extremitez") situated the *Essays* between two extremities; the second ("Ils pourroient vivoter en la moyenne region") placed them not just somewhere between two extremes but more precisely in the middle.

2. This middle chapter is a chapter about middles—middles between extremes that touch. Montaigne writes that at his house he and his friends had just been trying to see who could think of the greatest number of things "qui se tiennent par les deux boutz estremes" [that are connected by two extremes], such as the title "Sire," used only for kings and the lower social levels, nowhere in-between; similarly, "Dames." He cites Democritus's opinion that gods and beasts have senses more acute then men, "qui sont au moyen estage" [who are on the middle level] (I: 54, 311a, DM 577; 226*).

Sometimes the middle is a good place to be: "La foiblesse qui nous vient de froideur & desgoutement aux exercices de Venus, elle nous vient aussi d'un appetit trop vehement & d'une chaleur desreglée" [The incapacity that comes over us in the sports of Venus from lack of ardor and loss of attraction comes as well from too vehement a desire and an unruly lust] (I: 54, 312a; DM 477–78; 226*). "L'enfance & la decrepitude se rencontrent en imbecilité de cerveau. L'avarice & la profusion en pareil desir d'attirer & d'acquerir" [Infancy and decrepitude meet in weakness of the brain; avarice and extravagance, in a like desire to take and acquire] (I: 54, 312a, DM 479; 226).

Sometimes the middle is a bad place to be:

> La bestise & la sagesse se rencontrent en mesme point de gout & de resolution à la souffrance des accidens humains. Les sages gourmandent & commandent le mal, & les autres l'ignorent. Ceux cy sont, par maniere de dire, au deça des accidens : les autres au dela, lesquels apres en avoir bien poisé & consideré les qualitez, les avoir mesurez & jugez telz qu'ils sont, ils s'eslancent au dessus par force d'un vigoreus courage. . . . L'ordinaire & moyenne condition des hommes loge entre ces deux extremitez, qui est de ceuz qui aperçoivent les maux, les goustent, & ne les peuvent supporter.

> [Stupidity and wisdom meet at the same point of feeling and of resolving to endure human accidents. The wise curb and control the evil; the others are not aware of it. The latter are, so to speak, on this side of accidents, the former beyond them; for the wise man, after having well weighed and considered their qualities and measured and judged them for what they are,

springs above them by the power of a vigorous courage. . . . The ordinary and middle condition of men lodges between these two extremes, which is that of those who perceive evils, feel them, and cannot endure them.] (I: 54, 312a, DM 478–79; 226*)[19]

3. In I: 54 Montaigne refers to the overall shape of certain literary texts. "Nous voyons des oeufz, des boules, des aisles, des haches façonnées ancienement par les Grecs avec la mesure de leurs vers en les alongeant ou accoursissant: en maniere qu'ilz viennent à representer telle ou telle figure" [We see eggs, balls, wings, hatchets, shaped by the Greeks of old with the measure of their verses, by lengthening some lines and shortening others so as to represent one or another of these figures] (I: 54, 311a, DM 475; 225). In aligning his chapters in symmetrical pairs so that within each book those extremes touch, Montaigne gives a certain form to his *Essays*. What that form resembles is not a physical object like an egg or a hatchet but what he goes on to describe in "Des vaines subtilitez": extremes that meet and a middle that is sometimes valorized and sometimes put into question. This is most readily apparent in Book One, whose middle is unlike any other chapter and is presented as a text by another hand, and one which turned up at the last minute by chance. Later on, in "De la vanité," Montaigne would speak of the overall form of the *Essays* thus:

> Mon livre est tousjours un. Sauf qu'à mesure qu'on se met à le renouveller, afin que l'acheteur ne s'en aille les mains du tout vuides, je me donne loy d'y attacher (comme ce n'est qu'une *marqueterie* mal jointe), quelque embleme supernumeraire. Ce ne sont que surpoids, qui ne condamnent point la premiere forme, mais donnent quelque pris particulier à chacune des suivantes par une petite *subtilité* ambitieuse. De là toutesfois il adviendra facilement qu'il s'y mesle quelque transposition de chronologie, mes contes prenans place selon leur opportunité, non tousjours selon leur aage.

---

19. Bernard Sève, in "Les 'vaines subtilitez': Montaigne et le renversement du pour au contre," *Montaigne Studies* 16.1–2 (March 2004): 185–96), seems not to have realized that this passage appears in the 1580 version, which he criticizes for lacking "the idea of a passage from one healthy situation to another healthy situation by traversing a vain one" (194), a "dialectic" he finds in certain post-1588 additions. For the wise were once ignorant, as all are in infancy, and then like most men aware and troubled by the slings and arrows of outrageous fortune, but progressed beyond that middle position by their intelligence and courage. Sève also misrepresents Montaigne in the 1580 version when he claims that although he mentions the intermediate zone there "it is not this zone that interests him there but what interests him is the *topos* of the extremes that touch" (193). But as we have seen, Montaigne does pay attention to middle zones in 1580, differentiating between the desirable and the undesirable.

[My book is always one. Except that at each new edition, so that the buyer may not come off completely empty-handed, I allow myself to add, since it is only a badly joined *marquetry,* some extra ornaments. These are only overweights, which do not condemn the original form, but give some special value to each of the subsequent ones, by a bit of ambitious *subtlety.* Thence, however, it will easily happen that some transposition of chronology may slip in, for my stories take their place according to their timeliness, not always according to their age.] (III: 9, 964c; 736*)

It is a *marqueterie,* "un ouvrage de menuiserie, composé de feuilles de différents bois plaquées sur un assemblage, et représentant diverses figures, ou d'autres ornements" [a piece of woodwork composed of veneers of different woods affixed to a structure and representing various figures or ornaments] (*Littré*).[20] The number of chapters does not change; additions do not become new chapters but are added within existing ones, without destroying the original form. Despite his denigration of "vaines subtilitez" in I: 54, in this passage he reveals that he delights in incorporating from time to time "une petite subtilité ambitieuse." His anecdotes are placed where they are by their "opportunité," not their chronology. He writes, for example, of texts whose components are lengthened and shortened to fit an overall pattern in I: 54, for it is there that the opportunity presents itself to allude to such subtleties, as well as to middles between extremes that meet, in the central chapter of the *Essays*' 107. Montaigne shortened and lengthened too, like the poets he pretends to criticize: to produce three volumes of roughly equal size despite the second volume having 35% fewer chapters than the first, the third having 65% fewer than the second and 77% fewer than the first, he made most of the 13 chapters of the third volume much longer than those in the preceding volumes, and he made one chapter in the second volume, the immense "Apologie de Raimond Sebond" (II: 12), 22 times longer than the average of the volume's other chapters.

---

20. In "What does Montaigne mean by 'marqueterie'?," *Studies in Philology* 67. 2 (1970): 147–55, Barbara Bowen cites engravings of Androuet du Cerceau dating from about 1560 as evidence that Montaigne could have been familiar with floors constructed of marqueterie featuring complicated symmetrical and circular patterns. These engravings may be viewed at http://architectura.cesr.univ-tours.fr/ Traite/Images/INHA-4R84BIndex.asp. Bowen suggests that the composition of each of the chapters is circular: "these patterns are strikingly reminiscent of the structure of an *essai*. If you select one line and follow it through the pattern, its progress seems to have no logic or symmetry, but if you stand back and consider the overall effect it is obvious that every line and shape is necessary to the symmetry of the whole. It is very tempting indeed to assume that Montaigne is thinking of a pattern of this type when he uses the word *marqueterie*" (154). But one needs to stand back at an even greater distance to see what Montaigne was actually alluding to, the symmetry of each of the *Essays*' three books.

4. There is a mathematical reason that suggests, apart from what Montaigne wrote in "Des vaines subtilitez," that he had already decided before the 1580 edition appeared that he would write 13 more chapters. It is not the reason Butor gave, which is far from convincing. Butor's argument is based on his notion that Book One "is divided into three principal regions, whose articulations are chapters 19 and 39" (129). He arrives at this conclusion by reading groups of chapters as if they were all about the same thing (as he does with regard to these on pp. 73–74), which is not a good way to read them. He finds three thematic groups of 18 chapters in Book One, not including I: 19, I: 29, and I: 39; he divides Book Two into two groups of 18 chapters separated by II: 19, and Book Three into two groups of 6 separated by III: 7. Then he concludes, "Apart from the *middles,* the number of chapters in Book Two [36] is equal to ⅔ of those of Book One [54], and that of Book Three [12] to ⅓ of that of Book Two" (Butor's italics, 174). He is right to see that the three middle chapters (I: 29, II: 19, III: 7) stand apart from the rest, but he is talking about *five* middles here because he includes I: 19 and I: 39.

I have a mathematically based observation of my own to make. It does not attempt to say why the first book has 57 and the second 37, but does suggest why, if those first two numbers have already been selected, the third number should be 13. It is that if we assign A to the number 57, B to 37, and C to 13, B/A + C/B = unity. That is, 37/57 + 13/37 = 1. Unity, one, as in "Mon livre est tousjours un." There are other trios of numbers that could be plugged in to come up with 1, but if A and B are determined as 57 and 37, then for unity to be achieved C has to be 13.[21]

---

21. There is another consideration that I do not present as proof of anything but that is immensely interesting though it has remained, I believe, unknown until now. Rabelais's *Quart Livre* (1552), as Edwin M. Duval has shown, is symmetrically constructed (so too, he demonstrates, the *Tiers Livre*). In the numerical center of the *Quart Livre* (as in the *Essays,* the symmetry is determined by the number of chapters and their arrangement), a symmetrical pattern of 107 elements appears, when Pantagruel slays a whale that threatens to sink his fleet:

> In chapter 34, the numerically central chapter of the book . . . Pantagruel fills the skin of the attacking monster with 107 well-placed harpoons hurled with deadly precision. The first harpoon strikes the beast dead center in the middle of its forehead, at a point equidistant from the second and third harpoons, which pierce its eyes on either side of its head. . . . Pantagruel multiplies patterns in which symmetry around a central point predominate. Between the triangle planted on the forehead and a single harpoon planted in the tail, he places three more harpoons equally spaced along the spine. . . . And around this second triad he constructs yet a third symmetrical pattern in which the three harpoons sticking perpendicularly out of the whale's back mark the median position between two rows of 50 harpoons placed symmetrically along each flank. That these obvious geometrical representations of centered symmetry should appear at the precise numerical midpoint of the *Quart Livre,* and that Pantagruel should construct exactly *three triads* in a chapter that is both preceded and followed by exactly *thirty-three* chapters is impossible

Although I: 54 is the center of the *Essays* in their totality, the middle that occupies us here is the one in the center of Book One (I: 29) that makes it possible for such chapters as I: 1, I: 2, and I: 3 to find their counterparts in I: 57, I: 56, and I: 55—and "Des vaines subtilitez" (I: 54) in "Comme l'ame descharge ses passions sur des objects faux, quand les vrais luy defaillent" (I: 4), a title that by itself suggests that I: 4, like I: 54, will concern itself with examples of wasted effort.[22] But more than that unites the chapters thematically. I: 54 is about extremes that—surprisingly, because of the great distance that separates them—touch. I: 4 is about the need for an object to touch, whether to strike in anger or to embrace in love. A man suffering from gout rejects his doctor's advice to give up salted meats because, he says, he wanted to know who to get angry at, and in cursing now the beef tongue, now the ham, he feels better. The losing gambler chews up his cards; Xerxes whipped the sea. There must be something to take it out on: "le bras estant haussé pour frapper, il nous deut si le coup ne *rencontre*" [when the arm is raised to strike, it hurts us if the blow does not *hit*] (I: 4, 22a, DM 17; 14*). That *rencontre* encounters its like twice in "Des vaines subtilitez" when "La bestise & la sagesse se *rencontrent* en mesme point . . . de resolution à la souffrance des accidens humains" [Stupidity and wisdom *meet* at the same point . . . of resolving to endure human accidents] (I: 54, 312a, DM 478; 226*) and "L'enfance & la decrepitude se *rencontrent* en imbecilité de cerveau" [Infancy and decrepitude *meet* in weakness of the brain] (I: 54, 312a, DM 479; 226). This is a self-naming encounter, extremes—separated by the distance of fifty chapters—that meet.

Another encounter is completed in the very first sentence of I: 54: "Il est de ces subtilitez *frivoles & vaines*, par le moyen desquelles les hommes

---

> to attribute to chance. Whatever else may be signified by the patterns inscribed on the « Physetere » [the Whale] . . . the sign at the center of the *Quart Livre* serves first of all to *signal the center* of the epic with a conspicuous representation of its own median position in the book. (Duval, *Quart Livre*, 126; emphasis in original)

> Was Montaigne aware of the *Quart Livre*'s symmetrical construction and its valorization of the center? Could he have known about the symmetrical arrangement of 107 harpoons? In his one passing mention of Rabelais he calls his books "simplement plaisans" [simply pleasant], like Boccaccio's *Decameron*. But what did he really think? It is remarkable in any case that the two greatest prose authors of sixteenth-century France should have created symmetries around the same number. Perhaps it can be chalked up to chance. But just as it was not due to chance that Rabelais should "signal the center" of his book in the center of his book, so too in the case of "Des vaines subtilitez." It *is* the center of the *Essays* and Montaigne signals that fact, particularly when its last line places the book whose middle it is in a certain middle region.

> 22. Looking for extremes that touch is not presented as wasted effort in I: 54, nor as a vain subtlety. But constructing poems in the shape of eggs and hatchets is, as well as throwing grains of millet through the eye of a needle.

cerchent quelque fois de la recommandation" [There are those *frivolous and vain* subtleties by means of which men sometimes seek commendation] (I: 54, 311a, DM 475; 225*). For in I: 4, pet owners who lavish affection on their little dogs because they don't have a human being to devote their passion to, "à faute de prise legitime, plustost que de demeurer en *vain*" [lacking a legitimate object, rather than remain in *vain* (that is, remain idle)], their "partie amoureuse . . . s'en forge ainsi, une faulce *& frivole*" [loving part . . . thus creates a false *and frivolous* one] (I: 4, 22a, DM 18; 14*).

The first words of I: 54 ("Il est de ces subtilitez *frivoles & vaines*") echo not only the "vain . . . & frivole" of I: 4, but also the last words of Montaigne's address to the reader at the beginning of the *Essays:* "Ainsi, lecteur, je suis moy-mesme la matiere de mon livre: ce n'est pas raison que tu emploies ton loisir en un subject si *frivole & si vain*" [Thus, reader, I am myself the matter of my book; you would be unreasonable to spend your leisure on so *frivolous and vain* a subject] ("Au lecteur," 3; 2). What Montaigne calls vain subtleties in I: 54—the man throwing millet grains through the eye of a needle, poets who lengthen and shorten their lines for the sake of an overall design, words like "Dame" and "Sire" that meet across great distances—are therefore not to be dismissed as silly and pointless even though he presents them that way, for inasmuch as they are "frivoles & vaines" they are the matter of which the book is composed, consubstantial with its author.

Indeed, the parlor game of finding the same *word* reappearing in distantly separated contexts (and indeed it was a game: "Nous venons presentement de nous *joüer* chez moy") duplicates what is going on in the *Essays*. Montaigne invites his readers to play it too, to look for *words* that appear in distantly separated chapters and nowhere in between. Thus *plomb* [lead] can be found in I: 4 and in I: 54 but nowhere between—and nowhere else in Book One. In I: 4 it is one of those true but lacking objects in the chapter's title that are the true culprits, the real causes of the passions the soul consequently discharges on false ones: "Ce ne sont pas ces tresses blondes, que tu deschires, ny la blancheur de cette poitrine, que despite tu bas si cruellement, qui ont perdu d'un mal'heureux *plomb* ce frere bien aymé: prens t'en ailleurs" [It is not those blond tresses that you are tearing, nor the whiteness of that bosom that in your anger you beat so cruelly, that have made you lose by an unlucky *lead bullet* that well-loved brother: place the blame elsewhere] (I: 4, 23a, DM 18; 14–15*) (the tresses and bosom are the bereaved's own, in this extreme expression of grief). In I: 54 *plomb* is an element in which extremes meet: "Aristote dict que les cueus de *plom* se fondent & coulent de froid & de rigueur de l'hyver, comme d'une chaleur vehemente" [Aristotle says that pigs of *lead* will melt and run with the cold and the rigor of winter as with intense heat] (I: 54, 312a, DM 478; 226). Like the *Sire* and *Dame* that appear in two opposite social strata but nowhere in between, *plomb* appears in these two distant (though structurally related) chapters and nowhere else in Book One. Thus the *plomb* in I: 54 is where extremes meet in two different ways, one with regard to what the chapter is talking about, the other with regard to what it does.

As do some of the other words I will cite, *plomb* does appear elsewhere in Montaigne (twice each in Books Two and Three). But it is important to remember that although Books One and Two appeared at the same time in 1580, Montaigne evidently made the decision to present them to the public as two separate books, each with its own possibilities of structure and subtlety. Why did he not simply issue one book with 94 (57 + 37) chapters? His decision to divide them into two suggests his interest in the form his text would take, a form in which the chapters and their placement would play a role. Separating them into two books made it easier for him to place the two lone appearances of certain words and word combinations in meaningful locations, for it meant he would not have to avoid using them in the other book. We will later see that dividing those 94 into two volumes also had the virtue of allowing him to create two significant centers, I: 29 and II: 19, that will prove to be linked to each other (and to the center of Book Three, III: 7) by the kind of singular lexical echoes that link the symmetrically arranged chapters.

Montaigne concludes that extremes that touch are not so rare a phenomenon as he had first thought: "j'ay trouvé . . . que nous avions pris pour un exercice malaisé & d'*un rare subject,* ce qui ne l'est aucunement, & qu'apres que *nostre invention* a esté eschaufée, elle descouvre un nombre infiny de pareilz exemples" [I have found . . . that we had taken for a difficult exercise and *a rare subject* what is not so at all; and that after *our inventiveness* has been warmed up, it discovers an infinite number of similar examples] (I: 54, 313a, DM 479; 227*). The word *subject,* treated this way, is in fact rare, for the only other place in 1580 where it is preceded by an indefinite article and an adjective is I: 4: "Nous voyons que l'ame en ses passions se pipe plustost elle mesme se dressant *un faux subject* & fantastique, voire contre sa propre creance, que de n'agir contre quelque chose. Quelles causes n'*inventons nous* des mal'heurs, qui nous adviennent?" [We see that the soul in its passions will sooner deceive itself by setting up *a false subject* and a fantastical one, even contrary to its own belief, than not act against something. What causes *do we* not *invent* for the misfortunes that befall us?] (I: 4, 22a, DM 18; 14*). Particularly striking is the combination in both passages of "un + adjective

+ subject" with "n'inventons nous" and "nostre invention." The passage in I: 54 ("qu'apres que *nostre invention* a esté eschaufée, elle descouvre un nombre infiny de pareilz exemples") now reveals a self-referential dimension, for it is itself one of those "pareilz exemples" of extremes that touch. At the very moment that Montaigne writes "nostre invention" he is creating an instance of distantly spaced words that touch.[23]

5. In or Out

"Si le chef d'une place assiegée doit sortir pour parlementer"
[Whether the head of a besieged place should go out to parley]
(I: 5) and *"D'un mot de Caesar"* [On a saying of Caesar's] (I: 53)

Each of these chapters focuses on an assertion presented as having attained the status of a proverb. In I: 5 it is this: "c'est une reigle en la bouche de tous les hommes de guerre de nostre temps, qu'il ne faut jamais que le gouverneur en une place assiegée sorte luy memes pour parlementer" [it is a rule in the mouth of all military men of our time, that the governor of a besieged place must never go out himself to parley] (I: 5, 26a, DM 21–22; 17*). In I: 53 it is what Caesar said: "Il se faict par un vice ordinaire de nature, que nous ayons & plus de fiance & plus de crainte des choses que nous n'avons pas veu & qui sont cachées & inconnues" [It happens by a common vice of nature that we have both more trust and more fear of things that we have not seen and that are hidden and unknown] (I: 53, 310a, DM 475; 225*)—I am quoting Montaigne's own translation as given in the 1580 and 1588 editions. Both sayings give the same advice, though in different contexts: stay inside. Stay inside yourself (I: 5); stay inside the fort (I: 53).

Montaigne quotes Caesar at the end of this brief chapter to support the argument he has been making since the beginning that we spend too much time trying to know things that are "hors de nous" [outside us] (I: 53, 309a, DM 473; 224). We are never satisfied with what "tombe en nostre connoissance & jouissance" [falls within our knowledge and enjoyment] but instead "allons beant apres les choses avenir & inconues, d'autant que les presentes ne nous soulent pas" [we go gaping after things to come and unknown, inas-

---

23. As Ian Maclean points out, I: 54 is itself a "mise en abyme" in its "relationship . . . to the *Essais* as a whole; the chapter could be construed as an example of *subtilité* denouncing *subtilité* in a work of *subtilité* denouncing *subtilité*" (p. 149 of "Montaigne, Cardano: The Reading of Subtlety/The Subtlety of Reading," *French Studies* 37.2 [1983]: 143–56).

much as things present do not satiate us] (I: 53, 309a, DM 474; 225). Caesar was not speaking in a military context, despite his professional expertise in that domain, but was making an observation about human behavior in general. Yet his remark finds specific application in the military context to which I: 5 is devoted, where what is at issue is the grave risk one runs in going outside of one's domain in a literal way, outside of the fortress one is charged with defending. As Montaigne's examples show, treachery lurks; capture or worse may ensue for the governor of a besieged fortress who, however briefly, leaves the protecting walls behind.

But there are occasions when the conflicting claims of fear and trust can balance each other out. That is what Henry de Vaux discovered when he decided to accept the besieger's invitation to come out and parley, for when he did, the enemy pointed out to him the extent to which his castle had been mined with explosives, set to go off at the touch of a spark. De Vaux "s'en *sentit* singulierement obligé à l'ennemy, à la discretion duquel apres qu'il se fut rendu & sa trouppe, le feu estant mis à la mine les estansons de bois venant à *faillir* le chasteau fut emporté de fons en comble" [*felt* remarkably obliged to the enemy, to whose discretion he surrendered himself and his forces. After this, the fire was set to the mine, the wooden props began to *fail*, and the castle was demolished from top to bottom] (I: 5, 27a, DM 23–24; 17*). These, the last words of I: 5 in 1580, echo some of the first words of I: 53:

> Si nous nous amusions par fois à nous considerer, & le temps que nous mettons à contreroller autruy & à connoistre les choses qui sont *hors* de nous, que nous l'amploissions a nous sonder nous mesmes, nous *sentirions* aisément combien toute cète nostre contexture est bastie de pieces foibles & *defaillantes*.

> [If we sometimes spent a little consideration on ourselves, and employed in probing ourselves the time we put into checking up on others and learning about things that are *outside* us, we would easily *sense* how much this fabric of ours is built up of feeble and *failing* pieces.] (I: 53, 309a, DM 473; 224)

Having decided to "sortir" [come out], de Vaux "s'en sentit" [felt] obliged to the enemy for informing him that what was holding up his castle was about to "faillir" [fail], the besiegers "ayant *par dehors* fait sapper la plus part du chasteau" [having *from the outside* sapped the greater part of the castle] (I:

5, 27a, DM 23; 17*). The same words reappear when just the opposite happens in I: 53: if we were to decide to stop investigating the things that are "hors" [outside] us, and instead remained inside ourselves, we "sentirions" [would sense] the alarming extent to which our fabric, our inner structure, is about to collapse because it is constructed out of "defaillantes" [failing] pieces. In both situations, the fabric—de Vaux's castle, our "contexture"—is about to collapse because of its "pièces défaillantes," but de Vaux had to come out to discover the imminent collapse while we have to stop going out. He had to look at the structure from the outside; we have to look at it from within.

In 1588 Montaigne intensified the connections between these chapters by adding this sentence to the end of I: 5, by way of commentary on the de Vaux episode: "Je me fie ayseement à la foy d'autruy, mais mal-aiseement le fairoi je lors que je donrois à juger l'avoir plustost faict par desespoir & *faute de coeur,* que par franchise, & *fiance* de sa loyauté" [I put my trust easily in another man's word. But I should do so reluctantly whenever I would give the impression of acting from despair and *want of courage* rather than freely and through *trust* in his honesty] (I: 5, 27b; 17). This new final sentence of I: 5 sets up a parallel with the final sentence of I: 53, Montaigne's translation into French of what Caesar said: "Il se faict par un vice ordinaire de nature, que nous ayons & plus de *fiance* & plus de *crainte* des choses que nous n'avons pas veu & qui sont cachées & inconnues" [It happens by a common vice of nature that we have both more *trust* and more *fear* of things that we have not seen and that are hidden and unknown] (I: 53, 310a, DM 475; 225*). The *fiance* in Montaigne's translation of Caesar's "mot" is now anticipated by the *fiance* of the new last words of I: 5, but even more than that, the fear, the *crainte,* against which Caesar balanced that trust has its parallel too, the *faute de coeur.* Montaigne's translation makes Caesar's two terms more nearly alike than they were in the original, thereby enhancing the parallel with the dilemma the equally balanced demands of fear and faith impose upon the governor of a besieged place who wonders whether he should go out to parley. Caesar's "we trust more, and fear *more violently* [magis confidamus, *vehementiusque* exterramur]" Montaigne renders as "nous ayons *et plus de* fiance *et plus de* crainte" [we have both *more* trust and *more* fear]. It is as if Caesar had written "magisque" instead of "vehementiusque" as the adverb modifying "exterramur." Trust and fear are not on an equal basis in what Caesar wrote, but they are in Montaigne's translation, the better to support the parallel with the other chapter.

6. Trouble Back Home

"L'heure des parlemens dangereuse" [Parley time is dangerous]
(I: 6) and *"De la parsimonie des anciens"* [On the parsimony of
the ancients] (I: 52)

Given its brevity, "De la parsimonie des anciens," the shortest chapter in the *Essays* (257 words in 1580,[24] with 28 added in 1588), seems to imitate the thrift it discusses: "a simple and brief enumeration of examples of the modest lifestyle of some great men of antiquity," according to Alexandre Tarrête, whose "dryness and concision seem perfectly adapted to this theme."[25] By itself it could indeed seem wanting. George Hoffmann is probably not alone in finding it "totally inadequate. . . . As if anticipating revision that never came, this chapter remains in the larva-like state of the *leçon*, a Renaissance exercise of collecting quotations and material for future use. . . . [N]o critique, reflection, or personal anecdote ever transformed these notes on parsimony into a full-fledged essay. Clearly, he was not trying to write a masterpiece in the traditional sense of the term."[26] But if Montaigne's masterpiece is something larger than any separate chapter, perhaps the answer to the question that reading I: 52 poses—Is this all there is?—is no.

As with the other chapter pairs, I: 52 will likely make more sense when read with its other half, I: 6. At first glance, however, the latter is hard to distinguish from I: 5, for both are about the dangers of parleying with a besieging enemy. Their continuity is obvious from the first word of I: 6: "Toutes-fois" [However] (I: 6, 28a, DM 24; 18) and from Montaigne saying early on in that chapter "comme je viens de dire" [as I have just said] (I: 6, 28a, DM 24; 18), sending the reader back to something he had just said in I: 5. This continuity poses a challenge to the commonplace notion that the textual unit to be analyzed is the individual chapter, as André Tournon acknowledges: "We will accept, except for occasional proof of the contrary (for example in the case of a syntactical suture between chapters, as there is between I: 5 and I: 6 . . .), that the objective unit to consider is the *chapter*."[27] But unless these two chapters about parleying with the enemy can be differentiated from each other it will be impossible to see how I: 6 is more connected to I: 52 than I: 5 is. For Frieda S. Brown there is no difference:

---

24. Though in 1580, I: 55 ("Des senteurs") was even shorter.
25. In a note on the chapter in Naya et al., *Essais de Michel de Montaigne*, I: 694.
26. George Hoffmann, *Montaigne's Career* (Oxford: Clarendon Press, 1998), 128. Similarly, M. A. Screech finds it a mere compilation "that failed to grow into a larger chapter" (in his translation, 345).
27. *Route par ailleurs,* 12. He also cites I: 39 and I: 40 as being linked in this way.

the two chapters "constitute and should be read as a single commentary on the subject."[28] For Tournon there is a difference, but I think he is mistaken about what it is. In a note on I: 5 in his edition of the *Essais* he writes that while both "treat of the risks in parleys" I: 5 does so "under the practical angle of the precautions one should take" but I: 6 discusses them "from the point of view of the ethics of war" (523). Yet battlefield ethics come up in I: 5 just as much as they do in I: 6. It is in I: 5 for example that Montaigne contrasts the Roman way of war to "la Grecque subtilité et astuce Punique, où le vaincre par force est moins glorieux que par fraude" [Greek subtlety and Punic cunning, according to which it is less glorious to conquer by force than by fraud] (I: 5, 25c; 16). Alexandre Tarrête points out that the same moral questions are raised in both chapters, writing in a note to I: 5, "Are all means legitimate in order to win? What place should be given to trustworthiness in dealings with the enemy? This chapter, like the one that follows it, asks these questions" (in Naya et al., 593).

A hint of the real difference between the two can be glimpsed in their titles: "Si le chef d'une place assiegée doit sortir pour parlementer" [Whether the head of a besieged place should go out to parley] (I: 5), where the focus is on a danger faced by one man vs. "L'heure des parlemens dangereuse" [Parley time Is dangerous] (I: 6), where the danger is general. A comparison of the anecdotes told in each brings the difference into clearer focus. Those in I: 5 concern the risk the negotiator runs when negotiating, but those in I: 6 are about what can happen to the city's inhabitants when he has left them behind to go parley. In I: 5's first story, the result of Lucius Marcius' treachery against the king of Macedonia, whom he had lulled into a temporary truce, was that "le roy encourut sa derniere ruine" [the king incurred his final ruin] (I: 5, 25a, DM 20; 16). No mention is made of what his subjects may have suffered. When Guy de Rangon, defending his city against the seigneur de l'Escut, went out to parley he remained close enough that when trouble unexpectedly broke out between the armies he could retreat back into the city, and Escut for his own safety went with him under his protection; here too the focus is on the danger to the negotiators (in fact, the danger to the negotiators for both sides). In the same chapter Henri de Vaux, as we saw a few pages ago, was saved from death by coming out to parley.

But in I: 6 the focus is placed on what can happen to a besieged city's inhabitants when they have been left behind by a leader who has gone out

---

28. On p. 79 of Frieda S. Brown, "«Si le chef d'une place assiegée doit sortir pour parlementer» and «L'heure des parlemens dangereuse»: Montaigne's Political Morality and Its Expression in the Early Essays." In *O un Amy! Essays on Montaigne in Honor of Donald M. Frame,* edited by Raymond C. La Charité (Lexington, KY: French Forum Publishers, 1977), 72–87.

to parley. In the first anecdote the citizens of Mussidan were cut to pieces by a surprise attack that took place during the negotiations. It was during a parley that the town of Casilinum was taken by surprise (in a post-1588 addition); likewise Capua, Yvoy, Genoa, and Ligny-en-Barrois (in the 1580 and subsequent editions). In fact in some cases the negotiator himself is not under attack, but only the citizens he left behind: Giuliano Romero went out to parley and "trouva au retour sa place saisie" [on his return found his place seized] (I: 6, 29a, DM 26; 19). Likewise, Bertheville "estant sorty pour parlementer, pendant le parlement la ville se trouva saisie" [went out to parley, and during the bargaining the town was taken] (I: 6, 29a, DM 26; 19*).

Civilians left behind when their leader attends to military matters are likewise surprised by treachery in the following anecdote, which is the first and by far the longest told in I: 52, comprising 112 of the chapter's 257 words, or 44%, in 1580; 39% in 1588.

> Attilius Regulus general de l'armée Romaine en Afrique, au milieu de sa gloire & de ses victoires contre les Carthaginois, escrivit à la chose publique qu'un valet de labourage qu'il avoit laissé seul au gouvernement de son bien, qui estoit en tout, sept arpens de terre, s'en estoit enfuy, ayant *desrobé* ses utils de labourage, et demandoit congé pour s'en retourner y pourvoir, de peur que sa femme et ses enfans n'en eussent à souffrir. Le Senat pourveut à commettre un autre à la conduite de ses biens, & luy fit restablir ce qui luy avoit esté *desrobé*, et ordonna que sa femme et enfans seroient nourris aux despens du public.

> [Attilius Regulus, general of the Roman army in Africa, in the midst of his glory and his victories against the Carthaginians, wrote to the Republic that a farm laborer whom he had left in sole charge of his estate, which was seven acres of land in all, had run away and *stolen* his farming tools; and he asked leave to return and look after this matter, for fear that his wife and children would suffer from it. The Senate provided another man to manage his property, caused what had been *stolen* to be returned to him, and ordered that his wife and children should be maintained at the public expense.] (I: 52, 308a, DM 471; 224)

It resembles what happens to Romero and Bertheville in I: 6, whose towns were seized in their absence. It is just the opposite, too, in a couple of ways: (1) the citizens in I: 6 suffered from someone coming into their city, while the family in I: 52 suffered from someone going away; (2) it was "au retour" [on his return] that Romero discovered the damage, while Attilius wanted to "retourner" in order to undo the damage. Montaigne would add to the parallel in 1588 by characterizing successes due to taking unfair advantage on the battlefield as "des victoires *desrobées*" [*stolen* victories] (I: 6, 29b; 19*), setting up an echo with the servant "ayant *desrobé* ses utilz de labourage" and the Senate's making good what had been "*desrobé.*"

7. Words, in Effect

"Que l'intention juge nos actions" [That intention judges our actions] (I: 7) and "De la vanité des paroles" [On the vanity of words] (I: 51)

Having alluded to how the Greeks praised the order and arrangement of the feast that Paulus Aemilius gave them after conquering Macedonia, Montaigne makes the remark "mais je ne parle point icy des *effects,* je parle des *motz*" [But I am not speaking at all here of *effects,* I am speaking of *words*] (I: 51, 307a, DM 468; 223*). Before that he had just been telling us about the inflated language in which the maître d'hôtel of a Roman cardinal spoke of his culinary responsibilities: "particularisant les qualitez des ingrediens & leurs *effectz* . . . tout cela enflé de riches & magnifiques *parolles,* & celles mesmes qu'on emploie à traiter du gouvernement d'un empire" [particularizing the qualities of the ingredients and their *effects* . . . all this swollen with rich and magnificent *words,* and the very ones we use to talk about the government of an empire] (I: 51, 306a; DM 467–68; 222–23). The "effects" that he says he is not talking about seem to refer to the "effectz" that the maître d'hôtel was speaking of a few lines before. In saying after he had alluded to the feast Paulus Aemilius prepared that he is speaking of "motz" instead of "effects" he seems to confess to wandering from the subject, that he erred in bringing up the Paulus Aemilius anecdote because it wasn't about words, but only about the effect his banquet had on the Greeks (they liked it). Indeed, he immediately goes back to talking about words, in particular about inflated ones, though here too he will oppose those problematic *motz* to a certain *effect:* "Je ne sçay s'il en advient aus autres comme à moy: mais je ne me puis garder quand j'oy noz architectes s'enfler de ces gros *motz* de palastres, architraves, cornices d'ouvrage Corinthien & Dorique et semblables de leur jargon, que mon imagination ne se saisisse incontinent du palais d'Apolidon. Et par *effet* je trouve que ce sont les chetives pieces de la porte de ma cuisine" [When I hear our architects puffing themselves out with those big words like pilasters, architraves, cornices, Corinthian and Doric work, and such-like jargon, I cannot keep my imagination from immediately seizing on the palace of Apollidon; and in *effect* I find that these are the paltry parts of my kitchen door] (I: 51, 307a, DM 469; 223*). The architects' inflated words are deflated by a certain "effect." The opposition between words and "effects" surfaces a fourth time in a post-1588 addition to this chapter in which Montaigne notes that L. Volumnius recommended Q. Fabius and P. Decius for consulships because being military men they were "grands aux *effects;* au combat du *babil,* rudes" [great in *deeds;* at combat in *prattle,* clumsy] (I: 51, 306c; 222). Throughout I: 51 Montaigne prefers deeds to words and attacks empty eloquence, true to his title's indication of the emptiness, the "vanité," of words.

Effects and *paroles* are brought into play and into a relationship with each other but in a quite different way in "Que l'intention juge nos actions." In that chapter *parole* is understood in the sense of a promise, Henry VII of England "faillant à sa *parole*" [breaking his *word*] (I: 7, 30a, DM 29; 20) when he provided in his will that after his death his enemy the Duke of Suffolk (Edmund de la Pole), whom he had promised Phillip of Burgundy he would not harm (and kept prisoner in the Tower of London), be put to death. That the execution took place after the king's death in no way freed the latter of his obligation to keep his word. In a similar yet contrasting case, the Count of Egmont, about to be executed together with the Count of Horn, asked to be beheaded[29] first so that his death might free him from his obligation to Horn, whom he had unwittingly lured in a trap set for both. It is in commenting on Egmont that Montaigne brings "effects" into conflict with "parole." Egmont in the essayist's view was freed from his obligation already, because

> Nous ne pouvons estre tenus au dela de nos forces & de nos moyens. A ceste cause, par ce que les *effaictz* & executions ne sont aucunement en nostre puissance, & qu'il n'y a rien en bon essiant en nostre puissance, que la volonté. . . . Par ainsi le Conte d'Aiguemond tenant son ame & volonté endebtée à sa promesse, bien que la puissance de l'*effectuer* ne fut pas en ses mains, estoit sans doubte absous de son devoir, quand il eut survescu le Conte de Horne. Mais le roy d'Angleterre faillant à sa *parole,* par son intention ne se peut excuser.

> [We cannot be bound beyond our powers and means. For this reason—that we have no power to *effect* and accomplish, that there is nothing really

---

29. As Montaigne made clear in the 1580 edition: the "Comtes de Horne & d'Aiguemond, ausquels il fit trancher la teste" [the Count of Horn and the Count of Egmont, both of whom he had beheaded] (DM 28). This phrase was deleted in 1588.

in our power but will—all man's rules of duty are necessarily founded and established in our will. . . . Thus the count of Egmont, considering his soul and will in debt to his promise, though the power to *carry it out* was not in his hands, was certainly absolved of his duty even had he survived the count of Horn. But the king of England, in intentionally breaking his *word*, cannot be excused.] (I: 7, 30a, DM 29; 20)

In I: 51 *paroles* and *effects* are opposed to each other (as words vs. deeds), while in I: 7 they are on the same side in the case of the count of Egmont and of hypothetical others who wish to put their *parole* (as promise) into effect but are prevented by circumstance from doing so. In the 1580 edition Henry VII "*faillant* à sa *parole*" found an inverted reflection in the *defaillance* [defect] of the common people that makes them liable to be manipulated by clever rhetoric, by "la vanité des *parolles.*" Rhetoric is

> un util inventé pour manier & agiter une tourbe & une commune desreiglée. . . . Il semble par là que les estatz qui dependent d'un monarque en ont moins de besoin que les autres. Car la bestise & facilité qui se trouve en la commune, & qui la rend subjecte à estre maniée & contournée par les oreilles au dous son de céte harmonie, sans venir à poisir & conoitre la verité des choses par la force de la raison, céte *defaillance,* ne se se trouve pas si aiséement en un seul.
>
> [an instrument invented to manipulate and agitate a crowd and a disorderly populace. . . . From that it seems that monarchical governments need it less than others: for the stupidity and facility that is found in the common people, which makes them subject to be led by the ears to the sweet sound of this harmony without weighing things and coming to know their truth by force of reason—this *defect* is not so easily found in a single ruler.] (I: 51, 305–6a, DM 465–66; 222*)

Their *defaillance* is that they are under the power of certain *paroles*, while Henry VII's *defaillance* was that he broke away from the power of a certain *parole*. (In 1588 "defaillance" would be replaced by "facillité.")

Montaigne follows the stories of Henry VII and the count of Egmont with a third instance of death freeing one (or not) from an obligation. Henry VII "ne se peut excuser, pour avoir retardé jusques apres sa mort l'execution de sa desloyauté, non plus que le masson de Herodote, lequel ayant loyallement conservé durant sa vie le secret des tresors du roy d'Egypte son maistre, mourant les descouvrit à ses enfans" [cannot be excused merely on the ground that he delayed the execution of his dishonest plan until after his death; any more than Herodotus' mason, who, having loyally kept during his life the secret of the treasures of his master the king of Egypt, revealed it to his children as he died] (I: 7, 30a, DM 29–30; 20). That is all he tells us of the mason, but a detail from the passage in Herodotus to which he alludes resonates so strongly here that he must have been thinking of it—and may have wanted those of his readers familiar with Herodotus to think about it too. It is that when the mason's two sons were stealing from the treasury, as he recommended they do after his death, one of them was caught in a trap the king had set and, realizing he could not get out of it, said to his brother, "cut off my head, lest I be seen and recognized and so bring you too to ruin."[30] Like the Count of Egmont, the doomed brother (1) asks to be beheaded now, (2) knowing that he will be executed eventually, and (3) makes this request out of a sense of obligation to his partner in crime.

Similarly, another part of the story he doesn't mention, though an even more essential one, may have a secret connection to something in its partner chapter, the humble kitchen door that the vanity of words—the fancy architectural terms—gives Montaigne the momentary illusion that he is staring at a palace. For Herodotus' mason gave his sons access to the king's treasure by making an opening—a kind of door—into the *palace:* "That he might store his treasure safely, [the king] made to be built a stone chamber, one of its walls abutting on the outer side of his palace. But the builder of it craftily contrived that one stone should be so placed as to be easily removed by two men or even by one" (Herodotus, 415). That is how the sons were able to go in and out with the treasure until the king began to notice it was disappearing. It is a hidden door in two senses: literally so in Herodotus' story, and figuratively in I: 7 in that it is hidden in Montaigne's allusion to the story. From there it may lead us to the imagined palace door in I: 51, the two ends of the intratext I: 7 and I: 51 together form connected by this secret passage.

8. Of Idleness and Horses

"De l'oisiveté" [On idleness] (I: 8) and "De Democritus et Heraclitus" [On Democritus and Heraclitus] (I: 50)

"De l'oisiveté" (I: 8) could almost have served as a preface to the *Essays,* for it is there that Montaigne speaks of the birth of his book:

---

30. Herodotus. *Herodotus,* tr. A. D. Godley (Cambridge: Harvard University Press / Loeb Library, 1981), 417.

Dernierement que je me retiray chez moy, deliberé autant que je pourray de ne me mesler d'autre chose, que de passer en repos & à part ce peu qui me reste de vie, il me sembloit ne pouvoir faire plus grande faveur à mon esprit, que de le laisser en pleine *oysiveté* s'entretenir soi mesmes & s'arrester & rasseoir en soy, ce que j'esperois qu'il peut meshui faire plus aisement devenu avec le temps plus poisant & plus meur, mais je trouve . . . que au rebours faisant le *cheval* eschapé il se donne cent fois plus d'affaire à soy mesmes qu'il n'en prent pour autruy, & m'enfante tant de chimeres & monstres fantasques les uns sur les autres, sans ordre, & sans propos, que pour en contempler à mon aise l'ineptie & l'estrangeté j'ay commancé de les mettre en rolle, esperant avec le temps luy en faire honte à luy mesmes.

[Lately, when I retired to my home, determined so far as possible to bother about nothing except spending the little life I have left in rest and seclusion, it seemed to me I could do my mind no greater favor than to let it entertain itself in full *idleness* and stay and settle in itself, which I hoped it might do more easily now, having become weightier and riper with time. But I find . . . that, on the contrary, like a runaway *horse,* it gives itself a hundred times more trouble than it took for others, and gives birth to so many chimeras and fantastic monsters, one after another, without order and without purpose, that in order to contemplate their ineptitude and strangeness at my pleasure, I have begun to write them down, hoping in time to make my mind ashamed of itself.] (I: 8, 33a; DM 31–32; 21*)

"De Democritus et Heraclitus" (I: 50) is likewise a meditation on Montaigne's manner of self-exploration and his writing. In this chapter too horses and idleness are linked, as they are in I: 8 when he compares his idle mind to a runaway horse. The Leake *Concordance* confirms that nowhere else in Books One or Two do the words *cheval* and *oisif/oisiveté* in any of their forms make a joint appearance than in I: 8 and in the following passage in I: 50:

Toute action est propre à nous faire connoistre céte mesme ame de Caesar, qui se faict voir à ordonner & dresser la bataille de Pharsale, elle se faict aussi voir à dresser des parties *oysives* & amoureuses. On juge un *cheval,* non seulement à le voir manier sur une carriere, mais encore à luy voir aller le pas, voire & à le voir en repos à l'estable.

[Every action is apt to reveal to us this same soul of Caesar that shows itself in ordering and arranging the battle of Pharsalis: it shows itself as well in arranging *idle* and amorous affairs. One judges a *horse* not only by seeing it handled on a race course but also in seeing it walk, and even at rest in the stable.] (I: 50, 302a, DM 461; 219*)

The horse's repose ("*en repos* à l'estable") actually constitutes a third element in this repeated cluster, for it was as a consequence of his retirement to his estate to "passer *en repos*" his declining years that Montaigne's idle mind began to behave like a runaway horse.

Richard Scholar points out another parallel between the chapters. He finds it in the opening lines of I: 50:

> Le jugement est un util à tous subjets, & se mesle par tout. À céte cause aus essais, que j'en fay icy, j'y employe toute sorte d'occasion. Si c'est un subjet que je n'entende point, à cela mesme je l'essaie, sondant le gué de bien loing, & puis le trouvant trop profond pour ma taille, je me tiens à la rive. . . . Tantost je le promene à un subject noble & fort tracassé, auquel il n'a rien à trouver de soy mesme, le chemin en estant si frayé & si batu qu'il ne peut marcher que sur la piste d'autruy. Là il faict son jeu à trier la route qui luy semble la meilleure, & de mille sentiers, il dict que cetuy cy ou celuy là a esté le mieus choisi.

> [Judgment is a tool to use on all subjects, and comes in everywhere. Therefore in the tests that I make of it here, I use every sort of occasion. If it is a subject I do not understand at all, even on that I essay my judgment, sounding the ford from a good distance; and then, finding it too deep for my height, I stick to the bank. . . . Sometimes I lead it to a noble and well-worn subject in which it has nothing original to discover, the road being so worn and so beaten that it can walk only in others' footsteps. There it plays its part by choosing the way that seems best to it, and of a thousand paths it says that this one or that was the most wisely chosen.] (I: 50, 301-2a, DM 459–60; 219*)

Scholar writes that Montaigne here describes his

> process of essaying . . . as a journey on which two characters have embarked: the first person "I" ("je"), and his judgement. We might be reminded here of an earlier chapter, "Of idleness" (I: 8), which also stages a psychodrama involving two characters internal to Montaigne. "Of idleness" . . . has the first person set off in hot pursuit of his runaway mind. In "Of Democritus and Heraclitus," the judgement has replaced the mind in the lead role alongside the first person, and the balance of power is different: the first

person does not pursue so much as accompany his judgement on a journey; and he sets his judgement tests along the way.[31]

Montaigne, as Scholar suggests, actually seems to speak of his judgment as if it were a horse, leading it (in fact, "walking" it: "je le promene"), fording a stream or not with it, letting it choose its own path when several are offered. Scholar, who like other readers of I: 8 finds it to be a "second preface" (Scholar, 24) to Book I, supplementing the "Au Lecteur," makes the same observation of I: 50, and finds that to be an additional similarity between them: I: 50 "acts like a belated preface to Book I and a mirror-image of an earlier prefatory exercise, 'Of idleness' (I: 8). But where . . . 'Of idleness' describes a writer in hot pursuit of his runaway mind, 'Of Democritus and Heraclitus' presents essaying as the best way for him to give his mind free rein—while remaining in the saddle" (Scholar, 90).

Montaigne in I: 8 writes of fallow fields whose teeming abundance needs to be tamed by subjection to "certaines *semences*" [certain *seeds*] (I: 8, 32a, DM 30; 20) and of women who on their own can produce pieces of formless flesh but who for a good and natural offspring need to receive "une autre *semance:* ainsin est-il des esprits" [another kind of *seed;* so it is with minds] (I: 8, 32a, DM 30; 21), which require a definite subject to keep them reined in. Particularly is it true of Montaigne's own mind, and this has implications for his writing, as he goes on to say, in the passage already quoted at length. In a post-1588 addition to I: 50, that sowing will return in a self-referential way, in the present participle *semant* [sowing], at a moment when Montaigne is talking about how he writes his *Essays*. It follows immediately the passage, already quoted, in which he speaks of his judgment as if it were a horse.

[B] Je prends de la fortune le premier argument. Ils me sont également bons. Et ne [C] desseigne jamais de les produire entiers. Car je ne voy le tout de rien: Ne font pas, ceux qui promettent de nous le faire veoir. De cent membres et visages qu'a chaque chose, j'en prens un tantost à lecher seulement, tantost à effleurer; et par fois à pincer jusqu'à l'os. J'y donne une poincte, non pas le plus largement, mais le plus profondement que je sçay. Et aime plus souvent à les saisir par quelque lustre inusité. Je me hazarderoy de traitter à fons quelque matière, si je me connoissoy moins. *Semant* icy un mot, icy un autre, eschantillons despris de leur piece, escartez, *sans dessein et sans promesse,* je ne suis pas tenu d'en faire bon, ny de m'y tenir moy mesme,

---

31. Richard Scholar, *Montaigne and the Art of Free-Thinking* (Oxford: Peter Lang, 2010), 70.

sans varier quand il me plaist; et me rendre au doubte et incertitude, et à ma maistresse forme, qui est l'ignorance.

[(B) I take the first subject that chance offers. They are all equally good to me. And I (C) never plan to develop them completely. For I do not see the whole of anything; nor do those who promise to show it to us. Of a hundred members and faces that each thing has, I take one, sometimes only to lick it, sometimes to brush the surface, sometimes to pinch it to the bone. I give it a stab, not as wide but as deep as I know how. And most often I like to take them from some unaccustomed point of view. I would venture to treat some matter thoroughly, if I knew myself less well. *Sowing* a word here, there another, samples separated from their context, dispersed, *without a plan and without a promise,* I am not bound to make something of them or to adhere to them myself without varying when I please and giving myself up to doubt and uncertainty and my ruling quality, which is ignorance.] (I: 50, 302ac; 219*)

The phrase "sans dessein et sans promesse" at the very moment it asserts an absence of a plan may actually reveal the presence of one, for it appears to echo a parallel statement in the symmetrically matching "De l'oysiveté": in retreating from active life, Montaigne let his mind fall into idleness but found that it "m'enfante tant de chimeres & monstres fantasques les uns sur les autres, *sans ordre, et sans propos*" [gives birth to so many chimeras and fantastic monsters, one after another, *without order and without purpose*] (I: 8, 33a; 21*) that he began to write them down, giving birth to the *Essays*. Although the construction "sans . . . et sans . . . " appears often in the *Essays*, only in these two instances are both of the following conditions met: (1) Montaigne is talking about his book and (2) the second term begins with the prefix *pro*. The manuscript evidence suggests that it was important to him that the second term begin with "pro-" because what he had first written (and then drew a line through, replacing it with "sans dessein et sans promesse") also contained that feature: "Sans corps, sans *pro*position" [without order, without *pro*position].[32]

---

32. The manuscript post-1588 edition may be consulted at http://artflx.uchicago.edu/images/montaigne/0126.jpg . It is reproduced on p. 85 of Scholar's book and transcribed by André Tournon on p. 186 of his article "La segmentation du texte: usages et singularités" (in Blum, Claude and André Tournon, eds. *Éditer les Essais de Montaigne: Actes du Colloque tenu à l'Université Paris IV-Sorbonne les 27 et 28 janvier 1995* [Paris: Honoré Champion, 1997]: 173–96).

9. Lying, After a Fashion

"Des menteurs" [Of liars] (I: 9) and *"Des coustumes anciennes"* [Of ancient customs] (I: 49)

Montaigne begins "Des menteurs" (I: 9) by talking about the faculty of memory, and about how poorly endowed his is. "Il n'est homme à qui il siese si mal de se mesler de parler de la memoire qu'à moy. Car je n'en reconnoy quasi nulle trasse chez moy: & ne pense qu'il y en aye au monde une si monstrueuse en defaillance" [There is no man whom it would so little become to meddle with talking about memory. For I recognize almost no trace of it in me, and I do not think there is another one in the world so monstrously deficient] (I: 9, 34a, DM 32; 21*). In the same passage (in the 1580 edition, at least—before some additions from 1588 and later came in between) he goes on to say that good liars better have a good memory: "Ce n'est pas sans raison qu'on dit, que qui ne se sent point assez ferme de memoire, ne se doit pas mesler d'estre menteur" [It is not unreasonably said that anyone who does not feel sufficiently strong in memory should not meddle with being a liar] (I: 9, 35a, DM 33; 23*).

But in "Des coustumes anciennes" (I: 49) he seems to say that he has a better memory than nearly anyone else:

> J'excuserois volontiers en nostre peuple de n'avoir autre patron & regle de perfection que ses propres meurs & usances: car c'est un commun vice, non du vulgaire seulement, mais quasi de tous hommes, d'avoir leur visée & leur arrest sur le train auquel ils sont nais. . . . Mais je me plains de sa particuliere indiscretion, de se laisser si fort piper & aveugler à l'authorité de l'usage present, qu'il soit capable de changer d'opinion et d'advis tous les mois, s'il plait à la coustume, & qu'il juge si diversement de soy mesmes.

> [I should be prone to excuse our people for having no other pattern and rule of perfection than their own manners and customs; for it is a common vice, not of the vulgar only but of almost all men, to fix their aim and limit by the ways to which they were born. . . . But I do complain of their particular lack of judgment in letting themselves be so thoroughly fooled and blinded by the authority of present usage that they are capable of changing opinion and ideas every month, if custom pleases, and that they judge themselves so diversely.] (I: 49, 296a, DM 450–51; 215–16)

Their problem is that they live only in the present, and they forget the past. Specifically, they forget how enthusiastically they approved a certain fashion that they now ignore in their infatuation with the new. Despite what Montaigne says in I: 9 about having a worse power of recollection than anyone else ("Il n'est homme" [There is no man] with less right to speak of memory than him), in I: 49 he shows that he has a *better* memory than "quasi de tous hommes" [almost all men], for only he can remember how things used to be: "Je veux icy entasser aucunes coustumes anciennes *que j'ay en memoire,* les unes de mesmes les nostres, les autres differentes: afin qu'ayant en imagination céte continuelle variation des choses humaines nous en ayons le jugement plus esclaircy & plus ferme" [I want to pile up here some ancient fashions *that I have in my memory,* some like ours, others different, to the end that we may strengthen and enlighten our judgment by reflecting upon this continual variation of human things] (I: 49, 297a, DM 452; 216). And then he provides, out of his storehouse of memory, a long list of ancient Roman customs that differ greatly from sixteenth-century practice.

It is as if his memory were so poor that when he writes I: 49 he has forgotten what he had said in I: 9 about how poor a memory he has. Either that, or he is lying—which in I: 9 he said one must have a superior memory to do. Montaigne, not for the first or last time, incarnates the Epimenidean paradox about the Cretan who may or may not be telling the truth about all Cretans being liars.[33] It is fitting that he should do so here, in a pair of chapters of which one is about liars.

Lying, the declared theme of I: 9, is metafictionally thematic in Montaigne's contradicting in I: 49 what he says in I: 9. But equally so is fashion, the declared subject of I: 49. For his self-contradiction is, in the experience of a reader who reads the *Essays* from beginning to end, situated in time, and in the realm of fashion "souvent les formes mesprisées reviennent en credit, & celles la mesme tumbent en mespris tantost apres, & qu'un mesme jugement preigne en l'espace de quinze ou vingt ans deus ou trois, non diverses seulement, mais contraires opinions, d'une inconstance & legereté incroyable" [despised fashions often return into favor, and these very ones soon after fall back gain into contempt; and the same mind, in the space of fifteen or twenty years, may be so incredibly inconsistent and frivolous as to adopt two or three opinions that are not merely diverse but contrary] (I: 49, 297a, DM 452; 216*). What happens in fashion happens in the *Essays,* at a distance of, say, forty chapters instead of twenty years. That is, Montaigne

---

33. Montaigne alludes to the Liar Paradox in the "Apologie de Raimond Sebond": "Si vous dictes: Je ments, et que vous dissiez vray, vous mentez donc" [If you say, "I lie," and if you are speaking the truth, then you lie] (II: 12, 527b; 392).

changes his opinion after a while as the fashionable change theirs, and into not just a different opinion but its opposite.

A parallel phenomenon is the return of the same: in the realm of fashion, after many years abandoned modes re-emerge; in the *Essays,* words return in one chapter after having been dormant since appearing in an earlier one, rarely seen words that sometimes never appear in the book except in two such distantly-spaced chapters structurally linked by the symmetry surrounding the center of the book. For example, one of the curious customs Montaigne relates is that the ancient Romans

> se torchoient le cul . . . avec une esponge. Voylà pourquoy SPONGIA est un *mot* obscoene *en Latin:* & estoit céte esponge atachée au bout d'un baston, comme tesmoigne l'histoire de celuy qu'on menoit pour estre presenté aus bestes devant le peuple, qui demanda congé d'aller à ses affaires, & là n'ayant autre moien de se tuer, il se fourra ce baston & esponge dans le gosier & s'en estoufa.

> [wiped their ass . . . with a sponge—that is why SPONGIA is an obscene *word in Latin*—and this sponge was attached to the end of a stick, as is shown by the story of the man who was being taken to be thrown to the beasts in front of the people, and who asked permission to go and answer the call of nature; and having there no other way to kill himself, he stuffed the stick and sponge down his throat and choked himself.] (I: 49, 298a; DM 454–55; 217*)

The phrase "mot . . . en Latin" appears also in I: 9, and nowhere else:

> Je sçay bien que les grammairiens font différence entre dire mensonge & mentir: & disent que dire mensonge c'est dire chose faulce, mais qu'on a pris pour vraye, & que la definition du *mot* de mentir *en latin,* d'ou nostre François est party, porte autant comme aller contre sa conscience, & que par consequence cela ne touche que ceux qui disent contre ce qu'ils sçavent.

> [I know very well that the grammarians make this distinction between telling a lie and lying: and they say that telling a lie means saying something false but which we have taken for true, and that the definition of the *word* "to lie" *in Latin,* from which our French is taken, implies going against our conscience, and thus applies only to those who say what is contrary to what they know.] (I: 9, 35a, DM 33; 23*)[34]

---

34. The passage to which Montaigne refers in Aulus Gellius, perhaps at second hand, makes the

66   I. Book One

It is a hardly a coincidence that the identical words "mot . . . en Latin" should be attached to words that rhyme ("esponge" and "mensonge") and that the story Montaigne tells to show what Romans did with sponges is also the story of a lie (the one the victim told to get to use it).

In 1588 Montaigne added a passage to I: 9 that created a new parallel between the chapters, echoing the following passage, already quoted: "*un mesme* jugement preigne en l'espace de quinze ou vingt ans deus ou trois, non *diverses* seulement, mais *contraires* opinions" [the *same* mind, in the space of fifteen or twenty years, might adopt two or three opinions that are not merely *diverse* but *contrary*] (I: 49, 297a, DM 452; 216*). The relevant addition has to do with negotiators who over the course of their career work for different masters and in different situations. The details of a lie one has concocted are likely to escape all but the most powerful memories, and he has seen and been amused by those who choose their words to suit their negotiations and please the great to whom they are speaking: "il faut que leur parole *se diversifie* quand et quand; d'où il advient que de *mesme* chose ils disent gris tantost, tantost jaune" [their words must *become diverse* accordingly. So it happens that they describe the *same* thing as now gray, now yellow], and what they say is reported as containing things "si *contraires*" [so *contrary*] that they trip themselves up, for how could they remember "tant de *diverses* formes, qu'ils ont forgées à *un mesme* subject?" [so many *diverse* forms into which they have cast the *same* subject?] (I: 9, 36b; 23*). With this addition Montaigne deepens the analogy between lying and fashion. What happens to the *same* mind ["*un mesme* jugement"] over the course of several years of changing fashions is that it becomes *diverse* and *contrary* as it adapts to those fashions; what happens to lies a negotiator tells as circumstances change is precisely the same: a *same* subject he will give *diverse* and even *contrary* accounts.[35]

10. Excess Baggage

"Du parler prompt ou tardif" [Of prompt or slow speech] (I: 10) and "Des destries" [Of war horses] (I: 48)

In "Des destries" (I: 48), Montaigne writes admiringly of how "nos

---

distinction between "mendacium dicere" and "mentiri." *Noctes Atticae* (*Attic Nights*), IX, 11. On the web at: http://penelope.uchicago.edu/Thayer/E/Roman/Texts/Gellius/home.html

35. Unaware of the metafictional dimension, the editors of the new Pléiade edition find that I: 49 is nothing but an "inventory" of "pointless or inconsequential practices with regard to fashion, hygiene, or food" and that Montaigne even seemed "tired" [fatigué] by the time he reached its conclusion (Balsamo et al., 1478).

ancestres ... en tous les combats solemnelz ... se mettoient tous à pié, pour ne se fier à nulle autre chose, qu'à leur force propre" [our ancestors ... in all serious engagements ... all fought on foot, so as to trust to nothing but their own strength] (I: 48, 289a, DM 446; 211*). For in the heat of battle a horse is less an advantage than a liability: "Ses playes & sa mort tirent la vostre en consequence, son effray ou sa fureur vous rendent ou temeraire ou lache" [His wounds and his death bring on yours as a consequence; his fright or his furor make you rash or cowardly] (I: 48, 289a, DM 447; 211*). For the same reason he prefers the sword to the pistol:

> Comme je conseilleroy de choisir les armes les plus courtes & celles dequoy nous nous pouvons le mieux respondre. Il est bien plus seur de s'asseurer d'une espée que nous tenons au poing, que du boulet qui eschappe de nostre pistole, en laquelle il y a plusieurs pieces, la poudre, la pierre, le roüet, desquelles la moindre qui viendra à faillir vous fera faillir vostre fortune.

> [Just as I should advise the choice of the shortest weapons, and those that we can answer for best. It is much surer to rely on a sword that we hold in our hand than on the bullet that escapes out of our pistol, in which there are several parts—the powder, the flint, the lock—the least of which, by failing, will make your fortune fail.] (I: 48, 290a, DM 447–48; 211*)

It is a mistake, in other words, to depend more than absolutely necessary on the paraphernalia one brings to the encounter. A certain Poyet learned this very lesson in a completely different sort of context in "Du parler prompt ou tardif" (I: 10). He was given the task "de faire la harangue au Pape" [of making the harangue to the Pope] (I: 10, 39a, DM 41; 26) when the latter met with François I at Marseilles. A lawyer renowned for his eloquence, Poyet had come with a speech all prepared, but at the last moment it was decided that a different theme than the one originally chosen would be more appropriate, so that "sa harangue demeuroit inutile & luy en falloit promptement refaire une autre" [so that his harangue was useless, and he had to draft another promptly] (I: 10, 39a, DM 41; 26). But this he was unable to do on such short notice, so Cardinal du Bellay had to give the speech in his place.

Montaigne begins this chapter by making a distinction between two kinds of public speakers: "les uns ont la facilité & la promptitude, & ... le boute-hors si aisé qu'à chaque bout de champ ils sont prests: les autres plus tardifz ne parlent jamais rien qu'élaboré et premedité" [some have facility and promptness, and ... can get it out so easily that at every turn they are ready; whereas others, slower, never speak except with elaboration and premeditation] (I: 10, 39a, DM 38; 25). As I: 10 is based on a distinction between the two categories of prompt and slow speech, I: 48 is based on a distinction between two ways of fighting, for each of which Montaigne gives two opposing instances: (1) fighting on foot vs. fighting on horseback, and (2) the simple and reliable sword vs. the complicated and unreliable pistol. The trouble with fighting on horseback and with using a firearm is that one is encumbered with excess baggage—the horse liable to fright, impetuosity, wounds or death; the machinery of the pistol any of whose several parts might fail to function. The same trouble afflicts those who, like Poyet, are burdened with the useless encumbrance of a speech they have spent a long time preparing but which they cannot make fit the situation that suddenly presents itself, on those occasions when public speaking (as it does in a court of law or a meeting of heads of state at a politically charged moment) resembles a field of battle, when "les commoditez de l'advocat le pressent à toute heure de se mettre en lice" [the lawyer's opportunities press him at every moment to enter the lists] (I: 10, 39a, DM 40; 25*).

By contrast, Severus Cassius did better when he relied on his improvisatory powers instead of preparing in advance. It was said of him "qu'il disoit mieus sans y avoir pensé, qu'il devoit plus à la fortune qu'à sa diligence" [that he spoke better without having thought about what he was going to say; that he owed more to fortune than to diligence] (I: 10, 40a, DM 42; 26). Montaigne puts himself in this category: "Je cognois, par experience, cette condition de nature, qui ne peut soustenir une vehemente premeditation et laborieuse. . . . Mais, outre cela, la solicitude de bien faire, et cette contention de l'ame trop bandée et trop tenduë à son entreprise, la met au *rouet*, la rompt, et l'empesche" [I know by experience this sort of nature that cannot bear vehement and laborious premeditations. . . . But besides this, the anxiety to do well, and the tension of straining too intently on one's work, put the soul on the *rack*, break it, and make it impotent] [I: 10, 40ac; 26]. In "Des destries" the problem with the pistol as opposed to the sword is that "il y a plusieurs pieces, la poudre, la pierre, le *rouët*, desquelles la moindre qui viendra à faillir, vous fera faillir vostre fortune" [there are several parts—the powder, the flint, the *lock*—the least of which, by failing, will make your fortune fail] (I: 48, 290a, 211*). This *rouët*, a piece that, though small, is essential to a firearm's mechanism, is on the metafictional level a small yet significant part of the *Essays*' mechanics, echoing its homonym in the structurally related chapter I: 10. In both chapters, a *rouët* is connected with the failure of a system to work. Its gives the lie to the notion that Montaigne's avowed preference for speaking without lengthy preparation applies as well to his writing. I: 10's *rouët* was in fact long in coming, only appearing as a post-1588 addition.

That preparation may well extend, as others have suggested, to a system of sequential echoes paralleling the symmetrical ones. For *rouet* occurs but one other time in Book One, in the chapter that immediately precedes 1: 10, when François I bragged of having "mis au *rouet*" [trapped by encirclement] (I: 9, 37a; 24*). Francesco Taverna, catching him in a lie by inducing him to say too much and thus reveal his master's guilt in murdering the King's envoy in Milan. The sequential and the symmetrical echoes among this word's only appearances in Book One—in chapters I: 9, I: 10, and I: 48—are of equal strength but are based on different parallels. The sequential echo of "avoir mis au rouet" (I: 9) with "la met au rouet" (I: 10) includes *mettre + à* as well, and in both instances involves speaking. Taverna was caught saying too much; the speaker in I: 10 has too much to say, since he has thought in advance about what he is going to say, to say anything at all. The symmetrical echo between "la met au *rouet*" (I: 10) and the "*rouët*" as part of the firing mechanism in I: 48 draws out the parallel between the inability of an over-prepared speaker to speak and the inability of a pistol to fire when one of its pieces fails. Anticipating the bullet that, when the *rouët* does not fail, "eschappe de nostre pistole" [escapes out of our pistol] (I: 48, 290a, DM 447; 211), speech placed on the rack is likened to water that "par force de se presser de sa violence et abondance, ne peut trouver issuë en un goulet ouvert" [because of the violent pressure of its abundance cannot find its way out of an open gutter pipe] (I: 10, 40a; 26*). The "fortune" that will fail in the case of the man who tries to fire the jammed pistol in I: 48 also finds a parallel in the "fortune" of the speaker in the 1: 10 passage. For the passage about putting one's soul on the *rouët* derives from the example of Severus Cassius, who "devoit plus à la *fortune* qu'à sa diligence" [owed more to *fortune* than to his diligence] (I: 10, 40a, DM 42; 26*) because he was a speaker who, like Montaigne himself, excelled in an impromptu setting but was likely to fail when encumbered with advance preparation. The fortune that fails in one instance succeeds in the other.

More evidence about the long-term preparation that went into the *Essays*, particularly as they evolved over time, arises from a 1588 addition to I: 48 which responds to the anecdote in I: 10 about the two harangues for the Pope—the one Poyet had prepared but couldn't give, and the one Cardinal du Bellay gave in his place. The Indians in Mexico were so amazed by the sight of conquistadors on horseback that they thought both the men and the horses must be either gods or animals of a nobler nature than their own. "Aucuns, apres avoir esté vaincus, venant demander paix et pardon aux hommes, et leurs chevaux, avec une toute pareille *harengue* à celle des hommes, prenant leur hannissement pour langage de composition et de trefve" [Some, after being vanquished, coming to ask for peace and pardon of the men and bring gold and food, did not fail to go and offer the same to the horses, with a *harangue* just like one for the men, taking their neighing for a language of conciliation and truce] (I: 48, 293b; 214). These two harangues answer the two in I: 10. There are other harangues in the *Essays,* but only here do they come in pairs.

11. Enough Already

"Des prognostications" [Of prognostications] (I: 11) and "De l'incertitude de nostre jugement" [Of the uncertainty of our judgment] (I: 47)

While chapters I: 9 and I: 49 deal with the past (with the way it resurfaces in the present in both lies and fashion), and chapters I: 10 and I: 48 with the need to act effectively on the spur of the present moment, I: 11 and I: 47 concern the future, for in both Montaigne writes of the impossibility of predicting what will come from the limited perspective the present offers. In I: 11 he criticizes both ancient reading of entrails and present-day attempts to read the future in stars and dreams—"notable exemple de la forcenée curiosité de nostre nature s'amusant à preoccuper les choses futures, comme si elle n'avoit pas assez affaire à digerer les presantes" [a notable example of the frenzied curiosity of our nature, which wastes its time anticipating future things, as if it did not have enough to do digesting the present] (I: 11, 41a, DM 45; 27). In 1: 47 he writes of the impossibility of predicting the outcome of certain military behaviors and tactics, considering such questions as what might happen if one pursued a defeated adversary (pushed by despair, would he suddenly fight back with renewed vigor?); whether one's soldiers should be sumptuously accoutered or armed only for necessity (would they fight more valiantly in order to save their personal property or would they fight more tentatively for fear of losing it?); whether soldiers should be given licence to taunt the enemy (would it increase the courage of the taunters, making them think their opponents would then give them no mercy, or would it only make the enemy fight more courageously, now having a personal interest in the outcome?); or whether one should charge the enemy or stand firm to await his charge (would a charge give one's soldiers greater momentum or would it merely waste their strength?). You just cannot predict what will happen, despite the best laid plans and most well considered reasons. "Ainsi nous avons bien accoustumé de dire avec raison que les advenemens & issues dependent mesme en la guerre pour la pluspart de la fortune. Laquelle ne se veut pas renger & assujetir à nostre discours & prudence" [Thus we are quite wont to say, with reason, that events and outcomes depend for the most part, even in war, on Fortune, who will not fall into line and subject herself to our reason and foresight] (I: 47, 286a, DM 442; 209*).

Yet the specific language in which he expresses his contempt for the notion that the future can be predicted in I: 11, in the passage I quoted about our frenzied curiosity wasting its time anticipating future things "comme si elle n'avoit pas assez affaire à *digerer* les presantes" [as if it did not have enough to do *digesting* the present] (I: 11, 41a, DM 45; 27), appears to have some predictive power of its own, anticipating the language with which he will in I: 47 criticize those who do not pursue their military advantage. Perhaps, he writes, an exculpatory defense of the error we made in not pursuing the enemy at Montcontour, or of the King of Spain not pressing the advantage he had over us at Saint Quentin, was that one "pourra dire céte faute partir d'une ame enyvrée de sa bonne fortune, & d'un courage lequel plein & gorgé de ce commencement de bon heur, perd le goust de l'accroistre, des jà par trop empesché à *digerer* ce qu'il en a" [could say that this mistake came from a soul intoxicated with its good fortune and a heart full and gorged with such a happy beginning losing the hunger to increase it, already too overcome *to digest* what it already has] (I: 47, 281a, DM 429–30; 205*). While "à digerer" does appear elsewhere in the *Essays*, only in these two instances does it do so in the context of having enough on one's plate already. The echo points to an interesting case of the same and the precisely opposed, for neither our natural curiosity (in I: 11) nor the commander too soon sated with success (in I: 47) is able to digest what must presently be consumed, with the contrasting difference that the former errs in reaching for more while the latter errs in *not* doing so.

Thus despite the different routes they take to get there, the two chapters are in the end talking about the same thing: predicting the future. "Des prognostications" (I: 11) even presents its own instance of a failure to pursue a military advantage, the question to which "De l'incertitude de nostre jugement" (I: 47) devotes so much space. In fact, in the 1580 edition it was the only anecdote in I: 11 and took up half the chapter. It is ostensibly told to illustrate the force of superstition and false prophecy, yet it concludes with an instance of the same failure to pursue an advantage for which both

French troops and the Spanish king will be taken to task in I: 47. François, Marquis de Sallusse, was a lieutenant in the army of François I who owed his position to the French king's favor but decided to go over to the side of Charles V because of some prognostications predicting disaster for the French cause. But his defection was not nearly as great a catastrophe as it might have been, "Car ayant & villes & forces en sa main, l'armée ennemye . . . à trois pas de luy, & nous sans soubson de son faict, il estoit en luy de faire pis qu'il ne fist" [for having both cities and forces in hand, the enemy army . . . three steps away, and us without a suspicion of his action, he could have done worse than he did] (I: 11, 42a, DM 46; 28), as the French side lost but one town as a result. Torn between his belief in omens and his affection for François I, and thus "combattu de diverses passions" [conflicted by diverse passions], he was unable to act decisively and pursue the advantage that lay in his grasp.

12. Anagrams

"De la constance" [*Of constancy*] (*I: 12*) *and* "Des noms" [*Of names*] (*I: 46*)

Nicolas Denisot, we are told in "Des noms" (I: 46), anagrammatized his name into the "Conte d'Alsinois," under which pseudonym he produced paintings and poems (I: 46, 279a, DM 427; 203). Anagrammatization, the rearrangement of constituent elements in a meaningful manner, is a pertinent way to describe what happens when elements of an anecdote in one chapter reappear in a new arrangement in an anecdote in the symmetrically corresponding chapter. For instance, in both "Des noms" (I: 46) and "De la constance" (I: 12) a story is told of a man who suddenly sees the danger he is in and takes quick action to get out of it. In one instance, the peril arose when the man came "hors du *couvert*" [out from the *cover*] (I: 12, 46a, DM 49; 31*) that a building provided and exposed himself to artillery fire; in the other, a man realized the danger his sinful life posed for the salvation of his soul when, "ayant *recouvré* une garce" [having *picked up* a wench] (I: 46, 277a, DM 422; 201) (though *recouvrer* derives from "récupérer" and not "recouvrir," the echo does suggest itself), he found out that her name was Marie. The coincidence between her name and that of the Virgin mother of Christ struck him with such force that he suddenly sent the girl away, and made amends the rest of his life. In consideration of this miracle a chapel was built on the site of his house, which later became the cathedral of Poitiers. It happens that there is a coincidence of sorts between the wench named Marie—"[la] garce . . . Marie" (I: 46, 277a, DM 422–23; 201)—and the name of the man in the other story, the "Marquis de Guast": the *Mar* matching the *Mar,* the *is* the *ie* (in pronunciation), and the *Gua* the *ga.* One is nearly the anagram of the other.

The very first sentence of I: 12 makes *couvrir* a key word in the discussion carried out in that chapter: "La loy de la resolution & de la constance ne porte pas que nous ne nous devions *couvrir* autant qu'il est en nostre puissance, des maux & inconveniens qui nous menassent" [The precepts of resoluteness and constancy do not state that we must not *cover* ourselves as much as it lies in our power from the evils and troubles that threaten us] (I: 12, 45a, DM 47; 30*). Thus the Marquis de Guast could be forgiven for his lack of constancy in jumping out of the way of the cannonball he saw coming (he had seen the enemy apply the match), the danger to which he had inadvertently exposed himself by abandoning the *couvert* of the building he had just left. Buildings figure largely in both stories: in each story there are two, one of which offers protection and the other danger. The windmill from whose shelter the Marquis de Guast emerged had protected him momentarily as he stealthily approached the city of Arles on a reconnaissance mission; his opponents "se promenoient sus le theatre des arenes" [were walking on top of the city's amphitheater] (I: 12, 46a, DM 49; 31), which offered them the opportunity to aim a cannon at him with deadly precision. The house in which the young debauchee lived and entertained his wenches, and thereby endangered his soul, was replaced by one more likely to protect such souls from damnation: "en consideration de ce miracle il fut basti en la place où estoit la maison de ce jeune homme une chappelle au nom de nostre Dame, & depuis l'Eglise que nous y voyons" [in consideration of this miracle there was built, on the spot where this young man's house was, a chapel in the name of Our Lady, and, later on, the church that we see there] (I: 46, 277a, DM 423; 201).

Another pair of echoing anecdotes emerges with a post-1588 addition to I: 12. In this instance the recombinable elements are (1) the verb *reculer* [to retreat] in both instances designating a false retreat, (2) a plethora of insults (expressed as "force reproches" and "mille injures"), and (3) the honor of one's ancestors. Montaigne recounts that when Darius set out to conquer the Scythians he was frustrated because they kept retreating before his advance. Consequently he sent to their king "*force reproches* pour le voir tousjours *reculant* devant luy et gauchissant la meslée" [*many reproaches* because he saw him always *retreating* before him and avoiding battle]. The king replied that as nomads with no cultivated lands or settlements the Scythians were accustomed to being on the move, but that if he was really spoiling for a fight he should try approaching "le lieu de leurs anciennes sepultures" [the place of their ancient burials], ground the Scythians would defend to the death (I: 12, 45c; 30). In I: 46 Montaigne tells of a friend whose dinner guests began to make extravagant claims for their bloodlines on the flimsiest of evidence. Instead of taking his place at the table, the host "*se recula*" [retreated] with deep bows, pretending to beg their pardon for having dared to associate with such noble personages as themselves. Then he dropped the mask, and berated them with "mille injures" [a thousand insults] for their pretensions and admonished them, "ne desadvouons pas la fortune et condition de nos ayeulx" [Let us not disown the fortune and condition of our forefathers] (I: 46, 278b; 203). He berated them, that is, because there were abandoning their actual ancestry, which ought to have been good enough, for a fake one, and thereby being untrue to their forefathers, who had no such pretensions. The anecdote first appeared in 1588, but in a latter revision Montaigne added the point about their forefathers being content with the status they had: "[B] Contentez vous, de par Dieu, de ce [C] dequoy nos peres se sont contentez et de ce [B] que nous sommes" [(B) Content yourselves, by God, with (C) what our fathers contented themselves and with (B) what we are] (I: 46, 278bc; 203*). The post-1588 addition intensifies their connection to their ancestors, as if it were Montaigne's intent to make the anecdote even more closely parallel the one about the Scythians, whose devotion to their ancestors' honor was absolute.

13. A Waiting Game

"Ceremonie de l'entreveuë des roys" [Ceremony at the interview of kings] (I: 13) and "De la bataille de Dreux" [On the Battle of Dreux] (I: 45)

Both of these chapters are about waiting (*attendre*) and what it would be better (*mieux*) to do. In I: 13, it is alleged that "en toutes assemblées . . . il touche aux moindres de se trouver les premiers à l'assignation, d'autant qu'il est *mieux* deu aux plus apparans de se faire *attendre*" [in all assemblies . . . the lesser should be first at an appointment, since it is *more* seemly that the more prominent should make others *wait* for them] (I: 13, 48a, DM 51; 32*). In I: 45, those critical of Monsieur de Guise's conduct at the Battle of Dreux said that "il valloit *mieux* se hazarder prenant l'ennemy par flanc, qu'*attendant* l'avantage de le voir en queûe souffrir une si lourde perte" [it would have been *better* to take the risk of attacking the enemy by the flank than to suffer so heavy a loss by *waiting* for the advantage of catching him by the rear] (I: 45, 274a, DM 418; 200*).

Both chapters are also about whether it is better to go *ahead* (*devant*) to meet the party one is expecting—an invited guest in I: 13, the advancing enemy army in I: 45—or to wait for them to arrive. In 1: 13, it is suggested "que c'estoit incivilité à un gentil-homme de partir de sa maison . . . pour aller au devant de celuy qui le vient trouver, pour grand qu'il soit, & qu'il est plus respectueux & civil de l'attandre pour le recevoir" [that it would be incivility for a gentleman to leave his house . . . in order to go *ahead* to meet the person who is coming to see him, however great he may be; and that it is more respectful and civil to wait to receive him] (I: 13, 48a, DM 51; 32*). In 1: 45: "Philopoemen en une rencontre contre Machinidas ayant envoyé *devant* pour attaquer l'escarmouche bonne troupe d'archiers & gens de traict . . . " [Philopoemen, in an encounter with Machanidas, having sent *ahead* a good force of archers and darters to begin the skirmish . . .] (I: 45, 274a, DM 419; 200*). Although he did send his archers ahead, the point of the story is that once they engaged the enemy he did not then send the rest of his army ahead to save the archers from slaughter, despite the pleas of his soldiers that he do so, but wisely *waited* until the enemy came to him before attacking.

These two chapters apply the same principles in two very different—indeed opposite—contexts, hospitality (I: 13) and war (I: 45). In the *Essays*' metafiction they prove the truth of the assertion Montaigne makes in I: 45 that one should keep in mind the whole (the way the chapters fit together in the entirety of the work) and not just the part (the individual chapter): "que le but et la visée, non seulement d'un capitaine, mais de chaque soldat, doit regarder la victoire en gros, & que nulles occurrences particulieres, quelque interest qu'il y ayt, ne le doivent divertir de ce point là" [that the goal and aim not only of a captain but of every soldier must be the victory as a whole, and that no particular occurrences, of whatever interest to himself, should divert him from that goal] (I: 45, 274a, DM 418–19; 200).

14. More Than One Port in a Storm

> "*Que le goust des biens et des maux depend en bonne partie de l'opinion que nous en avons*" [*That the taste of good and evil things depends in large measure on the opinion we have of them*] (I: 14) and "*Du dormir*" [*On sleep*] (I: 44)

Montaigne writes in his chapter on sleep that "j'ay remarqué pour chose rare de *voir* quelquefois les *grands personnages*, aux plus hautes entreprinses et importans affaires, se tenir si entiers en leur assiette, que de n'en accourcir pas seulement leur sommeil" [it has struck me as a rare thing to *see* sometimes *great personages,* in the loftiest undertakings and most important affairs, remain so utterly unmoved as not even to curtail their sleep] (I: 44, 271a, DM 113; 198*). He cites, among others, two particular notable figures who had no trouble sleeping before they were about to commit suicide. One of them is the Emperor Otho, who decided to kill himself one night, but only *"apres avoir mis ordre à ses affaires domestiques"* [*after having put his domestic affairs in order*], after which he slept so deeply that his servants could hear him snoring. The other is Cato, who had resolved on suicide, but waited until the senators he was sending away had left the *"port d'Utique"* [*port of Utica*]. The messenger he sent to the port returned and awakened him to say that a *"tourmente"* [*storm*] had held them back; Cato went back to sleep until word would come that they had made it to safety (I: 44, 271a; DM 413–14; 198). Both anecdotes find echoes in I: 14 (hence my added italics). The "grands personnages" who face death so calmly (either by suicide in the cases of Otho and Cato, or in an impending battle in the other examples cited there) find their counterpart at the other end of the social scale:

> Combien *voit*-on de *personnes populaires & communes*, conduictes à la mort, & non à une mort simple, mais meslée de honte & quelque fois de griefs tourmens, y apporter une telle asseurance . . . qu'on n'y aperçoit rien de changé de leur estat ordinaire: *establissans leurs affaires domestiques*, se recommandans à leurs amis.
>
> [How many *persons from among the common folk* do we *see*, led to their death, and not to a simple death, but one mixed with shame and sometimes with grievous torments, bring to it such an assurance . . . that we notice nothing changed from their ordinary manner: *putting their domestic affairs in order*, commending themselves to their friends.] (I: 14, 51a, DM 55–56; 34*)

These two passages in I: 14 and I: 44 are the only ones in the *Essays* where anyone puts his "affaires domestiques" in order. Here Montaigne *sees* ("j'ay remarqué pour chose rare de *voir*," "Combien *voit*-on de . . . ") another instance of extremes that touch, as they do in chapters I: 4 and I: 54, when the humblest and the most exalted do the same things: face their certain death unmoved ("se tenir si entiers en leur assiette," "on n'y aperçoit rien de changé de leur estat ordinaire") and put their domestic affairs in order.

The story of Otho's suicide "a beaucoup de choses pareilles" [has many things like] those of the story of Cato's, and one of them is that the latter likewise echoes a passage in I: 14, one that appears just before the one that Otho's story echoes: "Or cete mort que les uns appellent des choses horribles la plus horrible, qui ne sçait que d'autres la nomment *l'unique port des tourmens* de cete vie? le souverain bien de nature? seul appuy de nostre liberté? & commune et prompte recepte à tous maux?" [Now this death, which some call the most horrible of horrible things, who does not know that others call it the *only port* of safety *from the torments* of this life, the sovereign good of nature, the sole support of our freedom, and the common and prompt remedy for all evils?] (I: 14, 51a, DM 55; 33–34*). The *unique port* in I: 14 finds its unique echo in the *port d'Utique* in 1: 44; the *tourmens* of this life in I: 14 find their counterpart in the *tourmente* [storm] that kept Cato's allies from leaving the *port* in I: 44. But this port means exactly the opposite of the other, because the senators would not be safe until they *left* it, while the port in I: 14 is the place of safety *to* which one goes. The reason the "unique port" is a refuge is that it is suicide, the act in which both Cato and Otho were about to engage. Their self-immolations, which loom so large in I: 44, are more than matched by those recited in I: 14: the twenty-five heads of households in Milan who killed themselves within a week (I: 14, 53a; 35), the Xantians (I: 14, 53a; 35), and even children (I: 14, 54a; 36). Post-1588 additions to the list include the wives of Narsinga (I: 14, 52c; 34–35), Turks and Greeks (I: 14, 53c; 35), and Portuguese Jews (I: 14, 53c; 35–36).

In another instance of a famously sound sleeper, Marius, even after he had drawn up his forces and given the word for the battle to begin, "se coucha dessoubs un *arbre*" [lay down under a *tree*] to rest and fell into such deep slumber that he was just barely awakened by the rout and flight of his men, having seen none of the combat. It was said that it was because he was so tired from lack of sleep "que *nature* n'en pouvoit plus" [that *nature* could hold out no longer] (I: 44, 272a, DM 417; 199). The only other passage in the *Essays* where trees bear witness to the unstoppable force of nature appears in I: 14: "forcerons nous la generale habitude de *nature*, qui se voit en tout ce qui est vivant sous le ciel, de trambler sous la douleur? Les *arbres* mesmes semblent gemir aux offences, qu'on leur faict" [Shall we violate the general law of *nature*, which can be observed in all that lives under heaven, that we shall tremble under pain? The very *trees* seem to groan at the blows that are given them] (I: 14, 55–56a, DM 64; 37).

Another famous personage in I: 44 who needed his rest was Alexander the Great, who on the day appointed for battle against Darius slept so soundly and so late that one of his generals was obliged to come into his room and call him by name two or three times to wake him up (I: 44, 271a; 198). But that same Alexander, in a 1588 addition to I: 14, is presented in an opposite light: "Qui rechercha jamais de telle faim la seurté et *le repos,* qu'*Alexandre et Caesar* ont faict l'inquietude et les difficultez" [Who ever with such hunger sought security and *repose* as *Alexander* and Caesar sought unrest and difficulties?] (I: 14, 61b; 42). Alexander in I: 44 provides an example of an unquenchable desire for repose, the sleep from which it was so hard to awaken him; here in I: 14, the same Alexander is cited as one hardly hungry for rest. Both chapters praise his courage in the face of danger, though in precisely opposed ways: in I: 14 he seeks out danger *instead of repose;* in I: 44 he is so unafraid of danger that he *can repose,* falling into unworried sleep just before he must face it.

15. Custom and Princely Grandeur

"On est puny pour s'opiniastrer à une place sans raison" [One is punished for stubbornly defending a place without reason] (I: 15) and "Des lois somptuaires" [On sumptuary laws] (I: 43)

Despite their disparate subjects—war and fashion—in both of these chapters the case is made that the lesser should respect the greater, the conclusion is drawn that the greater have certain prerogatives the lesser do not enjoy, and custom is said to sanction that distinction. In I: 15 those attacked by a more powerful enemy are justly punished with death for putting up a useless resistance (despite what Montaigne says in I: 1, where such behavior is sometimes rewarded with mercy). In I: 43 he addresses the problem of the lower classes wearing clothing appropriate only to their betters. In both situations princely grandeur is a determining factor.

In I: 15 a certain *coustume* obliges defenders facing long odds to respect the *grandeur* of a *prince.* Valor has its limits; when it goes too far, it turns into vice. Thus is born "*la coustume*" [*the custom*] of punishing with death those who defend a place that cannot be held. But one must take into account as well "la *grandeur du prince* conquerant" [the *grandeur of the* conquering *prince*], his reputation, the respect he is owed (I: 15, 68a, DM 75, 77; 47, 48). In I: 43 in the choice of what clothes to wear *la coustume* obliges one to respect the *grandeur* of a *prince:*

> [A] Car dire ainsi, qu'il n'y aura que les *princes* qui puissent porter du velours & de la tresse d'or, & l'interdire au peuple, qu'est ce autre chose que mettre en credit ces vanitez là, & faire croistre l'envie à chacun d'en user? Que les rois quittent hardiment ces marques de *grandeur,* ilz en ont assez

d'autres: [B] telz excez sont plus excusables à tout autre qu'à un *prince*. [A] Par l'exemple de plusieurs nations nous pouvons apprendre assez de meilleures façons de nous distinguer exterieurement & nos degrez (ce que j'estime à la verité estre bien requis en un estat) sans nourrir pour cet effect céte corruption & incommodité si apparente. C'est merveille comment *la coustume* en ces choses indifferentes plante aiséement & soudain le pied de son authorité.

[(A) For to say that none but *princes* shall be allowed to wear velvet and gold braid, and to forbid them to the people, what else is this but to give prestige to these vanities and increase everyone's desire to enjoy them? Let kings boldly abandon these marks of *grandeur*; they have enough others; (B) such excesses are more excusable in any other than in a *prince*. (A) From the example of many nations we may learn enough better ways of distinguishing ourselves and our rank externally (which I truly believe to be very necessary in a state), without for this purpose fostering such manifest corruption and harm. It is amazing how easily and quickly *custom,* in these indifferent things, establishes the footing of its authority.] (I: 43, 268–69ab, DM 409–10; 196*)

The "*grandeur du prince* conquerant" of I: 15 already found an echo in 1580 in the "marques de *grandeur*" that belong to "les *princes*" in I: 43. Montaigne would enhance the echo in 1588 by adding another *prince* with the insertion "telz excez sont plus excusables à tout autre qu'à un *prince* [such excesses are more excusable in any other than in a *prince*].[36] The new *prince* is much closer to *grandeur* than the first. The three terms *coustume, prince* and *grandeur* appear in other chapters but only in these two are all three logically connected: a custom that obliges one to respect princely grandeur.

In another 1588 addition to I: 43 Montaigne complains of the new custom of removing one's hat in the presence of the king, and even in the presence of the king's subalterns as well: "contre la forme de nos peres et la particuliere liberté de la noblesse de ce Royaume, nous nous tenons descouverts bien loing autour d'eux en quelque lieu qu'ils soient: et comme autour d'eux, autour de cent autres, tant nous avons de tiercelets et quartelets de Roys" [contrary to the ways of our fathers and the particular privilege of the nobility of this kingdom, we stand bareheaded at a long distance around our kings, wherever they may be, and not only around them but around a hun-

---

36. Villey, Tournon, and Balsamo et al. erroneously date these words from 1580. The only edition I could find that correctly shows it to be an addition from 1588 is Screech's translation (p. 300).

dred others, so many kinglets and semi-kinglets do we have] (I: 43, 270b; 107*). He subsequently found an anecdote paralleling this one to add to the corresponding chapter: the Portuguese invading the Indies "trouverent des estats avec cette loy universelle et inviolable, que tout ennemy vaincu du Roy en presence, ou de son Lieutenant, est hors de composition de rançon et de mercy" [found states with this universal and inviolable law, that any enemy conquered in the King's presence, or in that of his lieutenant, is excluded from consideration for ransom or mercy] (I: 15, 68–69c; 48*). In both anecdotes the king's presence causes a special rule to be observed (that of having to remain bareheaded in I: 43, that of not being eligible for ransom or mercy in I: 15), a custom that is equally observed in the presence of the king's lesser versions (his tiercelets and quarterlets in I: 43, his lieutenant in I: 15).

16. Judging Julian Judging

"De la punition de la couardise" [On the punishment of cowardice] (I: 16) and "De l'inequalité qui est entre nous" [On the inequality that is between us] (I: 42)

Consider these two passages, the first from I: 16, the second from I: 42.

> Ammianus Marcellinus raconte, que l'Empereur Julien condamna dix de ses soldats, qui avoyent tourné le dos à une charge contre les Parthes, à estre dégradés, et apres à souffrir mort, suyvant, dict il, les loix anciennes. Toutesfois ailleurs pour une pareille faute il en condemne d'autres, seulement à se tenir parmy les prisonniers soubs l'enseigne du bagage.

> [Ammianus Marcellinus relates that Emperor Julian condemned ten of his soldiers, who had turned their backs in a charge against the Parthians, to be degraded and afterward to suffer death, according, he says, to the ancient laws. Elsewhere, however, for a similar fault, he condemns others merely to stay among the prisoners under the baggage ensign.] (I: 16, 70a, DM 80; 49)

> Ses courtisans louoient un jour Julien l'Empereur de faire bonne justice: Je m'en orguillerois volontiers, dict il, de ces loüanges, si elles venoient de personnes qui osassent accuser ou mesloüer mes actions contraires, quand elles y seroient.

[One day the Emperor Julian's courtiers were praising him for being so just. "I would readily take pride in these praises," he said, "if they came from people who dared to accuse or dispraise my unjust actions, if there should be any."] (I: 42, 266–67a, DM 407; 195)

These are the only two mentions in Book One of Julian the Apostate, who is important enough to have a chapter devoted entirely to him in the 19th—and central—chapter of Book Two. Both I: 16 and I: 42 concern not only Julian, but the way he administered justice—a justice in both chapters contradictory or potentially so: in I: 16 he punishes cowardice in two contrasting ways; in I: 42 he opens up the possibility that while some of his judgments may be just others may be unjust. What is more, the second of these passages appears to refer to the first, since in it he dares his flatterers to remember such a contradictory administration of justice as the first passage in fact recounts. Both anecdotes come from the same source, the Ammianus Marcellinus to whom Montaigne credits the first story in I: 16 and from whom the second is also taken.

But how does this help us to read these two chapters? Are these just minor, decorative details and does the real sense of the chapters lie elsewhere? Or are they to be considered as some sort of sign pointing to what makes these chapters parts of a single text? On the face of it, it is hard to imagine a connection between the punishment of cowardice and the inequality between kings and their subjects (the "nous" of I: 42's title). Yet Montaigne treats of them in such a way as to make them related: what Julian is complaining about in I: 42 is that the overwhelming awe his subjects feel for his royal office prevents them from judging him for his real personal qualities. Montaigne complains at the beginning of the chapter that we do not properly judge men if we neglect to distinguish between innate qualities and extraneous considerations: "à propos de l'estimation des hommes, c'est merveille que sauf nous nulle chose ne s'estime que par ses propres qualitez. Nous loüons un cheval de ce qu'il est vigoureux & adroit, non de son harnois. . . . Pourquoy de mesmes n'estimons nous un homme par ce qui est sien?" [apropos of judging men, it is a wonder that, ourselves excepted, nothing is evaluated except by its own qualities. We praise a horse because it is vigorous and skillful, not for his harness. . . . Why do we not likewise judge a man by what is his own?] (I: 42, 259a, DM 393; 189). Now "De la punition de la couardise" (I: 16) is even more obviously about judging men. In considering whether cowardice should be punished by death or by shaming, Montaigne argues that we should make a distinction

> entre les fautes qui viennent de nostre foiblesse & celles qui viennent de nostre malice. Car en celles ici nous nous sommes bandés à nostre escient contre les regles de la raison, que nature a empreintes en nous: & en celles là, il semble que nous puissions appeller à garant cete mesme nature, pour nous avoir laissé en telle imperfection & defaillance.
>
> [between the faults that come from our weakness and those that come from our malice. For in the latter we have tensed ourselves deliberately against the rules of reason that nature has imprinted in us; and in the former it seems that we can call on this same nature as our warrantor, for having left us in such imperfection and weakness.] (I: 16, 70a, DM 78–79; 48)

Human weakness is excusable; malice is not. Hence perhaps the justice in Julian's decision to punish some with death, and others not. To appreciate the skill with which he could discern those who behaved in a cowardly manner out of malice from those who did so from natural weakness is to be granted an insight into his personal qualities that the flatterers in I: 42 were prevented from seeing.

I: 42 thus discusses the general problem (judging our fellow men) of which I: 16 considers a particular instance (judging the conduct, in this case the cowardly conduct, of some men). I: 42's opposition of extraneous considerations vs. innate qualities is paralleled by I: 16's opposition of cowardly acts vs. the inner motivation for those acts. It is in both cases the latter that must be judged—whether it was "malice" or "weakness" in the case of cowardice.

17. Glory, Given and Taken

> *"Un traict de quelques ambassadeurs"* [What some ambassadors did] (I: 17) and *"De ne communiquer sa gloire"* [On not sharing one's fame] (I: 41)

Montaigne tells in I: 17 of the decision certain French ambassadors made not to communicate to their king François I all that his enemy Charles V told them to tell him because they considered it too insulting. They left out two items in particular, an insult directed at the French army and a challenge to a duel. Montaigne comments, "j'ay trouvé bien estrange, qu'il fut en la puissance d'un ambassadeur de dispenser sur les advertissemens, qu'il doit faire *à son maistre*" [I found it very strange that it should be in the power of an ambassador to make his choice of the information that he should give *to his master*] (I: 17, 73a, DM 85; 188). I: 41 has an anecdote of its own about the same Charles V:

> Quand l'Empereur Charles cinquiesme passa en Provence l'an 1537 on tient que Anthoine de Leve voyant son maistre resolu de ce voyage, & l'estimant luy estre merveilleusement glorieux, opinoit toustefois le contraire, & le desconseilloit: a céte fin que toute la gloire & honneur de ce conseil en fut attribué *à son maistre*.

> [When the Emperor Charles V came into Provence in the year 1537, they say that Antonio de Lyva, seeing his master resolved on this expedition and believing that it would add wonderfully to his glory, nevertheless expressed a contrary opinion and advised him against it; to this end, that all the glory and honor of this plan should be attributed *to his master*.] (I: 41, 256a, DM 390; 188)

In both stories, a sovereign's subordinate takes it upon himself, for his sovereign's greater glory, not to communicate *à son maistre* [to his master] all that he could have said—Charles V's insulting remarks in I: 17, the subordinate's own opinion in I: 41. Montaigne approves of Antoine de Leve's behavior but disapproves of the ambassadors'.[37] Although the phrase "à son maistre" appears five other times in the *Essays* only in these two chapters does it involve not communicating to one's master. Both these stories—as was the case with those about Julian the Apostate in I: 16 and I: 42—were taken from a single source, in this instance the "histoire du Seigneur de Langey" (I: 17, 73a, DM 84; 50) (actually the *Mémoires* of Martin and Guillaume du Bellay) that he credits in one instance but not the other (noted by Balsamo et al., 1353, 1460), as he had likewise done with his source for the two Julian anecdotes, crediting Ammianus Marcellinus in I: 16 but not in I: 42. The two stories display a complementary symmetry in that the message that was supposed to have been communicated *from Charles V* in I: 17 is not received, while in I: 41 the message that might have been communicated *to Charles V* (Lyva's actual opinion about whether the Emperor should visit

---

37. Timothy Hampton writes that the ambassadors' decision not to tell all "became a test case for Renaissance writers on diplomacy" and that Montaigne was not the only writer to comment on it. "For Montaigne, the hierarchy of relations between master and servant structures the function of the ambassador, who does his duty to the extent that he reports accurately what he has seen" (*Fictions of Embassy: Literature and Diplomacy in Early Modern Europe* (Ithaca: Cornell University Press, 2009): 49. But the larger picture provided by the echoing and opposing passage in I: 41, where Montaigne *approves* of a subordinate not telling his sovereign all he might, suggests he might not have felt all that strongly about it. The ambassadors' silence, for the *Essays*, serves a larger purpose.

Provence) is not sent. In no other chapter is a message from or to Charles V not communicated.

It is as if the two chapters were communicating with each other. What is more, while I: 41, as its title indicates, is about *communicating* (or not communicating) and *glory,* so too is I: 17. Montaigne writes that when he travels he always hopes to learn something "par la *communication* d'autruy" [by *communication* with others] (I: 17, 72a, DM 82; 49), trying to get people he meets to talk about subjects they know best. Unfortunately what most often happens is that they prefer to talk about a profession other than their own, "estimant que c'est autant de nouvelle *reputation* acquise: tesmoing le reproche qu'Archidamus feit à Periander, qu'il quittoit la *gloire* de bon medecin, pour acquerir celle de mauvais poëte" [thinking this is so much new *reputation* acquired; witness the reproach Archidamus made to Periander, that he was abandoning the *glory* of a good doctor for that of a bad poet] (I: 17, 72a, DM 82; 49). In symmetrical contrast to Periander's abandoning his own *gloire* for one he didn't deserve but sought for his own aggrandizement to acquire, in I: 41 Catulus Luctatius flees the enemy with his soldiers so that they would still appear to be obeying his orders: "c'estoit abandonner sa *reputation* pour couvrir la honte d'autruy" [that was abandoning his *reputation* to cover the shame of others], thereby showing that he is willing to "communiquer son honneur & d'estrener autruy de sa *gloire*" [communicate his honor and endow another with his *glory*] (I: 41, 256a, DM 389; 188*). Both abandon their rightful glory, but one of them does it to selfishly acquire a glory that isn't his and the other to selflessly give up a glory that is. While Periander hoped to acquire "autant de nouvelle *reputation*," Luctatius was willing to "abandonner sa *reputation*" to cover his soldiers' shame.

18. Empty Signs

"De la peur" [On fear] (I: 18) and "Consideration sur Cicéron" [A consideration on Cicero] (I: 40)

In 1: 18 Montaigne illustrates the power of fear with the story of a "port'enseigne" [standard-bearer] at the siege of Rome who panicked and ran out through a hole in the ruins with the standard in his hand, thinking he was fleeing the enemy but in fact advancing toward them. But when he saw the latter "*se renger pour le soutenir*" [*draw up their ranks to resist him*] he turned around and went back in through the same hole, having ventured three hundred paces toward the enemy (I: 18, 75a, DM 88; 52*). Some three hundred pages later in the 1580 edition, something of that incident crops up again in Montaigne's description of what Seneca's and Epicurus' letters were not, and by implication what Cicero's letters were: "ne sont ce pas lettres vuides & descharnées, qui ne *se soutienent* que par un delicat chois de motz entassez & *rangez* à une juste cadence, ains farcies & pleines de beaux discours de sapience" [these are not mere empty and fleshless letters, *holding together* only by a delicate choice of words piled up and *arranged* in precise cadence, but letters stuffed full of the fine arguments of wisdom] (I: 40, 252a, DM 387; 185). Seneca's and Epicurus' letters, that is, contain wisdom lacking in Cicero's, which are empty and fleshless, holding together only by the way their words are chosen and arranged. The words that repeat here are themselves, in a self-naming metafiction, chosen and arranged. These are the only two places in the *Essays* where any form of the words "ranger" and "soutenir" appear together, and in both instances it is the former that enables the latter to happen: the besieging troops arrange themselves (*se rengent*) to bear up against (*soutenir*) the sortie of which they think the sudden appearance of the *enseigne* is the sign; it is because Cicero's delicately chosen words are arranged (*rangez*) a certain way that his letters hold together (*se soutiennent*). Cicero's letters find themselves in a position akin to that of the *port'enseigne:* "sustained" [*soutenues*] by that which is "arranged" [*rangez*], as the standard-bearer was "resisted" [*soutenu*] in a different sense (indeed, an opposite sense) of the word by the soldiers who were lined up [*rangés*] against him.

What is the point behind *this* delicate choice of echoing words? The answer may lie in the nature of Montaigne's criticism of the letters' author as well as in what happens to those letters. The problem Montaigne claims to have with Cicero's letters is that they are empty signifiers, devoid for the public of what private meaning they may have originally had, devoid even of that private meaning because they (both Cicero's and Pliny's) were never even delivered in the first place:

> Mais cecy surpasse toute bassesse de coeur en personnes de tel rang, d'avoir voulu tirer quelque principale gloire du caquet & de la parlerie, jusques à y employer les lettres privées écriptes à leurs amis: en maniere, que aucunes ayant failli leur saison pour estre envoyiées, ils les font ce neantmoins publier avec céte digne excuse, qu'ils n'ont pas voulu perdre leur travail & veillées.

> [But this surpasses all baseness of heart in persons of such rank: to have wanted to derive some great glory from mere babble and talk, to the point of publishing their private letters written to their friends; and even though some of these failed to be sent, they were published nonetheless, with this

worthy excuse, that the writers did not want to lose their labor and their vigils.] (I: 40, 249a, DM 383; 183)

Now the *enseigne* [the standard] that the standard-bearer carried when he rushed out of the city would in normal circumstances have borne a very specific meaning: that there was an army right behind it charging out to meet the enemy. Such is the meaning that the enemy troops read into it, "estimant que ce fut une sortie que ceux de la ville fissent" [who thought this was a sortie made by those in the city]. But, like the letters Cicero published even though they never reached their addressees—letters that, when published, meant nothing and that never did successfully convey a meaning to a private reader—the *enseigne* the unwitting soldier bore was a sign devoid of content. Though his gesture, however unintentional, did for one brief moment have a certain magnificent, if empty—and unconscious—eloquence. Montaigne may have seen himself in that unwitting sign-bearer, for elsewhere he writes of how one can create meaning without meaning to: "la fortune montre . . . la part qu'elle a en tous ces ouvrages, par les graces et beautez qui s'y treuvent, non seulement sans l'intention, mais sans la cognoissance mesme de l'ouvrier" [Fortune shows . . . the part she has in all these works by the graces and beauties that are found in them, not only without the workman's intention, but even without his knowledge] (I: 24, 127a; 93). The *Essays* are rich in such graces and beauties that closer inspection reveals not to be due to chance after all.

One emerges in a post-1588 addition to I: 40 in which Montaigne praises his own writing in the same terms with which he criticized Cicero's. Cicero's letters "ne se soutienent que par un *delicat* chois de motz *entassez* & *rangez* à une juste cadence" [hold together only by a *delicate* choice of words *piled up* and *arranged* in precise cadence] (I: 40, 252a, DM 387; 185). Montaigne says of his *Essays* that no writer has sown his text with more material, so much so that "Pour en *ranger* davantage, je n'en *entasse* que les testes" [In order to *line up* more, I *pile up* only the *heads*]. His anecdotes, he adds, often bear the seeds of a material richer and bolder than their immediate use, sounding "un ton plus *delicat*, et pour moy qui n'en veux exprimer d'avantage, et pour ceux qui rencontreront mon air" [a more *delicate* note, both for myself, who does not wish to express anything more, and for those who get my drift] (I: 40, 251c; 185*). How strange that Montaigne should castigate Cicero's style for being nothing but a *delicate* choice of words *piled up* [*entassez*] and *arranged* [*rangez*], when he should also say that his own practice of writing is to *ranger* and *entasser* in order to create something *delicat!* Nowhere in the *Essays* do two of these words, *ranger* and *entasser,* appear together but on these two neighboring pages from the post-1588 "Consideration sur Cicéron." That is certainly "un delicat chois de motz" [a delicate choice of words].

Yet his dismissal of Cicero is not absolute: "Fy de l'eloquence qui nous laisse envie de soy, non des choses. Si ce n'est qu'on die que celle de Cicero estant en si extreme perfection se donne corps elle mesme" [Fie on the eloquence that leaves us craving itself, not things. Unless we say that Cicero's, being of such extreme perfection, gives itself substance] (I: 40, 252a, DM 388; 185*). Montaigne gives substance to a hidden text within his text by his delicate choice of words, and this is true not only of the choice of words that makes his criticism of Cicero's writing strangely relevant to his praise of his own but also of the word choices that make that praise parallel the story of the misguided "*port*'enseigne qui . . . se jetta l'enseigne au poing *hors* la ville droit aux ennemis . . . & . . . en fin voiant la troupe de monsieur de Bourbon *se renger* pour le soutenir . . . tournant *teste* rentra" [standard-*bearer* who . . . threw himself, standard in hard, *outside of* the city right toward the enemy . . . and . . . at last seeing Monsieur de Bourbon's men *arrange themselves* to resist him . . . turning his *head* back, returned] (I: 18, 75a, DM 88, 52*). We recall that Montaigne in that post-1588 addition to "Consideration sur Cicéron" says of his *Essays* that he has put so much material in them that "Pour en *ranger* davantage, je n'en entasse que les *testes*" [To *cram in* more, I pile up only the *heads*]. Neither his

> histoires . . . ny mes allegations ne servent pas toujours simplement d'exemple, d'authorité ou d'ornement. Je ne les regarde pas seulement par l'usage que j'en tire. Elles *portent* souvent, *hors* de mon propos, la semence d'une matiere plus riche et plus hardie, et sonnent à gauche un ton plus delicat, et pour moy qui n'en veux exprimer d'avantage, et pour ceux qui rencontreront mon air.

> [stories . . . nor my quotations serve always simply for example, authority, or ornament. I do not esteem them solely for the use I derive from them. They often *carry*, *outside of* my subject, the seeds of a richer and bolder material, and sound off to the side a more delicate note, both for myself, who do not wish to express anything more, and for those who get my drift.] (I: 40, 251c; 185*)

I suggested a moment ago that Montaigne may have seen himself in the standard-bearer. His delicate choice of words indeed points to that possibility, as well as reveals that the anecdote of the "port'enseigne" is an example of what he is referring to when he says that his stories carry the seeds of a richer and bolder material and can mean something more than what they mean in their immediate context. Like the "*port'enseigne*" [the sign *carrier*] who carried his sign *hors* [outside] the place in which one would normally have expected him to remain, Montaigne's stories "*portent*" their signs *hors* [outside] the context in which one would have expected *them* to remain.

That delicate choice of words extends to his seeking to *ranger* so much into his text that only the *testes* show, for those two words occur together in no other chapter but these. The *testes* that show are, self-referentially, these—and the one the standard-bearer turned around once he saw the soldiers *se ranger* against him.

Here in summary form are the words repeated between the story of the standard-bearer in I: 18, Montaigne's description of how he wrote the *Essays* in I: 40, and his description of how Cicero wrote his letters in I: 40:

the standard-bearer:	the *Essays:*	Cicero:
(I: 18)	(I: 40)	(I: 40)
se renger	renger	rangez
	entasse	entassez
	delicat	delicat
soustenir		se soutiennent
teste	testes	
port'enseigne	portent	
hors	hors	

One word (*renger*) is found in all three; four (*renger, teste, porte, hors*) are shared by the standard-bearer's story and the description of the *Essays;* two (*renger, soutenir*) are shared by the standard-bearer and Cicero; three (*renger, entasser, delicat*) by the *Essays* and Cicero. Nowhere else in the *Essays* do *renger* and *entasser* appear together than in the two sequential passages in I: 40, nor *renger* and *teste* than in the standard-bearer's story and the description of the *Essays*.

19. Prolonging Life

> "*Qu'il ne faut juger de nostre heur, qu'apres la mort*" [That our happiness must not be judged until after death] (I: 19) and "*De la solitude*" [On solitude] (I: 39)

The exhortation in "De la solitude," to "s'en contenter, sans desir de *prolon-*

gement de vie ny de nom" [be content, with no desire of *prolonging life* or reputation] (I: 39, 248a, DM 382; 183*) echoes the warning implicit in the cautionary tale of Pompey in I: 19, who died too late, exchanging his status of conqueror of half the world for that of a miserable suppliant to officials of the king of Egypt: "tant cousta à ce grand Pompeius *l'alongement* de cinq ou six mois *de vie*" [such was the cost to this great Pompey of *lengthening his life* five or six months] (I: 19, 79a, DM 92; 54). It is a significant echo, a good example of Montaigne's penchant for a delicate choice of words: these are the only places where either *prolongement* or *alongement* appear in the *Essays*. He tightened the resemblance in a post-1588 alteration, changing *alongement* in I: 19 to *prolongation*.

In both passages the same message is conveyed: do not seek to prolong your life. Yet in all other regards the two chapters are opposed. In I: 19 Montaigne keeps insisting that no man should be judged happy until his death, because you never know what might happen: "la fortune quelque fois guette à point nommé le dernier jour de nostre vie pour monstrer sa puissance de renverser en un moment ce qu'elle avoit basty en longues années" [Fortune sometimes lies in wait precisely for the last day of our life, to show her power to overturn in a moment what she has built up over many years] (I: 19, 79a, DM 92–93; 54–55). But in I: 39 he insists that we can prepare for our declining years in such a way as to minimize risk. All we have to do, it seems, is to depend on ourselves and not others, as if we were the masters of our fate: "faisons que nostre contentement dépende de nous. Desprenons nous de toutes les liaisons qui nous attachent à autruy. Gaignons sur nous de pouvoir à bon escient vivre seulz & y vivre à nostre aise" [let us make our contentment depend on ourselves; let us cut loose from all the ties that bind us to others; let us win from ourselves the power to live really alone and to live that way at our ease] (I: 39, 240a, DM 364; 177).

Both chapters focus in these contrasting ways on the "bout" [end] of one's "vie" [life], thanks to a 1588 addition to I: 19, "Au jugement de la *vie* d'autruy, je regarde toujours comment s'en est porté le *bout*" [In judging the *life* of another, I always observe how the *end* turned out] (I: 19, 80b; 55*)—which set up an echo to this passage in I: 39: "Or c'est assez vescu pour autruy, vivons pour nous au moins ce *bout* de *vie*" [Now that's enough lived for others; let us live for ourselves at least this *end* of *life*] (I: 39, 242a, DM 368; 178*). In I: 19 this *bout* of *vie* is unpredictable, liable to be different from what we expect; in I: 39, on the contrary, it appears that with prudent planning the same *bout de vie* can be made predictably comfortable, that our future happiness can be made to depend on ourselves.

At the same time he made an alternation in I: 39 so that another echo would emerge. In 1580 the text was: "Il faut avoir femmes, enfans, biens

& sur tout de la santé, qui peut, mais non pas s'y attacher en maniere que *nostre bon heur* en despende" [One must have wife, children, goods, and above all health, if one can, but not attach ourselves to them in such a way that *our happiness* depends on them] (I: 39, DM 365–66; 177*). In 1588 he deleted the *bon*, so that the text would henceforth read "que tout *nostre heur* en despende" (I: 39, 241b).[38] From then on the passage would echo the title of the other chapter: "Qu'il ne faut juger de *nostre heur*, qu'après la mort"—a title that I: 39, by arguing that we can guarantee "nostre heur" by depending only on ourselves, contradicts. Nowhere else will "nostre heur" appear.

20. Unmasking Masks

> "*Que philosopher c'est apprendre à mourir*" [That to philosophize is to learn to die] (I: 20) and "*Comme nous pleurons et rions d'une mesme chose*" [How we cry and laugh at the same thing] (I: 38)

Montaigne seeks to unmask death, particularly on the last page of "Que philosopher c'est apprendre à mourir":

> Les *enfans* ont peur de leurs amis mesmes quand ilz les voyent *masquez*, aussi avons nous. Il faut oster le *masque* aussi bien des choses que des personnes. Osté qu'il sera, nous ne trouverons au dessoubz, que cete mesme mort, qu'un valet ou simple chambriere passerent dernierement sans peur.
>
> [*Children* fear even their friends when they see them *masked*, and so do we ours. We must strip the *mask* from things as well as from persons; when it is off, we shall find beneath only that same death which a valet or a mere chambermaid passed through not long ago without fear.] (I: 20, 96a, DM 120; 68)

Another unmasking can take place, however, if we pay attention to where masks and children appear in Montaigne. Beneath the disguise, that is, of their ostensibly different subjects—learning to die vs. laughing and crying at the same thing—chapters I: 20 and I: 38 turn out to be, like the playfellow beneath the mask, surprisingly familiar.[39] I: 38 certainly begins with what

---

38. Though given as 241a in Villey, who ignores the change; in a post-1588 alteration, Montaigne deleted "tout."

39. As Jean Starobinski also points out, finding that in both essays Montaigne tears away the

Montaigne tells us we will find once we remove the mask, namely death: Antigonus weeping when presented with the head of his enemy Pyrrhus, the Duke of Lorraine grieving at his enemy's burial, the count of Monfort showing sorrow over the body of his, and finally Caesar turning his eyes away from the head of his archrival Pompey. As the children at the end of I: 20 were surprised to discover the face of a friend beneath the scary mask, onlookers in the scenes recounted at the beginning of I: 38 may have been surprised to discover Antigonus and Caesar behaving as if the severed head of their enemy were that of a friend. Children—and masks—indeed have a role to play here, as they did in I: 20, for Montaigne goes on to say that

> il ne faut pas croire que céte contenance fut toute fauce & contrefaicte. . . . Car bien que à la verité la pluspart de nos actions ne soient que *masque* & fard . . . il faut considerer comme nos ames se trouvent souvent agitées de diverses humeurs. . . . D'où nous voyons non seulement aus *enfans* qui vont tout nayfvement apres la nature, pleurer & rire souvent de mesme chose.

> [We must not believe that his countenance was entirely false and counterfeit. . . . Although most of our actions are indeed only *mask* and disguise . . . we must consider how our soul is often agitated by diverse passions. . . . We see *children,* who quite spontaneously follow nature, often cry and laugh at the same thing.] (I: 38, 233–34a, DM 355–57; 172–73*)

Thus, at the moment in I: 38 when its title is implanted in the body of the chapter, Montaigne is alluding not only to that title but also to the chapter with which this one is paired, the one that closed, as this one begins, with a discussion of masks and of children.

In a typically Montaignian piece of metafiction, the "mesme chose" that is literally the same thing both in the body of I: 38 and in its title is at the same time the same thing—that is, death—that its associated chapter (I: 20) was almost entirely about, as *its* title made clear. For Montaigne has recourse to the example of children who laugh and cry at the same thing in order to say that we all do the same, and that this phenomenon is the reason why Antigonus wept when one would have expected him to rejoice. In a post-1588 addition to I: 20 Montaigne will even enunciate the central thesis of I: 38 (that we laugh and cry at the same thing): "La vie n'est de soy ny bien ny mal: c'est la place du bien et du mal selon que vous la leur faictes" [Life is neither a good nor an evil in itself: it is the scene of good and evil depending on how you make it for them] (I: 20, 93c; 65*).

"mask" of death (*Montaigne en mouvement* [Paris: Gallimard, 1982], 96–98, 107–8).

In two more post-1588 additions, one to each chapter, Montaigne creates yet another echo, one in which weeping, life, death, and the span of a hundred years are all linked. In I: 20 he writes: "c'est pareille folie de *pleurer* de ce que d'icy à *cent ans* nous ne vivrons pas, que de *pleurer* de ce que nous ne vivions pas il y a *cent ans*" [it is as foolish to *weep* because we shall not be alive *a hundred years* from now as it is to weep because we were not alive *a hundred years* ago] (I: 20, 92c; 64*). In I: 38, Xerxes, contemplating his army crossing the Hellespont, quivered with delight to see so many thousands under his command. "Et, tout soudain, en mesme instant, sa pensée luy suggerant comme tant de vies avoient à defailir au plus loing dans *un siècle*, il refroigna son front, et s'attrista jusques aux *larmes*" [And quite suddenly, in the same instant, as his thought suggested to him how all those lives would give out within *a century* at the latest, he knit his brows and was saddened to *tears*] (I: 38, 235c; 174*). That death is certain to come within a hundred years is a constant in both passages, though in I: 20 it is one's own death and in I: 38 the death of others.

21. Powers of Attraction

"De la force de l'imagination" [On the power of the imagination] (I: 21) and "Du jeune Caton" [On Cato the Younger] (I: 37)

Did Cato the Younger kill himself for less than noble motives? Montaigne rejects that idea. "Plutarque dict, que de son temps il y en avoit qui attribuoient la cause de la mort du jeune Caton *à la crainte* qu'il avoit eu de Caesar, dequoy il se picque avecques raison" [Plutarch is rightly annoyed that in his time there were some who attributed the cause of the younger Cato's death *to the fear* he had of Caesar] (I: 37, 231a, DM 352; 170), whose armies were about to overrun Cato's. In other words, "Il y en a, qui *de frayeur* anticipent la main du bourreau" [There are some who, *out of fear,* anticipate the hand of the executioner]. What is interesting is that those "other words" come from the companion chapter, "De la force de l'imagination" (I: 21, 98a, DM 121; 68–69). Fear is the supposed cause of death in both instances, even though Cato was not said (by those to whose slander Montaigne objects) to have died, as do those awaiting execution in I: 21, from the power of imagination itself, but by his own hand. Often not only do related topics emerge in these parallel chapters but the same words too. In the two passages concerning death by fright *"il y en avoit qui"* [*there were some who*] attributed the cause of Cato's death to the fear he had of Caesar, while *"Il y en a qui"* [*There are some who*], out of fear anticipate the executioner's hand.

Consider the multiple echoes that surface in this sentence from the chapter on Cato: "il ne se recognoit plus d'action vertueuse. Celles qui en portent le *visage* elles n'en ont pas pourtant l'*essence*. Car le profit, la gloire, la crainte, l'acoutumance, & autres telles causes estrangeres nous acheminent à les *produire*" [There are no more virtuous actions to be seen; those that wear virtue's *face* do not for all that have its *essence;* for profit, glory, fear, habit, and other such extraneous causes lead us to *produce* them] (I: 37, 230a, DM 351; 170*). This chapter, especially in its 1580 version, was about the difference between surface appearances and deeper truth, and thus about the desirability of penetrating to the *essence* of human behavior. Essence is at issue in the other chapter, the only other place in Book One in 1580 where the word appears: Gallus Vibius "banda si bien son ame, & la tendit à comprendre & imaginer *l'essence* de la folie" [strained his soul so hard, and stretched it to understand and imagine the *essence* of madness] (I: 21, 98a, DM 121; 68*) that he went mad. One thing these verbal and other echoes sometimes show is a playfulness on Montaigne's part, with one chapter undercutting the seriousness of the other. This is evident as well in the way the causality linking *visage* and *produire* in the sentence from I: 37 quoted above finds a weird parallel in the anecdote Montaigne tells in I: 21 of Cyppus, who having attentively watched a bullfight and then dreamed all night of horns on his head, "les *produit* en son front" [*produced* them on his forehead] (I: 21, 98a, DM 122; 69*) by the power of imagination. His visage was considerably altered by what was "produced" by the force of imagination, in a comic counterpart to the serious observation in the companion chapter that actions have the visage of virtue, but only the visage, because of the causes having nothing to do with virtue that lead us to *produce* those actions.

A substantial post-1588 addition at the end of I: 37 adds more parallels. From the beginning (i.e., 1580) the chapter had closed with five poetic quotations (from Martial, Manilius, Lucan, Horace, and Virgil) in praise of Cato. In the addition he prefaces them by imagining how an *"enfant* bien nourry" [well-educated *child*] (I: 37, 231c; 171*) would judge them, finding the third more vigorous than the first two but ruined by excess, clapping his hands at the fourth, and thunderstruck by the fifth. He sets up the well-educated child as an ideal reader, his response a good indication of Montaigne's own appreciation of the five passages he is about to quote. Now he matches this in a concurrent post-1588 addition near the end of the companion chapter in which he speaks of himself as a child *deficient* in literary prowess: "il n'est rien si contraire à mon stile qu'une narration estendue: je me recouppe si souvent à faute d'haleine, Je n'ay ny composition, ny explication qui vaille, *ignorant au-delà d'un enfant* des frases et vocables qui servent aux choses plus communes" [there is nothing so contrary to my style as an extended narration. I cut myself off so often for lack of breath; I have neither composition nor development that is worth anything; I am *more ignorant than a child* of the phrases and terms that serve for the commonest things] (I: 21, 106c; 76). In this post-1588 addition appearing in the same place in I: 21 as the other one does in I: 37, that is at the conclusion of the chapter, Montaigne also uses a child, though an ignorant one this time—thus conforming to his frequent practice in these symmetrical echoes of matching what is at once both the same and precisely the opposite—as a standard by which literary value may be judged. And he identifies himself with the child in both instances, despite the child being ignorant in one instance but well-informed in the other. In I: 37 the well-informed child's opinion of each poetic quotation is the same as his; in I: 21 the child's ignorance is the same as his.

This is a metafictional moment, for the genius of Montaigne's writing style, certainly that aspect of it that concerns us in this study, is that he writes in fragments (cutting himself off as he says for lack of breath) instead of in an extended narration, and yet the fragments are connected. The various parts of an extended narration are connected by continuity and context; even when they are not continuous they are still part of the same story. Montaigne connects his pieces in a radically different way, and what is metafictional about this passage is that his complaint that his literary ignorance is like a child's is itself one of the connections.

In an anecdote dating from the 1580 edition, he writes in I: 21 of a cat staring at a bird perched at the top of a tree, "et, s'estans fichez la *veuë ferme* l'un contre l'autre quelque espace de temps" [and, after they had been locked in a *firm gaze* one against the other for some time], the bird fell as if dead between the cat's paws, either intoxicated by its own imagination "ou *attiré* par quelque *force attractive* du chat" [or *drawn* by some *attracting force* of the cat] (I: 21, 105a, DM 151; 75*). In a post-1588 addition to I: 37 the "veuë ferme" and the situation of being "attiré par quelque force attractive" find their echoes (the beauty to which he is alluding is that of poetry when it is so good as to be "excessive" and "divine"):

> Quiconque en discerne la beauté d'une *veue ferme* et rassise, il ne la void pas, non plus que la splendeur d'un esclair. Elle ne pratique point nostre jugement: elle le ravit et ravage. La fureur qui espoinçonne celuy qui la sçait penetrer, fiert encores un tiers à la luy ouyr traitter et reciter: comme

l'aymant, non seulement attire un'aiguille, mais infond encores en icelle sa faculté d'en attirer d'autres.

[Whoever discerns its beauty with a *firm* and settled *gaze* does not see it, any more than he sees the splendor of a lightning flash. It does not persuade our judgment, it ravishes and overwhelms it. The frenzy that goads the man who can penetrate it also strikes a third person on hearing him discuss it and recite it, as a magnet not only attracts a needle but infuses into it its own faculty of attracting others.] (I: 37, 231–32c; 171*)

Divine poetry resembles the cat in having a strange attractive force, yet is just the opposite in that its attractive force *cannot* be received by regarding it with a "veuë ferme."

22. Complementarities and Buried Allusions

"Le profit de l'un est dommage de l'autre" [One man's profit is another man's loss] (I: 22) and "De l'usage de se vestir" [On the custom of wearing clothes] (I: 36)

At about three hundred thirty words one of the shortest chapters in the *Essays* (and the only one to which no addition was made), I: 22 compels the question, is this all there is? Of course by now we know that whatever is in any given chapter is not all there is, and that the rest of it can be found in its relation to its symmetrical complement. In the case of I: 22 and I: 36 Montaigne has planted the most obvious of clues to their complementarity by placing in both the expression "generale police"—whose two components appear separately 42 and 60 times respectively but together only in these two chapters. In I: 22, he writes of Demades of Athens condemning an undertaker for profiting from the death of others. Montaigne remarks that this condemnation was unjust, for "il ne se fait nul profit qu'au dommage d'autruy" [no profit is made except at the expense of others], and then reflects that it is an even broader phenomenon than that, for "nature ne se dément point en cela de sa *generale police*" [Nature here was not belying her *general polity*], since the birth and growth of anything is the change and corruption of another (I: 22, 107a, DM 132–33; 77*). In I: 36, he wonders whether the tendency of the natives of the New World to wear few or no clothes is forced on them by their warm climate or if it was humanity's original state. He remarks that we must distinguish man-made from natural laws, and "recourir à la *generale* *police* du monde, où il n'y peut avoir rien de contrefaict" [turn for advice to the *general polity* of the world, where there can be nothing counterfeit] (I: 36, 225a, DM 346; 166*).

What we would miss if we didn't read these chapters in twos is that the invention of clothing in I: 36, which goes against the "generale police" of a world in which there can be nothing artificial, is a specific instance of the rule obeyed by another "generale police," that of nature in I: 22 according to which the birth, nourishment, and growth of each thing is the alteration and corruption of another. For the human race began, he argues in I: 36, with sufficient natural covering against the elements, a protection every other living being still enjoys, "mais comme ceux, qui esteignent par artificielle lumiere celle du jour, nous avons esteint & estouffé nos propres moyens par les moyens empruntez & estrangiers" [but like those that block out the light of day with artificial light, we have extinguished and smothered our own means with borrowed and foreign means] (I: 36, 225a, DM 347; 167*). Our original innate protection has undergone alteration and corruption, extinguished by what has taken its place. Clothing's "profit" is the "loss" of that original tougher hide and hair.

Metafictionally, the complementarity that is the theme of one of these chapters (I: 22), that everything comes into existence at the expense of something else, is true of the way it relates to the other one. Indeed, all the chapters in pairs are each other's complement.

A post-1588 addition to I: 36 enhances the complementarity. I: 22 begins with the first of many examples of the general rule that one person profits from another's loss, the sale of things necessary for "enterremens" [burials] of which Demades complained. In the addition Montaigne comes up with an instance of a burial that serves the same function as clothing, protection from the cold (he never speaks in that chapter of it having any other purpose): "Alexandre veit une nation en laquelle on *enterre* les arbres fruittiers en hiver, pour les defendre de la gelée" [Alexander saw a nation in which they *bury* fruit trees in winter to protect them from the frost] (I: 36, 228c; 169*).

23. Here and There

> "*De la coustume et de ne changer aisément une loy receüe*" [On custom, and on not lightly changing an accepted law] (I: 23) and "*D'un defaut de nos polices*" [On a defect in our polities] (I: 35)

The lack to which I: 35's title alludes is one for which Montaigne's father, when he was mayor of Bordeaux, had a remedy in mind. It was to set up a sort of bulletin board where employers and job-seekers, and others with mutually complementary needs—"des conditions, qui s'entrecherchent" [situations that seek each other out]—could register their requests with an official appointed for that purpose. It would be a "moyen de nous entr'advertir" [a means of informing each other] and promote commerce and the common weal (I: 35, 223a, DM 343–44; 165*).

To this proposed remedy for a lack in our "polices" [polities] I: 23 counters with the assertion that any innovation in our "police" is dangerous:

> Il y a grand doubte, s'il se peut trouver si evident profit au changement d'une loy receüe telle qu'elle soit, qu'il y a de mal à la remuer: d'autant qu'une *police* bien instituée c'est comme un bastiment de diverses pieces jointes ensemble d'une telle liaison, qu'il est impossible d'en esbranler la moindre, que tout le corps ne s'en sente.
>
> [It is very doubtful whether there can be such evident profit in changing an accepted law, of whatever sort it be, as there is harm in disturbing it; inasmuch as a well set-up *polity* is like a structure of diverse parts joined together in such a relation that it is impossible to budge the least of them without the whole body feeling it.] (I: 23, 119a, DM 146; 86*)

Montaigne's father, of course, did not propose that a law be changed but that a new one (or a new state institution) be added. Yet that too is condemned in I: 23: the lawmaker of the Thurians ordained that whoever wanted to abolish an old law "ou en establir une nouvelle" [or establish a new one] (I: 23, 119a, DM 146; 86) present himself to the public with a rope around his neck so that if the proposal was not adopted he should be immediately strangled. Even just a new way of doing things is censured as well in I: 23. The ephor who cut the two strings Phrynis had added to the harp "ne s'esmaie pas, si elle en vaut mieux, ou si les accords en sont mieux remplis: il luy suffit pour les condamner, que ce soit une alteration de la vieille façon" [does not worry whether music is the better for it or the chords are richer; for him to condemn them, it is enough that they represent an alteration of the old way] (I: 23, 119a, DM 146–47; 86*). Like Phrynis' new strings, Montaigne's father's innovation would have enriched urban life and commerce, but because it was an innovation would have endangered the stability of the very polity it was intended to improve.

The contradiction is striking between Montaigne's approval of his father's innovation to remedy a defect in our "polices" in I: 35 and the argument he presents in I: 23 that any innovation whatsoever in our "police" is wrong. But we would probably not have noticed the contradiction unless we read the two chapters together. Of course, that is precisely the metafiction awaiting our discovery: I: 23's condemnation of change and I: 35's proposal for change are "des conditions, qui s'entrecherchent" [situations that seek each other out] (I: 35, 223a, DM 344; 165*). I: 35's proposal is a microcosm of what is going on *between* I: 35 and I: 23. To this I: 23 replies with a microcosm of its own, the polity as "un bastiment de diverses pieces jointes ensemble d'une telle liaison, qu'il est impossible d'en esbranler la moindre, que tout le corps ne s'en sente" [a structure of diverse parts joined together in such a relation that it is impossible to budge the least of them without the whole body feeling it.] (I: 23, 119a, DM 146; 86*). The *Essays* are such a structure, where important pieces fit together—the opposing chapters, pressing each against the other in the symmetrical design. Were one to go missing the whole structure would suffer.

24. How to Paint a Dog

> "*Divers evenemens de mesme conseil*" [Various outcomes from the same plan] (I: 24) and "*La fortune se rencontre souvent au train de la raison*" [Fortune is often met in the path of reason] (I: 34)

In I: 24 Montaigne recounts that Augustus, on the advice of his wife, pardoned Lucius Cinna when he plotted against his life, a clemency that appears to have preserved the emperor from subsequent conspiracies. But when François de Guise followed the same course of action, showing mercy to one would-be assassin, he did not do as well as Augustus, for he died at the hands of another assassin shortly thereafter. Montaigne meditates on how a diversity of outcomes can arise from the same plan, attributing it to the role chance plays in human affairs: "au travers de tous nos projects, de nos conseils & precautions la fortune maintient tousjours la possession des evenemans" [athwart all our plans, counsels, and precautions, Fortune still maintains her grasp on events] (I: 24, 127a, DM 158; 92*). Fortune is fully as much the subject of this chapter as it is of I: 34, where it is directly evoked in the title.

Fortune in I: 24 plays a major role not only in political conspiracies but in medicine too, as well as other arts:

> Il en est de mesmes en la peinture, qu'il eschape par fois des traitz de la main du peintre *surpassans* sa conception & sa *science*, qui le tirent luy mesmes en admiration, & qui l'estonnent. Mais la fortune monstre bien

encores plus evidemmant la part qu'elle a en tous ces ouvrages par les graces & beautez qui s'y treuvent, non seulement sans l'invention,[40] mais sans la cognoissance mesmes de l'ouvrier. Un suffisant lecteur descouvre souvant es escritz d'autruy des perfections autres que celles que l'autheur y a mises & aperceües, & y preste des sens & des visages plus riches.

[Sometimes there escape from the painter's hand touches so *surpassing* his conception and his *science* as to arouse his wonder and astonishment. But Fortune shows still more evidently the part she has in all these works by the graces and beauties that are found in them, not only without the workman's intention, but even without his knowledge. A sufficient reader often discovers in other men's writings perfections beyond those that the author put in or perceived, and lends them richer meanings and aspects.] (I: 24, 127a, DM 160–61; 93*)

Imitating Epimenides (the Cretan who said all Cretans were liars), Montaigne here poses us a paradox of astonishing subtlety. For at the same moment that he is telling us that certain readers are likely to discover things in a text the author never intended, and that the painter is sometimes surprised by the wonder of what he has, without intending to, done, he seems to be inviting us to discover just such perfections and richer aspects in the text of the *Essays*, and to dare us to decide whether it was Fortune that placed it there, or Montaigne himself. For in I: 34 we are told of just such a painter as the one in I: 24 whose science was surpassed by the hand of Fortune—and what is more significant, in the same turn of phrase.

Surpassa elle pas Protogenes en la *science* de son art? Cestuy cy estoit peintre, & ayant parfaict l'image d'un chien las & recreu, à son contentement en toutes les autres parties, mais ne pouvant representer à son gré l'escume & la bave, despité contre sa besongne prit son esponge, & comme elle estoit abreuvée de diverses peintures, la jetta contre pour tout effacer. La fortune porta tout à point le coup à l'endroit de la bouche du chien, & y parfournit ce à quoy l'art n'avoit peu attaindre. N'adresse elle pas quelque fois nos *conseils* & les corige?

[Did she not *surpass* Protogenes in the *science* of his art? He was a painter, and having completed the picture of a tired and panting dog to his satisfaction in all the other parts but unable to show the foam and slaver as he had

---

40. Changed to "l'intention" in a post-1588 revision.

desired, vexed with his work, he took his sponge, which was soaked with various colors, and threw it at the picture to blot it out completely. Fortune guided the throw with perfect aptness right to the dog's mouth, and accomplished what art had been unable to attain. Does she not sometimes address our *plans* and correct them?] (I: 34, 221a, DM 341–42; 64*)

The last sentence alludes to the "conseil" of I: 24's title, which is shown in that chapter to be in Fortune's hands; more remarkably, the combination of *surpasser* and *science* appears nowhere else than in these two passages about Fortune guiding the painter's hand. In the I: 24 passage Montaigne immediately goes on to say that the same thing happens in writing, virtually daring us to wonder if these symmetrically-placed twin instances of Fortune surpassing a painter's science are due to Fortune or to Montaigne. The latter seems far more likely, and the metafiction intentional. The fiction is that Fortune guides the writer's hand; the metafiction is that it doesn't. The fiction is that the grace, beauty, and perfection evident in the occurrence of these self-echoing passages in structurally-related parts of the work are the result of Fortune or of the cleverness of the able reader who finds them, and that Montaigne had no idea they were there; the metafiction is that Montaigne knows exactly what he was doing. Both passages are immediately preceded by a discussion of Fortune's role in medicine. In I: 24, we can see the connecting tissue in the following passage, when Montaigne says that not only in medicine but also in such other arts as poetry we can see Fortune at work:

> Nous appelons les medecins heureus, quand ilz arrivent à quelque bonne fin . . . la fortune preste la main à ses operations. . . . Or je dy que non en la medecine seulement, mais en plusieurs arts plus certaines la fortune y a bonne part. Les saillies poetiques, qui emportent leur autheur mesme & le ravissent hors de soy, pourquoy ne les atribuerons nous à son bon heur? puis qu'il confesse luy mesmes qu'elles surpassent sa suffisance & ses forces, & les reconnoit venir d'ailleurs que de soy.

> [We call doctors fortunate when they attain some good end. . . . Fortune lends her hand in their operations. . . . Now, I say that not only in medicine but in many more certain arts Fortune has a large part. Poetic sallies, which transport their author and ravish him out of himself, why shall we not attribute them to his good luck? He himself confesses that they surpass his ability and strength, and acknowledges that they come from something other than himself.] (I: 24, 127a, DM 160–61; 92–93)

In I: 34, he preceded the passage about Protogenes with this anecdote:

Quelque fois elle [la fortune] faict la medecine. Jason Phereus estant abandonné des medecins pour une apostume, qu'il avoit dans la poitrine, ayant envie de s'en défaire au moins par la mort, se jetta en une bataille à corps perdu dans la presse des ennemis, où il fut blessé à travers le corps si à point que son apostume en creva & guerit. Surpass elle pas Protogenes. . . . ?

[Sometimes she [Fortune] practices medicine. Jason of Pheres, given up by the doctors because of an abscess in his chest, wished to get rid of it by death if necessary, and threw himself bodily into the thick of the enemy in a battle, where he was wounded through the body so exactly that his abscess burst and he was cured. Did she not surpass Protogenes . . . ?] (I: 34, 221a, DM 341–42; 164)

In the story of Augustus and Cinna, Montaigne recounts that when the emperor was trying to decide whether to pardon him or not among the thoughts going through his mind was this one: "sera il absous ayant deliberé non de me meurtrir seulement, mais de me sacrifier? Car la conjuration estoit faicte de le tuer, comme *il feroit quelque sacrifice*" ["Shall he be absolved when he has decided not merely to murder me but to sacrifice me?" For the conspiracy was formed to kill him while *he would be performing some sacrifice*] (I. 24, 125a, DM 153–54; 91*). In a post-1588 addition to I: 34, Montaigne added an allusion to this passage in recounting another failed assassination attempt. Icetes had persuaded two soldiers to kill Timoleon. "Ils prindrent heure sur le point qu'*il fairoit quelque sacrifice*" [They chose the hour when *he would be performing some sacrifice*] (I: 34, 222c; 164*). The phrase occurs in no chapter other than these two.

A 1588 addition to I: 34 creates yet another connection to I: 24: "Pour la fin. En ce faict icy se descouvre il pas une bien expresse application de sa faveur, de bonté et pieté singuliere? Ignatius Pere et fils, proscripts par les *Triumvirs* à Romme, se resolurent à ce genereux office de rendre leurs vies entre les mains l'un de l'autre, et en frustrer *la cruauté des Tyrans*" [A final example. Does not the fact which is about to be related reveal a very express act of Fortune's favor, of her singular kindness and piety? The Egnatii, father and son, proscribed by the *triumvirs* at Rome, resolved on the noble device of giving up their lives at each other's hands, in order to frustrate *the cruelty of the tyrants*] (I: 34, 222b; 165). This b-stratum addition, which occurs at the end of the chapter (and would continue to despite later additions), as

Montaigne emphasizes by prefacing it by "Pour la fin," matches the last story in I: 24, which likewise tells of someone proscribed by the Triumvirate who decides, like the Egnatii, to die rather than flee. A Roman who, "fuyant *la tyrannie du Triumvirat*" [fleeing *the tyranny of the Triumvirate*] (I: 24, 132a; 97), and having escaped his pursuers a thousand times already, decided one day to give up himself up, coming out of his hiding place to call out to some soldiers who had passed right by him, thus "s'abandonnant volontairement à leur *cruauté*, pour oster eux et luy d'une plus longue peine" [abandoning himself to their *cruelty* in order to rid them and himself of further trouble] (I: 24, 132a; 97).

25. Well-Nourished Daughters

"Du pedantisme" [On pedantry] (I: 25) and "De fuir les voluptez au pris de la vie" [To flee from sensual pleasures at the price of life] (I: 33)

I: 33 is surely one of the strangest chapters in the *Essays*. Very brief (less than two pages in Balsamo et al.) and subject to no additions since its first appearance in 1580 (just some slight rewording), it devotes slightly more than half of its space to the story of Saint Hilary of Poitiers and his daughter Abra, "sa fille unique, . . . poursuivie en mariage par les plus apparens seigneurs du pais, comme fille tres bien nourrie, belle, riche, & en la fleur de son aage" [his only daughter, . . . sought in the marriage by the most eminent lords of the country, as a girl well brought up, beautiful, rich, and in the flower of her youth] (I: 33, 219a, DM 336; 162). Hilary wrote her from abroad to say that she should remove her affection from the pleasures and advantages those suitors offered, for he had found a much better husband for her in his travels, who would give her priceless riches. His intent had been to wean her from earthly distractions the better to fit her for heaven, but since it occurred to him that the quickest way to achieve that would be for her to die, he ceaselessly prayed for that to occur. Sure enough, shortly after his return she did succumb, which made him very happy. His wife, impressed with heaven's attractions and her spouse's power of prayer, successfully requested the same favor for herself.

The chapter begins with a brief exploration of the rather more reasonable notion that "il est heure de mourir lors qu'il y a plus de mal que de bien à vivre: & que de conserver nostre vie à nostre tourment & incommodité c'est choquer les reigles mesmes de nature" [it is time to die when there is more evil than good in living; and that to preserve our life to our torment and discomfort is to shock the very laws of nature] (I: 33, 218a, DM 333; 161*). But the ground shifts somewhat when Montaigne considers those who have urged others to consider leaving this life in order to withdraw not from torment but from "des honneurs, richesses, grandeurs, & autres faveurs & biens" [honors, riches, dignities, and other favors and goods] (I: 33, 218a, DM 334; 162). One he has found making such an exhortation is Seneca, who wrote to Lucilius that he should untie the knot that binds him to the pomp of public life and withdraw to a philosophical solitude, and that if he cannot untie it, then he should cut it by withdrawing from life itself.

Montaigne finds such advice unsurprising coming from a Stoic like Seneca, but it is "estrange qu'il soit emprunté d'Epicurus, qui escrit à ce propos, choses toutes pareilles à Idomeneus" [strange that it should be borrowed from Epicurus, who writes things just like it on this subject to Idomeneus] (I: 33, 218a, DM 335; 162). The chapter then concludes with the story of Saint Hilary, whose infanticidal prayer so shocks the laws of nature to which Montaigne appealed in the beginning that one imagines he (not Saint Hilary) must surely be joking. There does seem to be some hint of irony in the manner Montaigne introduces this dreadful account: "Si est ce que je pense avoir remerqué quelque traict semblable parmi nos gens, mais avec la moderation Chrestienne. S. Hilaire . . . " [Yet I think I have noticed something like it among our people, but with Christian moderation. Saint Hilary . . .] (I: 33, 219a, DM 335; 162). Christian moderation is more immoderate than the pagan variety, for Hilary "semble encherir sur les autres de ce qu'il s'adresse à ce moyen de prime face, qu'ilz ne prennent que subsidieremant, & puis que c'est à l'endroit de sa fille unique" [seems to outdo the others, in that he addresses himself from the first to this means, which the others adopt only as a subsidiary; and besides, it concerns his only daughter] (I: 33, 219a, DM 336–37; 162). What is repeated in this chapter, besides the motif of death's attractiveness, is repetition itself: the reappearance of a sentiment (death's seductiveness) in a context where it seems out of place. What was appropriate for the stoic Seneca to say was less so for the original Epicurean and still less so for a father with regard to his daughter.

Montaigne begins I: 25 by recalling that as a child he wondered why it is that schoolmasters are more often the butt of jokes than objects of respect. As an adult he began to see that in fact they often proved to be ridiculous figures, puffed up by borrowed wisdom that they were incapable of usefully applying to their own lives. Yet he continued to wonder why men who possessed such riches were not improved by them: "Mais d'où il puisse advenir qu'une ame garnie de la connoissance de tant de choses n'en deviene pas plus vive & plus esveillée, & qu'un esprit grossier & vulgaire puisse loger en soy, sans s'amender, les discours & les jugemens des plus excellens espritz que le monde ait porté, j'en suis encore en doute" [But how it is possible that a soul furnished with the knowledge of so many things should not thereby become keener and more alert, and that a crude and commonplace mind can harbor within itself, without being improved, the reasonings and judgments of the greatest minds that the world has produced—that still has me puzzled] (I: 25, 134a, DM 168; 98*). Borrowed knowledge doesn't seem to rub off on the new owner. "Nous de mesmes, nous prenons en garde les opinions & le sçavoir d'autruy, & puis c'est tout, il les faut faire nostres. . . . Que nous sert il d'avoir la panse pleine de viande, si elle ne se digere, si elle ne se transforme en nous?" [We do the same, taking the opinions and the knowledge of others into our keeping, and then that is all. We must make them our own. . . . What good does it do us to have our belly full of meat if it is not digested, if it is not transformed into us?] (I: 25, 137a, DM 174; 101*).

Both chapters, then, are about borrowed ideas, yet in precisely opposite ways. In 1: 25 Montaigne criticizes those who borrow opinions from others without making them their own, whereas in I: 33 the borrowed opinion paradoxically belongs more to the borrower (Seneca) than to the one he borrowed it from (Epicurus).

On a metafictional level, borrowing is what goes on between symmetrically linked chapters that repeat each others' discourse. In the case of these two, the borrowing is about borrowing itself. It is also about Hilary's daughter, who was "poursuivie en *mariage* . . . comme *fille* tres bien *nourrie*" [pursued in *marriage* . . . as a *girl well brought up*] (I: 33, 219a, DM 335; 162). For in I: 25 Montaigne writes of another daughter valued in the marriage market because of how she was "nourrie":

> François duc de Bretaigne . . . , comme on luy parla de son *mariage* avec Isabeau *fille* d'Escosse, & qu'on luy adjouta qu'elle avoit esté *nourrie* simplement & sans aucune instruction de lettres, respondit qu'il l'en aimoit mieux, & que une fame estoit assez sçavante quand elle sçavoit mettre difference entre la chemise & le pourpoint de son mary.
>
> [Francis, duke of Brittany . . . when they were talking to him about his marriage with Isabel, a *princess* of Scotland, and told him that she had been *brought up* simply and without any instruction in letters, replied that he

loved her the better for it, and that a woman was learned enough when she knew how to distinguish between her husband's shirt and his doublet.] (I: 25, 140a, DM 180; 103)

The verbal echo is not only striking but unique, as no other "fille nourrie" appears in the *Essays*. Villey explains in a footnote that when Montaigne says that Hilary's "fille" was "tres bien nourrie" he means "D'une très bonne éducation" [with a very good education] (219n), which is precisely the opposite of the way the "fille" in I: 25 was "nourrie": "simplement & sans aucune instruction de lettres" [simply and without any instruction in letters]. Abra would not have been seduced by her father's advice had she been, like Isabeau, illiterate, for Hilary had communicated it to her in a letter (as Seneca had to Lucilius and Epicurus to Idomeneus). As it was his theology that made Hilary desire his daughter's death, so too was it theology that kept Isabeau unlettered: "& nous & la Theologie ne requerons pas beaucoup de science aux fames" [neither we nor theology require much learning of women] (I: 25, 140a, DM 179–80; 103), Montaigne writes, in introducing the anecdote about Isabeau and her husband's contentment in her education, or lack thereof.

A third case of borrowing appears in the title of I: 33. For the motif of fleeing "les voluptez" was already present in I: 25's discourse on what ought to be taught to the young: in Sparta they were taught "à se desmeler des appats de la *volupté*" [to disentangle themselves from the lures of *sensual pleasure*] (I: 25, 143a, DM 184; 105).

A fourth instance of borrowing emerges when we realize that what Seneca advised Lucilius to do—"de se *retirer* de céte presse du monde, à quelque vie solitaire, tranquille & *philosophique*" [to *retire* from this crowded world to some solitary, tranquil and *philosophical* life] (I: 33, 218a, DM 334; 162*)—was anticipated in the companion chapter by the "*philosophes retirez* de toute occupation publique" [*philosophers retired* from all public occupation] who were "mesprisés par la liberté comique de leur temps: mais au rebours des nostres" [mocked by the comic license of their times, but treated in the opposite way in ours] (I: 25, 134a, DM 169; 98*).[41] What Seneca wants for Lucilius, in other words—short of death—is the vocation that was the ancient, and nobler, equivalent of the figure that in its debased modern form is the subject of the chapter with which this one is symmetrically paired, the pedant detached from the world.

---

41. A post-1588 revision deleted "mais au rebours des nostres."

26. God's Wrath and the Weather

"De l'institution des enfans" [On the education of children] (I: 26) and "Qu'il faut sobrement se mesler de juger des ordonnances divines" [That we should meddle soberly with judging divine ordinances] (I: 32)

Chapter I: 26 is obviously about the education of children, but in the following passage it also touches on the topic at the heart of I: 32, the difficulty of figuring out the will of God based on what happens around us:

> Quand les vignes gelent en son vilage mon prestre en argumente l'Ire de Dieu sur la race humaine, & juge que la pepie en tienne des-jà les Cannibales. A voir nos gueres civiles, qui ne crie que céte machine se bouleverse, & que le jour du jugement nous tient au colet, sans s'adviser que plusieurs pires choses se sont veües, & que les dix mille parts du monde ne laissent pas de galler le bon temps ce pendant. A qui il gresle sur la teste tout l'hemisphere semble estre en tempeste & orage.

> [When the vines freeze in his village my priest argues from it God's wrath on the human race, and judges that the Cannibals are already dying of the croup! Seeing our civil wars, who does not cry out that this mechanism is being turned upside-down and that the day of judgment has us by the throat, without reflecting that many worse things have happened, and that ten thousand parts of the world are meanwhile having a fine old time. To whom hail falls on the head the whole hemisphere seems to be in tempest and storm.] (I: 26, 157a, DM 206–7; 116*)

In I: 32 he argues that God's judgment is not behind the outcomes of those same civil wars, alluding in particular to the Protestants who were claiming that a recent victory meant that God favored their cause:

> aux guerres où nous sommes pour la religion, ceux qui eurent l'advantage au rencontre de la Rochelabeille faisans grand feste de cet accident, & se servans de céte fortune pour certain approbation de leur party: quand ils viennent apres à excuser leurs defortunes de Moncontour & de Jarnac, sur ce que ce sont verges & chastimemens paternelz, s'ilz n'ont un peuple du tout à leur mercy ilz luy font assez aisément sentir que c'est prendre d'un sac deux mouldures, & de mesme bouche souffler le chaud & le froid.

[In the wars we are in for the sake of religion, those who had the advantage in the encounter at La Rochelabeille make much ado about this incident and use their good fortune as a sure approbation of their party; but when they come later to excuse their misfortunes at Moncontour and Jarnac as being fatherly rods and chastisements, unless they have their following completely at their mercy, they make the people sense readily enough that this is getting two grinding fees for one sack, and blowing hot and cold with the same mouth.] (I: 32, 216a, DM 331–32; 160*)

In both chapters Montaigne argues that one cannot figure out God's intention from the outcome of events on earth, and in particular from the limited perspective of those trying to figure it out. In I: 26, his point is that as bad as the damage from France's civil wars may be, it doesn't mean that it is the end of the world for the rest of the world. In I: 32, though his point is that the Protestants who interpret their victories as a sign of God's favor and their defeats as his fatherly chastisements are speaking out of both sides of their mouth, at the same time he reveals that their point of view is just as limited as those in I: 26 who think the end of the world has come, since they think that the outcome of their battles is entirely determined by what is going on between them and God.

In I: 32 he complains of people who claim to discern God's designs,

faisans estat de trouver les causes de chasque accident, & de veoir dans les secretz de la volonté divine, les motifs incomprehensibles de ses operations. Et quoy que la varieté & discordance continuelle des evenemens les rejette de coin en coin, & *d'orient en occident,* ils ne laissent de suivre pourtant leur esteuf, & de mesme creon peindre le blanc & le noir.

[claiming to find the cause of every incident and to see in the secrets of the divine will the incomprehensible motives of his works; and although the variety and continual discordance of events tosses them from corner to corner and *from east to west,* yet they do not stop chasing their ball and painting black and white with the same pencil.] (I: 32, 215a, DM 331; 160)

The village priest in I: 26 had made the same mistake, claiming to discern God's judgments and to see their consequences on earth. But viewed from another angle, these two chapters are precisely opposed on this topic, for while the priest claimed to know what was happening in the land of the Cannibals, which is to say in the western hemisphere, because he assumed that what was true in his little locality was true everywhere else, those Montaigne criticizes in I: 32 are in fact confronted with the evidence that things are not the same everywhere, and this "discordance continuelle" sends them "d'orient en occident"—which just happens to be the same direction the priest's extrapolations took him, as he imagined what the weather in the western hemisphere was based on what was happening on his side of the Atlantic.

This mutual echoing and opposing symmetry has a metafictional resonance, for when in both chapters Montaigne argues against ignoring what may be happening in the rest of the world, in some other hemisphere, he may be nudging his readers toward the realization that there is more going on than they suspect, that something happening in a chapter in the book's other hemisphere (the one on the other side of the dividing line formed by the central chapter) may be relevant to what is happening in the chapter they are reading.

Things can happen together in both hemispheres on the lexical level, too. The passage in I: 32 in which the Protestants counted their losses at Montcontour and Jarnac as mere "verges & *chastimemens* paternelz" [paternal rods and *punishments*] (I: 32, 216a, DM 331; 160*) finds an echo in a post-1588 addition to I: 26 where Montaigne expresses his disgust with the "façon de *chastiement*" [manner of *punishment*] schoolmasters employed, which Villey in a note tells us was to strike the pupils with "verges" (166n4)—as in fact Montaigne makes explicit in the next sentence, though he does not use that word, when he writes of classrooms "jonchées . . . de tronçons d'osier sanglants" [strewn . . . with bloody birch rods] (I: 26, 166c; 123*). Nowhere else in Book One does a *chastiement* (as a noun) appear in the form of unspared rods.

As we have seen, Montaigne goes on in that passage about the Protestants to say that their boasting of a victory as proof that God is on their side and yet saying of their defeats that they are just a fatherly chastisement (as opposed to indicating he was *not* on their side) is to "de mesme bouche souffler le chaud & le froid" [blow hot and cold with the same mouth] (I: 32, 216a, DM 331–32; 160*). As he did with the post-1588 addition to I: 26 of an allusion to punishment by rods, he makes another post-1588 addition to I: 26 to set up an echo with this passage. It consists of four words inserted into a sentence dating from the 1580 edition. He writes that it is a widespread opinion that a boy should not be raised by his parents because their affection would prevent them from inuring him to hardship: "(A) Ils ne le sçauroient souffrir revenir suant et poudreux de son exercice, (C) *boire chaud, boire froid*, (A) ny le voir sur un cheval rebours" [(A)They could not endure his returning sweating dusty from his exercise, (C) *drinking hot, drinking cold,*

(A) or see him on a skittish horse] (I: 26, 153ac; 113). Nowhere else do *chaud* and *froid* appear in the same mouth.

In that same passage in I: 32 about the Protestants having it both ways, we can find, sandwiched between the chastising rods and the cold and the hot in the same mouth yet another lexical link to the companion chapter: "c'est prendre d'un sac deux mouldures" [it is to get two grinding fees for one sack] (I: 32, 216a; DM 331; 160*). This finds its parallel in what Montaigne says about the benefits of foreign travel for the child one intends to educate: "pour faire d'une pierre deux coups" [to make two blows with one stone] (I: 26, 153a, DM 199; 112), he should be taken at a very early age to neighboring countries where the language is most distant from our own because if the language acquisition does not begin early the tongue cannot be formed. The other "coup" for the "pierre" of travel for the child is to learn foreign customs and ways of thinking, and to "frotter et limer nostre cervelle contre celle d'autruy" [to rub and polish our brains by contact with those of others] (I: 26, 153a, DM 199; 112).

Both the passage in I: 32 and this one in 1: 26 are ones where more than one lexical echo appears, which suggests that Montaigne purposely planted them in both. The allusion to getting two payments for producing the same sack of grain appears, as noted, between the other two echoes of chastising rods and blowing hot and cold; the idea of getting two for one with regard to taking the young abroad occurs immediately before the passage about the disadvantage of doting parents raise their own child into which he inserted "boire chaud, boire froid" with its allusion to "souffler le chaud et le froid" in the other passage.

On the metafictional level, Montaigne gets two uses out of the topos itself of getting two uses out of the same thing by placing that topos in symmetrically matching chapters. One use is the purpose it serves in its immediate context in each chapter, as a way of advancing the argument being made; the other is that of pointing to the *Essays*' symmetrical structure.

27. Things to Come

"C'est folie de rapporter le vray et le faux à nostre suffisance"
[It is folly to measure the true and false by our own competence] (I: 27) and *"Des cannibales"* [On cannibals] (I: 31)

Julius Caesar held that "il est souvent advenu que la nouvelle a devancé l'accident" [it has often happened that the report has preceded the event] (I:

27, 180a, DM 247; 133). Ordinarily, writes Montaigne, we would dismiss such a claim had we heard it from a figure of lesser stature. He laughs, for example, at Froissart's assertion that the Comte de Foix learned of the defeat of King John of Castille in a distant city the day after it took place. Yet not only did Caesar make such a claim, but Plutarch did as well, writing that the news of Antonius' defeat in Germany was made public in Rome on the very day it happened. Montaigne argues that we should not dismiss such a seeming impossibility out of hand, for that would show a lack of respect for Caesar and Plutarch: "dirons nous pas que ces simples gens la *se sont laissés piper* apres le vulgaire?" [shall we say that these simple men *let themselves be tricked* like the common herd?] (I: 27, 180–81a, 133–34*). In a clever twist, Montaigne arranges for his denial that Plutarch and Caesar could have been "pipés" [tricked] into believing that the report could precede the event itself seem like the report of an event yet to come when in the accompanying chapter "Des cannibales" (I: 31) he writes that the Native Americans who were brought to Rouen were "bien miserables de *s'estre laissés piper*" [very much to be pitied for having *let themselves be tricked*] (I: 31, 213a, DM 326; 158–59) by the desire to see new things.

Montaigne is open not only to the possibility of reports anticipating events as Caesar and Plutarch allege but also to that of the "*prognostique des choses* futures" [*prognostication* of future *things*] (I: 27, 179a, DM 243; 132*) in general. That particular prognostication metafictionally prognosticates itself, for in I: 31 a prophet among the cannibals "*prognostique* les *choses* à venir" [*prognosticates things* to come] (I: 31, 208a, DM 313; 154*)—words that appear together nowhere else.

In both chapters Montaigne writes of simple folk and their ability or inability to discern the truth. He begins I: 27 with the suggestion that "Ce n'est pas à l'adventure sans raison, que nous attribuons à *simplesse* & à ignorance la facilité de croire & de se laisser persuader . . . à estre menés par les oreilles" [Perhaps it is not without reason that we attribute to *simplicity* and ignorance a readiness to believe and to be persuaded . . . to be led by the ears] (I: 27, 178a, DM 242–43; 132*). But he says the opposite in I: 31 in presenting a certain simple man as a reliable witness precisely because of his simplicity. The man had lived for a decade or more in the New World and was Montaigne's source for many details on the life of its inhabitants. "Cet homme que j'avoy, estoit homme *simple* & grossier, qui est une condition propre à rendre *veritable* tesmoignage. . . . Ou il faut un homme tres fidele, ou si *simple* qu'il n'ait pas dequoy bastir & donner de la *vrai-semblance* à des inventions *fauces*" [This man I had was a very *simple* and crude fellow, which is a condition likely to produce *true* testimony. . . . You need either a very honest man, or one so *simple* that he has not the stuff to build up *false* inventions and give them *verisimilitude*] (I: 31, 205a, DM 303–04; 152*). Clearly the two chapters are speaking the same language, as if they were conversing together, for the two terms "faux" and "vray semblable" appear when Montaigne in I: 27 points out that simple folk are not necessarily wrong in their belief in prophecy: "c'est une sotte presumption d'aller desdeignant & condamnant pour *faux* ce qui ne nous samble pas *vray semblable*" [it is foolish presumption to go around disdaining and condemning as *false* what does not strike us as *plausible*] (I: 27, 178a, DM 243; 132*).

A man less simple and ignorant than Montaigne's eyewitness would be inclined to embroider the truth to show off his knowledge.

> Je voudray que chacun escrivit ce qu'il sçait, & autant qu'il sçait, non en cela seulement, mais en tous autres subjectz. Car tel peut avoir quelque particuliere science ou experiance de la nature d'une *riviere* ou d'une fontaine, qui ne sçait au reste, que ce que chacun sçait. Il entreprendra toutes fois pour faire courir ce petit lopin, d'escrire toute la physique.
>
> [I would like everyone to write what he knows, and as much as he knows, not only in this, but in all other subjects; for a man may have some special knowledge and experience of the nature of a *river* or a fountain, who in other matters knows only what everybody knows. However, to circulate this little scrap of knowledge, he will undertake to write the whole of physics.] (I: 31, 205a, DM 305; 152)

The man projecting from his *knowledge* of a river useless conclusions about things of which he is as ignorant as anyone else finds a counterpart in I: 27 in a man who projects an inaccurate conclusion from his *ignorance* of a river: "Celuy qui n'avoit jamais veu de *riviere* à la premiere qu'il r'encontra il pensa que ce fut l'Ocean" [He who had never seen a *river* thought that the first one he came across was the ocean] (I: 27, 179a, DM 245; 133). But Montaigne himself comes close to resembling that man in a 1588 addition to I: 31 in which he says that if the Dordogne River doesn't stop eroding its banks it will change the face of the world—as if it had the destructive powers of an ocean:

> Quand je considere l'impression que ma riviere de Dordoigne faict de mon temps, vers la rive droicte de sa descente, & qu'en vingt ans elle a tant gaigné, & desrobé le fondement à plusieurs bastimens, je vois bien que c'est une agitation extraordinaire: car si elle fut tousjours allée ce train, ou deut aller à l'advenir, la figure du monde seroit renversée.

[When I consider the inroads that my river, the Dordogne, is making in my lifetime into the right bank in its descent, and that in twenty years it has gained so much ground and stolen away the foundations of several buildings, I clearly see that this is an extraordinary disturbance; for if it had always gone at this rate, or was to do so in the future, the face of the world would be turned topsy-turvy.] (I: 31, 204b; 151)

28. Of Immoderation

"De l'amitié" [Of friendship] (I: 28) and "De la moderation" [Of moderation] (I: 30)

From its first sentence—"Comme si nous avions l'attouchement infaict, nous corrompons par nostre maniement les choses, qui d'elles mesmes sont belles & bonnes" [As if our touch were infectious, by our handling them we corrupt things that of themselves are beautiful and good] (I: 30, 197a, DM 293; 146*)—chapter I: 30 enters into dialogue with chapter I: 28. For in the latter Montaigne presents La Boétie's *De la servitude volontaire* as something beautiful and good that has been corrupted by contagion. He begins the chapter by saying that he thinks so highly of his friend's text that he will put it in the middle of his own book, for lack of something good enough from his own pen to occupy that place of honor.

> Considerant la conduicte de la besoingne d'un peintre que j'ay, il m'a pris envie de l'ensuivre. Il choisit le plus noble endroit & milieu de chasque paroy, pour y loger un tableau elabouré de toute sa suffisance, & le vuide tout au tour il le remplit de crotesques, qui sont peintures fantasques, n'ayants grace qu'en la varieté & estrangeté. Que sont-ce icy aussi à la verité que crotesques & corps monstrueux, rappiecez de divers membres, sans certaine figure, n'ayants ordre, suite ny proportion que fortuite? . . . Je vay bien jusques à ce segond point avec mon peintre, mais je demeure court en l'autre, & meilleure partie. Car ma suffisance ne va pas si avant que d'oser entreprendre un tableau riche poly & formé selon l'art: je me suis advisé d'en emprunter un d'Estienne de la Boitie qui honorera tout le reste de céte besoigne. C'est un discours auquel il donna nom *De la servitude volontaire*. . . . Il court pieça es mains des gens d'entendement, non sans bien grande & meritée recommandation. Car il est gentil, & plein tout ce qu'il est possible.

[As I was considering the way a painter I employ went about his work, I was taken with the desire to imitate him. He chooses the noblest place, the middle of each wall, to place a picture labored over with all his skill, and the empty space all around it he fills with grotesques, which are fantastic paintings whose only charm lies in their variety and strangeness. What are these here[42] too, in truth, but grotesques and monstrous bodies, pieced together of diverse members, with no definite shape, having no order, sequence, or proportion other than by chance? . . . I do indeed go along with my painter in this second point, but I fall short in the first and better part; for my ability does not go far enough for me to dare to undertake a rich and polished picture, formed according to art. I have decided to borrow one from Estienne de la Boitie which will do honor to all the rest of this work. It is a discourse to which he gave the name *Of Voluntary Servitude*. . . . It has long been circulating in the hands of men of understanding, not without great and well-merited commendation, for it is a fine thing, and as full as can be.] (I: 28, 183–84a, DM 252–54; 135*)

He goes on to write of friendship in general and of his friendship with La Boétie in particular, before concluding—or at first appearing to conclude—the chapter with these words: "Mais oions un peu parler ce garson de dixhuict ans" [But let us listen a little to this eighteen-year-old boy speak] (I: 28: 194a, DM 273; 144*). That sentence is followed in the 1580 edition by a line of three asterisks and then this surprising declaration: "Parce que j'ay trouvé que cet ouvrage a esté depuis mis en lumiere & à mauvaise fin, par ceux qui cherchent à troubler & changer l'estat de nostre police sans se soucier s'ils l'amenderont, qu'ils ont melé à d'autres escris de leur farine je me suis dedit de le loger icy" [Because I have found that this work has since been brought to light, with evil intent, by those who seek to disturb and change the state of our government without worrying whether they will improve it, and because they have mixed his work up with some of their own concoctions, I have renounced placing it here] (I: 28, 194a, DM 273; 144*). The fine and beautiful thing that was the *Servitude volontaire* has been spoiled by the contagion of the "autres escris" [other writings] with which it has been "melé" [mixed]. Unlike La Boétie's essay, which, although it was an argument against tyranny, did not advocate that any current monarch be overthrown, the other writings with which the Protestants surrounded his text in *Mémoires sur l'Estat de France sous Charles IX* in 1576 did precisely that. In

---

42. Meaning the *Essays*.

such company, the *Servitude volontaire* risked guilt by association, as would Montaigne if he republished it in his *Essays*.

But what are we to make of the fact that what Montaigne presents as a surprising event of which he was not aware when he promised his readers that he would place the *Servitude volontaire* in the center of the first book of his *Essays*—the Protestants' contaminating it by their infectious touch— is itself echoed in the very first words of the other chapter? The event he recounts and I: 30's first words are not only parallel but each other's opposite, for the Protestants contaminated La Boétie's text with evil intent while the corrupting contagion in I: 30 is entirely innocent, or at worst comes from an excess of zeal. The "maniement" [handling] in this same first sentence of I: 30 ("Comme si nous avions l'attouchement infaict, nous corrompons par nostre maniement les choses, qui d'elles mesmes sont belles & bonnes") finds its own echo in I: 28: La Boétie's essay "court pieça es *mains* des gens d'entendement, non sans bien grande & meritée recommandation" [has long been circulating in the *hands* of men of understanding, not without great and well-merited commendation] (I: 28, 184a, DM 253; 135). That handling with good intent is just the kind of thing the first sentence of I: 30 would at first glance appear to be talking about except that the outcome is precisely the opposite. The *Servitude volontaire* was not corrupted by that handling, though it clearly was by the infection it received at the hands of the Protestants.

Much of what Montaigne says of La Boétie's essay turns out to function as a fiction in the metafiction I: 28 and I: 30 together form. The plot thickens when he informs us, after saying he will not include the *Servitude volontaire* after all, that he just happened to have been sent another text by La Boétie:

> Or en eschange de cet ouvrage serieux j'en substitueray un autre produit en céte mesme saison de son aage plus gaillard & plus enjoüé, ce sont vint & neuf sonnets que le sieur de Poiferré homme d'affaires & d'entendement, qui le connoissoit longtemps avant moy a retrouvé par fortune chez luy parmy quelques autres papiers, & me les vient d'envoyer.

> [Now in exchange for this serious work I will substitute another product of the same season of his life, more gallant and more playful. They are 29 sonnets that the Sieur de Poiferré, a man of business and of understanding, who knew him long before I did, found by chance at his house among some other papers, and has just sent to me.] (I: 28, 195a(n), DM 274–75; not in Frame)

I. Book One

As Gabriel-André Pérouse remarks, there is something fishy about this:

> Fate would have it that, during those same months, the good Sieur de Poiferré should send him the manuscript of Étienne's "Twenty-Nine Sonnets." Montaigne then begins a new chapter to put them in. . . . Can one really believe their publication was a mere stop-gap? If so, certain facts would be difficult to explain. To line up twenty-nine poems for a chapter that just happens to bear the number twenty-nine can hardly be laid to chance. What is more, the twenty-ninth chapter of a Book containing fifty-seven is not a neutral place—yet in the end these sonnets occupy it.[43]

Something else suggests that Montaigne is not telling the truth when he presents the twenty-nine sonnets as a last-minute stopgap. His very words "*je me suis dedit de le loger icy*" [I have renounced placing it here], when he announces that he will not give us the *Servitude volontaire* after all, are echoed in the sonnets themselves: "*je me desdiray / De mes sonnetz*" [I will renounce / My sonnets] (sonnet 16, lines 12–13; DM 285). Nowhere else in the 1580 edition will the first-person speaker "se dédire" [literally, to unsay oneself]. In both cases what is "unsaid," or going to be, is the inclusion of a text within the larger text. In I: 28 Montaigne "unsays" his promise to include the *Servitude volontaire* in the middle of his Book (that is, Book One); the speaker in the poem says he will "unsay" the two immediately preceding sonnets, numbers 14 and 15—at the center of the sequence of twenty-nine—because in them he criticized his beloved for her duplicitous "parler double" [double speech] (sonnet 14, line 8; DM 284). In the same way that what happened to the *Servitude volontaire* that supposedly made Montaigne not want to publish it was inscribed in the echoing parallels uniting chapters I: 28 and I: 30, his supposed renouncement of the *Servitude volontaire* was already inscribed in the text that would replace it, in which its middle—the position the *Servitude volontaire* would have occupied in Montaigne's first Book—is likewise to be excluded. Yet the speaker in the sonnets will not in the end have to

---

43. P. 78 of Gabriel-André Pérouse, "Montaigne, son lecteur et les Vingt-neuf sonnets d'Étienne de La Boétie," *Montaigne Studies* 11.1–2 (1999): 77–86. Raymond C. La Charité put forward the hypothesis that it was only after the 29 sonnets came into Montaigne's possession that he decided to make it the 29th of 57 chapters. "With the pre-publication of the *Servitude Volontaire*, it must have seemed appropriate to him to place the 29 sonnets in chapter 29. Thus, the 'plus bel endroit' would be numerically marked as well and, as a result, in order to remain central, 'chaque paroy' would have to consist of 28 chapters." But since (in La Charité's surmise) he had not yet divided the remaining 93 chapters into books, "37 leftover chapters would simply have to spill over into a separate unit or 'book.'" " . . . Book II as a separate entity is the product of an accident" (p. 41 of "The Coherence of Montaigne's First Book," in *L'Esprit Créateur* 20.1 [Spring 1980]: 36–45).

dislodge sonnets 14 and 15, for his beloved forgives him (in sonnet 19) for writing them and he decides to keep them in the sequence: "c'est pour vous punir" [it is to punish you], he declares, addressing the offending sonnets, "qu'ores je vous pardonne" [that I pardon you now] (sonnet 20, line 14; DM 287).[44]

I would like to return to the opening sentence of "De la moderation" in order to examine what immediately follows it:

> Comme si nous avions l'attouchement infaict, nous corrompons par nostre maniement les choses, qui d'elles mesmes sont belles & bonnes. Nous pouvons saisir la vertu: de façon qu'elle en deviendra vicieuse. Comme il advient quand nous l'embrassons d'un desir trop *aspre* & trop violent.
>
> [As if our touch were infectious, by our handling them we corrupt things that of themselves are beautiful and good. We can grasp virtue in such a way that it will become vicious. As it happens when we embrace it with a desire too *sharp* and too violent.] (I: 30, 197a, DM 293; 146*)

It happens that too sharp [aspre] a desire is a problem in I: 28 as well: "l'affection envers les fames" [love of women] creates a fire that is "plus actif, plus cuisant, & plus *aspre*" [more active, more scorching, and more sharp] than friendly affection, for "En l'amitié, c'est une chaleur generale & universele, temperée . . . qui n'a rien d'*aspre*" [In friendship it is a general, universal, and temperate warmth . . . that has nothing *sharp*] (I: 28, 185–86a, DM 258–59; 137*). Friendship is thus more moderate than heterosexual desire. But through a post-1588 addition to I: 28, that chapter joins I: 30 in speaking of what is immoderate in love as well, and these are the only chapters in Book One where the adjective "immoderé" in any form appears. It appears when Montaigne alludes to "les insolents et passionnez efforts que peut produire une ardeur *immoderée*" [the insolent and passionate acts that *immoderate* ardor can produce] (I: 28, 187c; 138) in a homosexual lover. In I: 30 immoderation likewise can arise from love that, like homosexuality, is out of the ordinary: the marriage of blood relatives. Montaigne writes that he seems to remember reading somewhere in Thomas Aquinas that in such a case

---

44. I will have more to say about the sonnets in chapter IV, including a discussion of the words and turns of phrase they feature that appear nowhere but in the other two middle chapters, II: 19 and III: 7—further evidence that Montaigne's promise in I: 28 to put the *Servitude volontaire* in that place of honor was always a fiction.

il y a danger que l'amitié qu'on porte à une telle femme soit *immoderée*. Car si l'affection maritalle s'y trouve *entiere & parfaicte,* comme elle doit, & qu'on la surcharge encore de celle qu'on doit à la parantelle: il n'y a point de doubte, que ce surcroist n'emporte un tel mary hors les barrieres de la raison, soit en l'amitié, soit aux effaitz de la jouissance.

[there is a danger that the affection a man bears to such a wife will be *immoderate;* for if conjugal love is *entire and perfect,* as it should be, and you add to it also that which is due to kinship, there is no doubt that this increase will carry such a husband beyond the barriers of reason, whether in friendship or in the effects of sexual enjoyment.] (I: 30, 198a; DM 294; 147*)

What Montaigne says in this passage about how conjugal love should be "entiere & parfaicte" echoes, strangely, what he said in I: 28 about his friendship with La Boétie: "céte amitié que nous avons nourrie, tant que Dieu a voulu, entre nous, *si entiere & si parfaite,* que certainement il ne s'en lit guiere de pareilles" [this friendship which together we fostered, as long as God willed, *so entire and so perfect* that certainly one could hardly read of the like] (I: 28, 184a, DM 255; 136*). As Montaigne was surely aware, one can indeed *read* of the like in the companion chapter, though nowhere else in Book One, from which the phrase is otherwise absent. Does this mean that his friendship with La Boétie had something conjugal about it? Françoise Charpentier suggests it might. "It is impossible, having arrived at this point," she writes, with reference to I: 28, "not to pose ourselves the problem of the homosexuality of Montaigne. All the less possible, or even more necessary, because he poses it himself, and thus invites the reader to do so."[45]

---

45. P. 184 of Françoise Charpentier, "Figure de La Boétie dans les 'Essais' de Montaigne," *Revue française de psychanalyse* 52 (Jan.–Feb. 1988): 175–89. What counts here is the story Montaigne tells in I: 28 of their friendship and its relation to I: 30, not whether their relation was homosexual. As David Lewis Schaefer suggests, it may all be a fiction: "a moving, if somewhat mawkish (and quite possibly fictitious) account of [their] affectionate union" (*The Political Philosophy of Montaigne* [Ithaca: Cornell University Press, 1990], 342). As Floyd Gray observed, "If we read the essay of 1580, and then read it as it appears in the edition of 1595, . . . then we are tempted to ask whether Montaigne wrote on friendship because of La Boétie, or if La Boétie came into the essay because he was writing an essay on friendship" (p. 205 of "Montaigne's Friends," *French Studies* 15.3 [July 1961]: 203–212). Todd W. Reeser, borrowing an expression of Robert D. Cottrell's (in the latter's *Sexuality / Textuality* [Columbus: Ohio State University Press, 1981], 34), writes that in I: 28 "La Boétie could be read not so much as a flesh-and-blood friend of Montaigne's but rather as . . . 'an operational concept,' an absence in the life of Montaigne that sparks him to create a discursive presence. Homosexuality, like La Boétie, is employed as an operational concept that helps create an ethical boundary" (*Moderating Masculinity in Early Modern Culture* [Chapel Hill: North Carolina Studies in the Romances Languages and Literatures, 2006], 214). However, William J. Beck writes, "As homosexuality is defined today,

Apart from the tantalizing hints about Montaigne and La Boétie's friendship that reading between the lines of these two chapters may give us, "De l'amitié" and "De la moderation" show, just like all the other symmetrically linked chapters in Book One, that they speak the same language to the extent of almost seeming to be having a friendly conversation. One striking instance has become invisible to most readers, ever since Montaigne in 1588 removed the words between "comme" and "richesses" in the following passage:

> Quand aux *mariages,* outre ce que c'est un marché qui n'a que l'entrée libre, sa durée estant contrainte & forcée, dependant d'ailleurs que de nostre vouloir, & marché qui ordinairement se faict à autres *fins:* comme de *la generation,* alliances, richesses. . . .

> [As for *marriages,* beyond the fact that it is a bargain to which only the entrance is free—its continuance being constrained and forced, depending otherwise than on our will—and a bargain ordinarily made for other *ends:* such as *generation,* alliances, riches . . .] (I: 28, 186a, DM 260; 137*)

Here, one of marriage's "fins" is "la generation"; the same point is made, though in a stronger way, in the companion chapter: "C'est une religieuse liaison & devote que le *mariage.* . . . sa principale *fin* c'est *la generation*" [*Marriage* is a religious and holy bond . . . its principal *end* is *generation*] (I: 30, 198–99a, DM 295; 147). In no other passage in the *Essays* is "generation" a "fin," nor of course is it said to be such in marriage.

---

it must be admitted that the friendship between Montaigne and La Boétie, as chaste as it could have been, remains, given the depth, intensity, and vigor with which Montaigne celebrates it, a homosexual one, at least at a rudimentary level, for the mind, if not the body" (p. 44 of William J. Beck, "Montaigne face à l'homosexualité," *Bulletin de la société des amis de Montaigne,* 6th series: 9–10 [1982]: 41–50).

II

BOOK TWO

1. Sorting Out the Pieces

"De l'inconstance de nos actions" [Of the inconstancy of our actions] (II: 1) and *"De la ressemblance des enfans aux peres"* [Of the resemblance of children to fathers] (II: 37)

"De la ressemblance des enfans aux peres" was the *Essays*' concluding chapter in the original 1580 edition. So it was appropriate that it should begin with a reflection, though brief, on the *Essais* themselves: "Ce fagotage de tant de diverses pieces se fait en céte condition, que je n'y metz la main que lors qu'une trop lâche oysiveté me presse, & non ailleurs que chez moi" [This bundle of so many disparate pieces is being composed in this manner: I set my hand to it only when pressed by too lax an idleness, and nowhere but at home] (II: 37, 758a, DM 599; 574*). Barbara Bowen remarks that "there is no reason why" the term "fagotage" should be taken as pejorative, for it is "the art of stacking lengths of wood in a wood-pile, which requires skill and practice."[1] But even if we do take it as pejorative we know that elsewhere such self-deprecating remarks are not what they seem. In "De l'oysiveté"

---

1. P. 147 of Barbara Bowen, "What does Montaigne mean by 'marqueterie'?," *Studies in Philology* 67. 2 (1970): 147–55.

(I: 8), the chapter of which the dominant role Montaigne here gives to his "oysiveté" should remind us, we recall that the "pleine oysiveté" [full idleness] he allowed to engulf him brought forth chimera and monsters "les uns sur les autres, sans ordre, & sans propos" [one after another, without order and without purpose] (I: 8, 33a; DM 32; 21*). We recall as well that this self-deprecating aside is echoed but ultimately contradicted by the way he describes his writing practice in "De Democritus et Heraclitus": "sans dessein et sans promesse" [without design and without promise] (I: 50, 302c; 219*)—contradicted, that is, by the evident order and design that led to those parallel descriptions appearing in symmetrically matching chapters. The metafiction (the order and design that the work as a whole reveals, particularly the part I: 8 and I: 50 play in it) contradicts the fiction (expressed separately in I: 8 and I: 50) that there is no order.

"De l'inconstance de nos actions" and "De la ressemblance des enfans aux peres" speak together in a metafictional way of the "pieces" of which this "fagotage" is composed. In both chapters, "pieces" is an almost obsessively repeated term. In II: 1 it chiefly refers to the various and usually contradictory aspects of a man's life, as seen by a potential biographer or by that man himself as he attempts to live his life in accord with certain consistent principles.[2] In II: 37, the context is medical (the principal resemblance between Montaigne and his father being their antipathy to doctors), and "pieces" refer both to patients' symptoms and their appropriate remedies. The doctor "a besoin de trop de *pieces*" [needs too many pieces] to properly calculate "son dessein" [his plan]. These "pieces" include the patient's constitution, his temperature, his humors, his symptoms, his actions, even his thoughts, such external circumstances as the weather and the position of the planets, and the properties of the drug to be administered. "Et faut que toutes ces *pieces*, il les sçache proportionner & rapporter l'une à l'autre, pour en engendrer une parfaicte symmetrie" [and he must know how to proportion all these *pieces* and relate them to one another to engender a perfect symmetry] (II: 37, 773a, DM 626–27; 587*).

It is an impossible task, as in the corresponding chapter is the task of "Ceux qui s'exercitent à contreroller les actions humaines" [Those who strive to account for human actions], for they "ne se trouvent en nulle partie si empeschez qu'à les *rappiesser* & mettre à mesme lustre. Car elles se contredisent quelque fois de si estrange façon, qu'il semble impossible qu'elles

---

2. As André Tournon remarks, "the same behavioral trait is presented now as an indication of moral weakness, now as an obstacle to understanding." André Tournon, *La Glose et l'essai* (Lyon: Presses Universitaires de Lyon, 1983), 76.

soient parties de mesme boutique" [are never more perplexed than when they try to *piece them together* and show them in the same light. For they contradict each other sometimes so strangely that it seems impossible that they have come from the same shop] (II: 1, 331a, DM 1; 239*). Young Marius is at one moment a son of Mars, at another a son of Venus. Nero, famous for his cruelty, was nevertheless sick at heart when he had to sign a death warrant. There are so many examples of this "que je trouve estrange de voir quelque fois des gens d'entendement se mettre en peine d'assortir ces *pieces*" [that I find it strange to see sometimes men of understanding taking pains to match these *pieces* together] (II: 1, 332a, DM 2; 239). "Nostre faict ce ne sont que *pieces rapportées*" [Our actions are nothing but a *pieced*-together patchwork] (II: I, 336a, DM 8; 243)—but we can "rapporter" [relate] these "pieces rapportées" with what Montaigne says in the passage just quoted about the doctor's task: "Et faut que toutes ces *pieces*, il les sçache proportionner & *rapporter* l'une à l'autre, pour en engendrer une parfaicte symmetrie" [and he must know how to proportion all these *pieces* and *relate* them to one another in order to create a perfect symmetry]. The astonishing thing is that what is engendered when we do this is indeed a "symmetrie," for these echoing passages appear in the first and last chapters of the *Essays'* second volume. Another passage in II: 1 likewise symmetrically anticipates the doctor's task: "Il est impossible de renger les pieces, à qui n'a une forme du tout en sa teste: à quoy faire la provision des couleurs, à qui ne sçait ce qu'il a à peindre" [A man who does not have in his head a picture of the whole cannot possibly arrange the pieces. What good does it do a man to lay in a supply of paints if he does not know what he is to paint?] (II: 1, 337a, DM 9; 243*). That it is impossible to arrange the pieces without a form of the whole in mind implies the converse, that with a mental image of the whole it might be possible to arrange them. We recall that in describing the way he arranged his *Essays* in "De l'amitié" (I: 28)—as "grotesques"—he said he was imitating a painter. Hence, perhaps, the relevance of laying in a supply of colors.

2. Slipping It In

"De l'yvrongnerie" [Of drunkenness] (II: 2) and "Des plus excellens hommes" [Of the most excellent men] (II: 36)

In II: 36 Montaigne justifies choosing Homer, Alexander, and Epaminondas as the three highest examples of human excellence, distinguishing each from his competitors for the title—Homer from Virgil, Alexander from Caesar,

Epaminondas from Scipio Aemilianus. In II: 2 he begins by making distinctions too, not among paragons of virtue but varieties of vice: "Les vices sont tous pareilz en ce qu'ilz sont tous vices . . . mais . . . ilz ne sont pas egaus vices" [Vices are all alike in that they are all vices . . . but . . . they are not equal vices] (II: 2, 339a, DM 11; 244). From then on he concentrates on one vice in particular, drunkenness.

But apart from their being devoted, respectively, to a consideration of virtue and of vice, II: 2 and II: 36 are exactly opposed with regard to the matter of deviating from the norm of the human condition. II: 36 is entirely devoted to praising men famous for having done exactly that: "trois excellans *au dessus* de tous les autres" [three who excel *above* all the rest] (II: 36, 751a, DM 591; 569*); Homer was "quasi *au dessus* de l'humaine condition" [almost *above* the human condition] (II: 36, 752a, DM 592; 569*), and Alexander, Montaigne would add in 1588, had he lived to a normal age would have become "quelque chose *au dessus* de l'homme" [something *superhuman*] (II: 36, 754b; 571). But in II: 2 Montaigne finds that going above (or below) the norm is far from a good thing: "Toutes actions hors les bornes ordinaires sont sujettes à sinistre interpretation, d'autant que nostre goust n'advient non plus à ce qui est *au dessus* de lui qu'à ce qui est au dessous" [All actions outside the ordinary limits are subject to sinister interpretation, inasmuch as our taste responds no more to what is *above* it than to what is below] (II: 2, 346a, DM 16–17; 250).

Montaigne counts Epaminondas among his three most "*excellens* hommes" because "quant à ses meurs & conscience il a de bien loing *surpassé* tous ceux, qui se sont jamais meslés de manier affaires" [as for his character and conscience, he very far *surpassed* all those who have ever undertaken to manage affairs] (II: 36, 756a, DM 598; 573). In the companion chapter the excellent surpass the human norm as well:

> Platon dit que pour neant hurte à la porte de la poesie un homme rassis. Aussi dict Aristote que null'ame *excellente* n'est exempte de quelque meslange de folie. Et a quelque raison d'appeller fureur tout eslancement tant louable soit il, qui *surpasse* notre propre jugement & discours: d'autant que la sagesse c'est un maniement reglé de nostre ame, & qu'elle conduit avec mesure & proportion.

> [Plato says that a sedate man knocks in vain on the door of poetry. Likewise Aristotle says that no *excellent* soul is free from an admixture of madness. And he is right to call madness any transport, however, laudable, that *surpasses* our own judgment and reason; inasmuch as wisdom is an orderly

management of our soul, which she conducts with measure and proportion.] (II: 2, 347–48a, DM 19; 251*)

In a post-1588 addition to II: 2, Montaigne writes at length of his father, to whom he had not alluded in previous versions of this chapter. It seems strange that he should do so, for his father is not, after all, here portrayed as greatly given to drink. Montaigne eases into this paternal reminiscence by remarking that the previous generation seemed to drink more, and that the reason the present one does not is that "nous nous sommes beaucoup plus jettez à la paillardise que noz peres. Ce sont deux occupations qui s'entrempeschent en leur vigueur" [we are much more addicted to lechery than were our fathers. These two occupations interfere with each other in their vigor] (II: 2, 343c; 247). His father could attest to his generation's lack of interest in erotic pursuits—"C'est merveille des comptes que j'ay ouy faire à mon pere de la chasteté de son siecle" [It is marvelous what stories I have heard my father tell of the chastity of his day] (II: 2, 343c; 247)—yet he personally was not at all typical of his times: "C'estoit à luy d'en dire, estant tresadvenant, et par art et par nature, à l'usage des dames" [He was the man to tell them, being very well suited to the service of the ladies, both by nature and by art] and "recitoit des estranges privautez, nommeement siennes, aveq des honnestes femmes sans soupçon quelconque" [would tell of remarkable intimacies, especially of his own, with respectable women, free from any suspicion] (II: 2, 344c; 248).

But there may be another reason for the insertion of this page about his father into this chapter: to provide more opportunity for echoes with II: 36—or perhaps even to pay homage to that father by showing (though in a somewhat indirect and veiled way) that he shared some of the excellence of those men, particularly of Epaminondas and Alexander. For of Epaminondas Montaigne writes that "jamais homme ne sçeut tant, et *parla* si *peu* que luy*"* [never did a man know so much, and *speak* so *little,* as he] (II: 36, 756a; 573), while his father too "*parloit peu* et bien" [*spoke little* and well] (II: 2, 343c; 247). In a post-1588 addition to the discussion of Epaminondas immediately after "parla si peu que luy," Montaigne inserts an echo to the other quality he at the same moment (that is, in his post-1588 revisions) attributes to his father, that he spoke not only little but well: "Car il estoit Pythagorique de secte. Et ce qu'il parla nul ne parla jamais mieux" [For he was a Pythagorean in sect. And what he did say, no man ever said better] (II: 36, 756c; 573).[3] As for Alexander, among his excellent virtues was the

---

3. The Pythagoreans were known for their vow of silence.

"*foy en ses parolles*" [*fidelity to his word*] (II: 36, 754b; 571). This was true of Montaigne's father as well: "Monstrueuse *foy en ses parolles*" [Prodigious *fidelity to his word*] (II: 2, 343c; 248*). Nowhere else does the phrase "foy en ses parolles" appear, nor do the expressions "parloit peu" (Montaigne's father, in II: 2) or "parla . . . peu" (Epaminondas, in II: 36) find an echo in any form of *parler* with *peu*.

Alexander was known for having "à l'aage de trente trois ans, passé victorieux toute la terre habitable" [at the age of thirty-three, passed victoriously over all the habitable earth] (II: 36, 754a; 571), wherein thirty-three is notable for being remarkably young—as Montaigne goes on to emphasize in a 1588 addition at this point, calling Alexander's span of years "une demye vie" [half a lifetime] and wondering what he might have accomplished had he lived "un juste terme d'aage" [a normal life span] (II: 36, 754b; 571). Montaigne's father, on the other hand, is noteworthy for having done something for which thirty-three is remarkably old: he "avoit eu fort longue part aux guerres delà les monts. . . . Aussi se maria-il *bien avant en aage,* l'an 1528—qui estoit son trente-troisiesme—retournant d'Italie" [he had taken a very long part in the Italian wars. . . . Consequently he married *well along in age,* in the year 1528, which was his thirty-third, on his return from Italy] (II: 2, 344c; 248). Not only does his age match Alexander's, and not only is there a symmetrical opposition in that for one the age is remarkably young yet for the other remarkably old, but for both that age marks the end of their military career.

Another post-1588 addition testifies to Montaigne's continuing desire to forge links between these chapters, for it is an interestingly roundabout way of inserting Epaminondas' name into "De l'yvrongnerie":

> Je n'eusse pas creu d'yvresse si profonde, estoufée et ensevelie, si je n'eusse leu cecy dans les histoires; qu'Attalus ayant convié à souper, pour luy faire une notable indignité ce Pausanias qui, sur ce mesme subject, tua depuis Philippus, Roy de Macedoine—Roy portant par ses belles qualitez tesmoignage de la nourriture qu'il avoit prinse en la maison et compagnie d'Epaminondas,—il le fit tant boire qu'il peut abandonner sa beauté, insensiblement, comme le corps d'une putain buissonnière, aux muletiers et nombre d'abjects serviteurs de sa maison.

> [I should not have believed in a drunkenness so deep, so dead and buried, if I had not read of this instance of it in the histories. Attalus, having invited Pausanias to supper in order to do him some notable indignity—that same Pausanias who for this same reason later killed Philip, king of Macedon, a

king who by his fine qualities bore witness to the education he had received in the house and company of Epaminondas—made him drink so much that he could abandon his body insensibly, like the body of some whore under a hedge, to the muleteers and a number of vile slaves of Attalus' household.] (II: 2, 341c; 246)

Montaigne's ability to slip in this allusion to the chapter to which this one is symmetrically linked—for Epaminondas has nothing to do with this story, being only tangentially related to another story involving a participant in this one—is only matched by the prowess of just such a low servant as the ones who took advantage of the situation here, for in the very next anecdote he tells (still in this post-1588 addition) how a young farmhand was able to insert himself unnoticed into a chaste but inebriated and hence unsuspecting young widow, leaving her to be greatly puzzled over her subsequent pregnancy (II: 2, 341–42c; 246). Perhaps Montaigne as well has taken advantage of the cover of drunkenness—as a topic of discourse, if not a condition—to slip in "la semence d'une matiere plus riche et plus hardie" [the seeds of a richer and bolder material] (I: 40, 251c; 185). It would be one way of imitating the prowess of that father who had been so adept at conducting "estranges privautez . . . aveq des honnestes femmes sans soupçon quelconque" [remarkable intimacies . . . with respectable women, free from any suspicion] (II. 2, 344c; 248).

3. Suicide is Painless

"Coustume de l'isle de Cea" [A custom of the island of Cea] (II: 3) and "De trois bonnes femmes" [Of three good wives] (II: 35)

What is done surreptitiously in II: 2 could not be carried out more openly than it is in II: 3 and II: 35. For a more obvious case of two symmetrically placed chapters linked by a common subject could hardly be imagined than that of these two treatises on suicide (unless it be the "cruauté" [cruelty] linking II: 11 and II: 27 in their titles). The custom in question in II: 3 is that of voluntarily ending one's life when one has lived enough, though the instance recounted of a ninety-year-old woman on Cea (and hence the resolution of the mystery of the title[4]) is saved until the end; her relatively happy

---

4. A mystery not entirely resolved, for Montaigne presents no other examples of inhabitants of Cea doing away with themselves. One instance hardly justifies calling it a custom. André Tournon points out that although the woman tells her fellow citizens why she has decided to take her life

self-inflicted exit is preceded by a veritable holocaust of less happy ones: a Lacedaemonian boy, Servius the grammarian, Speusippus, Cato, the virgins of Miletus, Therycion, Cleomenes, Cassius, Brutus, Damocritus, Antinous, Theodotus, the Sicilian of Gozo, the Jewish women besieged by Antiochus, Libo, Razis, Pelagia, Sophronia, Lucius Aruntius, Granius Silvanus, Statius Proximus, plus at least thirty-seven more together with the inhabitants of entire cities.

The three good wives in II: 35 are good precisely because they commit suicide, showing their love for their husband by accompanying them in death. The first two encourage their husbands to do this difficult thing by doing it themselves. The wife of a man who suffered from genital ulcers and who told him, upon examining them, that he had better kill himself, lashed her body to his and together they leapt into the sea. In doing so she and her husband, having resolved that they "*se precipiteroient en la mer*" [*would throw themselves into the sea*] (II: 35, 745a, DM 577; 564*) involuntarily (on their part, but perhaps not Montaigne's) echo two sets of suicides in the matching chapter: Cleombrotus of Ambracia, who was inspired by Plato's *Phaedo* to taste of the life to come, and consequently "*s'alla precipiter en la mer*" [went and *threw himself in the sea*] (II: 3, 360a, DM 32; 260), and the inhabitants of the Hyperborean region who, tired of life, decided to "*se precipiter en la mer*" [*throw themselves into the sea*] (II: 3, 362a, DM 35; 262). In the 1580 edition of the *Essays* these strikingly similar expressions would make their only appearances in these two chapters.

In the second case, Arria, the wife of Cecinna Paetus, who had taken part in an unsuccessful rebellion against the emperor Claudius but was reluctant to carry out his suicide, took her husband's dagger, plunged it into her stomach, then drew it back out and handed it to him, saying "tien Paetus il ne m'a point fait de mal" [See, Paetus, I felt no pain] (II: 35, 747a, DM 580; 565*). Shamed by her example, he followed suit. The third good wife was Seneca's young spouse, who did not need to encourage her husband but wanted to accompany him in death; Nero, however, had her wounds closed.

A 1588 addition to II: 3 counters the three good wives of II: 35 with three self-sacrificing wives of its own, of which the first two offer a clear and straightforward parallel to those in II: 35: "Sextilia, femme de Scaurus, et

---

"nothing tells us that she asked their permission" (*Route par ailleurs*, 93). Montaigne goes on to cite a genuine instance of suicide as a community custom: "Pline recite de certaine nation hyperborée... qu'estans las et sous de vivre ilz ont en *coutume*... se precipiter en la mer" [Pliny tells of a certain Hyperborean nation in which ... when they are weary and satiated with living it is their *custom* ... to throw themselves into the sea] (II: 3, 361–62a, DM 34–35; 262). The chapter could have been more appropriately entitled "Coustume hyperborée" [A Hyperborean Custom].

Paxea, femme de Labeo, pour encourager leurs maris à eviter les dangiers qui les pressoyent, ausquels elles n'avoyent part que par l'interest de l'affection conjugale, engagerent volontairement la vie pour leur servir, en cette extreme necessité, d'exemple et de compaignie" [Sextilia, wife of Scaurus, and Paxea, wife of Labeo, to encourage their husbands to avoid the dangers that pressed them, in which they themselves had no share except by virtue of conjugal affection, voluntarily sacrificed their own lives so as to serve in this extremity as example and company to their husbands] (II: 3, 358b; 258). The third, however, while duplicating the feat of killing herself in front of her husband to join him in his suicide, turns out to have been a *bad* wife:

> Il ne se peut rien adjouster à la delicatesse de la mort de la femme de Fulvius, familier d'Auguste. Auguste, ayant descouvert qu'il avoit esventé un secret important qu'il luy avoit fié, un matin qu'il le vint voir, luy en fit une maigre mine. Il s'en retourna au logis, plain de desespoir; et dict tout piteusement à sa femme qu'estant tombé en ce malheur il estoit resolu de se tuer. Elle tout franchement: Tu ne feras que raison, veu qu'ayant assez souvent experimenté l'incontinance de ma langue, tu ne t'en es point donné de garde. Mais laisse, que je me tue la premiere. Et, sans autrement marchander, se donna d'une espée dans le corps.

> [Nothing can be added to the delicacy of the death of the wife of Fulvius, a close friend of Augustus. Augustus, having discovered that Fulvius had aired an important secret he had confided to him, treated him bleakly one morning when he came to see him. Fulvius went back to his house full of despair, and said most piteously to his wife that because of this misfortune he was resolved to kill himself. She said very frankly: "You will only be doing the right thing, seeing that for all your experience of the incontinence of my tongue you did not guard against it. But here, let me kill myself first." And without further ado she ran a sword through her body.] (II: 3, 358b; 259)

She is bad enough as Montaigne tells it, having an incontinent tongue; but she is much worse in the story as Plutarch tells and which Montaigne quotes here almost word for word but leaves out what she is alluding to: it was she who had told Caesar's secret, which she had heard from her husband, to Livia, who then berated Augustus.

> Fulvius, the friend of Caesar Augustus, heard the emperor, now an old man, lamenting the desolation of his house: two of his grandsons were dead, and Postumius, the only one surviving, was in exile because of some false accu-

sation, and thus he was forced to import his wife's son into the imperial succession; yet he pitied his grandson and was planning to recall him from abroad. Fulvius divulged what he had heard to his own wife, and she to Livia; and Livia bitterly rebuked Caesar: if he had formed this design long ago, why did he not send for his grandson, instead of making her an object of enmity and strife to the successor to the empire. Accordingly, when Fulvius came to him in the morning, as was his custom, and said, "Hail, Caesar," Caesar replied, "Farewell, Fulvius." And Fulvius took his meaning and went away; going home at once, he sent for his wife, "Caesar has found out," he said, "that I have not kept his secret, and therefore I intend to kill myself." "It is right that you should," said his wife, "since, after living with me for so long a time, you have not learned to guard against my incontinent tongue. But let me die first." And, taking the sword, she dispatched herself before her husband.[5]

Thus the last of this 1588 insertion's three wives is both the same as (as a wife encouraging her husband to suicide) and yet the exact opposite of (not a good wife but a bad one, and not a comfort to her husband in his misfortune but the cause of it) the three good wives in the companion chapter.

No wonder Montaigne comments that all he had to do was to choose his stories and then arrange them according to what the beauty of the larger work they form requires, for that is clearly what he is doing here, in the interplay between chapters II: 3 and II: 35. He wonders why other writers do not assemble stories from books, from which they could "bastir un corps entier & s'entretenant" [construct and entire body that held together] for which the only thing of their own they need supply would be "la liaison" [the connection]. They could arrange and diversify the stories ("les disposant & diversifiant") as the beauty of the larger work would require, as Ovid sewed and pieced together his *Metamorphoses* (II: 35, 749a, DM 587–88; 567–68*).

It now appears even less likely that Montaigne's characterization of his book as a "fagotage de tant de diverses pieces" [bundle of so many diverse pieces] (II: 37, 758a, DM 599; 574) meant that it has no structure, for here he both likens it to the *Metamorphoses* and asserts that Ovid arranged and diversified his stories in such a way as to enhance the beauty of the whole. That beauty in the case of the *Essays* comes from his ability to "proportionner & rapporter l'une à l'autre" "toutes ces pieces . . . pour en engendrer une parfaicte symmetrie" [proportion and relate one to the other all those pieces to engender a perfect symmetry] (II: 37, 773a, DM 626–27; 587*).

---

5. Plutarch, "On talkativeness" (De garrulitate). In *Moralia* (Cambridge: Harvard University Press / Loeb Library, 1939) vol. 6, 429–31.

Another such symmetry is engendered when this statement near the beginning of II: 3—

> C'est ce que qu'on dit, que le sage vit tant qu'il doit, non pas tant qu'il peut.
>
> [That is what they say, that the wise man lives as long as he should, not as long as he can] (II: 3, 350a, DM 20; 252*)

—is echoed by this one near the end of II: 35:

> la loy de vivre aus gens de bien ce n'est pas autant qu'il leur plait, mais autant qu'ils doivent.
>
> [the law of living, for good men, is not as long as they please but as long as they ought] (II: 35, 750a, DM 589; 568)

They are not only parallel but also symmetrically opposed, for the first statement approves of suicide while the second counsels against it. The first appears in the midst of instances of voluntary suicides, seconding their resolution, as the words that follow it make clear: "& que le present que nature nous ait faict le plus favorable & qui nous oste tout moien de nous plaindre de nostre condition c'est de nous avoir laissé la clef des champs" [and that the most beneficent present Nature has given us, a present which takes from us any reason for complaining about our condition, is the gift of a way out] (II: 3, 350a, DM 20–21; 252*). The second appears in a letter of Seneca's in which he speaks of his realization that he has to live for his beloved wife and not just for himself. The sentences immediately following the one just quoted continue in that sense:

> Celuy qui n'estime pas tant sa femme ou un sien amy que d'en allonger sa vie & qui s'opiniastre à mourir, il est trop delicat & trop mol: . . . il faut par fois nous prester à nos amis: & quand nous vouldrions mourir pour nous interrompre nostre dessein pour autruy.
>
> [The man who does not value his wife or a friend of his so much as to prolong his life for them, and who stubbornly insists on dying, is too delicate and soft; . . . we must sometimes lend ourselves to our friends, even when for our sake we would like to die, break off our plan for the sake of others.] (II: 35, 750a, DM 589; 568*)

Montaigne here simply translates Seneca's words, at considerable length.[6] Hence the whole passage is essentially another one of those "histoires, qui se rencontrent dans les livres" [stories that are found in books] that he had just said he likes to choose and arrange for the sake of the beauty of his book as a whole. Part of that beauty is the way one particular sentence of it echoes yet opposes a sentence in the companion chapter. Here we can get a glimpse of how Montaigne went about writing these two chapters: he must have started with the sentence from Seneca, and then fashioned the other sentence to match it.

4. Caesar the Procrastinator

"À demain les affaires" [Let business wait till tomorrow] (II: 4) and "Observations sur les moyens de faire la guerre de Julius Caesar" [Observations on Julius Caesar's methods of making war] (II: 34)

Montaigne begins both chapters by heaping praise on a book, praise that culminates in his calling that book a breviary, and among the qualities he praises is the purity of its language, which in his estimation surpasses that of its competitors. In "À demain les affaires" it is Amyot's translation of Plutarch, among other qualities "*pour la* naifveté & *pureté du langage, en quoy il surpasse tous autres*" [*for the* naturalness and *purity of his language, in which he surpasses all others*]. Thanks to it we know how to speak and write, "*c'est nostre breviaire*" [it is our breviary] (II: 4, 363–64a; DM 35–36; 262). In the other chapter, the book called out for praise is Julius Caesar's *Commentaries* on the Gallic and Civil Wars. "Car à la verité *ce devroit estre le breviaire* de tout homme de guerre" [*it should be the breviary* of every warrior], characterized by "*une façon de dire si pure . . . que à mon goust il n'y a nuls escrits au monde, qui puissent étre comparables aus siens en céte partie*" [*that to my taste there are no writings in the world comparable to his in this respect*] (II: 34, 736a; DM 558–59; 556*). These two assertions, though they refer to each other in the way that the *Essays*' other symmetrically placed echoes do, are mutually contradictory, for it cannot both be true that Amyot's linguistic purity is unsurpassed and Caesar's incomparable.

The chapters are symmetrically opposed in that II: 4 focuses on delay in receiving messages while II: 34 features delay in sending them. In II: 4,

---

6. As the editors of the new Pléiade edition of the *Essais* point out (Balsamo et al., 1694n).

Montaigne cites Plutarch (in Amyot's translation) recounting how a certain Rusticus, in the audience at a lecture Plutarch himself was giving, was handed a letter from the Emperor but put off opening it until the lecture was over. Very courteous to Plutarch, Montaigne comments, but imprudent with regard to the Emperor. Montaigne cites several other addressees who delayed to a dangerous or fatal extent opening their messages. A fatal instance was Julius Caesar himself, according to (Amyot's) Plutarch: "ce mesme Plutarque m'a appris que Julius Caesar se fut sauvé, si, allant au senat, le jour qu'il y fut tué par les conjurez, il eut leu un memoire qu'on luy presenta contenant le faict de l'entreprise" [this same Plutarch has taught me that Julius Caesar would have saved his life if, in going to the Senate on the day when he was killed there by the conspirators, he had read a memorandum that was handed to him] (II: 4, 364a, DM 38; 263).

In II: 34, Julius Caesar delays *sending* three different kinds of messages:

(1) His orders to his soldiers: "Il accoustumoit sur tout ses soldats à obeir simplement sans se mesler de contreroller ou parler des desseins de leur capitaine, lesquels il ne leur communiquoit que sur le point de l'execution" [He accustomed his soldiers above all simply to obey, without meddling with criticizing or talking about their captain's plans, which he communicated to them only when he was about to put them into execution] (II: 34, 736a, DM 556; 556).

(2) His pep talks to his soldiers before they engaged the enemy: "il fait grand cas de ses exhortations aux soldatz avant le combat. Car là où il veut monstrer avoir esté surpris ou pressé, il allegue tousjours cela qu'il n'eust pas seulement loysir de haranguer son armée" [he sets great store by his exhortations to the soldiers before combat. For where he wants to show that he was surprised or hard pressed, he always mentions the fact that he had not even the leisure to harangue his army] (II: 34, 738a, DM 563; 557–58*). This kept happening, apparently, as Montaigne tells it ("il allegue tousjours" [he always mentions]). He tells of one instance in particular, when "il n'eust loisir de leur dire, sinon qu'ilz eussent souvenance de leur vertu acoustumée, qu'ils ne s'estonnassent point, & soustinsent hardiment l'effort des adversaires" [he had only time to tell them to remember their accustomed valor, not to be taken aback, and to sustain boldly the adversaries' attack] (II: 34, 738a, DM 563; 558*). But if he had had the time, he evidently would have said more than these platitudes, for his "eloquence militaire" was so highly regarded that "plusieurs en son armée recueilloint ses harengues. Et par ce moyen il en fut assemblé des volumes, qui ont duré

long temps apres luy" [several in his army took down his harangues; and that means there were volumes of them collected that lasted a long time after him] (II: 34, 738a, DM 564; 558). And what he said in his speeches to the troops when he had enough time to say it was evidently more interesting and specific than the commonplaces that were all he had time to say on that particular occasion to which Montaigne alludes: "Son parler avoit des graces particulieres, si que ses familiers & entre autres Auguste oyant reciter ce qui en avoit esté recueilli, reconnoissoit jusques aus phrases & aus mots ce qui n'estoit pas du sien" [His speech had particular graces, so that his intimates, and among them Augustus, hearing anyone recite what had been collected of them, could recognize what was not his, even to phrases and words] (II: 34, 738a, DM 564; 558).

(3) And his reply to a request for safe passage: when the Swiss asked him permission to travel through Roman territory but he decided to prevent them by force, he "print quelques jours de delay à leur faire responce pour se servir de ce loisir à assembler son armée" [took a few days' delay in answering them, so as to use this leisure in assembling his army] (II: 34, 737a, DM 560; 557). This instance differs from the other two in that he profited from his delay; nevertheless, it is yet another case of his delay in sending a message, the symmetrical response to his delay in receiving a message on the Ides of March, recounted in II: 4. Montaigne shows that he thinks that (2) and (3) are related by calling Caesar's delay in both cases—and twice in (2)—"loisir."

5. Suffering Innocence

"De la conscience" [Of conscience] (II: 5) and "L'histoire de Spurina" [The story of Spurina] (II: 33)

In "De la conscience" Montaigne argues that our innermost thoughts, especially our guilty ones, will show through on our face, despite our best efforts to conceal them. He tells of traveling during the religious civil wars and meeting a man who wore the outward marks of a Catholic, but whom he deduced must be a Protestant. He could see from the fear the man showed every time they passed through a town loyal to the king "que c'estoient *alarmes* que sa conscience luy donnoit" [that his *alarms* were caused by his conscience] (II: 5, 366a, DM 40; 262). "L'histoire de Spurina" is likewise about "alarmes," a word that appears in the plural nowhere else in Book Two save in this chapter and "De la conscience," and about how hard it is to prevent one's body from responding to an inner impulse: "Plusieurs ayans voulu delivrer leurs ames des *alarmes* continuelles que leur donnoit cet appetit, se sont servis d'incision & détranchement des parties esmeues & alterées" [Many, having wished to deliver their soul from the continual *alarms* that this appetite gave them, have resorted to the incision and amputation of the parts that were stirred and altered] (II: 33, 728a, DM 546; 550). The appetite in question is the sexual one, and Montaigne goes on in this passage to write of those who have fought it with, heat, cold, hair shirts and "des ceintures à *geiner* leurs reins" [girdles to *torture* their loins] (II: 33, 728a, DM 40; 550).

Torture, applied to the loins to kill desire in II: 33, is also central to the discussion of conscience in II: 5: "c'est une dangereuse invention que celle des *gehenes* & semble que ce soit plustost un essay de patience que de verité" [*tortures* are a dangerous invention, and seem to be a test of endurance rather than of truth] (II: 5, 368a, DM 43; 266). For pain is as likely to make the sufferer lie as tell the truth. There is, however, an effect on the conscience: torture makes the guilty weaken and confess, but fortifies the innocent. A 1588 and a post-1588 addition continue the discussion: "[B] Que ne diroit on, que ne feroit on pour fuyr à si griefves douleurs? . . . [C] D'où il advient que celuy que le juge *a geiné,* pour ne le faire mourir innocent, il le face mourir et innocent et *geiné*" [What would a man not say, what would a man not do, to escape such grievous pains? . . . Whence it happens that the man whom the judge *has tortured* so as not to make him die innocent, is made to die both innocent and *tortured*] (II: 5, 369bc; 266).

Pain and mutilation inflicted on innocence are what the story to which the title of II: 33 alludes is all about, though with the difference that they are self-inflicted. Spurina was a Tuscan youth so beautiful that he made virtuous women lust after him. Not content to refrain from abetting their desire, he "entra en furieux despit contre soy mesmes & contre ces riches presens, que nature luy avoit faits, comme si on se devoit prendre à eux *de la faute d'autruy*" [entered into furious spite against himself and against these rich presents that nature had made to him, as if these should be blamed *for the fault of others*] (II: 33, 734a, DM 558; 555) and cut his face, leaving such scars that he destroyed his beauty. His face, though innocent, was, like the innocent victim of torture, made to suffer for misdeeds for which others were responsible.

This intentionally self-inflicted destruction in II: 33 is the symmetrical opposite of a case of unintentionally self-inflicted destruction recounted in II: 5: the wasp who "picque & offence autruy, mais plus soi mesme, car elle y perd son eguillon & sa force pour jamais. Vitásque in vulnere ponunt" [stings and hurts others, but itself most, for there it loses its sting and its strength forever, "In the wound they make they leave their lives"] (II: 5, 367a; DM 41; 264).

Montaigne immediately follows this up with another insect analogy: "Les Cantarides ont en elles quelque partie qui sert contre leur poison de contrepoison, par une contrarieté de nature. Aussi à mesme qu'on prend le plaisir au vice, il s'engendre un desplaisir contraire en la conscience qui nous tourmente" [The Spanish fly has in itself something that serves as a counter poison to its own poison, by a contrariety of nature. So, even while we take pleasure in vice, there is engendered in our conscience a contrary displeasure which torments us] (II: 5, 367a, DM 41; 265). Balsamo et al. note Montaigne's source as Amyot's translation of Plutarch's "On the delays of divine justice" (1518), which is accurate (he nearly quotes it word for word), but their footnote gloss on the word "partie" as "qualité" (385n) is in error, revealing an ignorance of a passage from another essay of Plutarch's, also translated by Amyot, where he explains where the counter poison comes from: "les medecins disent que la mousche Cantharide est bien un mortel poison, et toutefois que les ailes et les pieds ont force d'aider au contraire, et de dissoudre sa mortelle puissance" [doctors say that the Spanish fly is indeed a fatal poison, and yet that its wings and feet have the power to counteract it, and to dissolve its fatal power].[7] So it is not a quality in the poison itself but another substance, made from other parts of the fly's body.

Unlike the wasp, the Spanish fly does not poison itself, so it forms no parallel with the self-harming Spurina. However, it will join with the wasp to find a counterpart poison in a post-1588 addition to "L'histoire de Spurina," the one that the father of a girl forced to become the mistress of Ladislas of Naples put on a handkerchief that she brought to the encounter:

> Elle estoit fille d'un medecin fameux de son temps, lequel, se trouvant engagé en si villaine necessité, se resolut à une haute entreprinse. Comme chacun paroit sa fille et l'attournoit d'ornements et joyaux qui la peussent rendre aggreable à ce nouvel amant, luy aussi luy donna un mouchoir exquis en senteur et en ouvrage, duquel elle eust à se servir en leurs premieres approches, meuble qu'elles n'y oublient guere en ces quartiers là. Ce mouchoir, empoisonné selon la capacité de son art, venant à se frotter à ces chairs esmeues et pores ouverts, inspira son venin si promptement, qu'ayant soudain changé leur sueur chaude en froide, ils expirerent entre les bras l'un de l'autre.

---

[7]. "Comment il faut que les jeunes gens lisent les poètes" [How young men should read the poets], available on the web at http://www.chass.utoronto.ca/~wulfric/rentexte/amyot/am_txt.htm.

[She was the daughter of a doctor famous in his time, who, finding himself entangled in so foul a necessity, resolved on a lofty attempt. As all were arraying his daughter and bedecking her with ornaments and jewels to make her pleasing to this novel lover, he too gave her a handkerchief, exquisite in fragrance and workmanship, which she was to use in their first embraces—an article they rarely forget in those parts. This handkerchief, poisoned according to the full capacity of his craft, coming to rub against the aroused flesh and open pores of both, infused its venom so promptly that, their warm sweat suddenly changing to cold, they expired in each other's arms.] (II: 33, 730c; 552)

M. A. Screech points out that this anecdote comes from Laonicus Chalcondylas' *De la décadence de l'Empire Grec*.[8] Montaigne made some telling departures from that source. In Chalcondylas' version, the father

> resolved to carry out a very strange thing that required no small courage. For with hemlock juice and other fatal drugs he soaked a kerchief [un couvrechef] richly worked with golden thread and crimson silk, which he gave to his daughter for her to put on when the King was with her, which she did. Now he no sooner cast his eye on this beauty, of which the renown, he said, had been too miserly in its praise, than all boiling and enflamed with love, without standing on ceremony, he immediately threw himself upon her. But he was no sooner touched by the kerchief, as heated as he was, than suddenly the poison went up to his heart, with such speed and force, that after having shed a few drops of a cold sweat, as if it were nature's last effort, he gave up the ghost in the arms of the girl, who also expired soon afterward.[9]

Montaigne's alterations allow the poison to recall more strongly II: 5's cantharides, known since antiquity for their alleged aphrodisiac powers. For in the original, it was not a handkerchief but a kerchief; it was not perfumed; the father had not instructed his daughter to use it in their first embraces; and it was not applied to the aroused flesh of *both* in the act of making love (though the daughter did succumb from contact with it; after all, it was on her head). Note as well that Montaigne's remark that a perfumed handkerchief was a "meuble qu'elles n'y oublient guere en ces quartiers là" [an article they rarely forget in those parts] has no basis in the source. It is not an apt

---

8. In his translation of the *Essais*, 827n.
9. Laonicus Chalcocondylas, *L'Histoire de la Décadence de l'Empire Grec, et Establissement de celuy des Turcs*, tr. Blaise de Vigenère, 1620 (orig. 1577). Available online at Google Books. My translation.

remark to make about a couvre-chef, which was not an item Italian (or Florentine) women wore with more frequency than French women in 1414 (the date of Ladislaus' death). To use a scented handkerchief in lovemaking is something one could reasonably assert that women in certain parts do more often than women elsewhere. Yet "ces quartiers là" may more likely connote not a geographical region but the bedroom. Montaigne's two insect examples in the other chapter, the wasp and the Spanish fly, together anticipate what will happen here, for like the latter, the daughter's seductive handkerchief was meant (in Montaigne's version of the story) to arouse her victim; but like the wasp, she would not survive the encounter.

6. Parallel Deaths

"De l'exercitation" [Of practice] (II: 6) and "Defence de Seneque et de Plutarque" [In defense of Seneca and Plutarch] (II: 32)

One can "s'exercer" [practice] for misfortune by voluntary poverty and other self-induced austerities, Montaigne writes, but practicing in advance is of no help as far as death is concerned. Yet we can try it out ("l'essayer") through sleep, which resembles death. But the closest we can come is through some violent accident that makes us lose conciousness. Those that have experienced such an event "ont esté bien pres de voir son vray & naturel visage" [have been very close to seeing death's true and natural face] (II: 6, 372a, DM 47; 268). Being knocked off his horse by another horseman and losing consciousness gave Montaigne such an opportunity, and he devotes "De l'exercitation" to recounting the event and its aftermath.

> [M]'estant alé un jour promener à une lieüe de chez moi, qui suis assis dans le moiau de tout le trouble des guerres civiles de France . . . j'avoy pris un cheval bien aisé mais non guiere ferme: à mon retour une occasion soudaine s'estant présentée de m'aider de ce cheval à un service qui n'estoit pas bien de son usage, un de mes gens grand & fort, monté sur un puissant roussin, qui avoit une bouche desesperée, frais au demeurant & vigoureus, pour faire le hardy & devancer ses compaignons, vint à le pousser à toute bride droit dans ma route, & fondre comme un colosse sur le petit homme & petit cheval, & le foudroier de sa roideur & de la pesanteur, nous envoyant l'un & l'autre les piedz contre-mont: si que voila le cheval abatu & couché tout étourdi, moy dis ou douze pas au dela mort estendu à la renverse, le

visage tout meurtry & tout escorché . . . n'ayant ny mouvement ny sentiment non plus qu'une souche.

[Having gone riding one day about a league from my house, which is situated at the very hub of all the turmoil of the civil wars of France . . . I had taken a very easy but not very strong horse. On my return, when a sudden occasion came up for me to use this horse for a service to which it was not accustomed, one of my men, big and strong, riding a powerful work horse who had a desperately hard mouth and was moreover fresh and vigorous— this man, in order to show his daring and get ahead of his companions, spurred his horse at full speed up the path behind me, came down like a colossus on the little man and little horse, and hit us like a thunderbolt with all his strength and weight, sending us both head over heels. So that there lay the horse bowled over and stunned, and I ten or twelve paces beyond, dead, stretched on my back, my face all bruised and skinned . . . having no more motion or sensation than a log.] (II: 6, 373a, DM 49–50; 268–69*)

His companions, unable to revive him, thought he was dead. They picked him up and carried him home. After two hours, he began to regain consciousness, but "mes premiers sentimens estoint beaucoup plus aprochans de la mort que de la vie. Céte recordation que j'en ay fort empreinte en mon ame me representant son visage & son idée si prez du naturel, me concilie aucunement à elle" [my first feelings were much closer to death than to life. This recollection, which is strongly implanted on my soul, showing me the face and idea of death so true to nature, reconciles me to it somewhat] (II: 6, 373–74a, DM 51; 269).

This encounter with death, singular as it was, finds a curious counterpart in "Defence de Seneque et de Plutarque" (II: 32). It emerges from a true story Montaigne tells to defend Plutarch from Jean Bodin's accusation that the instances he cited of stoic resistance to pain, such as the Spartan boy who continued to hide a stolen fox under his cloak even though he was biting him, were not to be believed. "Et qui s'enquerre à nos Argolets, des experiences qu'ils ont eues en ces guerres civiles, il se trouvera des effets de patience, d'obstination & d'opiniatreté parmi nos miserables siecles . . . dignes d'estre comparez à ceus que nous venons de reciter de la vertu Spartaine" [If anyone would ask our soldiers about the experiences they have had in these civil wars, there will be found acts of endurance, obstinacy, and stubbornness in this miserable age of ours . . . worthy to be compared to those we have just related of Spartan virtue] (II: 32, 724a, DM 539; 547*). Montaigne knows of peasants who have undergone excruciating tortures at the hands of their captors. He says he saw one left for dead naked in a ditch,

> ayant le col tout meurtry & enflé d'un licol qui y pendoit encore, avec lequel on l'avoit tirassé toute la nuict à la queüe d'un cheval, le corps percé en cent lieux à coups de dague qu'on luy avoit donné, non pas pour le tuer, mais pour luy faire de la doleur & de la crainte: qui avoit souffert tout cela & jusques à y avoir perdu parolle & sentiment, resolu, à ce qu'il me dit, de mourir plus tost de mille morts que de rien promettre, & si estoit un des plus riches laboureurs de toute la contrée.

> [his neck all bruised and swollen from a halter that was still hanging from it, by which he had been pulled all night behind a horse, his body pierced in a hundred places with stabs from daggers, which had been dealt him not to kill him but to hurt and frighten him; who had endured all that, even to the point of having lost speech and sensation, resolved so he told me, to die a thousand deaths rather than promise anything; and yet he was one of the richest farmers in the whole district.] (II: 32, 724a, DM 540; 548*)

The farmer was found in an unconscious state, "jusques à y avoir *perdu* parolle & *sentiment*" [to the point of having *lost* speech and *sensation*]; so too was Montaigne, being one of "ceus qui sont tombez par quelque violent accident . . . & qui y ont *perdu* tous *sentimens*" [those who by some violent accident . . . have *lost* all *sensation*] (II: 6, 372a, DM 47; 268), and in his own particular case "n'ayant ny mouvement ny *sentiment* non plus qu'une souche" [having no more motion or sensation than a log]. Consequently the farmer was "laissé *pour mort*" [left *for dead*]; so too was Montaigne: "Ceus qui estoint avec moy . . . me tenans *pour mort*" [Those who were with me . . . taking me *for dead*] (II: 6, 373a, DM 50; 269). He repeats the expression a few pages later, when he remembers seeing the other horse "à mes talons & me tins *pour mort*" [at my heels and took myself *for dead*] (II: 6, 377a, DM 55; 272*). That Montaigne is setting up, little by little and detail by detail, a double for himself in the man left for dead in this matching chapter becomes all the more apparent when we realize that the phrase "pour mort" appears nowhere else in the *Essays*.

The farmer was "tirassé"; so too was Montaigne. For the former, it was intentional torture by his enemies; for the latter, pain unintentionally inflicted by his friends. The farmer was "*tirassé* toute la nuict" [*pulled* all night] by a halter his tormentors had tied around his neck and attached to a horse's tail. As for Montaigne, "j'avois esté vilainement *tirassé* par ces pouvres

gens qui avoint pris la peine de me porter entre leurs bras par un long &
tresmauvais chemain & s'y estoint lassés deux ou trois fois les uns apres les
autres" [I had been villainously *pulled about* by those poor fellows, who had
taken the pains to carry me in their arms over a long and very bad road, and
had tired themselves out two or three times in relays] (II: 6, 376–77a, DM
56; 272*). The situation is hardly the same, but that's not the point: the
word is the same, giving rise to some irony. No one else is "tirassé" in Book
Two.

The same precision is evident in words describing their respective injuries. The farmer's neck was "*tout meurtry*" [*all bruised*] (II: 32, 724a, DM
540; 548) from the halter, while Montaigne's face was "*tout meurtry*" [*all
bruised*] (II: 6, 373a, DM 50; 269). Only in this pair of chapters does that
expression appear.

Perhaps the most important connection between Montaigne's story of his
own brush with death and the farmer left for dead in the ditch is that the
very thing that makes his own story so worth telling, that the event allowed
him to experience death without actually dying, is actually part of the other
man's experience too. For the suffering the latter endured, as Montaigne
makes clear in a 1588 addition, gave him the opportunity to die without
dying: he was "resolu, à ce qu'il me dict, de mourir plustost de mille morts
(comme de vray, quand à sa souffrance, *il en avoit passé une toute entiere*)
avant que rien promettre" [resolved, so he told me, to die a thousand deaths
(as in truth, so far as suffering goes, *he had died one whole death*) rather than
promise anything] (II: 32, 724ab; 548).[10]

But there are still more pieces to the puzzle. Like Montaigne, the man
was injured by a horse—the one he was tied to and by which he was "tirassé"
all night. But the way he was tied, the "licol" [halter] around his neck,[11]
almost turned him into a horse—though not so much in the context of his
own story as in the larger one of how Montaigne sets up this encounter of
echoing stories. It is in that larger metafiction that the halter can acquire
some significance. Another detail about him meaningful in the metafiction in
which these two stories converge is that he was a "laboureur," defined by Littré as "Celui qui laboure, soit l'ouvrier qui trace le sillon, soit le propriétaire
ou le fermier qui cultive une terre" [He who plows, whether it be the worker
who traces the furrow or the landowner or the farmer who cultivates a field].

---

10. The part in parentheses was added in 1588, as noted in DM 540, although neither of the Pléiade editions nor the Villey indicate it.
11. Screech and Frame both translate "licol" as "halter"; Cotgrave defines it as "A rope, halter; horse-collar." Randle Cotgrave, *A Dictionarie of the French and English Tongues* (London: 1611). Available on the web at http://www.pbm.com/~lindahl/cotgrave/

By strange coincidence, a "roussin," the kind of big horse that collided with Montaigne's smaller horse is a "cheval de *labour*," according to Balsamo et al. (391n), a *plow* horse.[12] So the "laboureur" is both a horse (by virtue of the horse's halter he is made to wear) and one who plows, making him a distant double of the plow horse that unhorsed Montaigne. If the *Essays* were a poem such a recombination of elements would be in no way surprising. But in fact they *are* a poem. And in that poem, Montaigne's run-in with the roussin is an allegory of the collision in the larger text between these stories. In the collision, the story in II: 6 may not escape unscathed. We can no longer think it unique, for example: both events take place during the "guerres civiles" [civil wars]; each man had "perdu . . . sentiment" [lost consciousness], was taken "pour mort" [for dead], was "tirassé" [pulled about] and "tout meurtry" [all bruised], each suffered from an encounter with a horse and experienced death without actually dying. But is Montaigne even telling the truth about what happened to him? How could so many details be true of both stories? Was one a true story and the other a fiction concocted to match so many details of the first?

If that is the case, Montaigne seems to want us to consider whether the story in II: 32 might not be the true one, for he appears to confirm the reality of the event by providing another source for it in "De l'experience": "Des paysans viennent de m'advertir en haste qu'ils ont laissé presentement en une forest qui est à moy un homme *meurtry de cent coups,* qui respire encores, et qui leur a demandé de l'eau par pitié et du secours pour le soubslever" [Some peasants have just informed me hastily that a moment ago they left in a wood that belongs to me a man *stabbed in a hundred places,* who is still breathing, and who begged them for pity's sake to bring him some water and help him to get up] (III: 13, 1070b; 819). The plowman in II: 32 had been stabbed a hundred times too: "le corps percé en *cent* lieux à *coups* de dague" [his body pierced in a *hundred* places with *stabs* from daggers]. There are sixty-four other appearances of "cent" in the *Essays* but these are the only two where it is combined with "coups" [blows].[13] Moreover, while the expression "tout meurtry" appears only twice, applied to Montaigne in II: 6 and to the plowman in II: 32, the word "meurtry" makes only one other appearance in the *Essays* at all, and this is it. As we have already seen in reading chapter pairs before now, Montaigne knows where he is putting certain words and he plants them where he does for a reason. In this instance, "meurtry" links the three passages. The only persons to whom it applies in the *Essays* are Mon-

---

12. Villey defines it similarly: "Fort cheval employé au labour ou aux charrois" [a strong horse employed in plowing or pulling carts] (373n5).
13. Both Frame and Screech (1214) translate these "coups" as stab-wounds.

taigne in II: 6, the plowman in II: 32, and the wounded man in III: 13—and the hundred blows connect the latter two.

Could then these two crime victims be the same? The peasants, Montaigne goes on to say, left the man where he lay because they were fearful of being accused of having attacked him themselves. Surely Montaigne would not have left him there too, but would have gone out and rescued the man, finding him in the ditch, left for dead yet still alive and able to tell his story. So that if we put the two stories together, as the unique repetition of "cent coups" and "meurtry" encourage us to do, this is where we pick up the story in II: 32. But if he wants us to believe that it could be the same man, he nevertheless wants us to believe it could not be the same man, for also he tells us in III: 13—a chapter first published in 1588—that the event had only just happened ("Des paysans viennent de m'advertir" [Some peasants have just informed me])—whereas the story in II: 32 was published eight years before. The metafictional plot thickens.

7. Rewards and Punishments

"Des recompenses d'honneur" [Of honorary awards] (II: 7) and "De la colere" [Of anger] (II: 31)

Montaigne begins "De la colere" by saying that it is not good to let a father bring up his own children. "Qui ne voit qu'en un estat tout dépend de l'education & *nourriture des enfans?* & ce pendant sans nulle discretion on les laisse à la merci de leurs parens tant fols & meschans qu'ils soient" [Who does not see that in a state everything depends on the education and *nurture of the children?* And yet, without any discernment, they are left to the mercy of their parents, however foolish and wicked these may be] (II: 31, 714a, DM 525; 539–40*). But in "Des recompenses d'honneur" he seems to express the opposite opinion, maintaining that for a father to be involved in his children's upbringing is appropriate, even if it is commonplace and thus not worth singling out for praise: "On ne remarque pas pour la recommandation d'un homme, qu'il ait soin de la *nourriture de ses enfans,* d'autant que c'est une action commune, quelque juste qu'elle soit" [We do not note in commendation of a man that he takes trouble over the *nurture of his children,* since this is a common action, however just] (II: 7, 382a, DM 61; 276*). The contradiction is made particularly apparent by the parallel expressions "nourriture de ses enfans" (in II: 7) and "nourriture des enfans" (in II: 31). In a post-1588 alteration to II: 31 that echo will disappear but the meaning remain as "tout dépend de l'education & *nourriture des enfans*" becomes "tout dépend de son education et nourriture" [everything depends on its education and nurture], the possessive adjective "son" [its] finding its antecedent in "enfance" [childhood] in a sentence inserted after 1588 just before this point. In it Montaigne reports that Sparta and Crete were the only states which "ont commis aux loix la discipline de l'enfance" [committed the education of children to the laws] (II: 31, 714c; 539). As I will show, however, in 1588 Montaigne added such significant new connections between these two chapters that he may have decided at the moment he made the later change that he no longer needed the verbal echo.

II: 7 is about how best to reward; II: 31, how best to punish. Specifically, the one doing the punishing should not be angry. Montaigne is revolted by the sight of an irate father or mother beating their child. "Il n'est passion qui esbranle tant la sinceritè des jugemens, que la colere. Nul ne feroit doubte de punir de mort le juge, qui par colere auroit comnamné son criminel" [There is no passion that so shakes the clarity of our judgment as anger. No one would hesitate to punish with death a judge who had condemned his criminal through anger] (II: 31, 715a, DM 526; 540). Consequently, neither parents nor schoolmasters should chastise children in anger, nor masters their servants.

In the other chapter Montaigne focuses on honorary rewards, as opposed to monetary ones, and on one in particular, the Order of Saint Michel, debased in recent years because too many have received it. Not only can rewards become too common to convey the meaning they should, but certain kinds of virtuous behavior can be so common as not to deserve a reward. It is this point in the discussion that he brings in the example of fathers' taking pains for the education of their children being so common a good trait as not to be worth commendation.

In 1588 Montaigne added a new dimension to his chapter on anger that enabled it to echo more strongly the central point of the other chapter, that honorary awards can lose their efficacy if they are given indiscriminately and too often, for precisely the same is true, he will argue in these new pages, of anger. "J'advertis ceux qui ont loy de se pouvoir courroucer en ma famille : premierement, qu'ils *mesnagent* leur cholere et ne l'*espandent* pas à tout pris, car cela en empesche l'effect et le poix : la criaillerie temeraire et ordinaire passe en usage et faict que chacun la *mesprise*" [I admonish those in my family who have the right to get angry, first to be *thrifty* with their anger and not *spread* it about at random, for that impedes its effect and its weight. Heedless and continual scolding becomes a habit and makes everyone *discount* it] (II: 31, 719b; 543–44*). The three terms I have italicized had been part of the discussion when he was making the same point in the other chapter about honorary awards: "Auguste avoit raison d'estre beaucoup plus *mesnagier* & espargnant" [Augustus was right to be much more *thrifty* and sparing] (II: 7, 382a, DM 61; 276) of an honorary award than monetary ones. It is unfortunate that the powers that be decided to award the Order of Saint Michel in so spendthrift a manner, to "*espandre* indignement & avilir cet honneur [post-1588: cete marque]" [unworthily *spread* and debase this honor (post-1588: this distinction)] (II: 7, 383a, DM 63; 277*). If the new honorary award (the Order of the Holy Spirit) intended to regain the prestige the Saint Michel lost is to succeed, people will have to lose their memory of the first and the "*mespris* auquel il est cheu" [*contempt* into which it has fallen] (II: 7, 383a, DM 64; 277).

By contrast with honorary rewards, monetary ones are not as dignified because "on les *employe* à toute autre sorte d'*occasions*" [they are *used* for all other sorts of *occasions*] (II: 7, 382a, DM 60; 276)—to reward valets, couriers, dancers, acrobats. Those words reappear in the 1588 addition too: when Montaigne gets angry with his servants, he does not have recourse to violence, but "je n'y *employe* communement que la langue. Mes valets en ont meilleur marché aux grandes *occasions* qu'aux petites" [I ordinarily *use* nothing but my tongue. My servants get off better on big *occasions* than small] (II: 31, 720b; 544*) because the small ones take him by surprise, and his anger flares, whereas on the big occasions he is prepared in advance not to give in to rage.

This is a good example of how Montaigne polished his chapter pairs in subsequent editions to make them even more mutually reflective.

8. Hidden Monsters

"De l'affection des peres aux enfans" [Of fathers' affection for their children] (II: 8) and "D'un enfant monstrueux" [Of a monstrous child] (II: 30)

These two chapters advertise some sort of connection by their titles, the beloved "enfants" of one anticipating the monstrous "enfant" of the other. That every monstrosity has its hidden twin is the astonishingly self-referential revelation Montaigne will make in a post-1588 addition to II: 30's conclusion: "cette figure qui nous estonne, se rapporte et tient à quelque autre figure de mesme genre inconnu à l'homme . . . mais nous n'en voyons pas l'assortiment et la relation" [this figure that astonishes us is related and linked to some other figure of the same kind unknown to man . . . but we do not see their arrangement and relation] (II: 30, 713c; 539*). On the immediate level—the fictive one in which he pretends in any given chapter to be talking about some particular subject—he is speaking of God and His creation; but on the metafictional level, he is talking about his own creation, the *Essays*' "assortiment" [arrangement] and "relation."

The monstrous child was profitable because of its strangeness: "Je vis avant hier un enfant que deux hommes & une nourrisse . . . conduisoient, *pour tirer quelque liard* pour le monstrer à cause de son *estrangeté*" [The day before yesterday I saw a child that two men and a nurse . . . were leading about *to get a penny or so* from showing him, because of his *strangeness*] (II: 30, 712a, DM 523; 538). So too, Montaigne hopes, are the *Essays:* "si *l'estrangeté* ne me sauve & la nouveleté, qui ont accoustumé de donner *pris* aus choses, je ne sors jamais à mon honneur de céte sote entreprinse: mais elle est si fantastique, & a un visage si esloigné de l'usage commun que cela luy pourra donner passage" [if *strangeness* and novelty, which customarily give *value* to things, do not save me, I shall never get out of this stupid enterprise with honor; but it is so fantastic and has a face so remote from common usage that that may enable it to pass] (II: 8, 385a, DM 66; 278*). The "stupid enterprise" is the *Essays,* which will turn out to have a lot more in common with the monstrous child than just strangeness.

For one thing, Montaigne's assertion that his book has "un visage si esloigné de l'usage *commun*" [a face so remote from *common* usage] finds its mirror-reversed image in what he says about the monstrous child: "Il estoit en tout le reste d'une forme *commune*" [In all other respects he was of a *common* shape] (II: 30, 712a, DM 523; 538*). That is, the two passages have "commun[e]" in common, though the uses made of that word are opposite, Montaigne in II: 8 insisting on the uncommonness of the *Essays*, while saying in II: 30 that in all respects other than what he is about to describe—the headless trunk, and the arms and legs of its conjoined twin—the child's appearance was *not* uncommon. Indeed to the "visage" [face] of the *Essays* corresponds the face of the child, which is evidently one of the few things about him that have a normal aspect.

To make the connection between his book and the monstrous child even more explicit, Montaigne goes on to say in "De l'affection des peres aus enfans" that the *Essays* have "un dessin farouche et *monstreus*" [a wild and *monstrous* plan] (II: 8, 385a, DM 67; 278*). That's how the passages read in 1580 and 1588; subsequently he changed "monstreus" to "extravagant." But the monstrosity of his chapters was already evident, and would remain so, in the passage at the beginning of "De l'amitié" where he characterized them as "corps monstrueux, rappiecez de divers membres" [monstrous bodies, pieced together of diverse members] (I: 28, 183a, DM 251; 135).[14]

The monstrous child was composed of a "double corps . . . *se rapportans* à une seule teste" [double body . . . *connected with* a single head] (II: 30, 713a, DM 524; 539). In the post-1588 addition to which I alluded at the outset the same verb relates such natural monsters to their undiscovered counterparts:

> Ce que nous appellons monstres, ne le sont pas à Dieu, qui voit en l'immensité de son ouvrage l'infinité des formes qu'il y a comprinses; et est à croire que cette figure qui nous estonne, *se rapporte* et tient *à* quelque autre figure de mesme genre inconnu à l'homme. De sa toute sagesse il ne part rien que bon et commun et reglé; mais nous n'en voyons pas l'assortiment et la relation.

> [What we call monsters are not so to God, who sees in the immensity of his work the infinity of forms that he has comprised in it; and it is for us to believe that this figure that astonishes us *is related* and linked *to* some other figure of the same kind unknown to man. From his infinite wisdom there proceeds nothing but that is good and common and regular; but we do not see their arrangement and relationship.] (II: 30, 713c; 539*)

One instance of the verb "se rapporter" self-namingly "se rapporte" [is related] to the other, for the two conjoined bodies are related to each other (and to the single head) as one monstrous event in God's creation is related to its unnoticed double, and as one chapter is related to its symmetrical counterpart.

Those relations are multiple. Three times the headless child attached to the other is called imperfect: "cet enfant imparfait . . . l'imparfait . . . cet imparfaict" [this imperfect child . . . the imperfect one . . . this imperfect

---

14. Gisèle Mathieu-Castellani (*Montaigne: L'écriture de l'essai* [Paris: Presses Universitaires de France, 1988]) reads "D'un enfant monstrueux" in light of Montaigne's comments in "De l'amitié" (I:,28) about the monstrosity of the *Essays,* and finds, as I do, that II: 30 is a "mise en abîme" of his book, but for quite different reasons. In her view, the *Essays* are "monstrous" in that they have no order other than a fortuitous one. But when he said that in I: 28 he was in my estimation referring to their sequence (from monster to monster), not their symmetry. Chapter II: 30 "emblematizes in the figure of the monster . . . the disproportioned and irregular structure of the essays, pieced together of divers members like the body of the child, and whose order is something other than 'normal'" (222). She also argues that the text itself of II: 30, with its 1588 and 1595 accretions, comes increasingly to assume the doubleness of the monstrous child (228). But then so would any of dozens of chapters that grew enormously through their own accretions.

one] (II: 30, 713a, DM 524; 539*). Three times in the companion chapter does Montaigne speak of producing, by contrast, a *perfect child*. In the first instance, the "perfect child" would be something like the *Essays*, a literary production proceeding from Montaigne himself and the muses:

> Ce seroit à l'adventure impieté en Sainct Augustin (pour exemple) si d'un costé on luy proposoit d'enterrer ses escrits, dequoy nostre religion reçoit un si grand fruit, ou d'enterrer ses *enfans*, au cas qu'il en eut, s'il n'aimoit mieux enterrer ses *enfans*. Et je ne sçay si je n'aimerois pas mieux beaucoup en avoir produict ung, *parfaictement* bien formé, de l'acointance des muses, que de l'acointance de ma femme.

> [It would perhaps be impiety in Saint Augustine, for example—if it were proposed to him on the one hand to bury his writings, from which our religion receives such great fruit, or else to bury his *children*, in case he had any—if he did not prefer to bury his *children*. And I do not know whether I would not like much better to have produced one *perfectly* formed one by intercourse with the muses than by intercourse with my wife.] (II: 8, 401ab; 292–93*)

The second and third instances occur in the same passage. In the former, the imagined perfect child would be a real one, though to which deeds of valor might be preferred; in the latter, the child is once more an artistic production:

> Il est malaisé à croire . . . que Alexandre et Caesar ayent jamais souhaité d'estre privez de la grandeur de leurs glorieux faicts de guerre, pour la commodité d'avoir des *enfans* heritiers, quelques *parfaits* et accompliz qu'ils peussent estre; voire je fay grand doubte que Phidias, ou autre excellent statuere, aymait autant la conservation et la durée de ses *enfans* naturels, comme il feroit d'une image excellente qu'avec long travail et estude il auroit *parfaite* selon l'art.

> [It is hard to believe . . . that Alexander and Caesar ever wanted to be deprived of the grandeur of their glorious deeds of war for the satisfaction of having *children* and heirs, however *perfect* and accomplished they might be. Indeed I very much doubt that Phidias or any other excellent sculptor would be so pleased with the preservation and long life of his natural *children* as with that of an excellent statue that his long labor and study had *perfected* according to the rules of his art.] (II: 8, 402a; 293*)

Although perfection and imperfection make other appearances in the *Essays,* nowhere but in these two chapters do they refer to a child. So the imperfect child in II: 30, one of the monsters that Montaigne in that chapter declares has a counterpart somewhere else which we would perceive if we could only see "l'assortiment et la relation," finds its symmetrical (that is, opposite) counterpart in the perfect children in the symmetrically paired chapter.

The fathers of those perfect children would in each instance have willingly given them up for more prestigious progeny of a different sort—writings, deeds of war, a statue. Indeed, father-child relations are sometimes problematic in II: 8, despite the chapter's title, not only in those three instances but also when the son and the father are competing for the same shot at success:

Voulons nous estre aimés de nos enfans, leur voulons nous oster l'occasion de souhaiter nostre mort? . . . Pour cela il ne nous faudroit pas marier si jeunes que nostre aage vienne quasi à se confondre avec le leur. . . . Un gentil'homme qui a trante cinq ans, il n'est pas temps qu'il face place à son fils qui en a vint. Il est luy mesme au train de paroitre & aus voyages des guerres & en la court de son prince; il a besoin de ses pieces: il en doit certainment faire part, mais telle part, qu'il ne s'oublie pas pour autruy.

[Do we want to be loved by our children? Do we want to take away from them the occasion for desiring our death? . . . For that purpose, we should not marry so young that our age comes to be almost confounded with theirs. . . . When a gentleman is thirty-five, it is not time for him to give place to his son who is twenty: he is himself in the midst of appearing on military expeditions and in the court of his prince; he needs his resources, and should certainly share them, but not so as to forget himself for others.]
(II: 8, 389–90a, DM 74–75; 282–83)

That unwise proximity of years, in which the age of one is likely to be confused with ("quasi à se confondre avec") that of the other, makes father and son uncomfortably alike in their abilities and needs. They look more like brothers, strangely paralleling the monstrous child who was in fact a pair of brothers, conjoined twins linked at the chest (the smaller one headless but having arms), "comme si un plus petit enfant en vouloit *accoler* un plus grandet. . . . Voilà comme ce qui n'étoit pas attaché, comme bras, fessier, cuisses & jambes de cet imparfaict demouroient *pendans* & branslans sur l'autre, & luy pouvoit aller sa longueur jusques à my jambe" [as if a smaller child were trying to *embrace* a bigger one *around the neck.* . . . In this way all of this imperfect child that was not attached, as the arms, buttocks, thighs, and legs, remained *hanging* and dangling on the other and might reach halfway down his legs] (II: 30, 713a, DM 524; 538). As if he were hanging onto the neck of his brother, he resembles the kind of imperfect child Montaigne accuses mothers of unjustly favoring and who consequently pose a problem for a father's intention: it is dangerous to leave our wives in charge of our succession and of which children to award it to, for "Communement on les void s'adonner aux plus foibles & malotrus, ou à ceux, si elles en ont, qui leur *pendent* encores *au col*" [We commonly see them devote themselves to the weakest and most ill-favored, or those, if they have any, who are still *hanging about their necks*] (II: 8, 399a, DM 83; 290). The weaker, headless, brother is at the same time weaker and more ill-favored by nature *and* hanging onto the other *and* giving the illusion of embracing him around the neck. The son of a father too close to him in age can only succeed at the latter's expense; likewise the weaker brother may ultimately drain the fully formed one of his strength. As it is, the latter, though already fourteen months old, cannot ingest solid food.

Montaigne suggests that "Ce double corps & ces membres divers se rapportans à une seule teste" [This double body and these several limbs, connected with a single head] (II: 30, 713a, DM 524; 539) might be a favorable omen for the king's holding the diverse factions of his kingdom together, but that it would be better to let events take their course, "car il n'est que de deviner en choses faictes" [for there is nothing like divining about things past] (II: 30, 713a, DM 525; 539). In 1588 he would add this: "Comme on dict d'Epimenides qu'il devinoit *à reculons*" [As they said of Epimenides that he prophesied *backward*] (II: 30, 713b; 539). This could be a wink at the reader who has a good enough memory to recall (or rather who, having caught on Montaigne's game of writing his chapters in symmetrical pairs, can go back and discover) that in "De l'affection des peres aux enfans" he wrote that although the care every animal takes for the conservation of its progeny is the second law of nature (the first being the instinct for self-preservation), "parce que nature semble nous l'avoir recommandée, regardant à estandre et faire aller avant les pieces successives de cette sienne machine, ce n'est pas merveille si, *à reculons*, des enfants aux peres, elle n'est pas si grande" [because Nature seems to have recommended it to us with a view to extending and advancing the successive parts of this machine of hers, it is no wonder if, looking *backward*, the affection of children for their fathers is not so great] (II: 8, 386a, DM 69; 279*). Montaigne is inviting us in 1588, in other words, to prophesy backwards, to look back to find what was already there in 1580 (and backwards in the nominal order of the chapters), to find that other *à reculons*.

9. Only When You Need It

"Des armes des Parthes" [Of the armor of the Parthians] (II: 9) and *"De la vertu"* [Of virtue] (II: 29)

In "Des armes des Parthes" Montaigne remarks that "Plusieurs *nations* vont encore & *alloient* anciennement *à la guerre* sans armes" [Several *nations* still go, and *used to go, to war* without wearing armor] (II: 9, 404a, DM 94; 294). In "De la vertu" he gives an example of just such a nation: the "Bedouins *nation* meslée aux Sarasins . . . *alloient à la guerre* nudz, sauf un glaive à la Turquesque & le corps seulement *couvert* d'un linge blanc" [Bedouins, a *nation* mingled with the Saracens . . . *used to go to war* unarmed except for a Turkish-style sword, their body *covered* only with a white linen cloth] (II: 29, 709a, DM 521–22; 536*). In 1588, Montaigne added to the II: 9 passage (after "sans armes") "sans se *couvrir*, d'autres se *couvroient* de vaines armes" [without *covering* themselves; others *covered* themselves with useless armor].[15] In a post-1588 revision, he changed that to "sans se *couvrir*; ou se *couvroient* d'inutiles defances" [without *covering* themselves; or *covered* themselves with useless armor]. The latter alteration did not change what the 1588 insertion added: the *couvrir* and *couvroient* that set up more echoes with the II: 29 passage, in addition to the echoes already present between *nations* and *nation, alloient . . . à la guerre* and *alloient à la guerre*, and of course the notion itself of going to war without armor.

II: 9 is about armor—the armor of Montaigne's own time, the armor of the Romans, and that of the Parthians. But II: 29 is about virtue. So how does it happen that Montaigne finds himself talking about armor—specifically, the lack thereof—in a chapter on virtue? And why does the statement in II: 9 about how some nations go to war without it find its only specific illustration in II: 29?

What Montaigne appears to mean by "vertu" in II: 29 is impassibility, the ability to withstand pain. There is a big difference, he writes, between leaps of the soul and a resolute and constant habit. It is a greater thing "de se rendre *impassible* de soy, que d'estre tel de sa condition originelle" [to make oneself *impassible* by one's own efforts than to be so by one's natural condition] (II: 29, 705a, DM 514; 532–33*). He cites as paragons of impassibility: Pyrrho, indifferent not only to what was around him (a disappearing interlocutor, carts crossing his path in the street) but also to the pain of surgery;

---

15. *Essais de Michel seigneur de Montaigne (Cinquiesme édition augmentée d'un troisiesme livre et de six cens additions aux deux premiers)* (Paris: L'Angelier, 1588), 367. Available on the web at http://gallica.bnf.fr/ .

two men who cut off their genitals to make a point; Indian widows who perform suttee; Indian Gymnosophists who perform similar self-immolation; and the Bedouins whose belief that fate has already determined when they will die is so strong that they go into battle without armor.

That "resolue & constante habitude" is hard to come by. Pyrrho in fact did not always have it (he quarreled with his sister and took defensive measures against menacing dogs). But the Indian widows did, as it was "leur coustume" [their custom] (II: 29, 707a, DM 519; 534) to throw themselves like that on their husband's funeral pyre. And unlike most of us, the Gymnosophists proved their virtue (in burning themselves up without moving a muscle) "non par l'impetuosité d'un'humeur soudeine mais par expresse profession de leur regle" [not by the impetuosity of a sudden impulse, but by the express profession of their order] (II: 29, 708a, DM 519; 535). We, on the other hand, can only attain such heights on special occasions, "par secousse" [fitfully], only in the form of "les boutées & saillies de l'ame" [the leaps and sallies of the soul] (II: 29, 705a, DM 514; 533*).

> Il nous advient à nous mesmes qui ne sommes qu'avortons d'hommes, d'eslancer par fois nostre ame esveillée par les discours ou exemples d'autruy, bien loing au dela de son ordinaire : mais c'est une espece de passion, qui la pousse & agite, & qui la ravit aucunement hors de soy : car franchi ce tourbillon, nous voyons que sans y penser elle se débande & reláche d'elle mesme, sinon jusques à la derniere touche, au moins jusques à n'étre plus cele-la. De façon que lors, à toute occasion, pour un oiseau perdu, ou un verre cassé, nous nous sentons esmouvoir à plus pres comme l'un du vulgaire.
>
> [It happens to us, who are but abortions of men, sometimes to launch out our soul, arouse by the ideas or examples of others, very far beyond her ordinary range; but it is a kind of passion that impels and drives her, and which to some extent tears her out of herself. For when this whirlwind is over, we see that without thinking about it she unbends and relaxes of herself, if not down to the lowest key, at least until she is no longer the same; so that then, for any occasion, for a lost bird or a broken glass, we let ourselves be moved just about like one of the vulgar.] (II: 29, 705a, DM 515; 533*)

In contrast to extraordinary cases like the Indians and the Bedouins, virtue defined as impassibility is something we put on only at certain critical moments, and cast off when we no longer think we need it. We treat it like some sort of protective armor that would be too heavy to wear day in and day out—and this is precisely the parallel Montaigne has set up between this chapter and its symmetrical double, which begins: "C'est une façon vitieuse de la noblesse de nostre temps, & pleine de mollesse, de ne prendre les armes que sur le point d'une extreme necessité & s'en descharger aussi tost qu'il y a tant soit peu d'apparance que le danger soit esloigné" [It is a vicious practice of the nobility of our time, and full of softness, to put on armor only on the point of extreme need and to take it off as soon as there is the slightest appearance that the danger has gone] (II: 9, 403a, DM 93; 293). The Romans wore heavy armor, typically sixty pounds as Montaigne points out, but "ils estoient si acoustumés à les porter, qu'elles ne les empeschoient non plus que leurs membres" [they were so accustomed to wearing it that it impeded them no more than their limbs] (II: 9, 405a, DM 96; 295*). But just as it was "leur coustume" that made it possible for Indian widows to die with their husbands, so too with armor: "Or il n'est que la *coustume* qui nous rende insupportable la charge de nos armes" [Now it is only *custom* that makes the burden of our armor insupportable to us] (II: 9, 404a, DM 95; 294*).

10. Act Your Age

"Des livres" [Of books] (II: 10) and "Toutes choses ont leur saison" [There is a season for everything] (II: 28)

In "Des livres" Montaigne tells us that at his advanced age he is in no mood to read for much more than pleasure:

> Mon dessein est de passer doucement non laborieusement ce qui me reste de vie. Il n'est rien pourquoy je me vueille rompre la teste, non pas pour la science mesme, de quelque grand pris qu'elle soit. Je ne cherche aux livres qu'à m'y donner du plaisir par un honneste amusement: ou si j'estudie je ny cerche que la science, qui traicte de la connoissance de moy mesmes, & qui m'instruise à bien mourir & à bien vivre.

> [My intention is to pass pleasantly, and not laboriously, what life I have left. There is nothing for which I want to rack my brain, not even knowledge, however great its value. I seek in books only to give myself pleasure by honest amusement; or if I study, I seek only the learning that treats of the knowledge of myself and instructs me in how to die well and live well.] (II: 10, 409a, DM 101; 297)

This is just what the companion chapter, "Toutes choses ont leur saison," is all about, that there is a time for everything, and old age is the time to take one's pleasure: "Le jeune doit faire ses apprets, le vieil en jouir" [Youth should make preparations, Old Age should enjoy them] (II: 28, 702a, DM 512; 531*). It is not the time for hard work or for learning something new, as Eudemonidas implied in his jab at the aged Xenocrates, who was still going to school: "quand sçaura cetui cy, ce dit il, s'il apprend encore?" [When will this man know, he said, if he is still learning?] (II: 28, 702a, DM 512; 531*).

In II: 28 Montaigne criticizes Cato the Elder for taking up the study of Greek in his declining years: "qu'en son extreme vieillesse, il se mit à apprendre la langue Grecque . . . ne me semble pas luy estre fort honnorable. C'est proprement ce que nous disons, retomber en enfantillage. Toutes choses ont leur saison, les bonnes & tout" [That in his extreme old age he set himself to learn Greek . . . does not seem to me to be much in his honor. It is exactly what we call falling back into childhood. All things have their season, good ones and all] (II: 28, 702a, DM 512; 531). In II: 10 he says that trying to read Greek in old age is not an appropriate activity for himself either. Concerning his own taste in books, he writes, "Je ne me prends guiere . . . aus Grecs, par ce que mon jugement ne se satisfait pas d'une moyenne intelligence" [I do not much take . . . to those in Greek, because my judgment is not satisfied with a mediocre understanding] (II: 10, 409–10a, DM 102; 297*). In a post-1588 rewording of this passage, he would enhance the parallel by changing "une *moyenne* intelligence" to "une *puerile et apprantisse* intelligence" [a *childish and apprentice* understanding] (II: 10, 410ac; 297), now closely matching the remark that Cato's taking up Greek in his old age was to "retomber en enfantillage." There would now be something childish about reading Greek both for the aged Cato and for the aging Montaigne, but for different reasons. Learning to read Greek was infantile for Cato because only the young should learn new things; reading Greek for Montaigne was to have to put up with only a childlike understanding of a text whose language he had not learned well enough.

Before taking Cato the Elder to task for learning Greek in his dotage, Montaigne compares him unfavorably to his great-grandson and namesake, Cato the Younger. In the 1580–1588 editions, he had written "Ceux qui apparient Caton le censeur au jeune Caton meurtrier de soy-mesme, font à mon opinion grand honneur au premier. Car je les trouve eslongnés d'une extreme distance" [Those who liken Cato the Censor with the younger Cato, who was his own murderer, do great honor to the former; for I find them separated by an extreme distance] (II: 28, 702a and 702n, DM 512; 531). On the Bordeaux copy he replaced this assertion with one that says just the opposite: that those who compare the two "apparient deux belles natures et de formes voisines" [are comparing two beautiful natures of neighboring (that is, similar) forms] (II: 28, 702c; 531*). But after initially elevating Cato the Elder to near-equal status with his grandson (and in fact saying that he exceeded the Younger in military and public service), he again stresses their difference, saying that the Elder could hardly be compared to the Younger in terms of virtue: "Mais la vertu du jeune, outre ce que c'est blaspheme de luy en apparier nulle autre en vigueur, fut bien plus nette. Car qui deschargeroit d'envie et d'ambition celle du censeur, ayant osé chocquer l'honneur de Scipion, en bonté et en toutes parties d'excellence de bien loin plus grand et que luy et que tout homme de son siecle?" [But the virtue of the Younger, besides the fact that it is blasphemy to compare any other with it in vigor, was much more spotless. For who can acquit the Censor of envy and ambition, when he dared to attack the honor of Scipio, a man in goodness and all aspects of excellence far greater than he or any other man of his time?] (II: 28, 702c; 531*).

I bring this up because the contrast between an elder and younger Cato finds a suggestive parallel in the contrast in "Des livres" between the elder and younger Cicero (a name that likewise begins with C and ends with o): Cicero the orator and "Le jeune Cicero, qui n'a ressemblé son pere que de nom" [The younger Cicero, who resembled his father only in name] (II: 10, 415a, DM 114; 302). Montaigne tells an unflattering anecdote about the son, who once had a dinner guest flogged when reminded that the latter had once bragged that his own eloquence was greater than the elder Cicero's. "Voilà un mal courtois hoste" [That was a discourteous host!] (II: 10, 415a, DM 114; 302). To say that the two Ciceros resembled each other in name only is pretty close to saying (from 1580 to 1588) that the two Catos were separated by a great distance or (post-1588) that they could not be compared in virtue, given the elder Cato's attack on a man (Scipio) whose excellence far excelled his own. In fact, the post-1588 addition restates the notion of distance originally present in "je les trouve *eslongnés* d'une extreme distance" when it replaces it with the distance between Cato the Elder and the man he dishonorably attacked, who was "en toutes parties d'excellence de bien *loin* plus grand . . . que luy." And the *excellence* that Cato the Elder so greatly lacked was lacking as well in the elder Cicero: "Quant à Cicero, je suis du jugement commun, que hors la science, il n'y avoit pas beaucoup d'*excellence* en luy" [As for Cicero, I am of the common opinion, that except for learning there was not much *excellence* in him] (II: 10, 415a, DM 113; 302*).

There wasn't much excellence in Cicero's writings, either: "sa façon d'escrire me semble lasche & ennuyeuse" [his writing style seems to me flaccid and boring] (II: 10, 413a, DM 110; 301*). The only good thing about them is that they won't interrupt your sleep: "Ils sont bons pour l'escole, pour le barreau, & pour le sermon, où nous avons loisir de *sommeiller:* & sommes encore un quart d'heure apres asses à temps pour rencontrer le fil du propos" [They are good for the school, for the bar, and for the sermon, where we have leisure to *nap* and are still in time a quarter of an hour later to pick up the thread of the discourse] (II: 10, 414a, DM 111; 301).

The funny thing is, this sets up yet another connection to one of the Catos. Cato the Younger spent the last evening of his life reading a dialogue of Plato's on the immortality of the soul (the *Phaedo*). Montaigne stresses that he did not read it to buck up his courage before committing suicide but rather that "comme celuy *qui n'interrompit pas seulement son sommeil* pour l'importance d'une telle deliberation, il continua aussi sans chois & sans changement ses estudes avec les autres actions acoustumées de sa vie" [but like a man *who would not even interrupt his sleep* out of concern over such a resolve, he also continued, without choice and without change, his studies together with the other customary actions of his life] (II: 28, 703–704a, DM 513–14; 532). So reading Plato is like sleeping in that both are activities that Cato refused to interrupt. But reading or listening to Cicero's orations is an activity that sleep itself can interrupt with no damage done! Nothing is lost by dozing off; you can always pick up the thread because Cicero takes so long to get to the point anyway. Although "sommeil" and "sommeiller" appear forty-one times in the *Essays,* and an entire chapter ("Du dormir," I: 44) is devoted to sleep, nowhere else is sleeping ever associated with texts.

When Montaigne gives us in II: 10 a sample of Cicero's words, they turn out to address the very topic that takes up so much of II: 28, the issue of acting one's age: "Ego vero me minus diu senem esse mallem, quam esse senem, antequam essem" [For my part, in truth, I would rather be old less long than be old before I am old] (II: 10, 416a, DM 115; 303). It is not surprising that the two chapters should not agree, but it is worth noting that they are talking about the same thing. Wise men, Montaigne writes, find that the greatest vice among the old, in whose company he counts himself, is that "nos desseins rajeunissent sans cesse: nous recommençons toujours à vivre: nostre estude & nostre desir devroient quelque fois sentir la vieillesse" [our desires incessantly renew their youth. We are always beginning to live over again. Our study and our desire should sometimes reek of old age] (II: 28, 702a, DM 512–13; 531*). It would appear that Cato the Elder and the elder Cicero agree with each other (Cato living according to the Ciceronian dictum Montaigne quotes) while disagreeing with Montaigne, who would rather be old when he is old than young when no longer young.

In writing in "Des livres" about what he likes and doesn't like to read, Montaigne provides an additional parallel to his assertion in the matching chapter that for every activity there is an appropriate time and an inappropriate one, and that old age is often a determinant: "céte vieille ame poisante ne se laisse plus chatouiller, non seulement à l'Arioste, mais encores au bon Ovide: sa facilité & ses inventions qui m'ont ravy autres-fois, à peine m'entretiennent elles à céte heure" [this heavy old soul of mine no longer lets itself be tickled, not merely by Ariosto, but even by the good Ovid: his facility and inventions, which once enchanted me, hardly entertain me at all now] (II: 10, 410a, DM 102; 298). His taste in reading changes with age, in other words, as the title of the matching chapter asserts: "Toutes choses ont leur saison."

11. Doubly Cruel

"De la cruauté" [Of cruelty] (II: 11) and "Couardise mere de la cruauté" [Cowardice, the mother of cruelty] (II: 27)

Beyond displaying the same key word in their titles, these chapters feature a pair of nearly identical sentences: "Quant à moy en la justice mesme *tout ce qui est au dela de la mort simple me semble pure cruauté*" [As for me, even in justice, *all that is beyond plain death seems to me pure cruelty*] (II: 11, 431a, DM 144; 314) and *"Tout ce qui est au dela de la mort simple, me semble pure cruauté"* [*All that is beyond plain death seems to me pure cruelty*] (II: 27, 700a, DM 511; 530).[16] In both passages (that is, in both chapters) Montaigne goes on to express concern for the state of the souls of those subjected to an execution that goes beyond plain death, and who should not be driven to despair: "nous . . . devrions avoir respect d'en envoyer les *ames* en bon *estat*, ce qui ne se peut, les ayant agitées & *desesperées* par tourmens insuportables" [we ought to have some concern about sending *souls* away in a good *state;* which cannot happen when we have agitated them and made them *desperate* by unbearable tortures] (II: 11, 431a, DM 145; 314*); "je ne sçay ce pendant si nous les jettons au *desespoir.* Car en quel *estat* peut estre *l'ame* d'un homme attendant vintquatre heures la mort brisé sur une rouë . . . ?" [I do not know but that we meanwhile drive them to *despair.* For what can be the *state* of a man's *soul*

---

16. Pierre Villey notes the resemblance in a note on the second passage: "Characteristic sentence that we have read already in essay II: 11" (700n). But he doesn't say what it is characteristic of—the insistent doubling of words and phrases in symmetrically connected chapters.

who is waiting twenty-four hours for death broken on a wheel . . . ?] (II: 27, 701a, DM 511; 530).

In looking for common ground as we have with previous chapter pairs, this time it might seem we find no resistance to overcome, no opportunity to exercise what Montaigne at the outset of one of these chapters calls "La vaillance (de qui c'est l'effect de s'exercer seulement contre la resistence)" [Valor (which acts only to exert itself against resistance)] (II: 27, 693a, DM 507; 524*) and near the beginning of the other he calls virtue: "il semble que le nom de la vertu presupose de la difficulté du combat & du contraste: & qu'elle ne peut estre sans partie" [it seems that the name of virtue presupposes difficulty and contrast, and that it cannot be without an opponent] (II: 11, 422a, DM 127; 306–7*). In a telling post-1588 alteration, Montaigne changed "estre" to "s'exercer," so that those last words would become "et qu'elle ne peut *s'exercer* sans partie" [and that it cannot *exert itself* without opposition]. It seems more than likely that he made this change to complete the parallel with the equivalent passage in the companion chapter: "La vaillance (de qui c'est l'effect de *s'exercer* seulement contre la resistence)." Nowhere else does the infinitive *s'exercer* appear in a context in which something is potentially exerted *against* anything. In the passage from II: 11, there is no "partie" for it to exert itself against; in II: 27, it can only exert itself if there is "resistence."

Furthermore, nowhere else does "exercer" (as either pronominal or non-pronominal infinitive) appear with "contre" [against] than in this passage from II: 27—and in *another* passage from II: 11: "Il faut *exercer* ces inhumains excez *contre* l'escorce, non *contre* le vif" [These inhuman excesses should be *exercised against* the skin, not *against* the living core] (II: 11, 432b; 315). These instances of *[s']exercer* (whether we consider II: 11's "s'exercer sans partie" in conjunction with II: 27's "s'exercer . . . contre" or the latter with II: 11's "exercer . . . contre") "exert themselves" [s'exercent], self-referentially, "against" [contre] each other alone, for they have no counterparts but themselves.

Although Montaigne talks about cruelty in both chapters, he arrives at the topic in different ways. In II: 27 it is announced in the very first sentence: "J'ay souvent oui dire, que la coüardise est mere de cruauté" [I have often heard it said that cowardice is the mother of cruelty] (II: 27, 693a, DM 507; 523). But in II: 11 it is not until past the mid-point (on the eighth of fourteen pages in the Villey edition, the sixteenth of twenty-five in 1580) that cruelty makes its first appearance apart from the title: "Je hay entre autres vices cruellement la cruauté, & par nature & par jugement, comme l'extreme de tous les vices" [Among other vices, I cruelly hate cruelty, both by nature and by judgment, as the extreme of all vices] (II: 11, 429a, DM 141; 313). Up until this point in II: 11 Montaigne had been consistently speaking about how souls like his give only the semblance of virtue, since they are not subject to temptations that must be mastered. "Je ne me suis mis en grand effort pour brider les desirs dequoy je me suis trouvé pressé. Ma vertu c'est une vertu, ou innocence, pour mieux dire, accidentale & fortuite" [I have not put myself to great effort to curb the desires by which I have found myself pressed. My virtue is a virtue, or I should say an innocence, that is accidental and fortuitous] (II: 11, 427a, DM 137–38; 311). Because he comes by it naturally, his aversion to cruelty, for example, is no virtue.

In a strange and striking opposition, while Montaigne in II: 11 has an *aversion* to cruelty because of his own "mollesse" [softness]—"Je hay . . . *cruellement la cruauté* . . . jusques à telle *mollesse* que je ne voy pas égorger un poulet sans desplaisir, & *ois* impatiemment *gemir* un lievre sous les dens des chiens: quoy que ce soit un plaisir violent que la chasse" [I hate . . . *cruelty cruelly* . . . to such a point of *softness* that I cannot see a chicken's neck cut without distress and I cannot bear to *hear* a dying hare *groan* beneath the dogs' teeth, although the chase is a violent pleasure] (II: 11, 429a, DM 141; 313*)—in a 1588 addition to II: 27 he says that men characterized by "mollesse" have a *propensity* to cruelty!

> Et ay par experience apperçeu que cette aigreur et aspreté de courage malitieux et inhumain s'accompaigne coustumierement de *mollesse* feminine. J'en ay veu des plus *cruels,* subjets à pleurer aiséement et pour des causes frivoles. Alexandre, tyran de Pheres, ne pouvoit souffrir d'*ouyr* au theatre le jeu des tragedies, de peur que ses citoyens ne le vissent *gemir* aus malheurs de Hecuba et d'Andromache, luy qui, sans pitié faisoit *cruellement* meurtrir tant de gens tous les jours.
>
> [And I have found by experience that the bitterness and hardness of a malicious and inhuman heart are usually accompanied by feminine *softness*. I have observed that some of the most *cruel* are subject to weeping easily and for frivolous reasons. Alexander, tyrant of Pheres, could not bear to hear tragedies played in the theater for fear that his citizens might see him groaning at the misfortunes of Hecuba and Andromache, he who, without pity, had so many people *cruelly* murdered every day.] (II: 27, 693b; 523–24*)

Just as Montaigne cannot stand to see a chicken slaughtered nor to *hear* the *groan* ("& *ois* impatiemment *gemir*") of the dying hare, the tyrant Alexander could not bear to see and *hear* ("ne pouvoit souffrir d'*ouyr*") the sufferings of fictional characters on the stage, for fear his subjects would see him *groan* [*gemir*]. Montaigne hates cruelty *cruelly* [*cruellement*]; the tyrant *cruelly* [*cruellement*] put people to death every day. These lexemes (*cruauté / cruel / cruellement, ouïr, gémir*) appear together in no other chapter.

It is cowardly camp-followers who are cruel, not the brave. Valor acts only to overcome resistance and therefore

> s'arreste à voir l'ennemi à sa merci: mais la lascheté pour dire qu'elle est aussi de la feste, n'ayant peu se meslier à ce premier rolle prend pour sa part le second, du massacre & du sang. Les meurtres des victoires se font ordinairement par le peuple & par les officiers du bagage: & ce qui fait voir tant de cruautés inouies aus guerres populaires, c'est que céte canaille de vulgaire s'aguerit & se gendarme à s'ensanglanter jusques aus coudes & à deschiqueter un corps à ses piedz, n'ayant resentiment de null'autre vaillance. Comme les chiens coüards, qui deschirent en la maison & mordent les peaus des bestes sauvages, qu'ilz n'ont osé attaquer aux champs.
>
> [stops when it sees the enemy at its mercy. But cowardice, in order to say that it is also in the game, having been unable to take part in this first act, takes as its part the second, that of massacre and bloodshed. The murders in victories are usually done by the mob and the baggage officers. And what causes so many unheard-of cruelties in wars in which the people take part is that that beastly rabble tries to be warlike and brave by ripping up a body at their feet and bloodying themselves up to their elbows, having no sense of any other kind of valor. Like cowardly dogs, that in the house tear and bite the skins of wild beasts that they did not dare attack in the fields.] (II: 27, 693–94a, DM 507–8; 524*)

In a 1588 addition to the matching chapter, Montaigne inserted a counterpart to what those dogs do: Artaxerxes softened the harshness of Persia's ancient laws by ordaining that the lords who had failed in their charge, "au lieu qu'on les souloit *foïter,* fussent despouillés, et leurs vestements *foitez* pour eux" [instead of being whipped, as was the custom, should be stripped, and their clothes whipped in their place] (II: 11, 432b; 315). As dogs took out their aggressions on the animals' skins (skins that could be turned into clothing), Artaxerxes whipped clothes instead of their owners. In a post-1588 addition to II: 27, Montaigne found an equivalent to match this painless whipping: Aristotle, upon hearing that someone had spoken ill of him, said "Qu'il face plus . . . qu'il me *fouëtte,* pourveu que je n'y soy pas" [Let him do more . . . let him *whip* me, provided I am not there] (II: 27, 695c; 525).

In another late addition, he inserts into II: 11 a subtle allusion to the baggage officers and rabble in II: 27 who display "la lascheté pour dire qu'elle est aussi de la *feste*" [the cowardice that wants to say it is also in the *game*] and consequently behave like dogs (the dogs who attack the skins of beasts they were afraid of confronting when alive), and that do so at an inappropriate time (when the battle is over): "Je ne creins point à dire la tendresse de ma nature si puerile que ne je puis pas bien refuser à mon *chien la feste* qu'il m'offre hors de saison ou qu'il me demande" [I am not afraid to admit that my nature is so tender, so childish, that I cannot well refuse my *dog the play* he offers me or asks of me outside the proper time] (II: 11, 435c; 318). There is softness in both instances (the *mollesse* of the cruel, whether they be tyrants like Alexander of Pheres or the post-battle crowd in one passage, and Montaigne's childishly tender nature in the other), as well as the untimely (after the battle is already decided in one case, "hors de saison" in the other) demand for "la feste." Here as in so many other instances Montaigne takes elements from a story or a discussion on one chapter and rearranges them in the matching one, often with a reversal: all of these dogs demand a "feste," those in II: 27 because of their softness, the one in II: 11 because of Montaigne's, whose softness is elsewhere in that chapter called by the same name as that of the rabble and the dogs in II: 27, "mollesse."

12. Opposable Thumbs

"Apologie de Raimond Sebond" [Apology for Raymond Sebond] (II: 12) and "Des pouces" [Of thumbs] (II: 26)

Of all the chapter pairings, this seems the most unlikely. Eventually running to more than 60,000 words, "Apologie de Raimond Sebond" is a book-length disquisition on the limits of human reason; "Des pouces" focuses its fewer than 300 words on thumbs. Yet that very disparity brings them together, for as II: 12 is the longest chapter in the Book Two, II: 26 is the shortest—extremes that, as we will see, touch.

We can rest assured Montaigne has something up his sleeve when we discover that in all editions published in his lifetime the only other thumbs to be found in all the *Essays* show up—you guessed it—in the "Apologie": "Il ne faut que sçavoir que le lieu de Mars loge au milieu du triangle de la main, celuy de Venus au *pouce* & de Mercure au petit doigt" [A man need only know that the seat of Mars is located in the middle of the triangle of the hand, that of Venus on the *thumb,* that of Mercury on the little finger]

(II: 12, 560a, DM 328; 420). The context for this is palm reading influenced by astrology, which Montaigne dismisses as yet another instance of human folly. But that the thumb is the seat of Venus is not so easily dismissed, for he shows how sexy it can be in "Des pouces": "Les Grecz l'appellent αντι-χειρ, comme qui diroit une autre main. Et il semble que parfois les Latins les prennent aussi en ce sens de main entiere. Sed nec vocibus excitata blandis / Molli *pollice* nec rogata surgit" [The Greeks call it αντιχειρ, as though to say "another hand." And it seems that sometimes the Latins also take it in the sense of the entire hand: "Neither sweet words of persuasion nor the help of her voluptuous thumb can get it erect"[17]] (II: 26, 691a, DM 507–8; 523*). These two erotic thumbs (one of which may be a metonym for a hand) were spotted by Fausta Garavini, though without reference to the structural connection that secretly links these chapters.[18] She calls the chapter on thumbs "perhaps the most disconcerting" of all the chapters, "an absolutely opaque text, that seems to reveal no reason for why Montaigne decided to discuss this topic" (105). Garavini notes as well that it disproves Villey's theory that the 1580 edition was imperfect but perfectible as Montaigne added more revealing comments about himself in subsequent editions, for he adds none to this chapter. For her, "this text seems to enclose the knot of something unsaid" (108), some unspeakable psychic phantasm, because thumbs for Montaigne are a stand-in for the penis. After quoting the following passage—

> Tacitus recite que parmy certains rois barbares, pour faire une obligation asseurée, leur maniere estoit de joindre estroitement leurs mains droites l'une à l'autre & s'entrelasser les pouces: & quand à force de les presser le sang en estoit monté au bout, ils les blessoient de quelque legiere pointe & puis se les entresucçoint.
>
> [Tacitus reports that among certain barbarian kings, to make an obligation binding, the custom was to join their right hands tightly together and to interlace their thumbs; and when by dint of pressing them the blood had risen to the tips, they pricked them lightly and then sucked each other's blood.] (II: 26, 691a, DM 505; 523*)

—she comments: "The pierced thumb and the blood that comes out of it are here metaphors for the engorged member and ejaculation" (107). I would

---

17. I have adopted Screech's translation (784), enhanced by the "voluptueux" by which Balsamo et al. render "Molli," which Screech does not translate.

18. *Monstres et chimères: Montaigne, le texte et le fantasme*. Translated by Isabel Picon (Paris: Honoré Champion, 1993), 106.

go even farther, and say that the whole scene suggests mutual fellatio—not in Tacitus' text, but in Montaigne's quoting it just before quoting Martial's epigram about the thumb's (or hand's) failure to bring about an erection.

But there is something else going on in "Des pouces." As in other chapter pairs, here too there emerge a number of allusions passing from one chapter to the other and they are not all sexual. The passage about thumb-sucking kings includes two: (1) The only other instance of sucking in the *Essays* (apart from a post-1588 substitution of "sucent" [suck] for "espuisent" [exhaust] in Book Three[19]) appears in the "Apologie": "L'humeur que *succe* la racine d'un arbre, elle se faict tronc, feuille et fruit" [The moisture that the root of a tree *sucks* up becomes trunk, leaf, and fruit] (II: 12, 599a, DM 388; 453). (2) What barbarian kings did to their thumbs before they pierced and sucked them—"*s'entrelasser* les pouces" [to *interlace* their thumbs]—happens to fingers in the "Apologie": "À manier une balle d'arquebouse soubs le second doigt, celuy du milieu estant *entrelassé* par dessus, il faut extremement se contraindre, pour advouer qu'il n'y en ait qu'une, tant le sens nous en represente deux" [When rolling a harquebus bullet under the forefinger, the middle finger being *entwined* above it, we have to force ourselves hard to admit that there is only one, so strongly does our sense represent two to us] (II: 12, 592a, DM 376; 448*). Entwined fingers, entwined thumbs: this only happens in II: 12 and II: 26, where enough other *entrelassements* occur that it seems to be a running theme:

> Aux spectacles de Rome il se voyoit ordinairement des elephans dressez à se mouvoir & dancer au son de la voix des dances à plusieurs *entrelasseures,* coupures & diverses cadances tres-difficiles à aprendre. Il s'en est veu, qui en leur privé rememoroient leur leçon & s'exerçoient par soin & par estude pour n'estre tancez & batus de leurs maistres.

> [In the spectacles in Rome it was quite usual to see elephants trained to move and dance, to the sound of the human voice, dances with many *interlacing movements,* changes of step and cadenzas, all very hard to learn. Some of them have been seen in private going over their lesson and practicing with care and study, so as not to be scolded and beaten by their masters.] (II: 12, 465a, DM 195; 341*)

---

19. In "De la vanité": "s'il advenoit, comme disent aucuns jardiniers, que les roses et violettes naissent plus odoriferantes pres des aulx et des oignons, d'autant qu'ils espuisent et tirent à eux ce qu'il y a de mauvaise odeur en la terre" [if it happened to be true, as some gardeners say, that roses and violets spring up more fragrant near garlic and onions, because these exhaust and draw to themselves whatever there is that smells bad in the ground] (III: 9, 972b, DM 418; 742*).

These *entrelasseures* were evidence of the surprising intelligence of animals; so too are those from which halcyons build their floating nests (and even more so, since the elephants were taught their dances but the birds construct their nests without human help):

> Mais nulle suffisance n'a encores peu attaindre à la cognoissance de céte merveilleuse fabrique, de quoy l'halcyon compose le nid pour ses petitz & en deviner la matiere. Plutarque qui en a veu & manié plusieurs, pense que ce soit des arestes de quelque poisson qu'elle conjoint et lie ensemble, les *entrelassant* les unes de long, les autres de travers, & adjoustant des courbes & des arrondissemens, tellement qu'en fin elle en forme un vaisseau rond prest à voguer.
>
> [But no cleverness has yet been able to attain the knowledge of the marvelous workmanship by which the halcyon builds the nest for her young, and to guess the material of it. Plutarch, who saw and handled several of them, thinks that they are the bones of some fish that she joins and binds together, *interlacing* them, some lengthwise, the others crosswise, and adding ribs and hoops so that at last it forms a round vessel ready to float.] (II: 12, 480–81a, DM 228–29; 354*)

Montaigne added yet another to the series at some point after 1588, the "*entrelassemens* des corps celestes" [*interlacings* of the heavenly bodies] (II: 12, 536c; 400), bringing the number to four.

There are *entrelasseures* elsewhere in the *Essays*. Curiously, none of them involve material objects (the elephants themselves in their dances, fish bones in halcyons' nests, heavenly bodies, fingers—and thumbs, in "Des pouces"), but instead are composed entirely of words: "l'imposture des mots captieusement *entrelassez*" [the imposture of words captiously *interlaced*] (I: 25, 143a; 105); "On tient quatre ou cinq ans à entendre les mots et les coudre en clauses . . . et autres cinq . . . à les sçavoir brefvement mesler et *entrelasser* de quelque subtile façon" [Schoolmasters keep us for four or five years learning to understand words and stitch them into sentences . . . another five . . . learning how to mix and *interweave* them briefly in some subtle way] (I: 26, 168a; 124–25*); "cette implication et *entrelasseure* de language" [this complication and *interlacing* of language] (III: 8, 927b; 707); "sans l'*entrelasser* de paroles" [without *interlacing* it with words] (III: 9, 995b; 761*). Montaigne's consistency in making the interlacings outside of II: 12 / II: 26 consist of words, by contrast to those within that intratext, suggests he knew what he was doing, which has the effect of tightening the link between the *entrelasse-*

ment going on in "Des pouces" and those taking place in the "Apologie." Of these the most striking is the entwining of fingers that not only matches that other entwining of digits in II: 26 but by creating the illusion of two from one uncannily replicates its own duplication.

It is yet more evidence that Montaigne distributes certain words and expressions with extreme care, so that they create a hidden network of allusions; those of particular interest to us appear in symmetrically-related chapters. Here is another instance: "Les medecins disent que les pouces sont les maitres doig[t]s de la main, & que leur etymologie Latine vient de *pollere*, qui signifie *exceller sur les* autres" [The doctors say that the thumbs are the master fingers of the hand and that their etymology in Latin is from *pollere*, which means to *excel over the* others] (II: 26, 691a, DM 505–06; 523*). The last six words disappeared in a post-1588 alteration, but until then—which is to say in all editions published in Montaigne's lifetime—they found a unique echo in a passage in the "Apologie" where Montaigne makes fun of the philosophers who said that Ulysses on Circe's island would have done better to drink the cup of folly than to allow himself to be changed into a beast: "Ce n'est donc plus par la raison, par le discours & par l'ame que nous *excellons sur les* bestes? c'est par nostre beauté" [Then it is no longer by our reason, our intelligence, and our soul that we *excel over the* beasts? It is by our beauty] (II: 12, 486a, DM 236; 358*). The echoing expression composed of the verb *exceller* + "sur les" appears nowhere else. It suggests that the superiority of thumbs to fingers parallels the superiority of man over the other animals, although in a typical Montaignian reversal man's alleged superiority is undercut throughout the "Apologie" while the thumb's is stoutly maintained in "Des pouces."

The same passage in "Des pouces" is the site of another unique echo, the one formed by "pollere" with its only other appearance in the *Essays*, in the "Apologie":

> Voilà de nostre siecle une grandeur infinie de terre ferme, . . . une partie esgale à peu prez en grandeur à celle que nous cognoissons, qui vient d'estre descouverte. Les Geographes d'à céte heure ne faillent pas d'asseurer que meshuy tout est trouvé & que tout est veu,
> Nam quod adest praesto placet, & *pollere* videtur.
>
> [Behold in our century an infinite extent of terra firma, . . . a portion nearly equal in size to the one we know, which has just been discovered. The geographers of the present time do not fail to assure us that now all is discovered and all is seen, "For what is at hand pleases, and seems *to be best*."] (II: 12, 572a, DM 351; 430*)

It was perhaps not by chance that Montaigne chose to plant the "pollere" that points to the other "pollere" (in II: 26) here, in an evocation of what in "Des cannibales" he calls "cet *autre monde* qui a esté descouvert" [that *other world* which has been discovered] (I: 31, 203a; 150), for in "Des pouces" we have seen him characterize the thumb as "une *autre main*" [*another hand*]. As one "pollere" points to the other, the other world points to the other hand. The new world is "esgale à peu prez en grandeur" [nearly equal in size] to the one we know, which isn't true of the chapters when we count their pages, but is true of them when we recognize that each occupies an equal place in the collection of symmetrical pairs, as well as in the list of chapters without regard to their symmetry. The discoveries we are making about them help assuage the dismay we might feel that as puny and seemingly silly a chapter as "Des pouces" should be set up to counterbalance as important and imposing a chapter as the "Apologie."

Montaigne was fully aware of the scandalous inequality of their length. He was in on the joke (he should have been, since it was his). That's why he calls the thumb "une autre main," and claims its etymology means to excel over the others (over the other fingers, apparently). Thumbs have the power of life and death, as he goes on in "Des pouces" to show when he alludes to audiences at gladiatorial contests using their thumbs to decide the fate of the combatants.[20] In the only other appearance of a thumb in the *Essays,* in a post-1588 addition to "De l'yvrongnerie," he brags about his father's ability to "faire le tour de la table sur son pouce" [to do a turn over the table on his thumb] (II: 2, 344c; 248)—a paternal thumb strong enough to take the place of a hand. In balancing "Des pouces" against the "Apologie" (itself a defense, ostensibly, of the theological treatise by Sebond his father had set him the task of translating), Montaigne duplicates in letters the feat his father performed in reality, showing the unexpected power of a thumb to bear weight.

More than that, the "Apologie" is in fact about a hand, God's:

> Aussi n'est il pas croyable que toute céte machine n'ayt quelques marques empreintes de *la main* de ce grand architecte. . . . Il a laissé en ces haults ouvrages le caractere de sa divinité: & ne tient qu'à nostre imbecillité que

---

20. Contrary to popular opinion today, Montaigne reports that thumbs up meant death and thumbs down life. Anthony Corbeill in a recent survey of Latin and other texts on the subject ("Thumbs in Ancient Rome: 'Pollex' as Index," *Memoirs of the American Academy in Rome* 42 [1997]: 1–21), says that "Des pouces" is "The only discussion I have found that corresponds with my own conclusions" (1n2).

nous ne le puissions descouvrir. . . . Sebond s'est travaillé à ce digne estude & nous monstre comment il n'est nulle piece du monde, qui desmante son facteur.

[It is not credible that this whole machine should not have on it some marks imprinted by *the hand* of this great architect. . . . He has left the stamp of his divinity on these lofty works, and it is only because of our imbecility that we cannot discover it. . . . Sebond has labored at this worthy study, and shows us how there is no part of the world that belies its maker.] (II: 12, 446–47a, DM 163–64; 326)

"Des pouces" opposes itself to the "Apologie" as the thumb to the hand, an equal contest, if we can believe Montaigne. But at the same time the *Essays* are Montaigne's creation, as the world is God's, and just as we can see God's handprint in the latter we can see Montaigne's thumbprint in the former, particularly in the intratext these two chapters form. We have seen that when he wrote one he was thinking of, and was writing or rewriting, the other. We have seen that in the beginning—in 1580, and up until some point after 1588—the only thumbs in French to be found in the *Essays* were in II: 12 and II: 26, prominently displayed in the latter, tucked away almost out of sight in the huge mass of out of the former but we would have only our imbecility to blame if we could not discover it. Not only that, but at first (from 1580 to 1588) the only other Latin thumb besides those in II: 26 ("Molli *pollice* nec rogata," "laudabit *pollice* ludum," "converso *pollice* vulgi") was this one in II: 12:

Ce que ma force ne peut descouvrir, je ne laisse pas de le sonder & essayer: & en retastant & pestrissant céte nouvelle matiere, la remuant & l'eschaufant j'ouvre à celuy, qui me suit, quelque facilité pour en jouir plus à son ayse, & la luy rendz plus souple, & plus maniable. Ut hymettia sole / Cera remollescit, tractataque *pollice,* / multas / Vertitur in facies, ipsoque fit utilis usu.

[I do not leave off sounding and testing what my powers cannot discover; and by handling again and kneading this new material, stirring it and heating it, I open up to whoever follows me some facility to enjoy it more at his ease, and make it more supple and manageable for him: "As Hymettian wax grows softer in the sun, / Takes many shapes when molded by the *thumb,* / And thus by usage useful does become."] (II: 12, 560a, DM 330; 421)

In a self-naming way, this *pollice* bears Montaigne's thumbprint, as he worked and reworked the "Apologie" to make it a worthy partner for "Des pouces," handling and kneading the text so that some future reader—"qui me suit" [who follows me]—could find that *pollice,* and discern its importance. Significantly, this passage does not occur in isolation but is part of the same discussion in which the other thumb, the one in French (the seat "de Venus au *pouce*" [of Venus on the *thumb*]), appeared—on the same page in the Villey edition (560a). The argument goes thus: palmistry is bunk; human knowledge has certain defined limits, but progress is possible as one seeker may succeed where another has failed; the arts and sciences do not come out fully formed from a mold but are worked and reworked as a bear licks her cubs into shape, as in my own case I handle and knead material in such a way that someone coming after me (who follows me in both senses: comes after and understands what I am up to) will find it more useful, like Hymettan wax molded by the thumb.

But as Mary McKinley reminds us,[21] the passage he quotes ("Ut hymettia . . . ") comes from Ovid's version of the story of Pygmalion, from which Montaigne had quoted lines that immediately precede this passage at the conclusion to "De l'affection des peres aux enfans" in the context of an author's paternal affection for the book that is his child:

> Pygmalion, qui, ayant basty une statue de femme de beauté singuliere, il devint si éperdument espris de l'amour forcené de ce sien ouvrage, qu'il falut qu'en faveur de sa rage les dieux la luy vivifiassent, Tentatum mollescit ebur, positóque rigore / Subsedit digitis.
>
> [Pygmalion, who after building a statue of a woman of singular beauty, became so madly and frantically smitten with love of his work that the gods, for the sake of his passion, had to bring it to life for him: "Its hardness gone, the ivory softens, yields / Beneath his fingers."] (II: 8, 402a; 293)

Thus the material he molds with his thumb really is the book itself, the text in which thumbs self-referentially appear in symmetrically placed chapters. He invites "celuy, qui me suit" to imitate Pygmalion and to place his own thumbs on the mold that he has softened for us. But part of his softening is to have left for his reader to find and apply to this passage in II: 12 the literal

---

21. In *Words in a Corner: Studies in Montaigne's Latin Quotations* (Lexington, KY: French Forum Publishers, 1981), 20–26. The two quotations from Ovid are also discussed by Richard L. Regosin in *Montaigne's Unruly Brood: Textual Engendering and the Challenge to Paternal Authority* (Berkeley: University of California Press, 1996), 125.

thumbs he has placed in the matching chapter, II: 26. Even here, when he seems particularly open to letting his readers bring his text to completion, he is already there before us; he has already done that completing work. It just remains for his readers to discover it.

13. Eyes Wide Shut

"De juger de la mort d'autruy" [*Of judging someone else's death*] *(II: 13) and "De ne contrefaire le malade"* [*Of not pretending to be sick*] *(II: 25)*

It is hard to tell if someone is really being courageous when confronted by his imminent demise, according to Montaigne, because so many in that situation lull themselves into a false sense of security. Few with a terminal illness really believe they will die. We think of others who have been just as sick but haven't died, and imagine that God can always pull off a miracle. We think of everything in relation to ourselves, and that the universe would be affected by our demise and has compassion for us.

> D'autant que nostre *veüe alterée* se represente les choses de mesmes, & nous est advis qu'elles luy faillent à mesure qu'elle leur faut: comme ceus qui voyagent en mer, ausquels il semble que les montaignes, les campaignes, les villes, le ciel & la terre aille mesme bransle, & quant & quant eus. D'ou il s'ensuit que nous estimons grande chose nostre mort, & qui ne se passe pas si aisément ny sans solenne consultation des astres.
>
> [because our *altered vision* represents things to itself as being likewise altered and we think they are failing it in proportion as it is failing them, like travelers at sea, for whom mountains, countryside, cities, heaven, and earth move right along with them and at the same pace. And so it follows that we reckon our death to be a great event, something which does not happen lightly nor without solemn consultations among the heavenly bodies.][22] (II: 13, 605–6a, DM 398–99; 458*)

---

22. I adopt Screech's translation of the last sentence (685). Unlike Frame, who renders the last words as "not without solemn consultation of the stars," Screech understands "des" in "consultation des astres" to be a subjective, not an objective, genitive. Montaigne's post-1588 addition at this point of Seneca's words "tot circa unum caput tumultuantes deos" [so many gods in an uproar about one single head] makes it all the more likely that he meant the stars consulting among themselves, as the gods were themselves in tumult.

Such people are unaware of the danger they are in. Pretending to be healthier than they are, they find their counterpart in the counterpart chapter in people who pretend to be sick. Those in II: 13 counterfeit health; those in II: 25 counterfeit illness. Not only do the terminally ill in II: 13 have false hopes of survival, but they also have an altered vision of the universe that leads them to think that unless the stars are concerned by their demise they aren't going to die. It is a question of seeing clearly or not, a theme to which Montaigne will return a little later in II: 13 when he writes of those facing a violent death:

> Nul ne se peut dire être resolu à la mort . . . qui ne peut la soutenir *les yeux ouvers*. Ceux qu'on voit aux supplices courir à leur fin . . . ne le font pas de vraye resolution, ils se veulent oster le temps de la considerer . . . comme ceux qui se jetent dans les dangiers, comme dans la mer *à yeux clos*.
>
> [No man can be said to be resolute in death . . . who cannot sustain it *with open eyes*. Those whom we see at executions running to meet their end . . . do not do so out of resolution; they want to deprive themselves of the time to consider it . . . like those who plunge into dangers, as into the sea, *with their eyes closed*.] (II: 13, 608a, DM 403; 460–61*)

This "veüe alterée," these "yeux ouvers" and these "yeux clos"—these variations on impaired vision find their counterpart in II: 25, for there Montaigne gives us six instances of impaired vision (four of which are voluntary and two involuntary), and four out of the six examples he provides of counterfeiting illness involve the eyes. Here they all are in the order in which they appear:

> 1. Martial tells of a man who in order to avoid court functions pretended to suffer from gout. To be more convincing, he oiled and wrapped his legs, and completely imitated the behavior and countenance of a gouty man. In the end, fortune did him the favor of giving him the condition for real.
> 2. Appian tells of a man fleeing the Roman triumvirs who to disguise himself put a patch on one eye, but when it was safe to remove it discovered he had become blind in that eye.
> 3. Reading in Froissart about the vow some young Englishmen made to keep their left eye covered until they had accomplished some feat of arms against the French, Montaigne amuses himself with the thought that they might have found themselves "tous éborgnés" [all

one-eyed] (II: 25, 689a, DM 502-3; 521) when they got back home to the sweethearts to whom they had made that vow.

4.-6. "Les meres ont raison de tancer leurs enfans, quand ilz contrefont *les borgnes, les boiteux & les bicles* & tels autres defautz de la personne" [Mothers are right to scold their children when they imitate *one-eyed, lame, and cross-eyed* people, and other such personal defects] (II: 25, 689a, DM 503; 521). For young bodies can acquire a bad twist by such behavior; besides, fortune loves to take us at our word and I have heard tell of many who have become sick after faking an illness.

The "tels autres defautz" being too vague to put into either category, this amounts to two counterfeit leg ailments (the "gouteux" and the "boiteux") vs. four counterfeit eye ailments (three "borgnes" and one allusion to "bicles"). But so intent is Montaigne on focusing on instances of altered vision that he introduces two more instances of blindness that have nothing to do with counterfeiting a malady, even though that is what the chapter is supposed to be about. Here is the first:

Mais alongeons ce chapitre & le bigarrons d'une autre piece à propos de la cecité. Pline conte d'un qui songeant estre aveugle en dormant s'en trouva l'endemain sans aucune maladie precedente. La force de l'imagination peut bien ayder à cela, comme j'ay dit ailleurs, & semble que Pline soit de cet advis. Mais il est plus vray-semblable, que les mouvemens que le corps sentoit au dedens, desquels les medecins trouveront s'il veulent la cause, qui luy ostoient la veüe, furent occasion du songe.

[But let us lengthen this chapter and variegate it with another piece apropos of blindness. Pliny tells of a man who, dreaming in his sleep that he was blind, found himself so the next day, without any previous illness. The power of imagination can indeed contribute to such results, as I have said elsewhere, and Pliny seems to be of this opinion. But it is more likely that the movements which the body felt within, of which the doctors may find out the cause, if they will, and which deprived him of his sight, were the occasion of the dream.] (II: 25, 689a, DM 503)

So it is not even a case of involuntarily counterfeiting blindness, nor of the thought (the dream) bringing about the change in the body, but of the ailment creating the thought.

The other instance of blindness that he tacks on to the chapter, unlike this one, has no connection at all to the relation between imagination and illness, mind and body (a relation that does have some relevance to faking illness: one is aware of the malady one is counterfeiting). But it has a very strong connection to what he says in II: 13 about how "nostre veüe alterée se represente les choses de mesmes, & nous est advis qu'elles luy faillent à mesure qu'elle leur faut" [our *altered vision* represents things to itself as being likewise altered and we think they are failing it in proportion as it is failing them]:

> Adjoutons encore un'histoire voisine de ce propos, que Seneque recite en l'une de ses lettres. Tu sçais, dit il, . . . que Harpaste la folle de ma femme est demeurée chez moy pour charge hereditaire. . . . Céte folle a subitement perdu la veüe. Je te recite chose estrange, mais veritable. Elle ne sent point qu'elle soit aveugle, & presse incessamment son gouverneur de l'en emmener, par ce qu'elle dict que ma maison est obscure.
>
> [Let us add one more story close to this subject, which Seneca tells in one of his letters. "You know," he says, . . . "that Harpaste, my wife's fool, has stayed at my house as a hereditary charge. . . . This fool has suddenly lost her sight. I am telling you something strange, but true. She does not realize that she is blind, and constantly urges her keeper to take her out, because she says my house is dark."] (II: 25, 689a, DM 504; 522)

Harpaste's attitude toward her blindness is about as good an illustration one could imagine of how our "veüe alterée" makes us think the things around us are failing our sight, as in her case they are making themselves invisible to her eyes (making her think there is not enough light in the house), and do so in proportion to our altered vision failing in its duty to represent those things around us. Our vision, like hers, is failing. We project our own failing onto our surroundings, as boat passengers project their own movement onto the shore. Seneca draws a moral from Harpaste's behavior: "Ce que nous rions en elle, je te prie croire qu'il advient à chacun de nous: nul ne connoit estre avare, nul convoiteux. Encore les aveugles demandent un guide, nous nous fourvoions de nous mesme" [What we laugh at in her, I pray you to believe happens to each one of us: no one knows that he is avaricious or covetous. The blind at least ask for a guide; we go astray of our own accord] (II: 25, 689a, DM 504; 522). While Seneca, as Montaigne paraphrases him, draws from Harpaste's unawareness of her condition a lesson about our blindness to our moral shortcomings, the essayist uses Seneca's words for his own purposes, making them echo what he writes in the other chapter. There, he says that most who are so sick they are going to die refuse to acknowledge that fact; here, he quotes Seneca speaking of another group of people who don't acknowledge how sick they are either:

> Et cela mesme que *nous ne sentons pas estre malades* nous rend la guerison plus malaisée. Si nous ne commençons de bonne heure à nous penser, quand aurons nous pourveu à tant de plaies & à tant de maus. Si avons nous une tres-douce medecine que la philosophie.
>
> [And the very fact that *we do not realize that we are sick* makes our cure more difficult. If we do not soon begin to tend ourselves, when will we have provided for so many sores and so many maladies? Yet we have a very sweet medicine in philosophy.] (II: 25, 689–90a, DM 504–5; 522)

He means moral sickness, but the parallel with the physical sickness in the other chapter is striking, and surely intentional. All the more so for the fact that in both chapters the unawareness of the seriousness of one's malady (bodily illness in II: 13, moral sickness in II: 25) is due to impaired vision: the "veüe alterée" that prevents those about to die from taking cognizance of that fact, and the way Seneca likens us to "les aveugles" (except that the latter know they need a guide, while we "nous nous fourvoions de nous mesme").

Montaigne follows his paraphrase of Seneca with these words: "Voila ce que dit Seneque, qui m'a emporté hors de mon propos: mais il y a du profit au change" [That is what Seneca says, which has carried me away from my subject, but there is profit in the change] (II: 25, 690a, DM 505; 522*). The profit is that both Seneca's story of Harpaste and his commentary on it allow Montaigne to enhance this chapter's connections to the other, even though it carries him away from the stated topic of the danger of pretending to be ill. Indeed, those of us to whom Seneca refers who do not realize how sick we are come close to counterfeiting health, which is just the opposite of counterfeiting illness—but is precisely what Montaigne accuses the terminally ill in II: 13 of doing.

Consequently, when Montaigne gives a scientific explanation for the blindness that can result from keeping a patch over one's eye for too long, his words may have a self-referential dimension:

> Il est possible que l'action de la veüe s'estoit hebetée, pour avoir été si long temps sans exercice & que la force vifve s'étoit toute rejetée en l'autre oeil. Car nous sentons evidemment que l'oeil que nous tenons couvert r'envoie à son compagnon quelque partie de son effect.

[It is possible that the power of sight had been weakened through having been so long without exercise, and that the visual power had wholly transferred itself to the other eye. For we palpably feel that an eye which we keep covered up sends some part of its activity to its companion.] (II: 25, 688a, DM 502; 521*)

In these paired chapters (as in all other paired chapters, but especially these because both focus on impaired vision) it seems that something is communicated in a strange way between them, something like the "force vifve" that can pass from one eye to its symmetrical other. Put another way, we need to read the chapters stereoscopically, gazing at two chapters at once, an eye to each, and both properly aligned. As opposed to reading one at a time, as if we were one-eyed ("borgnes"), or to look in two unrelated directions at once, as if we were cross-eyed ("bicles").

14. Equivalent Equivalents

> *"Comme nostre esprit s'empesche soy mesmes"* [How our mind hinders itself] (II: 14) and *"De la grandeur romaine"* [Of the greatness of Rome] (II: 24)

Of II: 14 Balsamo et al. have this to say:

> This brief chapter . . . is no more than a note a few lines in length, a fragment of an argument on the limits of human knowledge and on the misery of the human condition, propped up by some mathematical paradoxes and a maxim of Pliny's. Maybe it was a page written in preparation for the *Apologie de Raimond de Sebond* that Montaigne preserved, though not without modifying some details through successive editions (1629).

Similarly, II: 24 is in their opinion simply a "brief note" (1667). Such are the conclusions to which the limitations of a one-eyed reading would condemn us. Fortunately, there is another way to look at these chapters—namely, to look at them together.

"C'est une plaisante imagination de concevoir un esprit balancé justement entre deux pareilles envyes" [It is an amusing conception to imagine a mind exactly balanced between two equal desires], Montaigne writes as he begins II: 14.

Car il est indubitable qu'il ne prendra jamais parti, d'autant que l'inclination & le chois porte inequalité & qui nous logeroit entre la bouteille & le jambon avec pareille envie de boire & de menger, il n'y auroit sans doute remede que de mourir de soif & de faim.

[For it is indubitable that it will never decide, since inclination and choice imply inequality in value; and if we were placed between the bottle and the ham with an equal appetite for drinking and for eating, there would doubtless be no solution but to die of thirst and of hunger.] (II: 14, 611a, DM 407–8; 462)

In reading the previous chapter pair (II: 13 and II: 25) we saw Montaigne warn us of the danger of being one-eyed when we don't have to be, and in a metafictional sense encourage us to read his chapters in twos, to look for how each is in a hidden way the other's double. In the current pair (II: 14 and II: 24) we see him once more talking of two things that are alike, though more obviously so, and of focusing one's attention simultaneously on both. But now the danger comes from focusing one's attention on two things that are *too much* alike! Yet that danger is illusory, for there is no such thing as absolute equality:

Pour pourvoir à cet inconvenient, les Stoiciens quand on leur demande d'où vient en nostre ame le chois de deux choses indifferentes, & que faict que d'*un grand nombre d'escus* nous en prenions plus tost l'un que l'autre estant tous pareilz & n'y ayant nulle raison qui nous pousse au chois. Ils repondent que ce mouvement de l'ame est extraordinaire & déreglé venant en nous d'une impulsion estrangiere, accidentale, & fortuite. Il se pourroit dire, ce me semble plustost, que nulle chose ne se presente à nous, où il n'y ait quelque difference, pour legiere qu'elle soit, & que ou à la veüe, ou à l'atouchement, il y a tousjours quelque chois, qui nous touche & attire, quoy que ce soit imperceptiblement.

[To provide against this difficulty, the Stoics, when they are asked whence comes the choice in our soul between two indifferent things and what makes us take one rather than the other out of *a large number of one-crown pieces* when they are all alike and there is no reason which inclines us to a preference, answer that this movement of the soul is extraordinary and irregular, coming from an external, accidental and fortuitous impulse in us. It might rather be said, it seems to me, that nothing presents itself to us in which there is not some difference, however slight; and that either to the sight or to the touch, there is always some choice that attracts us, though it be imperceptibly.] (II: 14, 611a, DM 408, 463*)

As a parallel to this "grand nombre d'escus" of which each coin is the equivalent of every other, Montaigne in the corresponding chapter presents us with another large number of *escus* that likewise provide an instance of monetary equivalence, though in a different way:

> Il n'estoit pas nouveau à un simple cytoien Romain, comme estoit lors Cesar, de disposer des royaumes, car il osta bien au roy Dejotarus le sien pour le donner à un gentil'homme sien amy de la ville de Pergame nommé Mithridates. Et ceux qui escrivent sa vie enregistrent plusieurs autres royaumes par luy vendus : & Suetone dit qu'il tira pour un coup du roy Ptoloméus *trois millions six cens mill'escus,* qui fut bien pres de luy vendre le sien.
>
> [It was no novelty for a simple Roman citizen, as Caesar then was, to dispose of kingdoms, for indeed he deprived King Deiotarus of his to give it to a gentleman of the city of Pergamum, named Mithridates. And those who write his life record several other kingdoms sold by him; and Suetonius says that at one stroke he extracted from King Ptolemy *three million six hundred thousand crowns,* which was very close to selling him his kingdom.] (II: 24, 686a, DM 500; 520)

As Villey points out, "Such exactions were almost equivalent to the sale of the kingdom" (686n). Caesar, that is, sold Ptolemy his kingdom back to him for this genuinely princely sum. This large sum of écus, like the one in the other chapter, is part of a monetary equivalence, but instead of each écu being the equivalent of every other as in II: 14, this time the whole sum is the equivalent of something else. Yet, in an elegant way, one sum of écus in one chapter is equivalent to the one in the other in that each is an instance of equivalence.

Chapter II: 24 begins with another equivalence, another case of two things seeming at first remarkably similar:

> Au septiesme livre des épitres familieres de Cicero . . . il y en a une qui s'adresse à Caesar estant lors en la Gaule, en laquelle Cicero redit ces motz, qui estoient sur la fin d'un'autre lettre, que Caesar luy avoit escrit, Quant à Marcus Furius, que tu m'as recommandé, je le feray roy de Gaule: & si tu veux, que j'advance quelque autre de tes amis, envoie le moy.

[In the seventh book of Cicero's *Epistulae ad Familiares* (*Letters to His Friends*), . . . there is one addressed to Caesar, who was then in Gaul, in which Cicero repeats these words, which were at the end of another letter that Caesar had written to him: "As for Marcus Furius, whom you have recommended to me, I will make him king of Gaul; and if you want me to advance some other friend of yours, send him to me."] (II: 24, 686a, DM 499–500; 519)

Now here, in an intriguing parallel to the hypothetical equality (of hunger and thirst) at the beginning of II: 14, are two absolutely equal things: the words that Caesar first wrote Cicero and their reappearance, word for word, in Cicero's letter to him. Yet, as Montaigne had predicted in II: 14, no matter how compelling the similarity between two things, there will always be some difference, "pour legiere qu'elle soit" [however slight], for Caesar's words, when restated by Cicero, convey something rather different from what they first meant. Originally an offer, they are now a claim on that offer, Cicero's request that Caesar perform what he promised. This instance of two correspondents writing the same words for different reasons parallels what keeps happening in the *Essays,* that the same words turn up in corresponding chapters, as in the case we have just seen of a great sum of *écus* exemplifying a monetary equivalence in both II: 14 and II: 24.

In a post-1588 addition to II: 24 Montaigne set up another corresponding echo, providing a reply to what he had already written in II: 14 concerning geometrical propositions that contradict common sense, in particular those "qui concluent par la certitude de leurs demonstrations, le contenu plus grand que le contenant, le centre aussi grand que sa *circonference*" [which conclude by the certainty of their demonstrations that the thing contained is greater than the container, the center as great as the *circumference*] (II: 14, 611a, DM 409; 463). In the addition to II: 24 he would tell the story of how C. Popilius came to demand of Antiochus, who ruled over Egypt, that he submit to the Roman Empire. "Popilius *circonscrit* la place où il estoit, à tout sa baguette, en luy disant: Ren moy responce que je puisse rapporter au senat, avant que tu partes de ce *cercle*" [Popilius *circumscribed* the place where he was with his stick, and said: "Give me an answer that I can take back to the Senate before you move out of this *circle*"] (II: 24, 687c; 520*). Antiochus complied, providing yet another example of a conquered monarch that the Romans left "en la possession de leurs royaumes sous leur authorité : à ce qu'ils eussent des roys mesmes, utilz de la servitude" [in possession of their kingdoms, under their authority, so that they might have even kings as instruments of slavery] (II: 24, 687a, DM 500–501; 520). While the center of the circle in II: 14 may be as great as its circumference, such is not the case with the one in II: 24, whose circumference is clearly greater than what was inside it, so much so that the line itself of that drawn circumference was enough to prevent Antiochus from stepping out of it. And yet when he consented to become, as other conquered kings had done, Rome's instrument by slavishly serving Rome in continuing to reign over Egypt he became an example of one of those other seemingly impossible geometrical propositions, that of the contained being greater than its container. For such vanquished but rethroned kings became the vessel of a power greater than their own, parodies of containers lesser than their content.

15. Civil War vs. Civil War

> "*Que nostre desir s'accroit par la malaisance*" [That our desire is increased by difficulty] (II: 15) and "*Des mauvais moyens employez à bonne fin*" [Of evil means employed to a good end] (II: 23)

Montaigne begins II: 15 by remarking that "Il n'y a nulle raison qui n'en aye une contraire" [There is no reason that does not have its opposite] (II: 15, 612a, DM 409; 463). To provide an example of this, he first cites the ancient saying "Nul bien ne nous peut apporter plaisir, si ce n'est celuy, à la perte duquel nous sommes preparez" [No good can bring us pleasure, unless it is one for whose loss we are prepared], and then contradicts it by observing that "Il se pourroit toutes-fois dire au rebours, que nous serrons & embrassons ce bien d'autant plus ferme, & avecques plus d'affection que nous le voyons nous estre moins seur, & que nous le craignons nous estre osté" [Yet it could be said, on the contrary, that we clutch and embrace this good all the more tightly and with more affection because we see that it is less secure and fear that it may be taken from us] (II: 15, 612a, DM 410; 463*). For our will is sharpened by opposition, as fire is by cold, and there is nothing so distasteful as the satiety that comes from desires too easily met. "Nous defendre quelque chose c'est nous en donner envie: nous l'abandonner tout à faict c'est nous en engendrer mespris : la faute & l'*abondance* tombent en mesme inconvenient" [To forbid us something is to make us want it. To give it up to us completely is to breed in us contempt for it. Want and *abundance* fall into the same discomfort] (II: 15, 613–14a, DM 412; 465).

In II: 23 as well, though in a quite different context, abundance can pose problems. Doctors "disent que la perfection de santé trop allegre & vigoreuse, il nous la faut essimer & rabatre par art . . . : ils ordonnent pour cela aux Athletes les purgations & les saignées, pour leur soubstraire céte *superabondance* de santé" [say that too blithe and vigorous a perfection of health must be artificially reduced and abated for us. . . . Therefore they order purges and bleedings for athletes to draw off this *superabundance* of health] (II: 23, 682a, DM 494 ; 517*). In II: 15, to have something good in abundance is as bad as not to have it at all; in II: 23, to have something good in abundance (or superabundance) is as bad as to have an abundance of its opposite. Either way, one can have too much of a good thing.

To illustrate his assertion that we value more what we are at risk of losing, he notes that "*Pour tenir l'amour en haleine*" [*To keep love in trim*] (II: 15, 612a, DM 410, 464*) Lycurgus ordered that married couples in Sparta have sexual relations only in secret, and that it would be as shameful for them to be found together as to be found in bed with someone else. The purpose of this edict is that the added challenge would spice up their love life.

Montaigne uses the same turn of phrase in II: 23 with regard to a similar situation but a quite different context. The Romans fostered wars with some of their enemies "*pour tenir leurs hommes en haleine, de peur que l'oysiveté mere de corruption ne leur apportat quelque pire inconvenient*" [*to keep their men in trim, for fear that idleness, mother of corruption, might bring them some worse mischief*] (II: 23, 683a, DM 495; 517*). Like Lycurgus, the Romans found that an added, indeed a seemingly unnecessary, challenge had its uses. In 1582 (unusually for that edition) Montaigne made a substantial addition to II: 15 that includes the following passage, in which he clearly intended to set up additional parallels with the lines from II: 23 I have just quoted:

> C'est un effect de la Providence divine de permettre sa saincte Eglise estre agitée, comme nous la voyons, de tant de troubles et d'orages, pour esveiller par ce contraste les ames pies, et les r'avoir de l'*oysiveté* et du sommeil où les avoit plongez une si longue tranquillité. Si nous contrepoisons la perte que nous avons faicte par le nombre de ceux qui se sont desvoyez, au gain qui nous vient *pour nous estre remis en haleine*, resuscité nostre zele et nos forces à l'occasion de ce combat, je ne sçay si l'utilité ne surmonte point le dommage.
>
> [It is an act of God's Providence to allow his Holy Church to be, as we can see she now is, shaken by so many disturbances and tempests, in order by this opposition to awaken the souls of the pious and to bring them back from the *idleness* and torpor in which so long a period of calm had

immersed them. If we weigh the loss we have suffered by the numbers of those who have been led into error against the gain which accrues to us *from our having been brought back into fighting trim,* with our zeal and our strength restored to new life for the battle, I am not sure whether the benefit does not outweigh the loss.] (II: 15, 615a'; 466*)

Montaigne here not only reiterates the expression "en haleine" [in fighting trim] but also opposes it to "l'oysiveté" as he had done in II: 23 when he wrote "pour tenir leurs hommes *en haleine,* de peur que l'*oysiveté* . . . ne leur apportat quelque pire inconvenient" [to keep their men *in trim,* for fear that *idleness* . . . might bring them some worse mischief]. The 1582 insertion adds as well the idea that a civil war (for that is what the religious troubles to which he alludes in fact were) is good for the church—as in II: 23 it is good for the state.

Astonishing as this apology for civil war may be, he makes another one on different grounds in II: 23, finding it less unjust in God's eyes to wage war against one's fellow citizens than against an innocent foreign country, and he explicitly refers to the religious civil war to which he would allude in that 1582 insertion to II: 15:

> Il y en a plusieurs en ce temps . . . souhaitans que cette emotion chalereuse, qui est parmy nous se peut deriver à quelque guerre voisine, de peur que ces humeurs peccantes, qui dominent pour céte heure nostre corps, si on ne les escoulle ailleurs, maintiennent nostre fiebvre tousjours en force, & apportent en fin nostre entiere ruine. Et de vray une guerre estrangiere est un mal bien plus doux que la civile. Mais je ne croy pas que Dieu favorisat une si injuste entreprise, d'offencer & quereler autruy pour nostre commodité. Toutes-fois la foiblesse de nostre condition nous pousse souvent à céte necessité de nous servir de mauvais moiens pour une bonne fin.

> [There are many at the present hour . . . wishing that this heated passion that is among us might be deflected into some war with our neighbors, for fear that these peccant humors which dominate our body at the moment, if they are not drained off elsewhere, may keep our fever still at its height and in the end bring on our total ruin. And indeed a foreign war is a much milder evil than a civil war. But I do not believe that God would favor so unjust an enterprise as to injure and pick a quarrel with others for our own convenience.] (II: 23, 683a, DM 496–97; 517–18*)

It is remarkable that Montaigne should be in such apparent contradiction with himself as to say in II: 15 that the French religious civil wars were useful (producing greater "utilité" than "dommage") but in II: 23 that they may bring the country to total ruin. It is especially so where there is such irrefutable evidence that he was quite aware when writing—and rewriting—one chapter of what he was writing or had written in the other. The intensification of the echoing instances of "en haleine" (already present in 1580, intensified in 1582) testifies to that awareness. While it is true that the apparent contradiction may be resolved by pointing out that the church and the nation are not the same and that what may be good for one may not be good for the other, the important thing from our perspective is that here again we have proof that Montaigne wants us to read his chapters in pairs, and that these two, in talking about civil wars but coming to opposite conclusions, seem to be fighting their own civil war.

16. Spreading the News

"De la gloire" [Of glory] (II: 16) and "Des postes" [Of couriers[23]*] (II: 22)*

La gloire, in Montaigne's estimation, is essentially news.[24] Like the noise made by the proverbial tree falling in the forest with no one to hear, its existence is

---

23. This seems to me a more accurate translation than Frame's "Of riding post" or Screech's "On riding 'in post.'" John Florio in his 1611 translation of the *Essais* (available at www.luminarium.org/renascence-editions/montaigne/) renders it as "Of Running Posts, or Couriers," reflecting the emphasis the chapter places on messengers, which is at least equal to (if not greater than) that placed on riding. In fact the only reference to riding itself apart from the riding that couriers perform is the new opening sentence added in 1588: "Je n'ay pas esté des plus foibles en cet exercice, qui est propre à gens de ma taille, ferme et courte; mais j'en quitte le mestier : il nous essaye trop pour y durer long temps" [I have been not of the weakest in this exercise, which is suited to men of my build, solid and short. But I give up the business; it is too trying to keep it up for long] (II: 22, 680b; 515). That he added this sentence at the beginning of the chapter instead of later may have led some to think that the chapter was going to be about horseback riding instead of the long-distance transmission of messages. But as Marianne S. Meijer suggests (on pp. 113–14 of "'Des postes' et 'Des pouces': Plaisanteries ou points de repère?," in *Columbia Montaigne Conference Papers,* ed. Donald M. Frame and Mary B. McKinley [Lexington, KY: French Forum Publishers, 1981: 105–18]), he may have been alluding in this new first sentence to the sexual sense of "postes," evident in "Sur des vers de Virgile" when a man suspected of impotence claimed to have made "vingt postes la nuict precedente" [love twenty times the night before] (III: 5, 867b; 659*) with his new bride. Cotgrave in his 1611 dictionary gives two separate entries for *postes,* of which the first is "A poste, currier, speedie messenger" and the second is "Post, posting, the riding post." They are two different words, the first a masculine noun, the second a feminine. Montaigne, especially after 1588, may be playing on all three senses, but in any edition what is discussed in the chapter is for the most part message transmission, not all of which is done on horseback. There are also swallows, pigeons, and men carrying other men.
24. *Gloire,* defined by Littré (Émile Littré, *Dictionnaire de la langue française* [Paris: 1877], available at http://francois.gannaz.free.fr/Littre/accueil.php), is "Célébrité grande et honorable" [great and honorable celebrity]; by Cotgrave, "Glorie, fame, reputation, renowne."

dependent on its being perceived, and (to employ what will prove, ultimately, a more relevant simile) like a letter consigned to the postal system, it does not always reach its destination:

> Ceux qui apprenent à nos gens de guerre . . . de ne cercher en la vaillance que la reputation, que gaignent ilz par là, que de les instruire de ne se hazarder jamais, qu'ilz ne soient à la veüe de leurs compagnons, & de prendre bien garde s'il y a des tesmoins avec eux, qui puissent raporter *nouvelles* de leur vaillance? là où il se presente mille occasions de bien faire sans qu'on puisse estre remarqué. Combien de belles actions particulieres s'ensevelissent dans la foule d'une bataille?

> [Those who teach our men of war . . . to seek in valor only reputation, what do they gain thereby but to instruct them never to hazard themselves unless they be within sight of their companions, and to take good care that there are witnesses with them who can bring back *news* of their valor? Whereas a thousand occasions of well-doing present themselves without one's being able to be noticed for it. How many fine individual actions are buried in the press of a battle!] (II: 16, 622a, DM 420; 471*; 605a)

"Des postes" (II: 22) is about sending and receiving news:

> Je lisois à cet'heure, que le Roy Cyrus pour recevoir plus facilement *nouvelles* de tous les cotez de son empire, qui estoit d'une fort grande estandue fit regarder combien un cheval pouvoit faire de chemin en un jour tout d'une traite, & à céte distance il establit des hommes, qui avoient charge de tenir des chevaux prets pour en fournir à ceux qui viendroient vers luy.

> [I was just this moment reading that King Cyrus, the more easily to receive *news* from all parts of his empire, which was of very great extent, ascertained how much distance a horse could do at a stretch in one day; and at that distance he stationed men whose business it was to keep horses ready to equip those who should be coming toward him.] (II: 22, 680a, DM 492–93; 515–16)

In 1588, Montaigne added another way of sending the news to the catalog this brief chapter provides:

> L'*invention* de Cecinna à renvoyer des *nouvelles* à ceux de sa maison avoit bien plus de promptitude: il emporta quand et soy des arondelles, et les

relaschoit vers leurs nids quand il vouloit r'envoyer de ses *nouvelles,* en les teignant de *marque* de couleur propre à signifier ce qu'il vouloit, selon qu'il avoit concerté avec les siens. Au theatre, à Romme, les maistres de famille avoient des pigeons dans leur sein, ausquels ils attacheoyent des *lettres* quand ils vouloient mander quelque chose à leurs gens au logis; et estoient dressez à en raporter responce.

[Cecinna's *invention* for sending back *news* to his household was much swifter; he took swallows along with him, and released them toward their nests when he wanted to send back *news* of himself, tinting them with some *mark* of color to signify his meaning, according as he had pre-arranged with his people. At the theatre in Rome the heads of families kept pigeons in their bosoms, to which they attached *letters* when they wanted to send instructions to their people at home; and these were trained to bring back an answer.] (II: 22, 680–81b; 516*)

I have italicized *invention, lettres,* and *marque* because that constellation of words also appears in the following passage from II: 16. Montaigne is scandalized, or at least amused, by the contradiction between Epicurus' preaching against seeking personal glory and what he actually said on his deathbed. His last words "sont grandes & dignes d'un tel philosophe, mais si ont elles quelque *marque* de la recommendation de son nom, et de cette humeur qu'il avoit décriée par ses preceptes. Voicy une *lettre* qu'il dicta un peu avant son dernier soupir" [are great and worthy of such a philosopher, and yet they bear the *mark* of commending his name and of that humor that in his precepts he had decried. Here is a *letter* that he dictated a little before his last gasp] (II: 16, 620ac; 469). In the letter Epicurus complains about the pain of his illness but says that it is compensated "par le plaisir qu'apportoit à mon ame la souvenance de mes *inventions* et de mes discours" [by the pleasure which the remembrance of my *discoveries* and my teachings brought to my soul] (II: 16, 620a; 469). Montaigne returns to this mention of *inventions* in a comment on the letter: "Voilà sa *lettre.* Et ce qui me faict interpreter que ce plaisir qu'il dit sentir en son ame, de ses *inventions,* regarde aucunement la reputation qu'il en esperoit acquerir apres sa mort, c'est l'ordonnance de son testament" [That is his *letter.* And what makes me infer that this pleasure, which he says he feels in his soul over his *discoveries,* somewhat concerns the reputation that he hoped to acquire from them after his death, is the provision in his will] (II: 16, 620a; 469) by which he sets aside money for the annual celebration of his birthday, as well as a monthly celebration partly in his honor.

So here we have a *lettre* whose author takes pleasure in his *inventions,* a statement that Montaigne sees as the *marque* that negates what the writer says elsewhere, while in the companion chapter we are told of an *invention* for conveying *lettres* in which the entire text consists of a *marque.* The *marque* in II: 22 is all there is to read; the one in II: 16 is a hidden message that only Montaigne, "suffisant lecteur" par excellence, can interpret.

But in writing all this (the passages in both II: 16 and II: 22 with this repeating trio of words), Montaigne constructed a hidden text for another sufficient reader to interpret. Though he took his time about it: the passage in II: 22 didn't appear until 1588; the telltale *marque* in II: 16 that tops it off didn't appear until he crossed out "goust" [taste] (DM 417) and replaced it with *marque* in the margin of the Bordeaux Copy at some point after 1588. As we have seen in other instances, here too Montaigne gradually perfected his metafictional echoes over the course of successive editions. M*arque(s)* appears 58 times in the *Essays, lettre(s)* 91 times, and *invention(s)* 91, but the three appear together only twice, in II: 16 and II: 22. Odds are that could not have happened by chance.

17. Spitting Images

"De la praesumption" [Of presumption] (II: 17) and "Contre la faineantise" [Against do-nothingness] (II: 21)

As the title of II: 21 would suggest, Montaigne is against *la fainéantise*—but only sometimes. For in this chapter's other half he is *for* it; he positively revels in it:

> J'ay une ame libre & toute sienne, accoustumée à se conduire à sa poste. Je n'ay eu jusques à cet'heure ny commandant ny maistre forcé. J'ay marché aussi avant & le pas qu'il m'a pleu. Cela m'a amolli & rendu inutile au service d'autruy: & ne m'a faict bon qu'à moy, estant d'ailleurs d'un naturel poisant, paresseus & *fay-neant:* car m'estant trouvé en tel degré de fortune des ma naissance, que j'ay eu occasion de m'y arrester je n'ay rien cerché & n'ay aussi rien pris.

> [I have a soul all its own, accustomed to conducting itself in its own way. Having had neither governor nor master forced on me to this day, I have gone just so far as I pleased, and at my own pace. This has made me soft and useless for serving others, and no good to anyone but myself, being

besides of a heavy, lazy, and *do-nothing* nature. For having found myself from birth in such a degree of fortune that I had reason to remain as I was, and having as much sense as I felt I had occasion for, I have sought nothing, and have also acquired nothing.] (II: 17, 643a, DM 449; 481*)

By remarkable coincidence this paradoxical quality—a character flaw in II: 21, but a virtue in II: 17—appears nowhere else in Book Two. But the paradox is resolvable. For Montaigne personally, having this quality is good because it denotes his independent spirit, his refusal to serve another. The *faineantise* he opposes in II: 21 is that of monarchs who do not take an active role in governing their kingdom or in leading their armies on the battlefield. The "commandement de tant d'hommes, n'est pas une charge oisive, & qu'il n'est rien qui puisse si justement dégouster un subject de se mettre en peine & en hazard pour le service de son prince, que de le voir apoltronny ce pendant luy mesme à des occupations lasches & vaines" [commanding so many men is not an idle charge, and there is nothing that can so justly spoil a subject's taste for putting himself at pains and in danger for the service of his prince as to see the prince himself meanwhile loafing about at paltry and frivolous occupations] (II: 21, 676a, DM 491; 512*). So it is not exactly a contradiction for him to speak approvingly of that quality in himself since he is not a king. But it is nevertheless true that Montaigne carefully planted these only two instances in Book Two in symmetrically matching chapters and that he presented their combination for the assiduous reader who would eventually discover it as an apparent opposition.

One of the monarchs Montaigne singles out for praise for not being a *fainéant,* for not engaging in "des occupations lasches & vaines" to the detriment of the state and the army, is Julian the Apostate.

L'empereur Julian disoit . . . qu'un philosophe & un galant homme ne devoient pas seulement respirer, c'est à dire ne donner aus necessitez corporelles que ce qu'on ne leur peut refuser, tenant tousjours l'ame & le corps *embesoignés à* choses *belles,* grandes & vertueuses. Il avoit honte si en public on le voyoit cracher ou suer . . . par ce qu'il estimoit que l'exercice, le travail continuel et la sobrieté devoient avoir cuit et asseché toutes ces superfluitez.

[The Emperor Julian used to say . . . that a philosopher and a gallant man ought not even to breathe; that is to say, they should grant to bodily necessities only what cannot be refused them, ever keeping the soul and body *busied in fair,* great, and virtuous things. He was ashamed if he was seen to spit or sweat in public . . . because he considered that exercise, continual

toil, and sobriety should have cooked and dried up all those superfluities.]
(II: 21, 677a, DM 491-92; 513)

This echoes in a surprising way what he has to say in the other chapter about the Greek general Philopoemen—surprising because Philopoemen's pathetic predicament forms such a contrast to Julian's grandeur. When he arrived before the rest of his company at a house where he was expected, his hostess, not realizing who he was, put him to work at menial tasks for the arrival of the distinguished guest. When his retinue got there, discovering him "*embesongné à céte belle* vacation" [*busy at* this *beautiful* occupation] (II: 17, 641a, DM 446; 486*), asked him why, he replied that he was paying the penalty for his ugliness.

Nowhere else does *embesogner* appear with *à* + *belles*. Not only do the symmetrically placed appearances of these words constitute a striking parallel, but the two situations are just as parallel, if also the opposite. In both cases, the dignity of an exalted personage—a general, an emperor—is under attack. The general does not stand on his dignity; the emperor does. The general is not ashamed to perform trivial though necessary tasks, nor to do them before his subordinates; the emperor "avoit honte" [was ashamed] to be seen by the public fulfilling trivial needs. The tasks Philopoemen performed were actually for himself, "pour le service de Philopoemen," although the woman who ordered him to do them did not realize it. So too were the things Julian was reluctant to do: to sweat and to spit. Montaigne was being ironic when he wrote that Philopoemen's officers were surprised at seeing him "embesongné à céte belle vacation"; now we realize that he was being even more ironic than that in applying the same words to him that he would apply to Julian. These words in the Julian anecdote, by contrast, have no immediate ironic charge, since presumably the fine and beautiful things a philosopher and a gallant man do are indeed so. But they certainly acquire one in retrospect.

The rest of the passage on Julian—

> Il avoit honte si *en public* on le voyoit *cracher ou suer* . . . par ce qu'il estimoit que l'exercice, le travail continuel et la sobriété devoient avoir cuit et asseché toutes ces superfluitez.

> [He was ashamed if he was seen *to spit or sweat in public* . . . because he considered that exercise, continual toil, and sobriety should have cooked and dried up all those superfluities.] (II: 21, 677a, DM 492; 513)

—forms a parallel of its own to still another passage in "De la praesumption," about another Roman emperor (in fact, Julian's immediate predecessor). Montaigne writes of

> la morgue de Constantius l'Empereur, qui *en publicq* tenoit tousjours la teste droite, sans la contourner ou flechir ni ça ny là, non pas seulement pour regarder ceux, qui le saluoient à costé, ayant le corps planté & immobile, sans se laisser aller au branle de son coche, sans oser ny *cracher,* ny se moucher, ny *essuyer le visage* devant les gens.
>
> [the arrogance of the Emperor Constantius, who *in public* always held his head straight, without turning or bending it this way or that, not even to look at those who saluted him from the side; keeping his body fixed and motionless, without letting himself move with the swaying of his coach, without daring either *to spit,* or to blow his nose, *or to wipe his face* in front of the people.] (II: 17, 633a, DM 435; 480)

The infinitive *cracher* makes only these two appearances in Book Two. More significantly, while there is spitting going on elsewhere in the *Essays* (including Book Two), in no other passage does it occur together with sweating. More significantly still, in Ammianus Marcellinus' account of Constantius, Montaigne's source for this account, there is no mention of the emperor's not wiping off his face to remove the sweat: "quod autem nec os tersisse umquam vel nares in publico, nec spuisse, nec transtulisse in partem alterutram vultum aliquando est visus, nec pomorum quoad vixerat gustaverit, ut dicta saepius praetermitto" [That no one ever saw him wipe his mouth or nose in public, nor spit, nor turn his face to this side or that, or that so long as he lived he never tasted fruit, I leave unmentioned, since it has often been related].[25] So Montaigne added this detail to complete the parallel with Julian. But again it is a parallel based on an opposition. The very behavior he praises in Julian he criticizes in Constantius. Julian dared not spit or sweat in public because of his lofty ideal of how a philosopher and a gallant man should devote his energies, but Constantius dared not spit or sweat in public out of a defect of character: his arrogance ("morgue"). Constantius's behavior was one of several "mouvemens . . . artificiels" [artificial gestures] (II: 17, 633a, DM 434–35; 479*) and "contenances desreglées" [extraordinary mannerisms] (II: 17, 633b; 480) to which Montaigne objects.

25. Ammianus Marcellinus, *The History,* tr. John C. Rolfe (Cambridge: Harvard University Press / Loeb Classical Library, 1937), vol. 2, 176–77 (xxi, 16, 7).

When Montaigne inserted the post-1588 anecdote of Muley Moloch, king of Fez, into "Contre la faineantise" he gave us the second half of yet another intratext to ponder. Moloch was a monarch who died with his boots on, a fine example of a king who was not a *fainéant.* Sebastian, the young king of Portugal, had invaded Morocco; in response, Moloch arose from his deathbed to command his forces.

Il dressa sa bataille en rond, assiegeant de toutes pars l'ost des Portugais: lequel rond, venant à se courber et serrer, les empescha non seulement au conflict, qui fut tres aspre par la valeur de ce jeune Roy assaillant, veu qu'ils avoient à *montrer visage à tous sens,* mais aussi les empescha à la fuitte apres leur routte.

[He drew up his army in a circle, besieging the camp of the Portuguese from all sides, and this circle, coming to bend and tighten, not only hindered them in the fighting, which was very bitter because of the valor of the young invading king, seeing that they had to *face in all directions,* but also hindered their flight after their rout.] (II: 21, 678c; 515)

In "De la praesumption" Montaigne writes that of men he has known "le plus grand . . . des parties natureles de l'ame & le mieux né c'estoit Estienne de la Boitie: c'étoit vrayement un'ame pleine, & qui *monstroit* un beau *visage à tout sens*" [the greatest one . . . for natural qualities of the soul, and the best endowed, was Etienne de La Boétie. He was truly a full soul, and *displayed* a handsome *face in every sense*] (II: 17, 659a, DM 470; 500*). This repeating sequence of words—*montrer / monstroit visage à tout / tous sens*—makes its only appearances here. The contexts and indeed the meanings of these words could hardly be more different, yet by now it should be apparent that such a repetition, especially in structurally related chapters, is likely to be meaningful. The young man in the middle of Moloch's encircling army finds a counterpart in another young man in the middle, Etienne de La Boétie, occupying the middle chapter of Book One and surrounded by Montaigne's "grotesques et corps monstrueux." Curiously, Montaigne's assertion in II: 17 that La Boétie displayed a handsome face in every sense is contradicted by what he will write in a post-1588 addition to chapter 12 of Book Three, where he will say that his young friend's face was actually ugly:

Mais nous appellons laideur aussi une mesavenance au premier regard, qui loge principalement au visage, et souvent nous desgoute par bien legeres causes: du teint, d'une tache, d'une rude contenance, de quelque cause inexplicable sur des membres bien ordonnez et entiers. La laideur qui revestoit une ame tres-belle en La Boitie estoit de ce predicament.

[But we also call ugliness an unattractiveness at first glance, which resides chiefly in the face, and often arouses our distaste for very slight causes: the complexion, a spot, a rough countenance, or some inexplicable cause, when the limbs are well ordered and whole. The ugliness which clothed a very beautiful soul in La Boétie was of this predicament.] (III: 12, 1057c; 807–8*)

If what Montaigne says in III: 12 is accurate, then as he did with Constantius—adding sweating to the list of what Ammianus Marcellinus said he was unwilling to do in public so that he could set up a better parallel with Julian in the matching chapter—he does with La Boétie as well, tweaking the truth to plant a parallel. And, as we approach the middle of Book Two, to allude to the middle of Book One and its surrounding chapters. For Book Two has the same structure, with Julian the Apostate occupying the corresponding place of honor.

18. Consubstantial Consubstantiality

"Du démentir" [Of giving the lie] (II: 18) and *"Nous ne goustons rien de pur"* [We taste nothing pure] (II: 20)

Lying is so pervasive, Montaigne complains in "Du démentir," that "Nostre verité d'à cette heure ce n'est pas ce qui est, mais ce qui se persuade à autruy: comme nous appellons monnoye non celle qui est loyalle seulement, mais la fauce aussi, qui a mise" [Our truth of nowadays is not what is, but what others can be convinced of; just as we call money not only that which is legal, but also the false that has currency] (II: 18, 666a, DM 477; 505*). Our public discourse, like the money supply, is impure. Nothing we taste, to borrow from the title of the companion chapter II: 20, whether it be what passes for truth or what passes for legal tender, is pure. As he says in the first sentence of II: 20,

La foiblesse de nostre condition faict que les choses en leur simplicité & pureté naturelle ne puissent pas tomber en nostre usage. Les elemens que nous joyssons, sont alterés, & les metaus de mesme, & l'or il le faut empirer par quelque autre matiere plus vile, pour l'accommoder à nostre service.

[The weakness of our condition is such that we cannot make use of things in their simplicity and natural purity. The elements that we enjoy are altered, and the metals likewise; and gold must be debased by some other, more vile material to accommodate it to our service.] (II: 20, 673a, DM 491; 510*)

One of the chief instances of the service to which gold is put of course is money, so that both chapters allude to the impurity of money but do so in different ways. In II: 18, the impurity results from the combination of the purity of some coins (the legal) versus the impurity of others (the counterfeit); in II: 20, the impurity is inherent in any legal coin, which of necessity (gold, for example, being too soft a metal to stand up alone to the normal wear-and-tear coins must undergo) is made up of both pure metal (e.g., gold) and some baser material.

When Montaigne says in II: 20 that gold must be debased to *accommodate* it to our *service*, he is echoing what he says in II: 18 about writing the *Essays* for a private audience only—a neighbor, a kinsman, a friend. His only "commerce" [contact] with the public is that he has been constrained to borrow the tools of their writing (that is, printing), and he has cast this image into a mold to save himself the trouble of making several copies by hand. "En recompense de céte *commodité*, que j'en ay emprunté, j'espere luy faire ce *service* d'empecher Ne toga cordyllis, ne penula desit olivis" [In return for this *convenience* which I have borrowed from the public I hope to provide it the *service* of preventing "tuna fish and olives from lacking something to wrap them in"] (II: 18, 664a, DM 476–77; 504*). Montaigne replaced much of this passage after 1588, including the sentence with "commodité" and "service." But in a section he introduced after 1588 just after this point, he added a passage that sets up a connection to the following passage in "Nous ne goustons rien de pur" that dates from 1588:

> Des plaisirs et biens que nous avons, il n'en est aucun exempt de quelque meslange de mal et d'incommodité. . . . Nostre extreme volupté a quelque air de gemissement et de plainte. Diriez vous pas qu'elle se meurt d'angoisse? Voire quand nous en forgeons l'image en son excellence, nous la fardons d'epithetes et qualitez maladifves et douloureuses: langueur, mollesse, foiblesse, defaillance, morbidezza; grand tesmoignage de leur consanguinité et *consubstantialité*.

> [Of the pleasures and good things that we have, there is not one exempt from some mixture of pain and discomfort. . . . Our utmost sensual pleasure has an air of groaning and lament about it. Wouldn't you say that it is

dying of anguish? Indeed, when we forge a picture of it at its highest point, we deck it with sickly and painful epithets and qualities: languor, softness, weakness, faintness, "morbidezza": a great testimony to their consanguinity and *consubstantiality*.] (II: 20, 673b; 508*)

Pain and pleasure, particularly in sex, are consubstantial. So too, according to what Montaigne added to "Du démentir" after 1588, are he and his book: "Je n'ay pas plus faict mon livre que mon livre m'a faict, livre *consubstantiel* à son autheur" [I have not made my book any more than it has made me—a book *consubstantial* with its author] (II: 18, 665c; 504*). There is no consubstantiality anywhere else in Book Two. In adding this passage to II: 18 Montaigne made an important statement about the *Essays* that is justly famous. But at the same time he added yet another connection to the consubstantiality of the *Essays* themselves: the way each chapter has another with which *it* is consubstantial. In a marvelous instance of metafictional self-referentiality, here consubstantiality names itself.

III

BOOK THREE

1. Distant Harmonies

"De l'utile et de l'honneste" [Of the useful and the honorable] (III: 1) and *"De l'experience"* [Of experience] (III: 13)

It is to be expected that in "De l'utile et de l'honneste" Montaigne should talk about the useful and the honorable: "Je suy le langage commun, qui faict difference, entre les choses *utiles*, & les *honnestes*: si que d'aucunes actions naturelles, non seulement *utiles*, mais necessaires, il les nomme *deshonnestes* & sales" [I follow the common language, which distinguishes between things *useful* and *honorable*, so that it calls *dishonorable* and foul some natural actions that are not only *useful* but necessary] (III: 1, 796b, DM 347v; 604). But it is a little surprising that he should also bring up those two topics in "De l'experience":

> Tout cecy me faict souvenir de ces anciennes opinions, qu'il est forcé de faire tort en detail, qui veut faire droict en gros, & injustice en petites choses, qui veut venir à chef de faire justice és grandes: que l'humaine justice est formée au patron de la medecine, selon laquelle, tout ce qui est utile est aussi juste & honneste.

[All this reminds me of these ancient opinions: that a man is forced to do wrong in detail if he wants to do right in gross, and injustice in little things if he wants to achieve justice in great ones; that human justice is formed on the model of medicine, according to which all that is *useful* is also just and *honorable*.] (III: 13, 1071b, DM 473v; 820*)

Within Book Three those two terms appear together only in these two chapters. "De l'utile et de l'honneste" is in large measure about the administration of justice, while in "De l'experience" the essayist writes at length about his experience with medicine and disease. In both domains, medicine and justice, he raises the question of combating evil with evil: "Je n'ayme point à guarir le mal par le mal" [I do not like curing one ill by another] (III: 13, 1086b, DM 481v; 832*), he declares in "De l'experience"; "La perfidie peut estre en quelque cas excusable" [Perfidy may in a given case be excusable], he asserts in the matching chapter, "lors seulement elle l'est, qu'elle s'employe à punir et trahir la perfidie" [it is so only when it is employed to punish and betray perfidy] (III: 1, 797c; 605).

But evil, as he points out elsewhere III: 13, is unavoidable, even necessary—and in fact natural.

Nostre vie est composée, comme l'armonie du monde de choses contraires, aussi de divers tons, douz & aspres, aigus & plats, mols & graves. Le musicien qui n'en aymeroit que les uns, que voudroit il dire? Il faut qu'il s'en sçache servir en commun, & les mesler, & nous, aussi les biens & les maux, qui sont consubstantiels à nostre vie. Nostre estre ne peut sans ce meslange, & y est l'une bande non moins necessaire que l'autre. D'essayer à regimber contre la necessité naturelle, c'est representer la folie de Ctesiphon, qui entreprenoit de faire à coups de pied contre sa mule.

[Our life is composed, like the harmony of the world, of contrary things, also of different tones, sweet and harsh, sharp and flat, soft and loud. If a musician liked only one kind, what would he have to say? He must know how to use them together and blend them. And so must we do with good and evil, which are consubstantial with our life. Our existence is impossible without this mixture, and one element is no less necessary for it than the other. To try to kick against natural necessity is to imitate the folly of Ctesiphon, who undertook a kicking match with his mule.] (III: 13, 1089–90b, DM 483v; 835)

What he means in III: 1 by the *utile* was the politically useful in a Machiavellian sense, treachery and illegality in the interest of a larger good. Tiberius, for example, refused to have Arminius assassinated, declaring that the Roman people were not accustomed to fight their enemies by fraud, prompting the essayist to remark that the emperor "quitta l'utile pour l'honneste" [gave up the useful for the honorable] (III: 1, 790b, DM 344r; 599). The good and evil of which he writes in the passage from III: 13 just quoted have a descriptive terminology in common with the honorable and the useful he discusses in III: 1. Montaigne writes in the passage I first quoted from III: 1 of dishonorable measures that are "actions *naturelles*, non seulement utiles, mais *necessaires*" [*natural* actions that are not only useful but *necessary*] (III: 1, 796b, DM 347v; 604)—as good and evil in III: 13 are each "non moins *necessaire* que l'autre" [no less *necessary* than the other] and part of "la *necessité naturelle*" [natural necessity] (III: 13, 1090b, DM 483v; 835).

Two other parallel passages address the same issue. Near the end of "De l'experience" Montaigne writes:

> Est-ce pas erreur, d'estimer aucunes actions moins dignes, de ce qu'elles sont necessaires? Si ne m'osteront-ils pas de la teste, que ce ne soit un tres-convenable mariage du plaisir avec la necessité. A quoy faire desmembrons nous en divorce, un *bastiment* tissu, d'une si joincte & fraternelle correspondance. . . . Il n'y a piece indigne de nostre soin, en ce present que Dieu nous a faict.
>
> [Is it not an error to consider some actions less worthy because they are necessary? No, they will not knock it out of my head that the marriage of pleasure with necessity is a very suitable one. To what purpose do we dismember by divorce a *building* whose fabric of such conjoined and brotherly correspondence? . . . There is no part unworthy of our care in this gift that God has given us.] (III: 13, 1114b, DM 495r; 855–56*)

The matching passage appears near the beginning of the matching chapter:

> Nostre *bastiment* & public & privé, est plain d'imperfection: mais il n'y a rien d'inutile en nature, non l'inutilité mesmes; rien ne s'est ingeré en cet univers, qui n'y tienne place opportune.
>
> [Our *building*, both public and private, is full of imperfection. But there is nothing useless in nature, not even uselessness itself. Nothing has made

its way into this universe that does not hold a proper place in it.] (III: 1, 790b, DM 344v; 599)

This recurring *bastiment* is itself an example of how the *Essays* are such a building, one in which every piece has its place, conjoined in a fabric of correspondences.

Another example arises from the allusion in "De l'experience," quoted above, to Ctesiphon's effort to imitate his mule's talent for "coups de *pied*." For in "De l'utile et de l'honneste" he writes of the artificial liberties some men take in their dealings with others that remind him of "l'asne d'Esope: lequel par emulation du chien, vint à se jetter tout gayement, à deux *pieds*, sur les espaules de son maistre" [Aesop's ass, who, in emulation of the dog, came and threw himself gaily with both *feet* on his master's shoulders] (III: 1, 795b, DM 347v; 604). The dog had received caresses for that behavior but the ass got a beating. These aren't the only asses or mules in Book Three, but they are the only two whose hooves come into play. Both Ctesiphon and Aesop's ass came to grief for trying to replicate what another could do so much more successfully with their feet—in Ctesiphon's case a mule; in the ass's, a dog.

In addition, the dog in this fable of Aesop is matched by dogs in another of Aesop's fables in the matching chapter, in the only other allusion to an Aesopian animal (or fable) in Book Three. The human mind imagines that it sees a glimmer of imaginary light and truth, but when it runs toward it so many difficulties and new quests get in the way that it strays from the path, not unlike what happened "aux chiens d'Esope, lesquels descouvrant quelque apparence de corps mort floter en mer" [to Aesop's dogs, who, discovering something that looked like a dead body floating in the sea] (III: 13, 1068b, DM 472r; 817*), but unable to approach it, tried to drink up this water to dry it up, and died. By alluding in Book Three to these two particular fables of Aesop and no other, and by placing the allusions in symmetrically placed chapters (III: 1 and III: 13), Montaigne has managed to give the first a metafictional resonance it did not originally have. The second (the one about the dogs), in the structural context he gives it in the fabric of the book, now echoes the first, which just happened to be about an ass trying to echo a dog's behavior.

But the content of the second has an echoing resonance of its own. Both the motifs of (1) dogs eating something already dead and (2) death brought about by drinking too much water appear together in an anecdote added after 1588 to the matching chapter, III: 1. Montaigne is discussing cases in which hired murderers and traitors were paid the reward they were promised but then put to death for having committed the crime, the demands of both contractual and criminal justice thereby served. He tells of Mohammed II, who wanted to do away with his half-brother. He suborned one of his officers, "qui le suffoqua, l'engorgeant de quantité d'eau prinse trop à coup" [who choked him by pouring a quantity of water too fast down his throat]. But to expiate this murder he handed the killer over to the victim's mother, who tore out the killer's heart and "le jetta à manger aux chiens" [threw it to the dogs to eat] (III: 1, 798c; 606). Aesop's dogs in III: 13 tried to eat what looked like a dead body; it was part of a dead body that fed the dogs in III: 1. These are the only dogs in Book Three to eat or to contemplate eating dead flesh.

Montaigne made two post-1588 changes to his account of Aesop's dogs in III: 13. The first is that he replaced "& s'y tuerent" [and died] (at the conclusion of what is quoted above) by "et s'y *estouffarent*" [and *choked*]. This ties the passage more closely to the one in III: 1, where Montaigne follows up the story of murder by forced overdrinking and the putting to death of the murderer with another instance of the latter (King Clovis hanging the servants whom he had suborned to betray their master) and then says that in putting to death those who have done one's evil bidding one seeks "par leur mort d'*estouffer* la connoissance et tesmoignage de telles menées" [by their death to *choke off* the knowledge and evidence of such proceedings] (III: 1, 798c; 606*). The other change is that he immediately follows the change from "s'y tuerent" to "s'y estouffarent" with this new comment:

> A quoy se rencontre ce qu'un Crates disoit des escrits de Heraclitus, qu'ils avoient besoin d'un lecteur bon nageur, afin que la profondeur et pois de sa doctrine ne l'engloutist et *suffucast*.

> [And that coincides with what Crates said of the writings of Heraclitus, that they needed a good swimmer for a reader, so that the depth and weight of Heraclitus' learning should not sink him and *choke* him.] (III: 13, 1068c; 817*)

—tying the passage all the more closely to the one in which Mohammed II's henchman "*suffoqua*" his victim. These two passages are the only ones in the *Essays* where one is "suffoqué" by water.

In the two sentences immediately preceding the story about the man whom Mohammed II caused to be killed after he had done his dirty work for him, Montaigne reports how other suborners have managed to satisfy their private promise of reward with the state's demand for justice: "Ils les font *pendre* avec la *bourse* de leur payement au col" [They have them *hanged* with the *purse* of their payment around their neck] (III: 1, 798c; 606). This post-1588 addition to III: 1 answers an anecdote already present in III: 13 in which purses and hanging play a major part. He was recalling a case in which certain men are condemned to death for a murder, but before the sentence can be carried out some others confess to the crime. The judges debate whether they have the right to alter a sentence duly passed according to law, conclude they do not, and the innocent are sent to the gallows. Montaigne then cites a case from antiquity, in which a judge had sentenced one man to pay a fine to another. New evidence emerged, and he found that the exaction had been unjust. This judge faced the same competing demands that the judges in the other case debated between actual justice and the demands of judicial form. He found a way to satisfy both, "laissant en son estat la sentence, & recompensant de sa *bourse* l'interest du condamné: mais il avoit affaire à un accident reparable, les miens furent *pendus* irreparablement" [letting the sentence stand and compensating the loss of the convicted man out of his own *purse*. But he was dealing with a reparable accident; my men were irreparably *hanged*] (III: 13, 1071b, DM 473v; 820). In both this case and the one in III: 1, giving a purse to the condemned makes it possible to satisfy conflicting demands, although the demands are very different in nature.

This passage in III: 13 featuring a purse and a hanging that so cleverly reworks the same elements from III: 1 leads directly into the statement I quoted at the beginning that so strikingly repeats the two most significant elements of III: 1, the ones named in its title: "Tout cecy me faict souvenir de ces anciennes opinions, . . . que l'humaine justice est formée au patron de la medecine, selon laquelle, tout ce qui est *utile* est aussi juste & *honneste*" [All this reminds me of these ancient opinions: . . . that human justice is formed on the model of medicine, according to which all that is *useful* is also just and *honorable*] (III: 13, 1071b, DM 473v; 820*). The "Tout cecy" [All this] is precisely the pair of stories about a hanging and a purse that recall the hanging and the purse combined in the post-1588 addition to the chapter about the useful and the honorable. Thanks to that addition there is now an additional dimension to the memory that "Tout cecy" evokes.

It was the passage in "De l'experience" about the function of good and evil in "l'armonie du monde," with its allusion to the man who got into a kicking contest with his mule, illustrative of the folly of those who try to buck natural necessity, that sent us bouncing back and forth between these two chapters, from Ctesiphon's mule to Aesop's ass to Aesop's dogs to the dogs of Muhammed II's half-brother's mother. The same passage with its talk of music and mixing—the "musicien" must know how to "mesler" the contrary elements of his art—anticipates a later passage in the same chapter that itself more strikingly echoes a parallel passage in "De l'utile et le l'honneste." Near the end of III: 13 Montaigne writes:

> Le relachement & *facilité*, honore ce semble à merveilles & sied mieux, à une ame forte & puissante. *Epaminondas* n'estimoit pas que de se *mesler* à la dance des garçons de sa ville, & de s'y embesongner avec attention fut chose qui desrogeat à l'honneur de ses glorieuses victoires, & à la plus reiglée reformation de *meurs* qui fut jamais en homme.

> [Relaxation and *ease*, it seems to me, are marvelously honorable and most becoming to a strong and generous soul. *Epaminondas* didn't think that to *mingle* with the dance of the boys of his city, and to concentrate attentively on these things, was at all derogatory to the honor of his glorious victories and the perfect purity of *manners* that were ever in a man.] (III: 13, 1109b, DM 493r; 633*)

Epaminondas was already associated with the verbal cluster *facilité, mesler* and *meurs* near the end of III: 1: "C'est miracle, de pouvoir *mesler* à telles actions quelque image de justice, mais il n'appartient qu'à la vigueur d'*Epaminondas*, d'y pouvoir *mesler* la douceur, & la *facilité* des *meurs* les plus molles" [It is a miracle to be able to *mingle* some semblance of justice to such actions; but it belongs only to the strength of *Epaminondas* to be able to *mingle* with them the sweetness and *ease* of the gentlest *manners*] (III: 1, 801–2b, DM 349v–50r; 609*). Epaminondas makes no other appearance in the first (1588) edition of Book Three (from which I am quoting here). What is mingled is different in the two passages: in III: 1 Epaminondas mingles the "plus rudes & violentes actions humaines" [the roughest and most violent of human actions] (III: 1, 801b, DM 349v; 609) on the field of battle in wartime with the ease of his manners, while in III: 13 he mingles himself with the dancing youth of the city (though in effect he is at the same time accomplishing a mingling of heroism and peaceful camaraderie that parallels that between the heroic and the humane of which the other passage speaks). Epaminondas in the III: 1 passage "*marioit* aux plus rudes & violentes actions humaines, la bonté & l'humanité" [*married* to the roughest and most of violent of human actions goodness and humanity] (III: 1, 801b, DM 349v; 609*). Though marriage (whether as noun or verb) in the concrete sense makes numerous appearances in Book Three, especially in III: 5, in no chapter in that book other than the first and last does it appear in this particular figurative sense of mingling disparate things. Both as Epaminondas' rare feat, that is, and in the passage from III: 13 cited earlier that echoed the *bastiment* in III: 1 with one of its own: "Si ne m'osteront-ils pas de la teste, que ce ne soit un tres-convenable *mariage* du plaisir avec la necessité. A quoy faire desmembrons nous en *divorce*, un *bastiment* tissu, d'une si joinct & fraternelle correspondance?" [No, they will not knock it out of my head that the *marriage* of pleasure with necessity is a very suitable one. To what purpose do we dismember by *divorce* a *building* made up of such close and brotherly correspondence?] (III: 13, 1114b, DM 495r; 855*). Despite the disparate contexts of the two passages about Epaminondas, the same trio of words (*facilité, mesler, meurs*) persists from one to the other, together with Epaminondas himself. The two chapters are themselves co-mingled in this sense, imitating by their distant harmonies "l'armonie du monde."

2. Distant Theft

"Du repentir" [Of repentance] (III: 2) and *"De la phisionomie"* [Of physiognomy] (III: 12)

A man knocks on Montaigne's door and begs to be let in, claiming to be pursued by an enemy. Soon a half-dozen of his armed companions also show up to ask for shelter, followed by twenty or more who remain on horseback in the courtyard. Wanting to help but afraid it may be a robber's ruse, Montaigne plays along, trusting to God for a safe outcome. Suddenly, to the surprise of his soldiers, the man mounts his horse and leads them away, having decided not to pursue what he later will confess to have been a less than honorable intent.

This story of a surprising change of heart is immediately followed by another. Montaigne is captured by armed men during the religious wars, his money stolen, and is told he will be held for ransom. After much negotiation, a surprising change comes over his captors, who let him go and restore what they had stolen.

> La vraye cause d'un changement si nouveau & de ce *ravisement*, sans aucune impulsion apparent, & d'un *repentir* si miraculeux, en tel temps, en une entreprinse pourpensé & deliberé . . . certes je ne sçay bien encores qu'elle elle est.

[The true cause of so unusual an about-face and *change of mind*, without any apparent motivation, and of such a miraculous *repentance*, at such a time, in a premeditated and deliberate enterprise . . . I truly do not even now well know.] (III: 12, 1062b, DM 469v; 813–14)

One might expect to find a *repentir* like that in "Du repentir." But that's not where Montaigne put it, and in fact there are hardly any examples of genuine repentance in that chapter. As Jules Brody observes, in "Du repentir"

> we are made to understand that "repentence"—at least in the deep and far-reaching sense of a self-scrutiny capable of producing effective change—is a profound illusion. In those later parts of the essay, actually quite few in number, which deal specifically with repentance . . . the same conclusion will recur: the examples that we see around us are more verbal than actual, more apparent than real; what passes for repentance is superficial and will not measure up to the deep implications of the word. ("'Du repentir' (III: 2): A Philological Reading," 241)

So too is the case with the house invader and the kidnappers in III: 12. They simply changed their mind about robbing or holding him for ransom; they weren't changing their wicked ways. But Montaigne calls what the kidnappers did both a "repentir" and a "ravisement." That first term is heavy with echoes from the chapter with which III: 12 is symmetrically paired. And the second appears in no other chapter of Book Three than in the following passage from the same chapter: "Si je ne suis chez moy, j'en suis tousjours bien pres: mes desbauches ne m'emportent pas fort loing : il n'y a rien d'extreme & d'estrange : & si ay des *ravisemens* sains & vigoureux" [My indulgences do not catch me away very far: there is nothing odd or extreme about them, though I do have some sane and vigorous *changes of heart*] (III: 2, 811b, DM 353v; 615).

Brody writes of "the absolutely uncanny way in which Montaigne's words respond to each other" and "that to read Montaigne philologically"—which is to say, as one in love with the words, which is both his case and mine—"is to be ready at every moment to obey a double solicitation, the contextual and the intratextual." Such a reader, "once he has been through the text linearly, will be drawn to pursue and compare observed lexical recurrences, synonymies or on occasion even sizeable passages which continue to impinge on one another in his memory even at several pages' distance" (269–70). He further asserts that "any reading that claims access to a reality or a unity located outside the pages of Montaigne's book imposes an enormous sacrifice and exacts an exorbitant price, namely, the palpable, objective reality and unity constituted by the unbroken string of words which spans the textual space of each individual essay" (270). I can only applaud such a cogent statement of what is worth looking for in the *Essays*.

But that textual space, as Brody does not acknowledge, extends beyond the individual chapter to its secret partner, as the "repentir" and "ravisement" of "Du repentir" extend to those of "De la phisionomie." Another instance of such a long-distance echo arises from a remarkable story of *non*-repentence in "Du repentir," the peasant known as the thief of Armagnac. He was born a beggar and figured he could never make enough to live on by his own toil. So in his youth

> il moissonnoit & vendangeoit des terres d'autruy : mais c'estoit au loing, & à si gros monceaux, qu'il estoit inimaginable qu'un homme en eust tant rapporté en une nuict sur ses espaules, & avoit soing outre cela, d'egaler, & disperser le dommage qu'il faisoit, si que la foule estoit moins importable à chaque particulier.

> [he reaped his harvest and vintage from other people's lands, but so far away and in such great loads that it was inconceivable that one man could have carried off so much on his shoulders in one night. And he was careful besides to equalize and spread out the damage he did, so that the loss was less insupportable for each individual.] (III: 2, 811–12b, DM 354r; 616)

Now advanced in years, he makes his peace with God by doing good deeds to the descendants of those from whom he stole, and will instruct his heirs to continue to do so according to the records he kept of what he stole from whom. He "regarde le larrecin, comme action des-honneste, & le hayt, mais moins que l'indigence : s'en repent bien simplement, mais en tant qu'elle estoit ainsi contrebalancée & compencée, il ne s'en repent pas" [regards theft as a dishonorable action and hates it, but hates it less than poverty; he indeed repents of it in itself, but in so far as it was thus counterbalanced and compensated, he does not repent of it] (III: 2, 812b, DM 354v; 616).

Montaigne, who tells us that "mes fantasies, se suyvent, mais par fois c'est *de loing* : & se regardent" [my fantasies follow each other, but sometimes it is *from afar*, and look at each other] (III: 9, 994b, DM 439v; 761*), may have seen himself in the thief of Armagnac, who stole from others' fields, "mais c'estoit au loing." Not only does he work at a distance, placing his examples of repentance at the other end of Book Three from his chapter on that subject, but he places in the same distant location some intriguing parallels between the thefts of Armagnac and some of his own. With regard to his borrowing from other authors, he writes that

> quelqu'un pourroit dire de moy, que j'ay seulement faict icy un amas de fleurs estrangeres, que je n'y ay fourny du mien, que le filet à les joindre. . . . Je *desrobe* mes *larrecins*, et les desguise. . . . Comme ceux qui *desrobent* les chevaux, je leur peins le crin & la queuë, & par fois je les esborgne.

[someone might say of me that I have here only made a bunch of other people's flowers, having furnished nothing of my own but the thread to tie them. . . . I conceal my thefts, and disguise them. . . . Like those who steal horses, I paint their mane and tail and sometimes blind them in one eye.] (III: 12, 1055–56b, DM 466v–67r; 808–09, 809n)

He contrasts his practice with that of other writers who make a point of letting their readers know that they are stealing from other authors and thereby advertise how learned they are. Only Montaigne knows the full extent of his "larrecin," like the Armagnac thief who alone has the knowledge of how much he stole and from whom. But Montaigne may be alluding as well to another kind of theft, the sort he commits upon himself, as he does here with the word *larrecin*, together with *desrober*. As he says in the passage from III: 12 just quoted, "Je *desrobe* mes *larrecins*" [I *conceal* my *thefts*]. The man of Armagnac, "que chacun surnomme le *larron* . . . regarde le *larrecin* comme une action des-honneste" [whom everyone nicknames the *Thief* . . . regards *theft* as a dishonorable action] but not does entirely repent of it because he takes such care to "satisfaire par bien-faicts, aux successeurs de ceux qu'il *a desrobez*" [compensate, by good deeds, the successors of the people he *robbed*] (III: 2, 812b, DM 354r; 616). The kind of theft to which Montaigne confesses in III: 12 and the kind he performs upon his *Essays* are both textual; the larceny to which he confesses and that to which the thief of Armagnac likewise "se confesse ouvertement" [openly confesses] are both rural: crops in one case, horses in the other. Montaigne removed the comparison to stealing horses after 1588, but replaced it with a sentence that retains the echoing *desrober*: "Parmy tant d'emprunts je suis bien aise d'en pouvoir *desrober* quelqu'un, les desguisant et difformant à nouveau service" [I, among so many borrowings of mine, am very glad to be able to *hide* one now and then, disguising and altering it for a new service] (III: 12, 1056c; 809). He did the same thing to the other echoing word, *larrecin[s]*, replacing "les" in the 1588 sentence "Ceux cy *les* mettent en parade & en compte" [The latter put *them* on parade and into account] (III: 12, DM 467r) (referring to writers who advertise their theft from other writers) with *larrecins*: "Ceuxcy mettent leurs *larrecins* en parade et en conte" [The latter put their *thefts* on parade and into account] (III: 12, 1056bc; 809). Despite his changes he wanted the echo to remain.

Changes in another instance not merely preserved echoes but increased them. In 1588 Montaigne had already set up a parallel between repentance and the French wars of religion. In both, what is generated "au dedans" [on the inside] is worse than what comes "du deshors" [from the outside]. In "Du repentir" he writes

> Le vice laisse comme un ulcere en la chair, une repentance en l'ame, qui tousjours s'esgratigne, & s'ensanglante elle mesme. Car la raison efface les autres tristesses & douleurs, mais elle engendre celle de la repentance: qui est plus griefve, d'autant qu'elle naist *au dedans*, comme le froid & le chaut des fiévres, est plus poignant, que celuy qui vient *du deshors*.
>
> [Vice leaves repentance in the soul, like an ulcer in the flesh, which is always scratching itself and drawing blood. For reason effaces other griefs and sorrows; but it engenders that of repentance, which is all the more grievous because it springs *from within*, as the cold and heat of fevers is sharper than that which comes *from outside*.] (III: 2, 806b, DM 351v; 612)

In "De la phisionomie," he writes that the civil war raging around him is a "Monstrueuse guerre : les autres agissent *au dehors*, cette-cy encore contre soy, se ronge & se desfaict par son propre venin" [Monstrous war: other wars act *from outside*; this one acts in addition against itself, eats and destroys itself by its own venom] (III: 12, 1041b, DM 461r; 796*). As repentance "s'esgratigne & s'ensanglante elle mesme" [scratches and bloodies itself], this internecine conflict "se deschire & desmembre" [tears and dismembers itself] (III: 12, 1041b, DM 461r; 796). In addition, he applies the motif of the internal threat being worse than the external one to another aspect of this war, to the breakdown in military discipline that it engenders. A commanding officer faces more danger from his own men than from the enemy: "il a plus affaire *au dedans qu'au dehors*, c'est à luy de suivre, courtizer & plier" [he has more trouble *within than without*. It is he who must follow, court, and bend] (III: 12, 1042b, DM 461v; 796*).

After 1588 he made two additions, one to each chapter, that reveal how intent he was on making each chapter echo the other. To "De la phisionomie" he added a quotation from Livy—"non armis sed *vitiis* certatur" [it is fought not with arms but with *vices*] (III: 12, 1041c; 796)—that echoes what he had already written in the passage quoted above from "Du repentir" about how vice creates inner turmoil in the soul: "*Le vice* laisse comme un ulcere en la chair, une repentance en l'ame, qui tousjours s'esgratigne, & s'ensanglante elle mesme" [*Vice* leaves repentance in the soul, like an ulcer in the flesh, which is always scratching itself and drawing blood]. He quotes Livy at a moment when he is complaining about the lawlessness the civil war brings in its wake: "J'avois d'une part, les ennemys à ma porte, d'autre part, les picoreurs, pires ennemys" [I had on the one hand the enemy at my door, on the other hand the freebooters, worse enemies] (III: 12, 1041b, DM 461r; 796). Not only does this addition set up an echo with *vice*, but it also forges a further connection between repentance as a cause of internal torment and the disorder among armed men that poses a greater internal than external threat.

The addition to "Du repentir" immediately precedes "Le vice laisse comme un ulcere en la chair, une repentance en l'ame . . . ," which suggests that Montaigne was thinking of these two additions together—that is, the two additions are textually connected, the one in III: 12, Livy on vices, echoing the "vice" immediately before which the III: 2 addition was placed. It is this: "La malice *hume* la plus part de *son propre venin* et *s'en empoisonne*" [Malice *sucks up* the greater part *of its own venom*, and *poisons itself* with it] (III: 2, 806c; 612). As Balsamo et al. note (1720), Montaigne is paraphrasing Seneca: "malitia ipsa maximam partem veneni sui bibit." It appears in this passage of Letter 81 (paragraph 22) to Lucilius:

> When we do wrong, only the least and lightest portion of it flows back upon our neighbor; the worst and, if I may use the term, the densest portion of it stays at home and troubles the owner. My master Attalus used to say: "Evil herself drinks the largest portion of her own poison." The poison which serpents carry for the destruction of others, and secrete without harm to themselves, is not like this poison; for this sort is ruinous to the possessor.[1]

By choosing to translate Seneca's "bibit" by "hume" (instead of, say, "boit"), Montaigne sets up an echo with this line in "De la phisionomie": "il n'est air qui *se hume* si gouluement, qui s'espande & penetre, comme faict la licence" [there is no air that *is inhaled* so greedily, that so spreads and penetrates, as does license] (III: 12, 1042b, DM 461v; 796). The word is rare, appearing in this form only these two times in the *Essays*. The license to which he is refer-

---

1. Seneca, *Ad Lucilium Epistulae Morales*. Tr. Richard M. Gummere (Cambridge: Harvard University Press / Loeb Library, 1920): 233–35.

ring is that of soldiers in the civil conflict who pose a greater threat to their officers than does the enemy. The words "son propre venin" find a precise counterpart in "Monstrueuse guerre : les autres agissent au dehors, cette-cy encore contre soy, se ronge & se desfaict par *son propre venin*" [Monstrous war: other wars act from outside; this one acts in addition against itself, eats and destroys itself by *its own venom*] (III: 12, 1041b, DM 461r; 796*). The "s'en empoisonne" is echoed by "Nostre mal *s'empoisonne* / Du secours qu'on luy donne" ["Our illness *poisons itself* / With the remedy it is given"] (III: 12, 1041b, DM 461r; 796*). The context is Montaigne's observation that this monstrous war of Catholic against Protestant "vient guarir la sedition, & en est pleine, veut chastier la desobeyssance, & en montre l'exemple, & employée à la deffence des loix, faict sa part de rebellion à l'encontre des siennes propres" [comes to cure sedition and is full of it, would chastise disobedience and provides an example of it, and while employed in defense of the laws, rebels against its own] (III: 12, 1041b, DM 461r; 796*). Like the "malice" in "Du repentir," it is a self-poisoning "mal."

The parallels are so extensive and so striking that one wonders whether Montaigne was really saying what he thought about repentance and about the French civil wars or whether he was just playing with words! As Brody remarks, "it is the peculiar power of Montaigne's words to lead us back repeatedly and relentlessly to a constant sub-text that parallels the surface text" (261).

3. Intercourse with the Lame

"De trois commerces" [Of three kinds of intercourse] (III: 3) and *"Des boyteux"* [Of the lame] (III: 11)

The pages of "Des boyteux" where the title's topic is addressed are particularly rich in connections to each of the three "commerces"—social, sexual and textual—with which its symmetrical companion is concerned.

> A propos, ou hors de propos, il n'importe, on dict en Italie en commun proverbe, que celuy-là *ne cognoit pas Venus* en sa parfaicte douceur, qui n'a couché avec la boiteuse.
>
> [Apropos or malapropos, no matter, they say in Italy as a common proverb that he *does not know Venus* in her perfect sweetness who has not lain with a cripple.] (III: 11, 1033b, DM 457v–58r; 791)

This forms a strange echo to something Montaigne says in "De trois commerces": "De moy, je *ne connois non plus Venus* sans Cupidon, qu'une maternité sans engence : ce sont choses qui s'entreprestent & s'entredoivent leur essence" [For my part, I *no more know Venus* without Cupid than maternity without offspring: they are things that lend and owe their essence to each other] (III: 3, 826b, DM 360v; 627*). As Balsamo et al. explain, "here Venus represents desire, physical pleasure, and Cupid represents love" (1729). No other instance of "ne pas / ne plus connaître Venus" appears in the *Essays*. The two assertions are paradoxically contradictory: one of them holds that you cannot really know Venus without engaging in casual sex with a cripple, the other that one cannot know Venus by engaging in casual sex from which love is absent.

> *La fortune*, ou quelque particulier accident, ont mis il y a long temps ce mot en la bouche du peuple, & se dict *des masles comme des femelles*.

> [*Fortune*, or some particular incident, long ago put this saying into the mouth of the people, and it is said *of males as well as of females*.] (III: 11, 1033b, DM 458r; 791)

In the first section of III: 3, in Montaigne's discussion of his social intercourse with other men, a post-1588 addition echoes this sentence's elements of (a) fortune, (b) the speech of the lower classes, and (c) what is true of males as well as females: "le conseil de Platon ne me plaist pas, de parler tousjours d'un langage maestral à ses serviteurs, sans jeu, sans familiarité, *soit envers les males, soit envers les femelles*. Car . . . il est inhumain et injuste de faire tant valoir cette telle quelle prerogative de *la fortune*" [I do not like Plato's advice, always to talk to our servants, *whether to males or to females*, in masterful terms, without playfulness and without familiarity. For . . . it is inhuman and unjust to make so much of this accidental privilege of Fortune] (III: 3, 821c; 623*). Fortune, in III: 11, may have been responsible for what is said *by* the lower social classes; that same Fortune, in III: 3, has something to do with what is said *to* them.

> Car la Royne des Amazonnes, respondit au Scyte qui la convioit à l'amour, arista xolos oiphei, le boiteux le faict le mieux.

> [For the Queen of the Amazons replied to the Scythian who was inviting her to make love: "The lame man does it best"] (III: 11, 1033b, DM 458r; 791*)

That one can tell from the way a person walks how well he would do at a somewhat more strenuous activity, as the Queen of the Amazons said of the sexual prowess of those who limp, is asserted as well in III: 3: "Hyppomachus disoit bien qu'il connoissoit les bons luicteurs, à les voir simplement marcher par une ruë" [Hippomachus used to say that he could tell good wrestlers by seeing them walk down the street] (III: 3, 824b, DM 360r; 625–26*). Montaigne's source is Plutarch's *Life of Dion*, but he made two telling changes. In Plutarch, Hippomachus wasn't claiming that he could recognize a good wrestler but that he could recognize his own wrestling pupils, and he didn't say he could tell them from how they used their legs but from how they used their hands. Here is Amyot's translation, which was the version Montaigne customarily used: "un certain maistre de lucte & d'escrime, nommé Hippomachus, disoit qu'il conoissoit bien de tout loin ceux qui avoyent apris ces exercices du corps sous lui, à les voir tant seulement revenir du marché aportans de la chair en leurs mains" [a certain teacher of wrestling and fencing named Hippomachus used to say that he recognized from afar all those who had learned those physical exercises from him, just from seeing them come back from the market carrying meat in their hands]. Plutarch's purpose in recounting this anecdote is to make a point about how alike students of the same master can be—Dion, who studied with Plato in person, and Brutus, who studied him through his writings. Montaigne's purpose is different, and this accounts for why he made Hippomachus say that he had a way of spotting a good wrestler instead of saying that he could recognize his own students: "Ce n'est pas au subject des substitutions seulement, que nostre esprit montre sa beauté & sa force, & aux affaires des Roys : il la monstre autant aux confabulations privées. Je connois mes gens au silence mesme, & à leur soubsrire, & les descouvre mieux à l'advanture à table, qu'au conseil" [It is not only on the subject of lineal substitutions or the affairs of kings that our mind shows its beauty and strength; it shows it as much in private confabulations. I know my men even more by their silence and their smiles, and perhaps find out more about them at table than in the council chamber] (III: 3, 824b, DM 360r; 625). Montaigne's saying "Je connois mes gens" [I know my men] may be a sly wink signaling that he was well aware of what Hippomachus really said, and that he knew he was misquoting Plutarch, but he wasn't saying he could recognize someone he already knew. He meant that he could recognize the kind of conversational partner he was looking for: "Les hommes, de la societé & familiarité desquels je suis en queste" [The men whose society and intimacy I seek] (III: 3, 824b, DM 359v; 625).

Of the two changes Montaigne made in Plutarch, the one concerning whom or what Hippomachus could recognize from a distance suits his immediate purpose in "De trois commerces," while the change from hands to feet suits his purpose in the larger context that chapter forms with "Des boyteux," anticipating the attention paid to the walking ability (or inability) of those whom the Amazons found to be so good in bed.

> En cette republique feminine, *pour fuir* la domination des masles, elles les stropioient des l'enfance, bras, jambes, & autres membres qui leur donnoient avantage sur elles, & se servoient d'eux, à ce seulement, à quoy nous nous servons d'elles par deçà.

> [In that feminine commonwealth, *to escape* the domination of the males, they crippled them from childhood—arms, legs, and other parts that gave men an advantage over them—and made use of them only for the purpose for which we make use of women over here.] (III: 11, 1033b, DM 458r; 791*)

The Amazons of antiquity seeking to flee male domination find their counterpart in women who have the same motivation in "De trois commerces":

> Or de cette trahison commune & ordinaire des hommes d'aujourd'huy, il faut qu'il advienne, ce que desja nous montre l'experience, c'est qu'elles se r'alient & rejettent à elles mesmes, ou entre elles, *pour nous fuyr* : ou bien qu'elles se rengent aussi de leur costé, à cet exemple que nous leur donnons, qu'elles jouent leur part de la farce, & se prestent à cette negotiation, sans passion, sans soing & sans amour.

> [Now the necessary outcome of this common and ordinary treachery of the men of today is what experience is already showing us, that they rally and fall back upon themselves or each other *to flee from* us; or else that they too, for their part, fall in line with this example that we give them, play their part in the farce, and lend themselves to this negotiation, without passion, without interest, and without love.] (III: 3, 825b, DM 360v; 626–27*)

Both the Amazons and women of Montaigne's time not only flee men, but imitate them too. The Amazons, having maimed their victims, "se servoient d'eux, à ce seulement, à quoy nous nous servons d'elles par deçà" [made use of them only for the purpose for which we make use of women over here]— that is, for sex. Montaigne divides the women of his time into two groups, one of which forms its own society, like the Amazons their republic ("elles se r'alient & rejettent à elles mesmes" [they rally and fall back upon themselves or each other]), but those in the other group "se rengent . . . à cet exemple que nous leur donnons" [fall in line . . . with this example that we give them], and engage in loveless sex with men. In III: 3, the women do either one thing or the other; in III: 11, the Amazons do both—for they evidently aren't engaging in sex with the lame out of affection but because they believe that the latter are better at it.

> J'eusse dict, que le *mouvement detraqué* de la boiteuse, apportast quelque nouveau goust à la besongne, & quelque point de douceur à ceux qui l'essayent.

> [I would have said that the *irregular movement* of the lame woman brought some new pleasure to the business and a spice of sweetness to those who try it.] (III: 11, 1033b, DM 458r; 791)

He writes in "De trois commerces" as well—in a post-1588 addition—of the possibility that a woman's *mouvement* could be sexually enticing, even if nothing else about her was: "[B] il n'y a aucune d'elles, pour malotruë qu'elle soit, qui ne pense estre bien aymable, [C] et qui ne se recommande par son aage ou par son ris, ou par son *mouvement*; car de laides universellement il n'en est, non plus que de belles" [(B) there is not a woman, however ill-favored she may be, who does not think herself worth loving, (C) and who does not think herself attractive for her youth or her laugh, or the way she *moves*. For there are no absolutely ugly women, any more than there are absolutely beautiful ones] (III: 3, 825bc; 626*).

> mais je viens d'apprendre, que mesme la philosophie ancienne en a decidé : elle dict que les *jambes* & cuisses des boiteuses, ne recevant à cause de leur imperfection, l'aliment qui leur est deu, il en advient que les *parties genitales*, qui sont au dessus, sont plus plaines, plus nourries, & vigoureuses. Ou bien, que ce defaut empeschant l'*exercice*, ceux qui en sont entachez, dissipent moins leurs forces, & en viennent plus entiers aux operations de Venus. Qui est aussi la raison, pourquoy les Grecs descrioient les tisserandes d'estre plus chaudes que les autres femmes, à cause du mestier sedentaire qu'elles font, sans grand *exercice* du *corps*.

> [but I have just learned that ancient philosophy, no less, has decided the question; it says that since the *legs* and thighs of lame women, because of their imperfection, do not receive the food that is their due, the result is that the *genital parts*, which are above, are fuller, better nourished, and

more vigorous. Or else that, this defect preventing *exercise*, those who are tainted by it dissipate their strength less and come more entire to the works of Venus. Which is also the reason why the Greeks decried women weavers as being hotter than other women: because of the sedentary trade they perform, without much *bodily exercise*.] (III: 11, 1033–34b, DM 458r; 791*)

He speaks of the first of his "trois commerces," interaction with men through the art of conversation, as a form of *exercise*: "La fin de ce commerce, c'est simplement la privauté, frequentation, & conference : l'*exercice* des ames, sans autre fruit. . . . Une ame bien née, & *exercée* à la practique des hommes, se rend plainement aggreable d'elle mesme" [The object of this intercourse is simply intimacy, fellowship, and conversation: the *exercise* of our souls with no other gain. . . . A wellborn mind that is *practiced* in dealing with men makes itself thoroughly agreeable by itself] (III: 3, 824b, DM 359v–60r; 625–26*). And we have seen how his changing Plutarch's anecdote about Hippomachus to focus on the way a man walks (as opposed to what he does with his hands) connects with that same passage, and in particular with this part of it, with its reasoning concerning the "jambes & cuisses" of the "boiteuses."

The focus here placed on the "parties genitales" forms an echo to certain "parties matrimoniales" that appear in the same post-1588 addition to his discussion of his second "commerce," that with women, in which he writes of an ill-favored woman's *mouvement* as sexually attractive. Then he goes on to write of how another group of women reveal their only claim to beauty: "les filles Brachmanes qui ont faute d'autre recommandation, le peuple assemblé à cri publiq pour cet effect, vont en la place, faisant montre de leurs *parties matrimoniales*, veoir si par là aumoins elles ne valent pas d'acquerir un mary" [the Brahman girls who have nothing else to recommend them go to the market place, when the people have been assembled by the public crier for this purpose, and display their *matrimonial parts*, to see if in this respect at least they are not good enough to get a husband] (III: 3, 825c; 626). Although there are seven other allusions in Book Three to *parties* in this sense (in III: 1 and III: 5) those others are all of the male variety. It is fair to say that these feminine *parties* are on display in this book of the *Essays* both in the Brahman village and in the description of the *boiteuses*, each answering the other as only Montaigne's symmetrically placed echoes know how.

What he says about his third "commerce," the one with books, likewise provides some textual parallels with the passage on the "boiteuses," where he notes that the weaving trade condemns the women who ply it to a life "sans grand *exercice du corps*" [without much *bodily exercise*] (III: 11, 1034b, DM

458r; 791). Reading, another sedentary activity, poses the same problem for Montaigne. This "commerce," rewarding as it is, "a ses incommoditez, & bien poisantes : l'ame s'y *exerce*, mais le *corps*, duquel je n'ay non plus oublié le soing, demeure ce pendant sans action, s'atterre & s'attriste" [has its disadvantages, and very weighty ones. The mind is *exercised* in books, but the *body*, whose care I have not forgotten either, remains meanwhile inactive, droops and grieves] (III: 3, 829b, DM 362v; 630). Indeed, he dreams of constructing a walkway next to his library to stretch his legs in, "un proumenoir. Mes pensées *dorment*, si je les assis. Mon esprit ne va, si les *jambes* ne l'agitent" [a place to walk. My thoughts *fall asleep* if I make them sit down. My mind will not budge unless my *legs* move it] (III: 3, 828c; 629).

Legs and sleep are combined in an opposite way in another passage in "Des boyteux," where he has not yet taken up the topic of the lame. A man suffering from gout had heard of a priest who could cure that malady, but he would have to travel a distance to reach him. Eager to make the journey, he "par la force de son apprehension persuada et *endormit ses jambes* pour quelques heures, si qu'il en tira du service qu'elles avoient desapris luy faire il y avoit long temps" [by the power of his imagination persuaded his legs and put them to sleep for a few hours, so that he derived from them a service that they had long since forgotten how to do for him] (III: 11, 1028–29b, DM 455r; 787). While he found that his thoughts *dorment* [fall asleep] if he doesn't get up and walk around a bit, the gout-sufferer found that if he could *endormir ses jambes* [put his legs to sleep] (that is, if he could anesthetize them from the pain of the gout) then he could walk. So while in III: 3 using one's legs prevents one's thoughts from falling asleep, in III: 11 a man puts his legs to sleep in order to use them.

4. The Little Things

"De la diversion" [Of diversion] (III: 4) and "De mesnager sa volonté" [Of husbanding your will] (III: 10)

"Peu de chose nous divertit & destourne : car peu de chose nous tient" [A little thing diverts and turns us, for a little thing holds us] (III: 4, 836a, DM 365v; 635*), Montaigne writes in "De la diversion." He goes on to elaborate: "Nous ne regardons gueres les subjects en gros & seuls : ce sont des circonstances ou des images menues & superficieles qui nous frapent, & des vaines escorces qui rejaillisent des subjects" [We scarcely look at things in gross and alone; it is the minute and superficial circumstances and notions that strike us, and the empty husks that peel off from the things]. We are distracted, that is, by the "superficial" aspects of a subject, its useless outer surface, this "little thing" that diverts us, with the implication that we should not allow ourselves to be thus diverted from the subject itself.

Such, however, might itself be a superficial reading of this passage, because if we could get past the surface of this apparent deprecation of surface we might find that things are not quite what they seem, on the surface, to be. For the words "peu de chose nous tient" find an intriguing echo in the very first words of III: 4's companion chapter, "De mesnager sa volonté." It is particularly intriguing because although it is almost word for word the same, it means just the opposite: "Au pris du commun des hommes, *peu de choses* me touchent, ou pour mieux dire, *me tiennent*" [In comparison with most men, *few things* touch me, or, to put it better, *hold me*] (III: 10, 1003b, DM 443r; 766). By the difference of a single letter, the *s* that distinguishes "peu de chose" from "peu de choses," Montaigne manages to say precisely opposite things, the "peu de chose nous tient" of III: 4 meaning "a little thing holds us" (or as Frame translates it, "it takes little to hold us"),[2] yet the "peu de choses ... me tiennent" of III: 10 telling us that "few things ... hold me." It is the difference between a positive and a negative. Montaigne may not be contradicting himself, however, because what he said in III: 4 applies to "us"—evidently to people in general—while the statement in III: 10 applies only to himself. But this in no way frees us from the obligation to give serious consideration to what is itself a phenomenon of the *surface* of the text, an obligation that a superficial reading of the passage in III: 4, with its apparent dismissal of the husk for the sake of the core, might have made us think we did not, with this text, have to assume. But what in fact we are called here to consider is the extent to which the surface penetrates that core. And when Montaigne complains in III: 4 that "We scarcely look at subjects in gross"—in their totality—he could be taken, were his words to be applied to his readers, to mean that we look at the whole picture all too seldom. It is a picture that in its entirety would take in just this kind of symmetrically-placed echo. In other words, this is a self-referential metafictional moment. This is especially true of the phrase "ou pour mieux dire" [or, to put it better] in the echoing passage ("Au pris du commun des hommes, peu de choses me touchent, *ou pour mieux dire*, me tiennent"), for it does indeed put it better. It is only when he supplements "me touchent" with "me tiennent" that the echo with "peu de chose nous *tient*" fully emerges.

---

2. My translation follows that of Montaigne's near-contemporary John Florio: "A little thing doth divert and turne us; for a small thing holds us."

Another instance of both chapters talking about the same subject but from opposite points of view arises from a particular use of the tactic of diversion that is thematic in "De la diversion" but is all the same a significant presence in "De mesnager sa volonté." As well it might, since diversion is employed in III: 4 to deal with one's desires in the interests of self-control, which itself is the announced topic of III: 10. The relevant passage in III: 4 has to do with diverting the mind from thoughts of vengeance:

> C'est une douce passion que la *vengeance* . . . pour *en distraire* dernierement un jeune prince, je . . . m'amusay à luy faire gouster la beauté d'une image contraire : l'honneur, la faveur, la bien-veillance qu'il acquerroit par clemence & bonté : je le destournay à l'ambition.
>
> [*Vengeance* is a sweet passion. . . . Recently, in order *to distract* a young prince *away from it*, I . . . applied myself to making him relish the beauty of a contrary picture, the honor, favor, and good will he would acquire by clemency and kindness. I diverted him to ambition.] (III: 4, 835b, DM 364v; 634)

Distracting someone *away* from vengeance, however, is not what Montaigne has in mind in a parallel passage in "De mesnager sa volonté." For there vengeance is not to be avoided but desired, and any distraction or diversion made use of there is geared toward making that vengeance all the more effective.

> La philosophie veut qu'au chastiment des offences receuës, nous *en distrayons* la cholere, non afin que la *vengeance* en soit moindre, ains au rebours, afin qu'elle soit d'autant mieux assennee & plus poisante : à quoy il luy semble que cette impetuosité porte empeschement.
>
> [Philosophy wills that in chastising injuries received we *distract* anger *away from it*, not so that the *vengeance* may be less, but on the contrary so that it may be all the better dealt out and heavier; which purposes, so philosophy thinks, this impetuosity hinders.] (III: 10, 1008b, DM 445v; 770–71*)

Vengeance (in any form of noun or verb) appears together with *distraire* (in any form) in no other chapter than these two.

Frivolity and blushing are united, though in opposite ways (as were vengeance and distraction) in the two chapters. In "De la diversion" Montaigne imagines a soldier on a battlefield "tout bouillant & *rougissant* de cholere" [all boiling and red with anger] for a "Frivole cause" [Frivolous cause][3] (III: 4, 839b, DM 366v; 637). In "De mesnager sa volonté" he again calls our attention to an imaginary warrior caught up in the heat of battle: "Regardez pourquoy celuy-là s'en va courre fortune de son honneur & de sa vie, à tout son espée & son poignart; qu'il vous die d'où vient la source de ce debat, il ne le peut faire sans *rougir*, tant l'occasion en est vaine, & *frivole*" [See why that man goes off to risk his honor and his life with his sword and dagger; let him tell you whence comes the source of this quarrel; he cannot do so without *blushing*, so vain and *frivolous* is the occasion of it] (III: 10, 1018b, DM 449v; 779). This time the reason the soldier is fighting is still frivolous though his face reddens from quite a different emotion, not anger but shame (at the frivolity of the occasion). Unlike the two passages about the distraction of vengeance, the two here are not at odds with each other on the sentiment the narrator appears to express. For in both the warrior's zeal is frivolous, artificially induced. In both of these anecdotes the same elements—frivolous causality and blushing combatants—appear, though disassembled and rearranged into a new combination. We should note that there are two additional recurrent elements: that Montaigne imagines the soldier being asked (by Montaigne in III: 4, by the reader in III: 10) why he is fighting and the way he invites the reader to "see": "Voyez le" (III: 4, 839b, DM 366v; 637) and "Regardez" (III: 10, 1018b, DM 449v; 779). Reddening (any form of *rougir*) and frivolity (any form of *frivole*) make a joint appearance in no other chapter.

For another example of the reassembled anecdote we could consider the case of the burning martyrs and the snowman. In "De la diversion" Montaigne questions the constancy of martyrs about to be burned at the stake. Praying out loud, their eyes and their hands raised to heaven, filling their senses as much as they can with ardent devotion, "On les doibt louer de religion : mais non proprement de *constance*. Ils fuyent la luicte : ils destournent de la mort leur consideration" [They are to be praised for piety, but not properly for *constancy*. They avoid the struggle; they turn their attention away from death] (III: 4, 833b, DM 364r; 632*). To this questionable constancy on the part of those confronted with fire Montaigne in "De mesnager sa volonté" opposes a questionable "constancy" on the part of one confronted with ice. Diogenes, stark naked, was embracing a snowman as a test of his endurance. A passerby asked if he was very cold. Not at all, the stoic said. "Or, suyvit l'autre, que penses-tu donc faire de difficile & d'exemplaire à

---

3. Actually, it is the reader he is addressing whom he imagines saying that it is frivolous. Montaigne goes farther, saying there was no cause at all, just a "resverie sans corps & sans suject" [daydream without body or subject] that motivated the soldier.

se tenir là? Pour mesurer la *constance,* il faut necessairement sçavoir la souffrance" ["Then," the other went on, "what difficult and exemplary thing do you think you are doing by remaining there?" To measure the *constancy* we must necessarily know the suffering] (III: 10, 1014b, DM 448r; 776*).

5. Sexual Vanity, Vain Sex

"Sur des vers de Virgile" [Of some lines of Virgil] (III: 5) and "De la vanité" [Of vanity] (III: 9)

In "de la vanité," Montaigne tells us that he is in the habit of affecting a studied nonchalance that is really a cover for a more secret preparation. Though he is talking about speaking in public, his words are doubtless relevant to his writing style, whose surface is just as likely to give the impression of improvisation: "mon dessein est, de representer en parlant, une profonde nonchalance, & des mouvemens fortuites & impremeditez, comme naissans des occasions presentes" [my plan in speaking is to display an extreme nonchalance and fortuitous and unpremeditated gestures, as if they arose from the immediate occasion] (III: 9, 963b, DM 424v; 735*). He compares his own experience to that of poor Lyncestes, who was accused of conspiring against Alexander and was brought before the army to give his defense. He had committed his carefully planned speech to memory, "de laquelle tout hesitant & begayant il prononça quelques paroles: comme il se trouboit de plus en plus, ce pendant qu'il luicte avec sa memoire, & qu'il la *retaste*" [of which, all hesitating and stammering, he pronounced a few words. As he was growing more and more troubled, wrestling with his memory and trying *to go over it again*] (III: 9, 962b, DM 424r; 735*), the soldiers nearby rushed up and killed him, taking his difficulty in expressing himself to be a confession of guilt. Just a few lines before, Montaigne had used the verb *retaster* (literally, to touch a second time) in relation to his writing the *Essays* and to his own wrestling with a poor memory: "Encores en ces ravasseries icy, crains-je la trahison, de ma memoire, que par inadvertance, elle m'aye faict enregistrer une chose deux fois. Je hay à me reconnoistre, & ne *retaste* jamais qu'envis ce qui m'est une fois eschappé" [In these ramblings of mine I fear the treachery of my memory, lest inadvertently it may have made me record something twice. I hate to reexamine myself, and never *go over again*, if I can help it, what has once escaped me] (III: 9, 962b, 423v; 734*).

Complaining about an imperfect memory that is likely to allow him to say the same thing twice in two different places is a good way to affect nonchalance.[4] To conceal, that is, under the excuse of forgetfulness the significance of what he does say twice, and does so intentionally. In fact it happens here. In commenting on Lyncestes' plight he says that the flow of his own discourse is easily stopped. But in "Sur des vers de Virgile" he also complains that it is easily stopped. The reasons are different. In "De la vanité" it will happen if he relies too much on his memory: "Pour moy, cela mesme, que je sois lié à ce que j'ay à dire, sert à m'en desprendre. Quand je me suis commis & assigné entierement à ma memoire, je pends si fort sur elle, que je l'accable" [For my part, the very fact of being bound to what I have to say is enough to break my grip on it. When I have committed and entrusted myself entirely to my memory, I lean so heavily on it that I overburden it] (III: 9, 963b, DM 424r–24v; 735). In "Sur des vers de Virgile" it will happen if someone interrupts him: "J'ay le parler un peu delicatement jaloux d'attention & de silence, si je parle de force. Qui m'interrompt, m'arreste" [In speech I am rather sensitively jealous of attention and silence if I am speaking in earnest: whoever interrupts me stops me] (III: 5, 876b, DM 384r; 668).

Nor long after the passage in "De la vanité" where he says he is afraid of having said the same thing twice, he again says the same thing twice: "*Les imperfections* mesme, ont leur moyen de se recommander" [Even *imperfections* have a way of recommending themselves] (III: 9, 964b, DM 425r; 737). For here he is repeating a sentiment expressed in III: 5: "Je corrigerois volontiers une erreur accidentale, dequoy je suis plain, ainsi que je cours inadvertemment, mais *les imperfections* qui sont en moy ordinaires & constantes, ce seroit trahison de les oster" [I would indeed correct an accidental error, and I am full of them, since I run on carelessly. But *the imperfections* that are ordinary and constant in me it would be treachery to remove] (III: 5, 875b, 383v; 667). In both chapters he is talking about imperfections in the *Essays*. Given that he says that if he were to "enregistrer une chose deux fois" [record something twice] it would be "par inadvertance" [inadvertently], then the second of these statements about the desirability of keeping imperfections in the book is a self-naming artifact because it is an imperfection he kept in the book.

But there is an interesting twist in this repetition, for in making it he seems to contradict himself. In the passage quoted from "Sur des vers de Virgile" he says there are some errors he would correct, the inadvertent ones ("*Je*

---

4. We are reminded by Sylvie Peytavin of the insistence with which Montaigne keeps telling us throughout the *Essays* that he has a monstrously bad faculty of memory in "L'exceptionnelle amnésie de Montaigne. Constat ou signe?" *Nouveau Bulletin de la Société Internationale des Amis de Montaigne* 50 (July–December 2009): 91–107. See also Eric Macphail, "Mémoire," in the *Dictionnaire de Montaigne*, 748–50.

corrigerois volontiers une erreur accidentale, dequoy je suis plain, ainsi que je cours *inadvertemment*"), and just a few lines later he says the same thing again (an inadvertent error?): "*je corrige* les fautes d'*inadvertence*, non celles de coustume" [I *correct* the faults of *inadvertence*, not those of habit] (III: 5, 875b, 383v; 667). Yet in the passage from "De la vanité" he says he does *not* correct the *Essays* from one edition to the next: "J'adjouste, mais *je ne corrige pas*" [I add, but *I do not correct*] (III: 9, 963b, DM 424v; 736). The seeming contradiction vanishes when he goes on to make clear that the errors he doesn't correct are the habitual ones, the imperfections that "ont leur moyen de se recommender." Yet on the level of the words themselves, which is where we have so often seen Montaigne at play, the parallels are substantial. In both passages he writes of what he does or doesn't correct and of imperfections worth keeping.

Here's another instance of his repeating himself. In "Sur des vers de Virgile" he advertises for a companion:

S'il y a *quelque personne d'honneur*, quelque bonne *compagnie*, aux champs, en la ville, en France, ou ailleurs, resseante, ou voyagere, à qui *mes humeurs* soient bonnes, de qui les humeurs me soient bonnes, il n'est que de siffler en paume, *je* leur *iray* fournir des essays, en cher & en os.

[If there *some person of honor*, some good *company*, in country or city, in France or elsewhere, residing or traveling, to whom *my humors* seem good, and whose humors seem good to me, they have only to whistle in their palm and *I will go* furnish them with essays in flesh and bone.] (III: 5, 843–44b, DM 368v; 640*)

In "De la vanité" he repeats the offer:

Outre ce profit, que je tire d'escrire de moy, j'en espere cet autre, que s'il advient que *mes humeurs* plaisent, & accordent à *quelque honneste homme*, avant que je meure, il recerchera de nous joindre. . . . Si à si bonnes enseignes, je sçavois quelqu'un qui me fut propre, certes *je l'irois* trouver bien loing. Car la douceur d'une sortable, & aggreable *compaignie*, ne se peut assez acheter à mon gré.

[Besides this profit that I derive from writing about myself, I hope for this other advantage, that if *my humors* happen to please and suit *some worthy man* before I die, he will try to meet me. . . . If by such good signs I knew of a man who was suited to me, truly I *would go* very far to find him; for the sweetness of harmonious and agreeable *company* cannot be bought too dearly, in my opinion.] (III: 9, 981b, DM 432v; 750)

Not only is the wish repeated, but so too the vocabulary: *quelque, compaignie, mes humeurs, je . . . iray / irois.* Is this really a case of saying the same thing twice by inadvertence? Or is it not rather another instance of the myriad of symmetrically and intentionally placed echoes in the text? Like the self-naming imperfections we encountered above, this repetition is self-referential: like the situation they describe, each reaches out to its distant double, each to the other across the pages that separate them. Or they would if they knew the other was there. Montaigne, that is, pretends not to know that he has said the same thing twice, saying that if he were ever to do so it would be inadvertent. He pretends that he never willingly goes over what he has written, that he "ne retaste jamais qu'envis ce qui m'est une fois eschappé." But we know that isn't true. As Marianne S. Meijer reminds us, "The *Exemplaire de Bordeaux* shows that Montaigne continuously reread his own book and commented on his own text by inserting additions of varying length."[5] Indeed, both of these passages, dating from the 1588 edition, are surrounded by post-1588 insertions.

Thus do III: 5 and III: 9 form, in hidden yet discernible ways, a single text. Their two great themes, not surprisingly, come together when Montaigne observes of sex that "Certes c'est une marque non seulement de nostre corruption originelle: mais aussi de nostre *vanité* & deformité" [Truly it is a mark not only of our original corruption but also of our *vanity* and deformity] (III: 5, 878b, DM 385r; 669*).[6] Or again: "C'est une passion qui mesle à bien peu d'essence solide, beaucoup plus de *vanité* & resverie fievreuse" [this is a passion that with very little solid essence mixes in much more *vanity* and feverish dreaming] (III: 5, 880b, DM 386r; 671*).

The two chapters share a different variety of common text as well. As André Tournon points out (*Route par ailleurs*, 347), an examination of the Bordeaux Copy reveals that a post-1588 addition to III: 9 was originally a post-1588 addition to III: 5. The following passage—

Plaisante fantasie: plusieurs choses que je ne voudroy dire à personne, je les dis au peuple, et sur mes plus secretes sciences ou pensées renvoye à une boutique de libraire mes amis plus feaux.

---

5. Page 168 of Marianne S. Meijer, "Guesswork or Facts: Connections between Montaigne's Last Three Chapters (III: 11, 12, and 13)," *Yale French Studies* 64 (1983): 167–79.

6. "Vanity" in the original sense of emptiness, which is predominant in "De la vanité."

[Amusing notion: many things that I would not want to tell anyone, I tell the public; and for my most secret knowledge and thoughts I send my most faithful friends to a bookseller's shop.] (III: 9, 981c; 750)

—was written in the margin of the other chapter[7] to be inserted just before "Celuy qui faict tout pour l'honneur & pour la gloire, que pense-il gaigner, en se produisant au monde en masque, desrobant son vray estre à la connoissance du peuple? Louez un bossu de sa belle taille, il le doit recevoir à injure" [A man who does everything for honor and glory, what does he think to gain by presenting himself to the world in a mask, concealing his true being from public knowledge? Praise a hunchback for his handsome figure, and he is bound to take it as an insult] (III: 5, 847b, DM 369v; 643). That *bossu*, we know, is itself the site of another intratextual echo. And where Montaigne finally put this addition in III: 9 was right inside another such echo, the appeal to a stranger with whom his "humeurs" might find favor that harks back to a similar appeal in III: 5. He broke up the original passage to place this insertion just after the sentence about the "humeurs" and before the part that echoes the "compaignie" of the equivalent passage in III: 5.

The two chapters were interchangeable for Montaigne in this sense: an addition originally intended for one could just as easily go into the other.[8]

6. Borrowed Wealth

"Des coches" [Of coaches] (III: 6) and "De l'art de conferer" [Of the art of discussion] (III: 8)

"Des coches" is memorable for its account of Spanish treachery and Aztec and Incan nobility of spirit. Montaigne writes at length, for example, about the stoic valor of the "*Roy de Mexico*, ayant long temps defendu sa ville assiegée, & montré en ce siege tout ce que peut & la souffrance, & la perseverance, si

---

7. There is slightly different wording at the end of what he had added in the margin of III: 5: "... renvoie à mon livre mes plus privez amis" [I send my most private friends to my book].

8. Another indication of the continuity of Montaigne's chapter on sex and his chapter on vanity is that in the former he argues that a marriage should devolve into a friendship ("Ung bon mariage, s'il en est, refuse la compaignie & conditions de l'amour, il tache à representer celles de *l'amitié*" [A good marriage, if such there be, rejects the company and conditions of love. It tries to reproduce those of *friendship*] [III: 5, 851b, DM 371v; 647]) and in the latter that is precisely what he calls it: "Quant aux devoirs de *l'amitié maritale*, qu'on pense estre interessez par cette absence, je ne le crois pas" [As for the duties of *marital friendship* that some people consider injured by absence, I do not believe it] (III: 9, 975b, DM 429v; 745*).

onques prince, & peuple, le monstra" [*king of Mexico*, having long defended his besieged city and shown in this siege all that endurance and perseverance can do, if ever prince and people did so] (III: 6, 912b, DM 400v; 696*). In their mad search for gold, the conquistadors tortured him, together with one of the chief notables of his court. The latter, unable to bear his pain, asked the king for permission to tell his tormentors what they wanted to hear, but

> *le Roy* plantant fierement & rigoureusement les yeux sur luy, pour reproche de sa lascheté & pusillanimité, luy dict seulement ces mots, d'une voix rude & ferme: & moy suis-je dans un bain, suis-je pas plus à mon aise que toy?

> [*the king*, fixing his eyes proudly and severely on him in reproach for his cowardice and pusillanimity, said to him only these words, in a stern firm voice: "And I, am I in a bath? Am I more comfortable than you?"] (III: 6, 912b, DM 400v–401r; 696–97*)

But even though Montaigne in "De l'art de conferer" sticks more closely to its declared subject—for in "Des coches" he spends more time talking about the New World (and the spectacles held in the Roman Coliseum) than about coaches—he manages to wander far enough from the topic his title announces to talk about the very same king: "A quoy, touche l'usage de tant de peuples, qui canonizent *le Roy*, qu'ils ont faict d'entre eux, & ne se contentent point de l'honnorer, s'ils ne l'adorent. Ceux de *Mexico* dépuis que les ceremonies de son sacre sont parachevées, n'osent plus le regarder au visage" [To this is related the custom of so many peoples who canonize *the king* they have created from among themselves, and are not content to honor him if they do not adore him. Those of *Mexico*, after the ceremonies of his coronation are completed, no longer dare to look him in the face] (III: 8, 935b, DM 412r; 714), but as if his royal status had made him a god, they have him swear to maintain their religion, their laws, their liberties, to be valiant, just and kind, to make the sun, rain, and rivers contribute all things necessary to the people. Montaigne drew the details about the Mexican monarch that he relates in both chapters from the same source, Gomara's *Histoire générale des Indes* (Villey 1320–22). Although the "Roy de Mexico" was mentioned twice in Book One (in I: 30 and I: 36), these are the only two chapters in which he appears in Book Three.

Edwin Duval, who has revealed so many architectural symmetries in Rabelais's books, finds a remarkable one in the construction of "Des coches." The newly discovered world of the Americas mirrors the world of ancient Rome:

1. Roman coaches: Mark Anthony, Heliogabalus, Firmus and their strange chariots
2. Roman pomp and magnificence: spectacles in the amphitheaters
3. Misconceptions concerning the age of the world: historical views of Lucretius and modern Europeans

...

3. Misconceptions concerning the age of the world: religious views of the Mexicans
2. New World pomp and magnificence: the Peruvian highway
1. New World coaches: the king of Peru and his golden litter[9]

It was a nice touch on Montaigne's part to have planted a "belle symmetrie" in his description of the Roman spectacles themselves, a kind of microcosm of the whole: "C'estoit pourtant une belle chose, d'aller faire apporter & planter en la place aus arenes, une grande quantité de gros arbres, tous branchus & tous verts, representant une grande forest ombrageuse, despartie en *belle symmetrie*" [It was, however, a fine thing to bring and plant in the amphitheater a great quantity of big trees, all branching and green, representing a great shady forest, arranged in *beautiful symmetry*] (III: 6, 905b, DM 396v; 691). But even the symmetry that Duval finds in "Des coches" is a microcosm of another, the symmetry in which that chapter finds its other (as the Old World finds its other in the New: "Nostre monde vient d'en trouver un autre" [Our world has just discovered another world] [III: 6, 908b, DM 398r; 693]) in "De l'art de conferer." That larger symmetry finds another metafictional moment in Montaigne's account of the architecture of those amphitheaters: "tous les coustez de ce grand *vuide, remplis* & environnez" [all the sides of this great *emptiness filled* and surrounded] (III: 6, 905b, DM 396v; 691*) with tiers of cushioned seats. For it repeats his description of the *Essays* themselves, when he likened them at the beginning of "De l'amitié" to what an artist did to the walls of his chateau: "Il choisit le plus noble endroit & milieu de chasque paroy, pour y loger un tableau elabouré de toute sa suffisance, & le *vuide* tout au tour il le *remplit* de crotesques" [He chooses the noblest place, the middle of each wall, to place a picture labored over with all his skill, and the *empty space* all around it he *fills* with grotesques] (I: 28, 183a, DM 252; 135). The central tableau will turn out to be La Boétie's sonnet sequence; the grotesques, he will go on to say, are the surrounding chapters. The word "vuide" and verb "remplir" appear together

---

9. On p. 106 of Edwin M. Duval, "Lessons of the New World: Design and Meaning in Montaigne's 'Des Cannibales' (1: 31) and 'Des coches' (III: 6)," *Yale French Studies* 64 (1983): 95–112.

nowhere else. In an interesting inversion, the "vuide" in I: 28 is the circumference, in III: 6 the center.

The reason why Montaigne begins his description of what takes place in the "vuide" (the symmetrically planted trees, etc.) with the concessive "pourtant" [however] is that he disapproves of the expense to which the Roman emperors went to put on those shows, since the people had to pay for them in the end. And therein lies a mirroring reflection at work in both symmetries, Duval's and my own. Duval does not go into this, but it fits with the parallel between the Amerindians and the Romans that is at the heart of the symmetry he reveals. Montaigne first applies his criticism to the expense of Roman triumphs: "il semble aus subjects, spectateurs de ces triomphes, qu'on leur faict montre de leurs propres richesses, & qu'on les festoye à leurs despens" [it seems to the subjects, spectators of these triumphs, that they are given a display of their own riches, and entertained at their own expense] (III: 6, 902–3b, DM 395r–95v; 688). Only private citizens have the right to be generous and not kings, for "un Roy n'a rien proprement sien, il se doibt soy-mesmes à autruy" [a king has nothing that is properly his own; he owes his very self to others] (III: 6, 903b, DM 395v; 689). In his criticism of the expense of public spectacles he quotes Cicero: "Pecuniarum translatio a justis dominis ad alienos non debet liberalis videri" [The transfer of money from its rightful owners to strangers should not be regarded as liberality] (III: 6, 905c; 690). But he has the Amerindians make the same complaint that he imagines the Roman people making about the triumphs and that he makes on his own about the spectacles, and in doing so sets up a parallel between the Roman emperors so lavish with the public treasury and the Roman pontiff who so generously allotted part of the New World to Portugal and part of it to Spain. The Spanish had told the inhabitants that they came in peace, sent by the King of Castille, "auquel le Pape, representant Dieu en terre, avoit donné la principauté de toutes les Indes" [to whom the Pope, representing God on earth, had given the principality of all the Indies]. The Americans replied that their king must be indigent and needy, "& celuy qui luy avoit faict cette distribution, homme aymant dissention, d'aller donner à un tiers, chose qui n'estoit pas sienne" [and he who had awarded their country to him must be a man fond of dissension, to go and give another person something that was not his] (III: 6, 911b, DM 399v; 695). As with the Roman emperors, it was not his to give.

In the larger symmetry, Montaigne in "De l'art de conferer" makes a similar observation in a different context: "aus disputes & conferences, tous les mots qui nous semblent bons, ne doivent pas incontinent estre acceptez.

La plus part des hommes sont riches d'une suffisance estrangere" [in arguments and discussions not all the words that seem good to us should be accepted immediately. *Most men are rich with a borrowed capacity*] (III: 8, 936b, DM 412r; 715*). In a post-1588 addition to this passage, he makes it clear that he is talking about borrowing and says he is guilty of it himself: "Qu'on ne tient pas tout ce qu'on emprunte, à l'adventure se pourra il verifier par moy mesme" [That we do not possess all we borrow may perhaps be verified in myself] (III: 8, 936c; 715). Indeed it may be verified at this very moment, for although on the surface he is alluding to his borrowing from other authors he is in a less obvious way borrowing from himself, for the motif of being rich with something that is not one's own had already appeared, as we have just seen, in "Des coches." In fact, it appeared there twice. The Roman emperors showed their largesse with money not their own; the Pope gave away lands that were not his to give. And Montaigne was borrowing from himself the second time he brought that up (when what the Amerindians said of the Pope echoed what he said of emperors), as he is borrowing again now. That borrowing continues when he says in "De l'art de conferer" that in judging a writer "il faut sçavoir ce qui *est sien*, & ce qui *ne l'est point*" [we must know what *is his* and what *is not*] (III: 8, 940b, DM 414r; 718), words that almost seem borrowed from what the Americans said of the Pope, that he was giving away "chose qui *n'estoit pas sienne*" [something that *was not his*]. Montaigne is the master of the metafictional moment, making borrowing itself something borrowed—as he committed theft upon himself in the intersection of III: 12 and III: 2. The assertion that most men are "*riches d'une suffisance estrangere*" [rich with a borrowed capacity] is "borrowed" in this sense from what he wrote of the Roman triumphs, that they borrowed their "richesses" from the "richesses" of the public to whom they were displayed: "il semble aus subjects, spectateurs de ces triomphes, qu'on leur faict montre de leurs propres *richesses*" [it seems to the subjects, spectators of these triumphs, that they are given a display of their own *riches*]. And then, in a post-1588 addition to "De l'art de conferer," he borrows from those triumphs themselves, in the only other appearance in Book III of the word in that sense (a victor's parade through the streets of ancient Rome): "le peuple Romain a souvent refusé le *triomphe* à des grandes et tres utiles victoires par ce que la conduite du chef ne respondoit point à son bonheur" [the Roman people often refused a *triumph* for great and very profitable victories because the conduct of the leader did not correspond to his good luck] (III: 8, 933c; 712).

Jules Brody makes two interesting points in his study of "De l'art de conferer"[10] that are even more interesting when we consider them in the context of that chapter's connections with "Des coches":

(1) "The attentive reader will not be slow to notice that this essay is saturated with passages where the *art de conférer* is modeled on one-on-one combat, whether in earnest or for sport" (77). Indeed, Montaigne is talking not so much about conversation as about debate, and he consistently casts it as a duel.[11] For example: "Si je confere avec une ame forte et un roide jousteur, il me presse les flancs, me pique à gauche et à dextre" [If I discuss with a strong mind and a stiff jouster, he presses on my flanks, prods me right and left] (III: 8, 923b; 764). Now in "Des coches" he recounts how both the Peruvians and the Mexicans were defeated in battle by the conquistadors, but he also narrates an encounter that took the form of a debate, and this one the Americans won. It is the passage alluded to earlier, in which the native inhabitants refuted what the invaders had to say point by point: if the invaders were peaceable, they sure didn't look it; as for their king, he must be indigent to be asking them for tribute; as for the man who claimed to have given them this land (the Pope), he was being generous with what wasn't his; as for worshipping the invaders' god, they were happy with the religion they had, and were not in the habit of taking advice from strangers (III: 6, 911b, DM 399v–400r; 695). And so forth. The Spanish went away empty-handed. It is as if the defenders won the debate—they certainly out talked the enemy.

(2) Brody notes that the substantial post-1588 addition to "De l'art de conferer" that comes just after "Stercus cuique suum bene olet" [Every man likes the smell of his own dung] (III: 8, 929b; 709) begins with "Nos yeux ne voient rien en derriere" [Our eyes see nothing behind us], develops the point that we criticize others for faults of which we are even more guilty, and concludes with Socrates saying that if a man, his son, and a stranger were guilty of some violent wrongdoing, he should present himself to the executioner, and then his son, and then the stranger. He notes as well that the reference to Socrates is immediately preceded by a return to the scatological theme: "Si nous avions bon nez, nostre ordure nous devroit plus puir d'autant qu'elle est nostre" [If we had a good nose, our excrement ought to

---

10. "Entre l'écrit et l'oral: *De l'art de conférer* (III, 8)," in his book *Nouvelles lectures de Montaigne* (Paris: Honoré Champion, 1994): 73–104.

11. As Yves Delègue explains, a "conference" in the sense Montaigne understands it "is a combat, a 'dispute' in the Latin sense of the term and not a friendly 'civil conversation.'" On p. 32n of "*De l'art de conferer* (III, 8) ou de la 'sottise,'" *Bulletin de la Société des Amis de Montaigne* 8: 29–30 (January–June 2003): 29–42.

stink worse to us inasmuch as it is our own] (III: 8, 930c; 710), and that this is eventually followed by another Latin quotation that is preceded by another allusion to Socrates:

> [C] Et les foibles, dict Socrates, corrompent la dignité de la philosophie en la maniant. Elle paroist et inutile et vicieuse quand elle est mal estuyée. [B] Voilà comment ils se gastent et affolent,
>
>> Humani qualis simulator simius oris,
>> Quem puer arridens pretioso stamine serum
>> Velavit, nudàsque nates ac terga reliquit,
>> Ludibrium mensis.
>
> [(C) And the weak ones, says Socrates, corrupt the dignity of philosophy in handling it. It appears both useless and harmful when it is badly encased. (B) This is how they spoil themselves and make fools of themselves,
>
>> Just like an ape, man's mimic, whom in jest
>> A prankish boy in silken clothes has dressed,
>> And left his buttocks and his backside bare,
>> To give the guests a laugh.] (III: 8, 932bc; 711)

Brody from this quite reasonably observes: "These two Latin quotations' retroactive focus on the word 'derrière' is enriched by a final trait they have in common: they are both connected, by the most curious of paradoxes, to the image and the moral presence of Socrates" (90). Reading that chapter together with "Des coches," however, would show that there too Montaigne focuses on Socrates and what is behind him:

> Alcibiades recite de Socrates, son compagnon d'armes: je le trouvay (faict-il) apres la route de nostre armée, luy & Lachez, des derniers entre les fuyans. . . . Je remerquay premierement, combien il montroit d'avisement & de resolution, au pris de Lachez, & puis la braverie de son marcher, nullement different du sien ordinaire: sa veue ferme & reglée, considerant & jugeant ce qui se passoit autour de luy, regardant tantost les uns, tantost les autres, amis & ennemis, d'une façon, qui encourageoit les uns, & signifioit aux autres, qu'il estoit pour vendre bien cher son sang & sa vie, à qui essayeroit de la luy oster.

[Alciabades reports of Socrates, his comrade in arms: "I found him," he says, "after the rout of our army, him and Laches, among the last of the fugitives. . . . I noticed first how much presence of mind and resolution he showed compared with Laches; and then the boldness of his walk, no different from his ordinary one, his firm and steady gaze, considering and judging what was going on around him, looking now at one side, now the other, friends and enemies, in a way that encouraged the former and signified to the latter that he was a man to sell his blood and his life very dear to anyone who should try to take them away."] (III: 6, 899–900b, DM 394r; 686)

The enemy was right behind him, for he was among the last to retreat. And he looked behind him as well as ahead: "regardant tantost les uns, tantost les autres, amis & ennemis," giving encouraging looks to his comrades and menacing ones to the foe. Socrates in "Des coches" is just the opposite of the rest of us mortals in "De l'art de conferer," whose "yeux ne voient rien en derriere" [eyes see nothing behind us], for he could indeed see, and even cast a significant gaze.

In a supremely metafictional (because self-naming) moment, Montaigne in that post-1588 addition to "De l'art de conferer" to which Brody calls our attention—"Nos yeux ne voient rien en derriere" [Our eyes see nothing behind us] (III: 8, 929c; 709)—dares us to do precisely what he complains we are unable to do: *to look back* . . . to look back to where he says the same thing, that we don't have the ability to look back, in "Des coches": "Je crains que nostre cognoissance soit foible en tous sens, *nous ne voyons* ny gueres loin, ny *guere arriere*" [I fear that our knowledge is weak in every direction; *we do not see* very far ahead or *very far behind*] (III: 6, 907b, DM 397v; 692).[12] Appropriately, in "Des coches" we not only cannot look back; we cannot look forward either. If we could look forward, as far as the parallel passage in "De l'art de conferer," we would feel a shock of recognition.

As I have been trying to show, Montaigne wants us to look both forward and back as we read the *Essays*. He has given us hundreds of clues about what to look *for*.

---

12. Brody cites and comments on this passage (as well as on Socrates's retreat) in an illuminating reading of "Des coches" but of course has no inclination to see its connection to the parallel statement in "De l'art de conferer" (on p. 66 of "Montaigne, *Des coches* (III: 6), anatomie d'une lecture 'philologique,'" in the *Bulletin de la Société des Amis de Montaigne* 7: 31–32 (July–December 2003): 47–75.

IV

JOURNEY TO THE CENTER OF THE BOOK

"Vingt et neuf sonnets d'Estienne de la Boetie" [Twenty-nine sonnets of Estienne de La Boétie] (I: 29), "De la liberté de conscience" [Of freedom of conscience] (II: 19), and "De l'incommodité de la grandeur" [Of the inconvenience of greatness] (III: 7).

WE RECALL that "De l'amitié" (I: 28), which immediately precedes the central chapter of Book One and serves to introduce it, begins with an account of how an artist decorated the walls of Montaigne's chateau with a noble example of his best work in the middle of each one, and filled the surrounding space with grotesques. We recall as well that he likens his *Essays* to those symmetrical decorations and said that since he could produce nothing good enough to put in the middle he would put his departed friend Etienne de la Boétie's *Discours de la servitude volontaire* there instead. Until the last pages of I: 28 he leads us to believe that the chapter to follow this one would be that text, and that it would form the center of his book. But just before the end something odd occurs. Immediately after he invites us to read the *Discours*—"Mais oions un peu parler ce garson de dixhuict ans" [But let us listen a little to this eighteen-year-old boy speak] (I: 28: 194a, DM 273r; 144*)—a line of three asterisks appears (in the 1580 edition), followed by the statement that because he has discovered that the *Discours* has already been published, and with malign intent, "je me suis dedit de le loger icy" [I have renounced placing it here] (I: 28, 194a, DM 273; 144*). He was alluding to certain Protestants, who had indeed published some of the *Discours* in 1574, and then all of it in 1576, bound together with some really incendiary pamphlets, as an incitement to murder the French Catholic king. He then devotes about two hundred words to exculpating La Boétie from any Protestant or regicidal leanings, after which he informs us that he has just received twenty-nine sonnets by the same author, a manuscript of whose existence he was apparently unaware—for the man who sent them had found them by chance ("par fortune") among some papers—and that he will substitute them for the *Discours*. It would appear that for at least a brief moment—the time represented perhaps by the three asterisks, and the words of exculpation—he was going to leave the place vacant, for he says that the sonnets had only just come into his possession. In other words, if Poiferré had only just sent them, it would seem that they arrived after he had already decided not to publish the *Discours,* and clearly he wishes us to believe that he arrived at the decision to remove it independently of the sonnets' coming to light. If the sonnets showed up after Montaigne had decided, and then reneged, on having the *Discours* be the middle, was that middle going to be the twenty-ninth chapter anyway—the middle of fifty-seven?

And how do we account for the fact that Montaigne pretends he has just discovered that the Protestants kidnapped the *Discours* when he must have known about it for four years if not six? Villey, who tried to date every chapter, was hard put to account for this contradiction without suggesting that "De l'amitié" was an incoherent piece of work: "We can therefore say, without being able to be more precise, that the first part is anterior to 1576, the second posterior to that date" (Villey's edition of the *Essais,* 183). In other words, Montaigne didn't bother to correct the first part of the chapter to bring it in line with the second—or more importantly, with the truth.

Richard Regosin put the question this way: "Why did he choose not to modify his opening remarks by explaining his change of mind? . . . Clearly the impact on the reader of this unrealized expectation"—that the *Discours de la servitude volontaire* would soon appear—"derives from the internal disposition of the essay, for the parallel between its culmination in the absence of both the friend and his work is too striking to be gratuitous."[1] Yves Delègue asks the same question: "This change of stage directions surprises: the pirated edition of the *Contre Un* took place in 1574, in part, and then in

---

1. Richard Regosin, *The Matter of My Book: Montaigne's* Essais *as the Book of the Self* (Berkeley: University of California Press, 1977), 19–20.

1576, in totality. Why does Montaigne pretend to discover the theft at the last minute? Why does he keep the preamble where he defines his project, instead of deleting or modifying it?" (*Montaigne et la mauvaise foi*, 60).[2]

François Rigolot casts doubt as well on Montaigne's assertion that he was intending to put the *Discours* there:

> Montaigne decided to honor his friend's memory by placing this booklet in the best spot . . . of his first volume of essays. Or, rather, this is what he *says* he decided to do, borrowing a "rich, artistic picture" from La Boétie and filling the space around it with poor, artless "grotesques," namely his "essays." . . . For the "masterpiece in the center" simile does not seem to function too well when we look closely at the text. . . . Montaigne tells us that La Boétie wrote his political discourse "par maniere d'*essay*." . . . This is indeed a curious way to refer to the "masterpiece."[3]

Not only does the promise to give us the *Discours* coexist with the declaration "je me suis dédit de le loger icy," but even in the first part of the chapter, when he is still making that promise, he lets slip that the sonnets are coming: "Sous céte parfaicte amitié ces affections volages ont autrefois trouvé place ches moy: affin que je ne parle de luy, qui n'en confesse que trop par ses vers" [Beneath this perfect friendship those fleeting affections have sometimes found a place in me, not to speak of him, who confesses only too many of them in his verses] (I: 28, 186a, DM 260; 137*). Balsamo et al. take note of the contradiction: "Montaigne is already alluding here to the twenty-nine love sonnets . . . yet he was claiming a few pages earlier that he was going to give us the *Discours de la servitude volontaire*" (1413). Stranger still, in the 1588 edition Montaigne would change "ses vers" [his verses] to "ces vers" [these verses], making it even clearer that he was alluding to the poems he was about to present even though at this point in the chapter he was still pretending that he was about to present the *Discours*.[4]

---

2. The author of a recent book on Montaigne for the general reader, alluding to the seeming awkwardness of the last-minute replacement of the *Discours* by the sonnets and then to the eventual disappearance of the latter, remarks: "One entire chapter, number 29 in Book I, became a double deletion: a ragged stub or hole which Montaigne deliberately refused to disguise. He even drew attention to its frayed edges. It is odd behavior, and has inspired a lot of speculation. Was Montaigne simply adding and subtracting material in a fluster, without bothering to tidy up the results, or was he trying to alert us to something?" Sarah Blakewell, *How to Live: Or, a Life of Montaigne in One Question and Twenty Attempts at an Answer* (New York: Other Press, 2010), 99.

3. Pp. 152–53 of François Rigolot, "Montaigne's Purloined Letters," in *Yale French Studies* 64: 145–66.

4. Incomprehensibly, although the Villey edition, reflecting the 1588 change, has "ces" the University of Chicago on-line text at http://www.lib.uchicago.edu/efts/ARTFL/projects/montaigne/index.

Although the sonnets of I: 29 appeared in all editions of the *Essais* published in his lifetime, Montaigne crossed them out on the Bordeaux Copy and wrote "Ces vers se voient ailleurs" [These verses may be seen elsewhere] (I: 29, 196c; 145). Where else could they have been seen (apart from the earlier editions)? Marie de Gournay replaced that statement by this one: "Ces vingt neuf sonnetz d'Estienne de la Boëtie qui estoient mis en ce lieu ont esté imprimez avec ses oeuvres" [These twenty-nine sonnets of Estienne de la Boëtie which had been put in this place have been printed with his works] (Balsamo et al., 202). Balsamo et al. provide this note: "Mlle de Gournay is perhaps alluding to the publication of the *Historique description du solitaire et sauvage pays de Médoc*, published in 1593 in Bordeaux by S. Millanges, which may have included these twenty-nine sonnets, but which today is lost (a copy was supposedly seen in 1765 in abbé Desbiey's library)" (1420). Until recently, scholars of Montaigne have almost ignored them, or have been more interested in La Boétie as the author of the *Discours de la servitude volontaire*. The sonnets are nowhere to be found in Pierre Villey's otherwise careful edition of the *Essais*, nor were they translated by either Donald Frame nor M. A. Screech.[5] Neither Donald Frame nor M. A. Screech translate them; in fact they have to my knowledge never appeared in English except once, in an out-of-print translation by Louis How in 1915.[6]

Their relative neglect is not surprising since (1) they are apparently not by the author of the *Essays*, (2) Montaigne leads us to believe that they were his second choice for I: 29, and (3) he marked them out on the Bordeaux Copy. In addition, as Philippe Desan points out, Montaigne never corrected what seems to have been a printing error dating from the first edition that on the title page of I: 29 numbered that chapter as the "vinthuitiesme" [twenty-eighth] (DM 275). In that same 1580 edition, the heading for "De la moderation" (I: 30) gave it as the "vintneufiesme" (DM 293) and "Des cannibales"

---

html has "ses"—even though the same site's photograph of the relevant page from the Bordeaux Copy (the 1588 edition) clearly shows "ces." Balsamo et al. give "ses," with no explanation, and no indication of the changes this word underwent.

5. Studies of the sonnets may be found in *Étienne de La Boétie: Sage révolutionnaire et poète perigourdin. Actes du Colloque International, Duke University 1999* (Paris: Honoré Champion, 2004). Other studies include: André Gendre, "Les 29 sonnets d'Estienne de La Boétie publiés dans les *Essais* de Montaigne" and Gabriel-André Pérouse, "Montaigne, son lecteur et les 29 sonnets d'Estienne de La Boétie," *Montaigne Studies* 6. 1–2 (October 1999): 45–60, 77–86; Michel Magnien, "De l'hyperbole à l'ellipse: Montaigne face aux sonnets de La Boétie," *Montaigne Studies* 2.1 (September 1990): 7–25; Patrick Henry, "Ces vers se voient ailleurs," *Bulletin de la Société des Amis de Montaigne* 3–4 (1980): 77–80; and Jeffrey Mehlman, "La Boétie's Montaigne," *Oxford Literary Review* 4 (1979): 45–61.

6. *Montaigne's Essay on Friendship, and XXIX Sonnets by Estienne de La Boétie*, tr. Louis How (Boston: Houghton Mifflin, 1915). I have also translated them, in *Freedom over Servitude: Montaigne, La Boétie, and* On Voluntary Servitude, ed. David Lewis Schaefer (Westport, CT: Greenwood Press, 1998), 223–35.

(I: 31) as the "trentieme" [thirtieth] (DM 298). The error finally stopped at that point, "Qu'il faut sobrement se mesler de juger des ordonnances divines" being correctly numbered as the "trentedeuxieme" [thirty-second] (DM 329). On the corresponding chapter title pages of the 1582 edition the error is corrected for I: 30 and I: 31 but not for I: 29. That error persists in the 1588 edition. Desan concludes that this "casts a doubt on the thesis that makes of chapter 29 the center or the heart of the first book of the *Essais*."[7] Yet I: 29 is correctly listed in the table of contents in every edition during Montaigne's lifetime (even I: 30 and I: 31 were correctly numbered there in 1580). Desan dismisses the significance of the table of contents:

> As for the famous table of contents invoked by critics, it was at that time, as it is today, created after the printing of the rest of the book. A Renaissance author furnished neither a table of contents, nor an index, nor a glossary. Those paratextual tools were entirely created by the printer-booksellers. One should not grant too much importance to the numbering followed in the table of contents. (54)

This is in part a straw-man argument: we aren't talking about indexes or glossaries. And to argue that Montaigne did not draw up the table of contents (or at least did not supply its page numbers) is not the same as to prove that he didn't know there were tables of contents in his books and that they gave I: 29 as I: 29.

Yet there is definitely something strange going on, just as strange as Montaigne pretending he was going to give his reader the *Discours de la servitude volontaire* when he knew he wasn't. Book One's 29th chapter both is (in the tables of contents) and isn't (on the chapter's title page) there. The same is true of the sonnets, which were (he claims) neither his first choice nor his last (because he marked them out of the Bordeaux Copy). At first they were not yet there, then they were, and then they were there no longer.

Their eventual disappearance is, curiously, anticipated by their own narrative. For the poet, the speaker of the poems, wants at one moment to make their own center disappear. Although the sequence for the most part expresses a lover's praise for his beloved, the two central sonnets, 14 and 15, do not. In them he charges his beloved with infidelity. In sonnet 16 he retracts his accusation and tries to make amends (sonnets 16–20 constituting a palinode) for his outburst.[8]

---

7. Philippe Desan, *Montaigne dans tous ses états* (Fasano, Italy: Schena editore, 2001), 43.

8. An outburst similar to the vituperative "Chanson" included among those Montaigne published in 1571. In sonnet 16 of the 29, the speaker says "je me desdiray" of the two offending sonnets

14

O coeur leger, o courage mal seur,
    Penses tu plus que souffrir je te puisse?
    O bonté creuze, o couverte malice,
    Traitre beauté, venimeuse doulceur.
Tu estois donc tousjours soeur de ta soeur?
    Et moy trop simple il failloit que j'en fisse
    L'essay sur moy? & que tard j'entendisse
    Ton parler double & tes chantz de chasseur?
Depuis le jour que j'ay prins à t'aimer,
    J'eusse vaincu les vagues de la mer.
Qu'est ce meshuy que je pourrois attendre?
    Comment de toy pourrois j'estre content?
    Qui apprendra ton coeur d'estre constant,
    Puis que le mien ne le luy peut aprendre?

15

Ce n'est pas moy que l'on abuze ainsi:
    Qu'à quelque enfant ses ruzes on emploie,
    Qui n'a nul goust, qui n'entend rien qu'il oye:
    Je sçay aymer, je sçay hayr aussi.
Contente toi de m'avoir jusqu'ici
    Fermé les yeux, il est temps que j'y voie:
    Et que meshui, las & honteux je soye
    D'avoir mal mis mon temps & mon souci.
Osereois tu m'ayant ainsi traicté
    Parler à moi jamais de fermeté?
Tu prendz plaisir à ma douleur extreme:
    Tu me deffends de sentir mon tourment:
    Et si veux bien que je meure en t'aimant.
    Si je ne sens, commant veux tu que j'aime?

16

O l'ai je dict? helas l'ai je songé?
    Ou si pour vrai j'ai dict blaspheme telle?
    Ça faulce langue, il faut que l'honneur d'elle

---

14 and 15; in the "Chanson" he says he will "[se] desdire" of all the poems he had previously written in praise of the beloved. Unsaying was already a theme in La Boétie's *oeuvre*, and Montaigne would have known that. *Oeuvres complètes d'Estienne de La Boétie*, ed. Louis Desgraves (Bordeaux: William Blake, 1991), vol. 2, 114.

De moi, par moi, desus moi, soit vangé.
Mon coeur chez toi, O madame, est logé:
    Là donne lui quelque geine nouvelle:
    Fis lui souffrir quelque peine cruelle:
    Fais, fais lui tout, fors lui donner congé.
Or seras tu (je le sçais) trop humaine,
    Et ne pourras longuement voir ma peine.
Mais un tel faict, faut il qu'il se pardonne?
    A tout le moings hault *je me desdiray*
    De mes sonnetz, & me desmentiray,
Pour ces deux faux, cinq cent vrais je t'en donne.

[14

O fickle heart! O uncertain virtue!
    Do you imagine that I could bear more?
    O hollow kindness! O covert malice,
    Treasonous beauty, sweetness envenomed!
And so you were your sister's sister still?
And I, too simple, had to try it out
    Upon myself, and all too late would hear
    Your double speech and your songs of the hunt?
Since the day that I started to love you
    I would have conquered the waves of the sea,
But from now on what can I hope to gain?
    How could I ever be happy with you?
    Who could ever teach your heart constancy,
    When mine was such a failure at that task?

15

I'm not a man to suffer such abuse—
    Try out those ruses on some ignorant child,
    Who, artless, takes in nothing that he hears.
    I know how to love, I know how to hate.
Content yourself with having until now
    Kept shut my eyes, for it is time I saw:
    And time as well, alas, that I, in shame,
    Regret such ill-spent use of time and care.
Would you dare then, in light of what you've done,
    Entreat me now to have a steadfast heart?
My bitter sorrow seems to you delight.

You even tell me not to feel my pain,
And then want me to die of loving you.
If I can't feel, why think you I could love?

16

Did I say that? Alas! Was it a dream?
    Or did in fact I speak such blasphemy?
    For that, false tongue, my lady's honor must
    Be by me, through me, over me, avenged.
My heart, belovèd, within you is lodged.
    There find some novel torture to inflict;
    Make it to suffer cruelly some pain;
    Do, do unto it all save give it rest.
But you will be (I know this) too humane,
    Unable long to watch my suffering.
But can a crime like mine seek clemency?
    The least that I can do is *to unsay*
    These guilty sonnets, which I'll now recant:
    For these two false I'll write five hundred true.]

In microcosm, the sonnets predict their own demise: "je me desdiray / De mes sonnetz" [I will unsay / My sonnets]. Montaigne unsaid the sonnets on the Bordeaux Copy, as he literally unsaid the *Discours* they replaced in writing "je me suis dedit de le loger icy" (I: 28, 194a, DM 273; 144). He may even have toyed with the idea of repeating in the middle of the sonnets the same error he allowed to persist in the numbering of his central chapter, for in the 1582 edition, which corrected so many of the printer's errors of the first, sonnet XIIII, correctly numbered that way in 1580, becomes a second sonnet XIII (1582, 173). It became sonnet XIIII again in 1588.

The poet's attempt at erasure in sonnet 16 was anticipated in a different context in sonnet 8: "Maulgré moy je t'escris, maulgré moy je t'efface" [Despite myself I write you, despite myself I efface you] (line 5). He was speaking of his desire to name his beloved before the world:

Quand viendra ce jour la, que ton nom au vray passe
    Par France, dans mes vers? combien & quantesfois
    S'en empresse mon coeur, s'en demangent mes doits?
    Souvent dans mes escris de soy mesme il prend place.

[When will that day come, when your name will truly pass
    Through France, in my verse? How often and how much

> Does my heart race ahead, my fingers itch to write?
> Many times in my verse on its own it appears.] (sonnet 8, lines 1–4)[9]

But "Maulgré moy je t'escris, maulgré moy je t'efface" is also what Montaigne could have been saying to his late friend, who on his death bed famously begged him "de luy donner une place" [to give him a place]. And when Montaigne seemed not to understand: "mon frere, me refusez-vous doncques une place?" [my brother, are you then refusing me a place?].[10] He gave him a place, but then he took it away.

The poet in sonnet 16 promises to write five hundred more to recant the preceding two; he actually writes five, this one and the four that follow. They constitute a palinode, anticipated by an allusion in sonnet 9 to the *locus classicus* of the genre, Stesichorus' recantation of his attack on Helen:

> Mesme race porta l'amitié souveraine
> > Des bons jumeaux, desquelz l'un à l'autre despart
> > Du ciel & de l'enfer la moitié de sa part,
> > Et l'amour diffamé de la trop belle Heleine.
>
> [From the same race sprang forth the sovereign friendship
> > Of the good twins of whom each to the other gave
> > Of heaven and of hell the half of his portion;
> > And the slandered love of the too beauteous Helen.] (sonnet 9, lines 11–14)

The twins are Castor and Pollux, who avenged their sister Helen by blinding Stesichorus for writing that Helen had been a willing abductee. Socrates tells that story in the *Phaedrus*:

> Now for such as offend in speaking of gods and heroes there is an ancient mode of purification, which was known to Stesichorus, though not to Homer. When Stesichorus lost the sight of his eyes because of his defama-

---

9. Those who believe that Montaigne's friendship with La Boétie had a homosexual component might find that fourth line intriguing in light of the fact that four out of the six times his name is written in the *Essays* it is spelled la Boitie, notably in "De l'amitié" (183a; also: I: 26, 156b; II: 17, 659a; III: 12, 1057c) combined with Montaigne's comment on the proverb "celuy-là ne cognoit pas Venus en sa parfaicte douceur qui n'a couché avec la boiteuse" [he does not know Venus in her perfect sweetness who has not lain with a cripple] to the effect that it "se dict des masles comme des femelles" [is said of males as well as females] (III: 11, 1033b, DM 458; 791).

10. Letter from Montaigne to his father recounting the death of La Boétie. Montaigne, *Oeuvres complètes,* ed. Albert Thibaudet and Maurice Rat (Paris: Gallimard / Pléiade, 1962), 1359.

tion of Helen, he was not, like Homer, at a loss to know why. As a true artist he understood the reason, and promptly wrote the lines:

> False, false the tale,
> Thou never didst sail in the well-decked ships
> Nor come to the towers of Troy.

And after finishing the composition of his so-called palinode he straightway recovered his sight.[11]

In *The Republic,* Socrates explains how Stesichorus' palinode differed from his first version: it wasn't Helen but her phantom (an *eidolon* that looked just like her) that went off to Troy in the arms of a man who was not her husband: "Stesichorus says the wraith of Helen was fought for at Troy through ignorance of the truth" (814; 586bc). The brothers' "amitié souveraine" recalls another, the one between Montaigne and La Boétie, described in the same terms in "De l'amitié": "cette *souveraine* et maistresse *amitié*" [this *sovereign* and masterful *friendship*] (I: 28, 190b; 140). The formulation "souveraine [. . .] amitié" appears nowhere else in the *Essays*. Its presence here could well have been influenced by its appearance in the sonnet, since it comes from 1588. But an even more striking anticipatory echo had already been in the chapter since 1580: "Nous estions à *moitié* de tout. Il me semble que je luy desrobe *sa part* . . . il me semble n'estre plus qu'à demy" [We went *halves* in everything. It seems to me that I am robbing him of *his share* . . . only half of me seems to be alive now] (I: 28, 193a, DM 271–72; 143). Montaigne is describing himself and his friend in the language La Boétie had used in sonnet 9, as the brothers who shared "Du ciel & de l'enfer la *moitié* de *sa part*" [Of heaven and of hell the *half* of *his share*]. Even though this passage appears when Montaigne is still leading the reader to believe that he is about to present the *Discours de la servitude volontaire,* before he receives the sonnets from Poiferré, it is evident that he had already read sonnet 9 and had decided to borrow the language in which it alludes to Castor and Pollux. The mention in both I: 28 and sonnet 9 of half portions alludes to the peculiar way the twins shared their immortality. Originally Castor was mortal and Pollux immortal. Castor died in battle; his brother wept because, being deathless, he could not follow him to Hades. Touched by such devotion, Zeus allowed Pollux to share his immortality with Castor, each twin living

---

11. *The Collected Dialogues of Plato,* ed. Edith Hamilton and Huntington Cairns (Princeton: Princeton University Press, 1961), 490 (243ab).

on alternate days.¹² In describing his friendship with La Boétie in "De la vanité," Montaigne enlarges this parallel in saying that they were more fully friends when they were not in the same place at the same time, as was the case with the Dioscuri: "Nous remplisions mieux et estandions la possession de la vie en nous separant : il vivoit, il jouissoit, il voyoit pour moy, et moy pour luy, autant plainement que s'il y eust esté. . . . La separation du lieu rendoit la conjonction de nos volontez plus riche" [We filled and extended our possession of life better by separating: he lived, he enjoyed, he saw for me, and I for him, as fully as if he had been there. . . . Separation in space made the conjunction of our wills richer] (III: 9, 977b; 746–47).

Françoise Charpentier suggests that Montaigne might have already had the sonnets in hand before he received a copy of them from Poiferré. In introducing them in I: 29, he addresses Madame de Grammont, "la belle Corisande" (later the mistress of Henri de Navarre), and promises he will some day whisper in her ear who it was they were written for. He tells her that the 29 were written earlier and are hotter ("plus bouillant") than the 25, which La Boétie wrote for his wife, Marguerite de Carle, and which are redolent of a certain "froideur maritale" [marital coolness] (I: 29, 196a, DM 277; 145). Charpentier comments: "Might Montaigne not have had in his possession and kept secret for the sake of decency, or out of regard for Marguerite de Carle, this collection of sonnets, whether M. de Poiferré later gave him a copy or not?"¹³ She then advances the hypothesis that the 29 might have been written *after* La Boétie married Marguerite de Carle, and recount an adulterous affair carried out *during* the marriage. All the more reason, she adds, for Montaigne to have kept them out of the 1571 collection of his friend's poems.

Whether he had them earlier or not, we already saw him signaling they were in his possession when he alluded to them as "ses vers" (and in 1588 as "ces vers") near the beginning of "De l'amitié." His repeating the terms of sonnet 9 in those two other passages of "De l'amitié" not only signals their existence but is evidence of the sonnets' presence in the *Essays* beyond their appearance in I: 29.

The immortality-sharing twins figure in the 25 sonnets too. When his beloved falls gravely ill, the poet asks heaven the favor of dying with her:

---

12. *New Larousse Encyclopedia of Mythology,* tr. Richard Aldington and Delano Ames (New York: Hamlyn, 1959), 190.
13. Françoise Charpentier, "Les poésies françaises d'Étienne de La Boétie," in *Étienne de La Boétie: Sage révolutionnaire et poète perigourdin. Actes du Colloque International,* Duke University 1999 (Paris: Honoré Champion, 2004), 107–8.

Ou s'il est, ce qu'on dit des deux freres d'Helene,
Que l'un pour l'autre au ciel, & là bas se promene,
Or accomplissez moy une pareille envie.

Ayez, ayez de moy, ayez quelque pitié,
Laissez nous, en l'honneur de ma forte amitié,
Moy mourir de sa mort, ell' vivre de ma vie.

[Or if it is true what they say of Helen's two brothers,
That one for the other in heaven and down below wanders,
Then fulfill a similar desire for me.

Have some pity on me.
Allow us, in honor of my strong love,
That I die of her death, and she live with my life.] (sonnet 3, lines 9–14; Desgraves, vol. 2, 117)

Montaigne, even if he didn't know the 29 sonnets (though it appears he did), was familiar with the 25, since he published them in 1571. So he would have been familiar with the Dioscuri motif in La Boétie. But the connection between the twins as they are evoked in the 29 sonnets and Montaigne's text (that is, "De l'amitié") is stronger than that between their presence in the 25 and that text (except perhaps for the fact that in the 25 they parallel a pair of lovers, as Montaigne and La Boétie may have been), for it is based on the words themselves: "l'amitié souveraine" and "la moitié de sa part."

In the 29 sonnets, Castor and Pollux find an explicit parallel in the Dordogne and the Vézère, two rivers of contrasting character to which the poet likens his beloved and her sister. Lacking her permission to name her publicly, he decides that "tu seras ma Dourdouigne" [you will be my Dordogne] (sonnet 8, line 10). In sonnet 10, however, we see that these siblings are far from similar:

Or ne charge donc rien de ta soeur infidele,
   De Vesere ta soeur: elle va s'escartant
   Toujours flotant mal seure, en son cours inconstant.
   Voy tu comme à leur gré les vans se joüent d'elle?
Et ne te repent point pour droict de ton aisnage
   D'avoir des-jà choisi la constance en partage.
Mesme race porta l'aimité souveraine
   Des bons jumeaux. . . .

[Now don't reproach your sister, faithless though she be,
   Vézère your sister river: Wandering she goes,
   Flowing never steady in her inconstant course.
   Can you see how the winds play with her at their whim?
And never regret, as the right of the elder,
   Having picked constancy for your inheritance.
   From the same race sprang forth the sovereign friendship
Of the good twins. . . .] (sonnet 10, lines 5–12)

This explains the complaint the poet expresses in sonnet 14: "Tu estois donc tousjours soeur de ta soeur?" [And so you were your sister's sister still?].[14] The Dordogne proves to be just as inconstant as the Vézère. Both rivers are part of a landscape shared by La Boétie and Montaigne. La Boétie's native Sarlat lies between the Dordogne and the Vézère; downstream, to the west, Montaigne's château is located just north of the Dordogne, some distance after the Vézère has joined forces with it. More intriguingly, perhaps, in "Des cannibales" (I: 31), at two chapters' distance from the sonnets, what for La Boétie was "ma Dourdouigne" becomes for Montaigne "*ma* riviere de *Dordoigne*" [*my* river *Dordogne*] (I: 31, 204b; 151*):

Quand je considere l'impression que ma riviere de Dordoigne faict de mon temps vers la rive droicte de sa descente, et qu'en vingt ans elle a tant gaigné, et desrobé le fondement à plusieurs bastimens, je vois bien que c'est une agitation extraordinaire: car, si elle fut tousjours allée ce train, ou deut aller à l'advenir, la figure du monde seroit renversée. Mais il leur prend des changements: tantost elles s'espendent d'un costé, tantost d'un autre; tantost elles se contiennent.

[When I consider the inroads that my Dordogne river is making in my lifetime into the right bank in its descent, and that in twenty years it has gained so much ground and stolen away the foundations of several buildings, I clearly see that this is an extraordinary disturbance; for if it had always gone at this rate, or was to do in the future, the face of the world would be turned topsy-turvy. But rivers are subject to changes: now they overflow in one direction, now in another, now they keep to their course.] (I: 31, 204B; 151*)

---

14. Erroneously printed as "*seur* de ta soeur" in 1580 and 1582, it was corrected to "*soeur* de ta soeur" in 1588.

The Dordogne, Montaigne is saying, is inconstant, like any river. It will not always be encroaching on the bank it is attacking now. Sometimes a river will eat away at its right bank, sometimes at its left, sometimes neither. Both Montaigne and La Boétie are saying almost the same thing, that the Dordogne is as inconstant as another river. The only difference is that La Boétie likens its inconstancy to only one other, the Vézère, while Montaigne likens it to all others.

The Dordogne makes another appearance in the *Essays,* in the chapter in Book Two that has the same numerical position as the sonnets, II: 29 ("De la vertu"). And there, as in I: 29 (with the Dordogne and the Vézère), it is a question of two sisters.

> Dépuis peu de jours, à Bragerac, à cinq lieues de ma maison, contremont la riviere de Dordoigne, une femme, ayant esté tourmentée et batue, le soir avant, de son mary . . . delibera d'eschapper à sa rudesse au pris de sa vie; et . . . prenant une sienne soeur par la main, la mena avecques elle sur le pont, et, apres avoir prins congé d'elle, comme par maniere de jeu, sans montrer autre changement ou alteration, se precipita du haut en bas dans la riviere, où elle se perdit.
>
> [A few days ago, at Bergerac, five leagues from my house up the Dordogne River, a woman who had been tormented and beaten the night before by her husband . . . resolved to escape his roughness at the price of her life, and . . . taking a sister of hers by the hand, brought her onto the bridge, and, after taking leave of her as if in jest, without showing any other change or alteration, she threw herself down headlong into the river, where she perished.] (II: 29, 706–7a; 534*)

There is no reason to think it didn't really happen, but we have seen ample evidence of Montaigne's propensity for taking material at hand, from real events to classical and other texts, and using it for his own artistic purpose, like a *bricoleur* in the Lévi-Straussian sense. The 29 sonnets, despite his claiming they were not his first choice, are part of the fabric of the *Essays.*

The reason the poet gives for keeping the two offending sonnets in the sequence sounds strangely like the reason Montaigne gives in "De l'oisiveté" for writing the *Essays.* Montaigne says he retired from active life and as a favor to his mind let it remain idle, hoping that with time it would become stronger and more mature. But he found that it gave birth to so many chimera and monsters with neither order nor pertinence that "pour en contempler à mon aise l'ineptie & l'estrangetté j'ay commancé de les mettre en rolle, esperant avec le temps luy en faire *honte* à luy mesmes" [in order to contemplate their ineptitude and strangeness at my leisure, I have begun to put them in writing, hoping in time to make my mind ashamed of itself] (I: 8, 33a; DM 32; 21*). The poet writes that sonnets 14 and 15 are the "*honte* de mes vers" [*shame* of my verses] and that if he doesn't destroy them it is because he wants to make their shortcomings public:

> O vous mauditz sonnetz, vous qui prinstes l'audace
> De toucher à ma dame: o malings & pervers,
> Des muses le reproche, & *honte* de mes vers:
> Si je vous feis jamais, il faut que je me fasse
> Ce tort de confesser vous tenir de ma race,
> . . .
> Si j'ai oncq quelque part à la posterité
> Je veux que l'un & l'autre en soit desherité.
> Et si au feu vangeur des or je ne vous donne,
> C'est pour vous diffamer, vivez chetifz, vivez,
> Vivez aux yeux de tous, de tout honneur privez:
> Car c'est pour vous punir, qu'ores je vous pardonne.

> [O you, my cursèd sonnets, you who had the nerve
> To do my lady harm! O evil and perverse,
> The reproach of the Muses, the *shame* of my verse!
> If ever I made you, if I must do myself
> The wrong of confessing that you come from my race,
> . . .
> If ever in posterity I have some share,
> I want you both to suffer disinheritance.
> If in the vengeful fire I do not throw you now,
> It's so I might defame you: live, stunted ones, live;
> Live in the sight of all, of all honor deprived;
> It's for your punishment that I pardon you now.] (sonnet 20: lines 1–4, 9–14)

The fate reserved both for the monsters of Montaigne's mind and the two shameful sonnets is punishment by publication. In addition to that similarity, the two sonnets in the middle resemble the sequence itself in that both are an extended quotation in the center of the book, presented to the public ("aux yeux de tous") but eventually disinherited ("Je veux que l'un & l'autre en soit desherité"), when Montaigne marked them out.

But the whole sonnet sequence is not so easily isolated from the rest of the *Essays*. We have seen how its influence extends to "De l'amitié."[15] In the same way that each chapter finds another, always symmetrically connected to it, with which it shares a common language and some situational parallels, the center of Book One finds its partner in the most structurally appropriate place, the other center that the 1580 edition—divided as it was into two volumes—provided, the middle chapter of Book Two, II: 19. And then when Book Three joins the other two books in 1588, its center, III: 7, joins the conversation, repeating the others' words and recycling some of their situations.

The sonnet sequence is about recanting (the poet recanting the terrible things he said about his beloved in sonnets 14 and 15), while "De la liberté de conscience" [Of freedom of conscience] (II: 19) is about one of the most notorious recanters in history, Julian the Apostate. The Emperor Constantine had made Christianity the official religion of the state. When Julian came to power, he reintroduced the worship of the gods, and fostered freedom of religion (the better to divide his enemies, Montaigne asserts). That he returned to the pagan religion gave him, in Montaigne's view, the unmerited name of "apostat, pour avoir abandonné la nostre. Toutesfois cête opinion me semble plus vray-semblable qu'il ne l'avoit jamais eue à coeur, mais que pour l'obeissance des loix il s'estoit feint jusques à ce qu'il tint l'empire en sa main" [Apostate for having abandoned ours; however, this theory seems to me more likely, that he had never had it at heart, but that, out of obedience to the laws he had dissembled until he held the Empire in his hand] (II: 19, 670a, DM 486–87; 508).

Montaigne, as so often elsewhere, creates a singular verbal echo as a tangible sign that the parallel is really there. Read again, in the very center of the sonnets, what the poet says he must later unsay:

Ce n'est pas moy que l'on abuze ainsi:
   Qu'à quelque enfant ses ruzes on emploie,

---

15. Lawrence D. Kritzman points out an interesting textual influence of at least the title of the "Discours de la servitude volontaire" on "De l'amitié." In friendships that law and family obligation impose "il y a d'autant moins de nostre chois & *liberté volontaire*. Et nostre *liberté volontaire* n'a point de production qui soit plus proprement sienne que celle de l'affection et amitié" [the less of our choice and *free will* there is in them. And our *free will* has no product more properly its own than affection and friendship] (I: 28, 185a, DM 258; 137). Kritzman sees Montaigne as "shifting the focus from 'servitude volontaire' to the 'liberté volontaire' of friendship" (*The Fabulous Imagination: On Montaigne's* Essais [New York: Columbia University Press, 2009], 86. Yet Montaigne by this point in the chapter had already cited this title ("C'est un discours auquel il donna nom *De la servitude volontaire*" [I: 28, 183a, DM 253]), so one could just as easily speak of the influence of this passage on the one a few pages later in the same chapter.

> Qui n'a nul goust, qui n'entend rien qu'il oye:
> Je sçay aymer, je sçay hayr aussi.
> *Contente toi* de m'avoir jusqu'ici
> Fermé les yeux, il est temps que j'y voie.

> [I'm not a man to suffer such abuse—
> Try out those ruses on some ignorant child,
> Who, artless, takes in nothing that he hears.
> I know how to love, I know how to hate.
> *Content yourself* with having until now
> Kept shut my eyes, for now it's time I saw.] (sonnet 15: lines 1–6)

And now read what Montaigne says Julian did *not* say:

> Aussi ce que plusieurs disent de luy, qu'estant blessé à mort d'un coup de traict, il s'escria, Tu as vaincu, ou comme disent les autres, *Contente toy* Nazarien, n'est non plus vraysemblable. Car ceux qui estoient presens à sa mort, & qui nous en recitent toutes les particulieres circonstances, les contenances mesmes & les parolles n'en disent rien.

> [Thus what several say of him, that being mortally wounded by an arrow he cried out, "You have conquered," or as others say, "*Content yourself,* Nazarene," is not plausible, either. For those who were present at his death, and who recount to us all the particular circumstances, even the countenances and the words, say nothing about it.] (II: 19, DM 484)

The words "Contente toi" make their only appearance in the two central chapters of the original edition. But in the 1582 edition they disappeared from the second of these centers, when Montaigne removed this anecdote from the chapter on Julian. In a post-1588 revision of that chapter they returned, but on the same Bordeaux Copy Montaigne removed the sonnets, so when one "Contente toi" reappeared the other one disappeared. In other words, from 1582 on they start behaving like Castor and Pollux.

Between the 1580 and 1582 editions, Montaigne traveled to Italy, and in Rome was told by the papal censor along with some other objections that he had been too favorable to Julian. But would he have satisfied the Vatican by deleting only this passage, in which he denies that the emperor had made something approaching a death bed conversion, but let all the rest of his praise of Julian stand? He did not delete such praise as this, for instance: "C'estoit, à la vérité, un tres-grand homme et rare . . . et, de vray, il n'est aucune sorte de vertu dequoy il n'ait laissé de tres-notables exemples" [He was, in truth, a very great and rare man . . . and indeed there is no sort of virtue of which he did not leave very notable examples] (II: 19, 669a; 507). Nor did he take away the good things he had to say about him in I: 42 or II: 21. André Tournon writes that Montaigne suppressed the anecdote and his criticism of it "by deference, *it seems [semble-t-il]*, to the censors" (my italics)—which suggests that Tournon is not entirely convinced of it being more than a seeming. He comments further, "The suppression of this passage in 1582 attests to the boldness the essayist detected within it; its reinsertion after 1588, by a sort of recidivism, marks its importance" (Tournon, *Route par ailleurs,* 308).¹⁶ But from Montaigne seeing how bold it was it does not necessarily follow that he knew that the papal censor could detect it.

When Montaigne put the story, and his refutation of it, back into the chapter after 1588, he put it in a different place, just after his account of Julian's death:

> [A] Il dit entre autres choses, en mourant, qu'il sçavoit bon gré aux dieux et les remercioit dequoy ils ne l'avoyent pas voulu tuer par surprise . . . et qu'ils l'avoient trouvé digne de mourir de cette noble façon, sur le cours de ses victoires et en la fleur de sa gloire. Il avoit eu une pareille vision à celle de Marcus Brutus, qui premierement le menassa en Gaule et depuis se representa à lui en Perse sur le poinct de sa mort. [C] Ce langage qu'on lui faict tenir, quand il se sentit frappé: Tu as vaincu, Nazareen; ou, comme d'autres: Contente toi, Nazareen, n'eust esté oublié, s'il eust esté creu par mes tesmoings, qui, estans presens en l'armée, ont remerqué jusques aux moindres mouvements et parolles de sa fin. . . .
>
> [(A) He said among other things, as he was dying, that he was grateful to the gods and thanked them because they had not willed to kill him by surprise . . . and that they had found him worthy to die in this noble fashion, in the course of his victories and in the flower of his glory. He had had a vision like that of Marcus Brutus, which first threatened him in Gaul and later reappeared to him in Persia just before his death. (C) These words that they have him say when he felt himself struck, "Thou hast conquered, Nazarene," or, as others have it, "Be content, Nazarene," would not have been forgotten if they had been believed by my witnesses, who, being present in the army, noted even the slightest movements and words at his end. . . .]
> (II: 19, 671ac; 509)

---

16. Donald Frame, though erroneously dating the deletion to 1588, says it "*may have been* in response to the observations of the papal censor" (508n—my italics).

Ammianus Marcellinus, one of Montaigne's acknowledged sources, recounts the vision the essayist alludes to here:

> Once when in the darkness of night he was intent upon the lofty thought of some philosopher, he saw somewhat dimly, as he admitted to his intimates, that form of the protecting deity of the state which he had seen in Gaul when he was rising to Augustan dignity, but now with veil over both head and horn of plenty, sorrowfully passing out through the curtains of his tent. And although for a moment he remained sunk in stupefaction, yet rising above all fear, he commended his future fate to the decrees of heaven, and now fully awake, the night being now far advanced, he left his bed, which was spread on the ground, and prayed to the gods with rites designed to avert their displeasure.[17]

It was perfectly appropriate for Montaigne to place his "Contente toi" anecdote just after mentioning this vision Ammianus recounts, as well as in the context of Julian's death. That is where he put it in the post-1588 alteration. The question arises, why did he not also put it there in 1580? The account of Julian's death and the allusion to the vision he did have (as opposed to the vision of Christ which Montaigne argues he did not have) were there as well in the 1580 edition. So he could have logically placed it there, but instead he put it here:

> Il nous estoit apre à la verité, mais non pourtant cruel ennemy: car nos gens mesmes recitent de luy céte histoire, que se promenant un jour autour de la ville de Calcedoine, Maris l'Evesque du lieu osa bien l'appeller meschant traistre à Christ, & qu'il n'en fit autre chose sauf luy respondre, Va miserable, pleure la perte de tes yeus. À quoy l'Evesque encore repliqua, Je rens graces à Jesus Christ de m'avoir osté la veue pour ne voir ton visage impudent. Affectant, disent ils, en cela une patience philosophique. Tant y a que ce faict là ne se peut pas bien rapporter aux cruautés qu'on le dict avoir exercées contre nous. Il estoit (dit Eutropius mon autre tesmoin) ennemi de la Chrestienté: mais sans toucher au sang. Aussi ce que plusieurs disent de luy, qu'estant blessé à mort d'un coup de trait, il s'escria, Tu as vaincu, ou comme disent les autres, Contente toy nazarien, n'est non plus vraysemblable.

> [He was a harsh enemy to us, in truth, but not a cruel one. For even our own people tell of him this story, that as he was walking about the city of

---

17. Ammianus Marcellinus, *The History*, vol. 2, pp. 486–87 (xxv, 2. 3–5).

Chalcedon one day, Maris, the bishop of the place, actually dared to call him a wicked traitor to Christ, and that he did nothing about it except to answer: "Go, wretched man, and weep for the loss of your eyes." To which the bishop further replied: "I give thanks to Jesus Christ for having taken away my sight, so that I may not see your impudent face." In this, they say, Julian was affecting a philosophic patience. At all events, that action cannot be reconciled with the cruelties that they say he exercised against us. He was (says Eutropius, my other witness) an enemy of Christianity, but without touching blood. And what several say of him, that being mortally wounded by an arrow he cried out, "You have conquered," or as others say, "*Content yourself,* Nazarene," is not plausible, either.] (II: 19, 669–70a, DM 483–84; 507–8*)

One reason he may have initially put the anecdote here in 1580 is that this is also the place where he makes another allusion through a unique verbal echo to the same lines in sonnet 15 where "Contente toi" appears. When the bishop says that he thanks Jesus Christ "*de m'avoir osté la veue*" [*for having taken away my sight*] he is repeating almost verbatim, minus the thanks, what the speaker in the poem said as the completion of the verbal construction that "Contente toi" began: "Contente toi *de m'avoir jusqu'ici / Fermé les yeux,* il est temps que j'y voie" [Content yourself *with having until now / Kept shut my eyes,* for it is time I saw] (sonnet 15, lines 5–6). The expression "de m'avoir" with blinding as its completion appears in no other passage. The coincidence between that singular echo and the structural connection linking the two places where they appear—the center of one book and the center of the other—make it hard to imagine that Montaigne was unaware of what he was doing. When he deleted the sonnets on the Bordeaux Copy and restored the "Contente toi" anecdote to II: 19 he separated it from the bishop's echo of the speaker in the sonnets, and put it where more logically it should have gone in the first place, in an account of Julian's death and of another vision he had had. The sonnets gone, there was no longer any reason to put the anecdote where it did not belong.

These singular echoes ("Contente toi" and "de m'avoir" + "osté la veue" / "Fermé les yeux") are matched by another that brings the remaining central chapter, III: 7, into the conversation. "De l'incommodité de la grandeur" (III: 7) is about the difficulty of being king when no one will play against you in earnest. A king is surrounded by such a strong radiance that his subjects are blinded: "Cette lueur estrangere qui l'environne, le cache, & nous le desrobe, nostre veüe s'y rompt & s'y dissipe, estant remplie & arrestée par cette *forte lumiere*" [That extraneous glare that surrounds him hides him and conceals him from us; our sight breaks and is dissipated by it, being filled and arrested by this *strong light*] (III: 7, 919a, DM 404v; 702). Where else do we find a "forte lumiere" in the *Essays?* Only in the 29 sonnets:

> J'ay veu ses yeux perçans, j'ay veu sa face claire:
>   (Nul jamais sans son dam ne regarde les dieux)
>   Froit, sans coeur me laissa son oeil victorieux,
>   Tout estourdy du coup de sa *forte lumiere*.
> Comme un surpris de nuit aux champs quand il esclaire,
>   Estonné, se pallist si la fleche des cieux
>   Sifflant, luy passe contre, & luy serre les yeux,
>   Il tremble, & veoit, transi, Jupiter en colere.
>
> [I have seen her piercing eyes, have seen her bright face
>   (Never does any man unharmed gaze on the gods);
>   Bereft of heart, and chilled, by her victorious eye,
>   All dazzled and awed by the force of its *strong light*.
> Like one surprised at night by lightning's sudden flash,
>   Who, astonished, turns pale—the arrow from the skies
>   Hissing, passes by, making him shut tight his eyes.
>   He trembles and, transfixed, sees Jupiter in rage.] (sonnet 5, lines 1–8)

The beloved of the sonnets, who prefigures Christ in II: 19 as the one to whom one says "Contente toi," prefigures the king in III: 7 as the one whose "forte lumiere" bedazzles and blinds. The puzzle pieces fall into place when we recollect that Christ in II: 19 is also the one who blinds: "Je rens graces à Jesus Christ de m'avoir osté la veue" [I give thanks to Jesus Christ for having taken away my sight]. That makes the parallel between the beloved of the sonnets and the Christ of II: 19 all the stronger.

III: 7 is further connected to II: 19 by the fact that when the bishop is addressing Julian he talking to a sovereign whom he cannot see. Montaigne's point in III: 7 is that we can never see a king, that we are always blinded when we get near one. Chapters I: 29, II: 19 and III: 7, in other words, just like the other chapters in their symmetrical pairings, recycle the same elements in beautiful and playful ways.

Montaigne gives royally induced sight impairment a fresh spin just a few lines after talking about the "forte lumiere" that blinds a king's subjects. As we cede all advantages of honor to kings,

> aussi conforte l'on & auctorise les deffauts & vices qu'ils ont: non seulement par approbation, mais aussi par imitation. Chacun des suyvans d'Alexandre portoit comme luy la teste à costé. Et les flateurs de Dionysius s'entrehurtoyent en sa presence, poussoyent & versoyent ce qui se rencontroit à leurs pieds, pour dire qu'ils avoyent *la veuë aussi courte que luy.*
>
> [so we confirm and authorize the defects they have, not only by approbation but also by imitation. Every one of the followers of Alexander carried his head on one side, as he did; and the flatterers of Dionysius bumped into one another in his presence, stumbled upon and knocked over what was at their feet, to signify that they were *as shortsighted as he.*] (III: 7, 919a, DM 404v; 702)

In a reversal reminiscent of the way a situation is recycled from one symmetrically related chapter to another, these subjects employ a *feigned* partial blindness in order to *flatter* their sovereign, while the bishop in II: 19 made use of his *genuine* blindness to *insult* his.

Before talking about Julian, Montaigne complains about the disappearance of texts due to religious zeal:

> Il est certain qu'en ces premiers temps que nostre religion commença à fleurir & à gaigner authorité & puissance avec les loix, le zele en arma plusieurs contre toute sorte de livres payens, de quoy les gens de lettre souffrent une merveilleuse perte. J'estime que ce desordre ait plus porté de nuysance aux lettres, que tous les feux des barbares.
>
> [It is certain that in those early times when our religion began to flower and to gain authority and power with the laws, zeal armed many believers against every sort of pagan books, thus causing men of letters to suffer an extraordinary loss. I consider that this excess did more harm to letters than all the bonfires of the barbarians.] (II: 19, 668a, DM 481; 506*)

La Boétie's *Discours de la servitude volontaire* comes close to being just such a missing text, not totally lost to posterity as were the pagan ones alluded to here, but missing all the same from the place where Montaigne says he wanted it to appear, thanks to a certain religious zeal. The pagan texts went missing because such zeal took them *out* of circulation, while the *Discours* is missing from the *Essays* because it *was* circulated. Emmanuel Naya suggests that Montaigne in II: 19 may be alluding to another missing text of La Boétie's:

One could point to the parallel, this time in the center of Book Two, between these pages and another text of La Boétie's that Montaigne had not published either when he edited his posthumous works in 1571: the *Mémoire touchant l'Édit de janvier,* in which he envisaged the positive effects of a temporary solution based on establishing freedom of conscience. Might this be homage by substituted praise, paralleling the substitution of the sonnets for the *Discours de la servitude volontaire* in Book One, before the ultimate removal of all foreign texts?[18]

In *Essais sur les Essais,* Michel Butor notes that the first words of "De l'incommodité de la grandeur"—"Puisque nous ne la pouvons aveindre, vengeons nous à en mesdire" [Since we cannot attain it, let us take our revenge by speaking ill of it] (III: 7, 916b, DM 402v; 509)—"are almost an echo" (173) of the last words of "De la liberté de conscience": "n'ayants peu ce qu'ils vouloient, ils ont faict semblant de vouloir ce qu'ils pouvoient" [having been unable to do what they would, they have pretended to will what they could] (II: 19, 672a, DM 489; 509). It is in fact both a sameness and a twist of the sort we have seen in symmetrically paired chapters. The sameness is that in both passages one wants what one cannot have. The twist is that in III: 7 one *pretends not to want* the thing one wants but cannot have ("Puisque nous ne la pouvons aveindre, *vengeons nous à en mesdire*" [Since we cannot attain it, *let us take our revenge by speaking ill of it*] while in II: 19 one settles for what one can get and *pretends to want* that. In III: 7, we would like to possess the "grandeur" to which the chapter's title alludes. In II: 19, kings of Montaigne's time would like a unified kingdom with no division between Protestants and Catholics, and the king of France in particular would like a unified Catholic nation. But the Protestants are too strong to extinguish, and civil war rages. So a truce is called and the Protestants are for a while no longer attacked by the state. The hope is that

> de *lâcher* la bride aus pars, d'entretenir leur opinion c'est les amolir & *relascher par la facilité & par l'aysance,* & que c'est emousser l'eguillon qui s'affine par la rarité, la nouvelleté & la *difficulté.* Et si croy mieux pour l'honneur de la devotion de noz rois, c'est que n'ayants peu ce qu'ils vouloint, ils ont faict semblant de vouloir ce qu'ils pouvoint.

---

18. *Essais de Michel de Montaigne II,* ed. Emmanuel Naya, Delphine Reguig-Naya, and Alexandre Tarrête (Paris: Gallimard Folio, 2009), 777. Gisèle Mathieu-Castellani also finds Montaigne alluding to La Boétie's *Mémoire* in II: 19, but in order to argue against it (in *Montaigne ou la vérité du mensonge,* 95–105).

[to *loosen* the rein for factions, allowing them to entertain their own opinions, is to soften and *relax them through facility and ease,* and to dull the point, which is sharpened by rarity, novelty, and *difficulty.* And I prefer to think, for the reputation of our kings' piety, that having been unable to do what they would, they have pretended to will what they could.] (II: 19, 672a, DM 489; 509*)

The words I have italicized return in what Montaigne has to say in III: 7 about the disadvantage of royal greatness, which is that a monarch cannot participate in "les essays que nous faisons les uns contre les autres, par jalousie d'honneur & de valeur, soit aux exercices du corps ou de l'esprit" [the trials of strength we have with one another, in rivalry of honor and worth, whether in exercises of the body or of the mind] (III: 7, 918b, DM 403v; 701) because his subjects offer no genuine resistance and always let him win.

Qui ne participe au hazard & *difficulté,* ne peut pretendre interest à l'honneur & plaisir qui suit les actions hazardeuses. C'est pitié de pouvoir tant, qu'il advienne que toutes choses vous cedent.... Cette *aysance* & *lâche facilité,* de faire tout baisser soubs soy, est ennemye de toute sorte de plaisir.... Concevez l'homme accompaigné de l'omnipotence, vous l'abismez: il faut qu'il vous demande par aumosne, de *l'empeschement* & de la resistance.

[He who does not share the risk and *difficulty* can claim no involvement in the honor and pleasure that follow hazardous actions. It is a pity to have so much power that everything gives way to you.... That *ease and slack facility* of making everything bow beneath you is the enemy of every kind of pleasure.... Imagine man accompanied by omnipotence: he is sunk; he must ask you for *hindrance* and resistance, as an alms.] (III: 7, 919b, DM 404v; 701–2)

These words make their only joint appearances in these two chapters.

When Julian came to power he wanted to re-establish the worship of the gods and to accomplish this he reopened the temples and decreed that his subjects, whether Christian or pagan, should follow "sans *empeschement* & sans crainte" [without *hindrance* and without fear] (II: 19, 671a, DM 488; 509) the tenets of their own religion. In doing so, he employed "pour attiser le trouble de la dissention civile de cette mesme recepte de liberté de conscience, que noz Roys viennent d'employer pour l'étaindre" [to kindle the trouble of civil dissension, that same recipe of freedom of conscience that

IV. Journey to the Center of the Book 249

our kings have just been employing to extinguish it] (II: 19, 671a, DM 489; 509). For our kings that would supposedly result in weakening the Protestants by giving them "facilité" and "aysance" and taking away all "difficulté."

In other words, Montaigne is saying the same thing about the disadvantage of royal grandeur that he says about Julian's and the modern-day kings' political strategies. In both chapters, one suffers from having difficulties smoothed away. But in a characteristic opposition, in II: 19 it is kings who hinder their opposing subjects by making things too easy for them, while in III: 7 it is subjects who do that to kings.

In a metafictional way, another remark he makes at this point about the disadvantage of greatness is applicable to what he is at this moment doing (as well as continually doing) in the *Essays:* "Leurs bonnes qualitez sont mortes & perdues, car elles *ne se sentent que par comparaison,* & on les met hors" [Their good qualities are dead and wasted, for these *are felt only by comparison,* and they are out of comparison] (III: 7, 919b, DM 404v; 702). It is only by comparing one chapter with its structurally related other (through their symmetry or, in this case, their being in the middle) that we can see their true excellence. Is it by chance that Montaigne calls these comparisons *"essays"* made "les uns contre les autres" [each against the other]?

LET US RETURN one last time to the sonnets. Given that they occupy the center of Book One, what might be the center of this center? Since French prosody is based on syllable count, it ought to be possible to find the central syllable or syllables of a collection of poems by simple arithmetic. It is a little more complicated in this case, since not only do fifteen of the sonnets have twelve-syllable lines and fourteen have ten-syllable lines, but in addition their arrangement with regard to syllable count is not entirely regular. They fall into six groups, composed respectively of 2, 2, 7, 6, 6, and 6 sonnets. Sonnets 1–2 are composed of 12-syllable lines, Sonnets 3–4 of 10, Sonnets 5–11 of 12, Sonnets 12–17 of 10, Sonnets 18–23 of 12, and Sonnets 24–29 of 10. But the math is still simple: the total number of syllables can be determined by adding the sum of decasyllables—14 sonnets x 14 lines x 10 syllables = 1960 syllables—to the number of alexandrine syllables: 15 sonnets x 14 lines x 12 syllables = 2520 syllables. This gives us 4480 syllables. The two central syllables will therefore be the 2240th and the 2241st. Where they fall in the sequence can be determined if we add the total number of syllables in each metric group and keep a running tally until syllables 2240 and 2241 are reached:

Sonnets 1 through 2: 2 sonnets x 14 lines x 12 syllables: 336 syllables. Total so far: 336.

Sonnets 3 through 4: 2 sonnets x 14 lines x 10 syllables: 280 syllables. Total so far: 616.

Sonnets 5 through 11: 7 sonnets x 14 lines x 12 syllables: 1176 syllables. Total so far: 1792.

Sonnets 12 through 17: 6 sonnets x 14 lines x 10 syllables: 840 syllables. Total so far: 2632.

The two central syllables are therefore somewhere in the group of decasyllabic sonnets between 12 and 17. To find precisely where, we bear in mind that each sonnet in this decasyllabic group has 140 syllables (14 lines x 10 syllables per line). Because 2240–1792 = 448, it will be the 448th in this metric group. Sonnets 12 through 14 = 3 sonnets x 140 syllables per sonnet = 420 syllables. This means that the 448th syllable in this group—syllable 2240 of the 29 sonnets' total—will be the 28th syllable in sonnet 15. The other central syllable (the 2241st) will be the 29th syllable in sonnet 15.

But this is a strange coincidence, for the number (448) that the first of these two syllables bears within its metric group (sonnets 12 through 17) is strangely similar to the total number of sonnets in the whole sequence, 4480; and the second of these two central syllables, as the 29th in its sonnet, bears the same number as the total number of sonnets: 29. So in this sequence of 29 sonnets comprising 4480 syllables each of the two central syllables seems to refer to one of two available numbers signifying the whole sequence: one to the total number of syllables and the other to the total number of sonnets. What would be the odds of this happening by chance? Astronomical, really.

If La Boétie did it on purpose, it does not follow that Montaigne was aware of it. But then Montaigne would have been blissfully ignorant of a particularly striking "vaine subtilité" at the heart of his first book, as Bellerophon (or Uriah the Hittite) was unaware of the content of the message he was carrying. Indeed, there is something like a message in this center. Here are the two central syllables, in context:

Ce n'est pas moy que l'on abuze ainsi:
    Qu'à quelque enfant ces[19] ruzes on emploie,
    Qui n'a nul goust, qui n'entend *rien qu'il* oyt.

[I'm not a man to suffer such abuse—

---

19. I have corrected the "ses" [her, his] that appears in 1580, 1582, and 1588 to "ces" because "ses" makes no sense, since he is addressing the beloved when he says "Contente toy." Albert-Marie Schmidt makes the same correction in his *Poètes du XVIe siècle* (Paris: Gallimard / Pléiade: 1953), 698.

IV. Journey to the Center of the Book   251

> Try out those ruses on some ignorant child,
> Who, artless, takes in *nothing that he* hears.] (Sonnet 15, lines 1–3)

The message, if there is one, is about nothing—that is, about nothingness. The speaker asserts that he is not naive, not a childlike being who understands nothing that he hears. Metafictionally, we may have permission to read this line a little differently: that it is a question of understanding or not understanding the *rien* that one hears. How then might we readers understand this *rien* that we read? At roughly the same time Montaigne was deleting this *rien* and the sonnets surrounding it, he added the following description of his book to "De la phisionomie": "[Je] ne traicte à point nommé de rien que du rien, ny d'aucune science que de celle de l'inscience" [there is nothing I treat of specifically except of nothing, nor of any knowledge except that of the lack of knowledge] (III: 12, 1057c; 809*). Long before Flaubert, Montaigne, it seems, wrote a book about nothing.[20] So it is weirdly appropriate that there should be a *rien* in the middle of the middle of Book One.

Montaigne quotes La Boétie's poetry twice more in Book One, and on both occasions the middle of the line that is quoted seems to refer to the middle of the sonnets. The first quotation is placed at the beginning of "Du parler prompt ou tardif" [Of prompt or slow speech]: "Onc ne furent à *tous, toutes* graces données" [Never to *all* were *all* graces given] (I: 10, 39a, DM 39; 25*). Totality is twice expressed in the central syllables of this alexandrine line, as totality is twice expressed in the central syllables of the sonnets: the total number of syllables, as the first syllable being exactly one-tenth of the total number of syllables, and the total number of sonnets, as the second syllable being the 29th in the sonnet in which the center appears. Not only that, but the sonnet from which Montaigne took this line (the fourteenth of the 25 sonnets Montaigne published in 1571) refers, just two lines before this one, to a hidden tenth:

> . . . du peuple ay pitié:
> De mil vertus qu'il voit en un corps ordonnees,
> *La dixme* il n'en voit pas, & les laisse pour moy:
> Certes j'en ay pitié; mais puis apres je voy
> Qu'onc ne furent à tous toutes graces donnees.
>
> [. . . I pity the common herd:
> Of a thousand virtues in one body arranged,
> They don't even see *the tenth,* and leave them for me.

---

20. As Terence Cave notes, in commenting on this passage (*The Cornucopian Text: Problems of Writing in the French Renaissance* [Oxford: Clarendon Press, 1979], 309).

Certainly I pity then, but afterwards I see
That never to all were all graces given.] (lines 11–14; Desgraves, vol. 2, 123)

The speaker of the poem is referring to the thousand virtues arranged in the body of his beloved, but in the new context Montaigne gives this passage by quoting it in Book One, where the 29 sonnets occupy center stage, they could be taken to refer to the hidden tenth that no one sees but himself (the common herd do not see the other nine tenths either). It might not be by chance that this quotation begins a *tenth* chapter.

The other line from La Boétie that Montaigne quotes in the First Book appears in "Que le goust des biens et des maux depend en bonne partie de l'opinion que nous en avons" [That the taste of good and evil things depends in large measure on the opinion we have of them]: "Aut fuit, aut veniet, *nihil* est praesentis in illa" [Either it (i.e., death) has been or is to come; *nothing* of the present is in it] (I: 14, 56a; DM 64; 37*). The nothingness that is at the center of the 29 sonnets is at the center again here, thanks to the fact that Montaigne quoted only this one line from his friend's Latin poem and none of the more than three hundred others. In quoting this line, as he did the other one, Montaigne made it stand alone, with a *nihil* in the middle.[21]

---

21. Charles S. Singleton discovered in Dante something analogous to La Boétie's having placed significant numbers at the numerical center of his sonnet sequence as well as to the variable in the poetic structure of the sequence that made such placement possible (Charles S. Singleton, "The Poet's Number at the Center," *MLN* 80 [1965]: 1–10). The variable in La Boétie's case is the meter; specifically, his decision to make some sonnets decasyllabic and some alexandrine, and to distribute these different metrical groups in the precise way he did. For Dante, writes Singleton, "the one variable in the component parts of this poem, as the poet has conceived it, is the length of the cantos," which vary from 115 to 160 verses. What he found was that the seven central cantos of *Purgatory* (in the center of the *Divine Comedy*) display an absolute symmetry in their respective length: 151 + 145 + 145 + 139 + 145 + 145 + 151 lines. What is equally remarkable is that this *seven* (the number of symmetrical cantos at the center) should repeat itself in the *seven*tieth line of this central canto, the exact center of the entire *Divine Comedy*. (Similarly, the 448th syllable at the center of the twenty-nine sonnets is one-tenth of his total number of 4480 syllables.) All this was possible only because of the variable Dante had to play with, just as all that happens in the center of the sonnets is possible only because of the variable the poet had up his sleeve. "Only such a canto length," Singleton writes, "could give us a verse numbered 70 at the precise midpoint of the whole poem." In responding to an attack on Singleton's argument by Richard J. Pegis, who held that such a construction was more likely to have been the product of chance, J. L. Logan invoked Occam's razor: "For it is surely questionable to assume that an organized poetic unit can be treated as if it were merely a random arrangement of unrelated elements" (J. L. Logan, "The Poet's Central Numbers," *MLN* 86 [1971]: 95–98). It is "questionable" because inconsistent with Occam's principle, which orders us to accept the theory which saves the phenomena "with the fewest possible assumptions." That such a phenomenon could have been intended in the *Divine Comedy*, "a special poem in connection with which the word 'random' does not come quickly to mind," seems more likely than not. Neither, in light of what secrets the sonnets reveal, may "random" be the best word to describe the *Essays*, nor the twenty-nine sonnets—nor the interplay between the two.

EPILOGUE
The Playful Text

"Every commentary," writes Yves Delègue in *Montaigne et la mauvaise foi,* adding that his own is no exception, "is in the final analysis only a montage of quotations reassembled in a certain order. It takes apart the work under the pretext of making the 'truth' come out at last. The commentator's avowed wish . . . is to disappear once he has thus redealt the cards, as if all by themselves they could play the game of transparency" (10–11). Given the barrage of quotations from the *Essays* with which I have assaulted the reader, Delègue's characterization seems especially apt. It has indeed been my hope that if I lined up side by side the passages in symmetrically related chapters where certain words and phrases repeated themselves, then it would become obvious that there is at least that element of structure in the *Essays,* that Montaigne planted those echoing words there on purpose, and that ever since 1580 he has been waiting for someone to realize that every symmetrical pair could be read as a single text. I would be glad to disappear once that truth has been unveiled and let the text speak for itself. I would only point out that the "certain order" in which I present these quotations is not mine but Montaigne's.

On different grounds, but with the reference to many of the same passages where we have seen Montaigne inviting the reader to complete his work, Michel Jeanneret argues that Montaigne doesn't want his work to die with him, but to continue coming into existence after his death with the assistance of the "lecteur suffisant" [sufficient reader] to whom he appeals in I: 24. Such a reader "descouvre souvant ès escritz d'autruy des perfections autres que celles que l'autheur y a mises & aperceües, & y preste des sens & des visages plus riches" [often discovers in others' writings perfections beyond those that the author put in or perceived, and lends them richer meanings and aspects] (I: 24, 127a; 93*). Given the wealth of parallels between the chapter where this passage appears and I: 34, its symmetrical counterpart, where Montaigne likewise writes of perfections emerging in a work of art independently of its creator's awareness, it is difficult to conceive of him being as unaware as such a creator. According to Jeanneret, Montaigne wants to make the reader "a partner" for whom he "created numerous occasions . . . to intervene" and "deliberately made the reception, or rather diverse receptions that would ensue an active posthumous destiny for the *Essays,* an integral part of the book." The reader "has to reconstruct missing articulations, put the disorder in order."[1] Jeanneret is not alluding to the overall structure of the *Essays* that concerns us here, but rather to what he calls "intentional failings in the organization of the text" of individual chapters. Yet this does speak to the kind of completion that I argue Montaigne has been waiting for, that of matching each chapter to its other half.

Montaigne appeals for a sharp-eyed reader to take in the whole picture: "Il est impossible de renger les pieces, à qui n'a une forme du tout en sa teste" [A man who does not have in his head a picture of the whole cannot possibly arrange the pieces] (II: 1, 337a, DM 9; 243*). "Dieu . . . voit en l'immensité de son ouvrage l'infinité des formes qu'il y a comprinses; et est à croire que cette figure qui nous estonne, se rapporte et tient à quelque autre figure de mesme genre inconnu à l'homme. De sa toute sagesse il ne part rien que bon et commun et reglé; mais nous n'en voyons pas l'assortiment et la relation" [God . . . sees in the immensity of his work the infinity of forms that he has comprised in it; and it is for us to believe that this figure that astonishes us is related and linked to some other figure of the same kind unknown to man. From his infinite wisdom there proceeds nothing but that is good and common and regular; but we do not see their arrangement and relationship] (II: 30, 713c; 539*).

The *Essays* are a playful book, hiding their artfulness in some ways and revealing it in others. André Tournon complains that Montaigne's "express declarations" deny the possibility of a hidden order ("Organisation des Essais," in *Dictionnaire de Michel de Montaigne,* 847). But François Rigolot

---

1. Michel Jeanneret, *Perpetual Motion: Transforming Shapes in the Renaissance from da Vinci to Montaigne,* tr. Nidra Poller (Baltimore: Johns Hopkins University Press, 2001), 275.

argues that Montaigne is part of a long tradition of concealing art with art: "From the 'corps rappiecez' to the 'pieces décousues,'" in reading the *Essays* "we are always in the enchanting aporia of *art without art*. 'Ars adeo latet arte sua' [Thus art is hidden by its own art], as Ovid wrote in the *Metamorphoses* (X, 252)."[2] Despite the concealment Montaigne keeps lifting the veil by making the very thing that repeats from one chapter to its symmetrical partner allude to the fact of its existence. For example, in I: 9, a chapter on lying ("Des menteurs"), he says that a liar better have a good memory, but that his is worse than anyone else's; but in I: 49 he claims he can remember what no one else can, showing himself to be a bad liar with a bad memory. In both I: 24 and I: 34 chance "surpasses" the "science" of an artist, allowing him to better his work without intending to, as if it were by mere chance that chance would do its works so well in symmetrically related chapters. The motif of getting two for one appears in both I: 26 and I: 32, giving us one motif in two places (that are, I argue, one place since symmetrical chapters form a unit). II: 30 prophesies backward, "à reculons," to the earlier appearance in II: 8 of that same expression. Fingers are intertwined in both II: 12 and II: 26, and in II: 12 they give the illusion of two for one. One's "veue" [sight] is altered in both II: 13 and II: 25, though it would take the stereoscopic sight discussed in II: 25 to see it. The motif of restated words is itself restated in II: 14 and II: 24. Chapters II: 15 and II: 23 fight their own civil war by presenting opposing opinions on the desirability of civil war. The *Essays* are famously "consubstantial" with their author in II: 18, but the chapter in which that assertion appears is itself consubstantial with II: 20, where the only other consubstantiality in Book Two appears. III: 2 and III: 12 steal from each other the theme of hiding one's theft by both speaking of "larrecins desrobés." III: 6 and III: 8 borrow from each other the theme of borrowing, each alluding to being rich with a borrowed capacity, with what is not "le sien" [one's own].

All this playful self-reference may mean that Montaigne does not always mean what he says. For the seriousness of many an assertion may be undercut—ironized—when its words crop up in a different and apparently unrelated context somewhere else, and when that somewhere else is a chapter that is not thematically or logically but structurally—which is to say, depending on one's point of view, esthetically, or arbitrarily—connected to the one in which it was originally found. Of course this irony does not overwhelm everything in the *Essays*. While the symmetrical doubling reveals the hidden

---

2. François Rigolot, *Les Métamorphoses de Montaigne* (Paris: Presses Universitaires de France, 1988), 82. The italics are Rigolot's.

value of the otherwise puzzling short chapters, it does not always touch at the heart of the longer ones. For instance, what is shared by I: 32 and I: 26 has nothing to do with the education of children, the latter's great theme. On the other hand, just about all of I: 32, one of the very brief chapters, finds its double in I: 26. Roughly the first half of II: 34 seems to be in conversation with the briefer II: 4, including what both say about Julius Caesar, but the entire second half, where Montaigne focuses on other aspects of the man, has no equivalent in the matching chapter. This makes one wonder if there might not be some other structural principle at work here connecting that second half to some other chapter; the most fruitful avenue of approach for finding it may well be the sequential approach championed by Sayce and Meijer.

Yet the "nothing" waiting to be discovered at the center of the first of the *Essays'* three interconnecting centers—"qui n'entend *rien* qu'il oye" [who understands *nothing* that he hears] (Sonnet 15, line 3)—does hold out the teasing suggestion that the *Essays* are about (at least in a literal sense: built about) precisely that, nothing. At the same time, another tease suggests itself: that he who focuses so intently on this "rien" is not understanding the "rien" he hears. But like the liar paradox, this reads both ways. If it is a warning, it was nevertheless put there on purpose. As Montaigne once said of his cat (II: 12, 452c; 331), who knows if his text is playing with the reader or the reader with the text?

APPENDIX

Below are most of the lexical echoes connecting symmetrical chapters. Indicated in **boldface** are those that appear only in the two chapters in question. Occurrences are based on Roy E. Leake's *Concordance des Essais de Montaigne* (Geneva: Droz, 1981).

I: 1 / I: 57
    1. "commune façon" / "façon commune"
    2. **"outre . . . prescript"** / **"prescript . . . outre-passée"** [within Book One]
    3. "piqué" / "pique"

I: 2 / I: 56
    1. in the "giron" of "la jouissance" / in the "giron" of "la loi divine"
    2. "en son escole & en public" / "publie . . . aux escoles"
    3. noncommunicative "contenance" / noncommunicative "contenance"

I: 3 / I: 55
    1. "descouvrir" / "couvrir" a defect
    2. "inhumer," "inhumer" / "Posthume"
    3. "s'emportent" (title), "porter," "raporter," "porter," "porter," "portoient" / "porter," "se portent"
    4. "attaché," "attachast"/ "s'attache"
    5. **"change . . . selon"** / **"changent . . . selon"**

I: 4 / I: 54
  1. "plomb" / "plomb" [within Book One]
  2. "un faux subject . . . n'inventons nous" / "un rare subject . . . nostre invention"
  3. "rencontre" / "rencontrent," "se rencontrent"
  4. "vain . . . frivole" / "frivoles et vaines"

I: 5 / I: 53
  1. "dehors . . . sentit . . . faillir" / "hors . . . sentirions . . . defaillantes"
  2. "faute de coeur . . . fiance" / "fiance . . . crainte"

I: 6 / I: 52
  1. "au retour" / "retourner"
  2. "desrobées" / "desrobé," "desrobé"

I: 7 / I: 51
  1. "effaictz . . . effectuer . . . parole" / "effects . . . babil," "effectz . . . paroles," "effects . . . mots," "motz . . . effect"
  2. "faillant à sa parole" / "defaillance" because of "paroles" [1580 only]

I: 8 / I: 50
  1. "l'oisiveté . . . cheval" / "oysives . . . cheval"
  2. "semences," "semance" / "Semant"
  3. "sans ordre, et sans propos" / "sans dessein et sans promesse" (only instances of "sans . . . et sans . . . pro- . . ." with regard to the *Essays'* construction)

I: 9 / I: 49
  1. "mot . . . en latin" / "mot . . . en Latin"
  2. "se diversifie . . . mesme . . . contraires . . . un mesme" / "un mesme . . . diverses . . . contraires"

I: 10 / I: 48
  1. "rouet" / "rouet" (both causing failure)
  2. "harangue" / "harangue" (both as one of two harangues)

I: 11 / I: 47
  1. "à digerer" / "à digerer" (both in the sense of having too much to digest)

I: 12 / I: 46
  1. "reculant" / "se recula" (both accompanied by reproaches and an allusion to ancestors)

1: 13 / I: 45
  1. "mieux . . . de se faire attendre" / "mieux . . . qu'attendant"
  2. "aller au devant" / "ayant envoyé devant"

I: 14 / I: 44
  1. "establissans leurs affaires domestiques" / "apres avoir mis ordre à ses affaires domestiques"
  2. "l'unique port" / "du port d'Utique"
  3. "Combien voit-on de personnes populaires & communes" / "voir . . . les grands personnages"
  4. Alexander seeking danger instead of repose / Alexander seeking repose in the face of danger

I: 15 / I: 43
  1. "la coustume . . . la grandeur du prince" / "grandeur . . . prince . . . la coustume"

I: 16 / I: 42
  1. "l'Empereur Julien" / "Julien l'Empereur" [within Book One]

I: 17 / I: 41
  1. not to communicate "à son maistre" / not to communicate "à son maistre"
  2. not relaying a message from "l'Empereur Charles cinquiesme" / not relaying a message to "l'Empereur Charles cinquiesme"
  3. "communication . . . gloire" / "De ne communiquer sa gloire" (title)
  4. acquiring a new "reputation" / abandoning one's "reputation"

I: 18 / I: 40
  1. "renger . . . soutenir" / "se soutienent . . . rangez"
  2. "se renger . . . teste" / "ranger . . . testes"

I: 19 / I: 39
  1. "alongement . . . de vie" ["prolongation . . . de vie" after 1588] / "prolongement de vie"
  2. "nostre heur" (title) / "nostre heur"
  3. the "bout" of a "vie" / "ce bout de vie"

I: 20 / I: 38
  1. "enfans . . . masquez" / "masque . . . enfans"
  2. "pleurer . . . cent ans" / "siecle . . . larmes"

I: 21 / I: 37
  1. suicide because of "frayeur" / suicide because of "crainte"
  2. "l'essence" / "l'essence" [1580 only]
  3. "produit en son front" / "visage . . . produire"
  4. un "enfant" as a poor judge of literary value / an "enfant" as a good judge of literary value
  5. "veue ferme" / "veue ferme"

I: 22 / I: 36
   1. "generale police" / "generale police"
   2. "enterremens" / "enterre"

I: 23 / I: 35
   1. against a new law because the "police" would suffer / in favor of a new law because of a defect in our "polices" (title)

I: 24 / I: 34
   1. "surpassans . . . sa science" / "Surpassa . . . la science"
   2. "il feroit quelque sacrifice" / "il fairoit quelque sacrifice"
   3. "Triumvirs . . . la cruauté des Tyrans" / "la tyrannie du Triumvirat . . . leur cruauté"

I: 25 / I: 33
   1. "fille . . . nourrie" / "fille . . . / nourrie"
   2. "se desmeler des appats de la *volupté*" / "De fuir les *voluptez* au pris de la vie" (title)
   3. "*philosophes retirez* de toute occupation publique" / "de se *retirer* de céte presse du monde, à quelque vie solitaire, tranquille & *philosophique*"

I: 26 / I: 32
   1. "chastiement" / "chastiemens" (both with rods) [within Book One]
   2. "boire chaud, boire froid" / "souffler le chaud & le froid"

I: 27 / I: 31
   1. "prognostique des choses futures" / "prognostique les choses à venir"
   2. "se sont laissés piper" / "s'estre laissés piper"
   3. "simplesse" associated with falsity / a "simple" person as a source of truth
   4. ignorance of a "riviere" leads to unfounded conclusions / knowledge of a "riviere" leads to unfounded conclusions

I: 28 / I: 30
   1. "si entiere & si parfaite" / "entiere & parfaicte" [within Book One]
   2. "la generation" one of the "fins" of "mariage" [1580 only] / the "principale fin" of "le mariage" is "la generation"
   3. "immoderée" / "immoderée" [within Book One]
   4. "ès mains" / "maniement"
   5. "aspre" / "aspre"

II: 1 / II: 37
   1. "assortir ces pieces" / "proportionner et rapporter" "ces pieces"
   2. "pieces rapportées" / "rapporter" "ces pieces"

II: 2 / II: 36
   1. "foy en ses parolles" / "foy en ses parolles"
   2. "parloit peu" / "parla si peu"

II: 3 / II: 35
1. "s'alla precipiter en la mer," "se precipiter en la mer" / "se precipiteroient en la mer" [1580 only]
2. "le sage *vit tant qu'il doit,* non pas tant qu'il peut" / "la loy de *vivre* aus gens de bien ce n'est pas autant qu'il leur plait, mais *autant qu'ils doivent*"

II: 4 / II: 34
1. Amyot's Plutarch is "nostre breviaire" / Caesar's Commentaries should be "le breviaire" of any man of war
2. Amyot's Plutarch praised for its "pureté du langage" / Caesar's Commentaries praised for "une façon de dire si pure"

II: 5 / II: 33
1. "alarmes" / "alarmes" [within Book Two]
2. "gehennes," "a gehenné" / "geiner"

II: 6 / II: 32
1. "pour mort," "pour mort" / "pour mort"
2. "tirassé" / "tirassé" [within Book Two]
3. "tout meurtry" / "tout meurtry"
4. "perdu ... sentimens" / " perdu ... sentiment"

II: 7 / II: 31
1. "nourriture de ses enfans" / "nourriture des enfans"
2. "espandre ... mespris" / "espandent ... mesprise"
3. "emploie ... occasions" / "employe ... occasions"

II: 8 / II: 30
1. "enfans ... parfaits" / "enfant imparfait"
2. "estrangeté" as a source of profit / "estrangeté" as a source of profit
3. malformed children who "pendent ... au col" / a malformed child who seemed to "accoler" another and whose limbs were "pendans"
4. "à reculons / "à reculons"

II: 9 / II: 29
1. "nations ... alloient à la guerre sans armes" [altered post-1588] / "nation[s] ... alloient à la guerre nudz, sauf un glaive"
2. "nations ... alloient à la guerre sans armes sans *se couvrir,* d'autres *se couvroient* de vaines armes" [altered post-1588] / "nation[s] ... alloient à la guerre nudz, sauf un glaive ... & le corps seulement *couvert* d'un linge blanc"

II: 10 / II: 28
1. reading that doesn't interrupt sleep: "sommeiller" / sleep that doesn't interrupt reading: "qui n'interrompit pas seulement son sommeil"

II: 11 / II: 27
1. "*De la cruauté*" (title) / "Couardise mere *de la cruauté*" (title)
2. "tout ce qui est au dela de la mort simple me semble pure cruauté" / "Tout ce qui est au dela de la mort simple, me semble pure cruauté"
3. "s'exercer" against something / "s'exercer" against something
4. "cruellement... cruauté... mollesse... ois... gemir" / "mollesse... cruels... ouyr... gemir... cruellement"
5. "ames... estat... desesperées" / "desespoir... estat... l'ame"
6. "foïter... foitez" / "fouëtte"
7. "chien la feste" / "la feste... chiens"

II: 12 / II: 26
1. "succe"/ "entresucçoint" [within Books One and Two]
2. "entrelassé" involving a finger / "s'entrelasser" involving thumbs
3. "entrelasseures," "entrelassant," "entrelassemens" / "s'entrelasser"
4. "excellons sur les" / "exceller sur les" [altered post-1588]
5. "pollere" / "pollere"
6. "pollice" / "pollice" [1580 only]
7. "pouce" / "Des pouces" (title), "pouces"

II: 13 / II: 25
1. "veüe alterée" / "à yeux clos," "l'oeil gauche bandé... éborgnés," "borgnes... bicles," "la cecité," "aveugle," "la veüe... hebetée"

II: 14: / II: 24
1. "un grand nombre d'escus" / "trois millions six cens mill'escus"
2. "circonference" / "circonscrit... ce cercle"

II: 15 / II: 23
1. problematic "abondance" / problematic "superabondance"
2. "Pour tenir l'amour en haleine," "pour nous estre remis en haleine" / "pour tenir leurs hommes en haleine"

II: 16 / II: 22
1. "raporter nouvelles" / "recevoir... nouvelles"
2. "marque... lettre... inventions... lettre... inventions" / "invention... marque... lettres"

II: 17 / II: 21
1. "fay-neant" / "la faineantise" (title) [within Book Two]
2. "*embesongné à* cête *belle* vacation" / "l'ame & le corps *embesoignés à* choses *belles*"
3. "en publicq... cracher... essuyer le visage" (from perspiration) / "en public... cracher ou suer"
4. "monstroit... visage à tout sens" / "montrer visage à tous sens"

II: 18 / II: 20
  1. "commodité . . . service" / "l'accommoder à nostre service" [altered post-1588]
  2. **"consubstantiel"** / **"consubstantialité"** [within Book Two]

III: 1 / III: 13
  1. **"De *l'utile* et de *l'honneste*"** (title), "qui faict difference, entre les choses *utiles*, & les *honnestes*" / "tout ce qui est *utile* est aussi juste & *honneste*" [within Book Three]
  2. "naturelles . . . mais necessaires" / "la necessité naturelle"
  3. a "bastiment" where everything has its place / a "bastiment" where everything has its place
  4. "pieds" of an "asne" / "coups de pied" from a "mule"
  5. **"Esope"** / **"Esope"** [within Book Three]
  6. **"chiens"** who eat a dead body / **"chiens"** who try to eat a dead body [within Book Three]
  7. "le suffoqua" by water / "soffucast" by water
  8. "pendre . . . bourse" / "bourse . . . pendus"
  9. "mesler . . . Epaminondas . . . mesler . . . facilité des meurs" / "facilité . . . Epaminondas . . . mesler . . . meurs"
  10. **"marioit"** disparate things / **"mariage"** of disparate things [within Book Three]

III: 2 / III: 12
  1. **"ravisemens"** / **"ravisement"** [within Book Three]
  2. "Du repentir" (title) / "repentir"
  3. "desrobez . . . larrecin" / "Je desrobe mes larrecins"
  4. "au dedans" worse than "de deshors" / "au dedans" worse than "au dehors"
  5. "hume" / "hume"
  6. "son propre venin" / "son propre venin"
  7. "s'en empoisonne" / "s'empoisonne"

III: 3 / III: 11
  1. "ne connois non plus Venus" / "ne cognoit pas Venus"
  2. "soit envers les males, soit envers les femelles . . . fortune" / "la fortune . . . se dict des masles comme des femelles"
  3. "pour . . . fuyr" (women fleeing men) / "pour fuir" (women fleeing men)
  4. an ill-formed woman's enticing **"mouvement"** / an ill-formed woman's enticing **"mouvement"**
  5. women's **"parties matrimoniales"** / women's **"parties genitales"** [within Book Three]
  6. "l'ame s'y exerce, mais le corps" does not / "sans grand exercice du corps"
  7. "dorment . . . les jambes" / "endormit ses jambes"

III: 4 / III: 10
  1. **"peu de chose nous tient"** / **"peu de choses . . . me tiennent"**
  2. "la vengeance . . . en distraire" / "en distrayons . . . la vengeance"
  3. "rougissant . . . Frivole cause" / "rougir . . . occasion . . . frivole"
  4. "constance" when confronted with fire / "constance" when confronted with ice
  5. golden "pommes" / golden "pomme"

III: 5 / III: 9
1. "les imperfections" / "Les imperfections"
2. "je corrige" / "je ne corrige pas"
3. "S'il y a quelque personne d'honneur . . . compagnie . . . mes humeurs . . . je . . . iray" / "s'il advient que mes humeurs . . . quelque honneste homme . . . je . . . irois"
4. "Misce stultitiam consilius brevem" / "Il faut avoir un peu de folie qui ne veut avoir plus de sottise"
5. "bossu" / "bossu" (as hunchback, and with this spelling)
6. "à un estomac tendre" / "Aux estomacs tendres"
7. "tendron" / "tendrons"
8. "vanité," "vanité / "vanité" (title)
9. "marriage" as "amitié" / "l'amitié maritale"

III: 6 / III: 8
1. "Roy de Mexico" / "Roy . . . de Mexico" [within Book Three]
2. "donner à un tiers, chose qui n'estoit pas sienne" / "il faut sçavoir ce qui est sien, & ce qui ne l'est point"
3. "triomphes" / "triomphe" in the sense of a triumphal procession [within Book Three]
4. "nous ne voyons . . . guere arriere" / "Nos yeux ne voient rien en derriere"

I: 28 / I: 29
1. "cette *souveraine* et maistresse *amitié*" / "l'amitié souveraine"
2. "Nous estions à *moitié* de tout. Il me semble que je luy desrobe *sa part*" / "la *moitié* de *sa part*"

I: 29 / II: 19
1. "Contente toi" / "Contente toy"
2. "de m'avoir . . . / Fermé les yeux" / "de m'avoir osté la veue"

I: 29 / III: 7
1. "forte lumière" / "forte lumiere"

II: 19 / III: 7
1. "n'ayants peu ce qu'ils vouloient, ils ont faict semblant de vouloir ce qu'ils pouvoient" / "Puisque nous ne la pouvons aveindre, vengeons nous à en mesdire"
2. "lascher . . . relascher par la facilité & par l'aysance . . . la difficulté" / "difficulté . . . aysance & láche facilité"

WORKS CITED

Ammianus Marcellinus. *The History.* Translated by J. C. Rolfe. Cambridge: Harvard University Press / Loeb Classical Library, 1937.
Aulus Gellius. *Noctes Atticae (Attic Nights).* On the web at: http://penelope.uchicago.edu/Thayer/E/Roman/Texts/Gellius/home.html.
Beaujour, Michel. "*Les Essais:* Une mémoire intratextuelle." In *Textes et Intertextes: Études sur le XVIe siècle pour Alfred Glauser,* edited by Floyd Gray and Marcel Tetel, 29–45. Paris: Nizet, 1979.
———. *Poetics of the Literary Self-Portrait.* Translated by Yara Milos. New York: New York University Press, 1991.
Beck, William J. "Montaigne face à l'homosexualité." *Bulletin de la société des amis de Montaigne.* 6th series: 9–10 (1982): 41–50.
Blakewell, Sarah. *How to Live: Or, a Life of Montaigne in One Question and Twenty Attempts at an Answer.* New York: Other Press, 2010.
Blum, Claude. "L'édition des *Essais* à travers les âges: histoire d'un sinistre." In Claude Blum and André Tournon, eds., *Éditer les* Essais *de Montaigne:* 5–19.
———. "La Pléiade en habits de Gournay." *Nouveau Bulletin de la Société Internationale des Amis de Montaigne* 3 (1er semestre 2008): 55–70.
Blum, Claude, and André Tournon, eds. *Éditer les* Essais *de Montaigne: Actes du Colloque tenu à l'Université Paris IV–Sorbonne les 27 et 28 janvier 1995.* Paris: Honoré Champion, 1997.
Bowen, Barbara. "What does Montaigne mean by 'marqueterie'?" *Studies in Philology* 67. 2 (1970): 147–55.
Brody, Jules. "'Du repentir' (III: 2): A Philological Reading." *Yale French Studies* 64 (1983): 238–72.

———. "Montaigne, *Des coches* (III: 6), anatomie d'une lecture 'philologique.'" *Bulletin de la Société des Amis de Montaigne* 7: 31–32 (July–December 2003): 47–75.

———. *Nouvelles lectures de Montaigne.* Paris: Honoré Champion, 1994.

Brooks, Cleanth. *The Well Wrought Urn.* New York: Harcourt Brace, 1947; 1975.

Brown, Frieda S. "'By Diverse Means We Arrive at the Same End': Gateway to the *Essays*." In *Approaches to Teaching Montaigne's Essays,* edited by Patrick Henry, 138–45. New York: Modern Language Association of America, 1994.

———. "« Si le chef d'une place assiegée doit sortir pour parlementer » and « L'heure des parlemens dangereuse »: Montaigne's Political Morality and Its Expression in the Early Essays." In *O un Amy! Essays on Montaigne in Honor of Donald M. Frame,* edited by Raymond C. La Charité, 72–87. Lexington, KY: French Forum Publishers, 1977.

Butor, Michel. *Essais sur les Essais.* Paris: Gallimard, 1968.

Cave, Terence. *The Cornucopian Text: Problems of Writing in the French Renaissance.* Oxford: Clarendon Press, 1979.

Corbeill, Anthony. "Thumbs in Ancient Rome: 'Pollex' as Index." *Memoirs of the American Academy in Rome* 42 (1997): 1–21.

Chalcocondylas, Laonicus. *L'Histoire de la Décadence de l'Empire Grec, et Establissement de celuy de Turcs.* Translated by Blaise de Vigenère. 1620 (orig. 1577). Available online at Google Books.

Charpentier, Françoise. "Figure de La Boétie dans les 'Essais' de Montaigne." *Revue française de psychanalyse* 52 (January–February 1988): 175–89.

———. "Les poésies françaises d'Étienne de La Boétie." In *Étienne de La Boétie: Sage révolutionnaire et poète perigourdin. Actes du Colloque International, Duke University 1999,* 107–8.

Claes, Paul. *Concatenatio Catulliana: A New Reading of the Carmina.* Amsterdam: J. C. Gieben, 2002.

Compagnon, Antoine. "A Long Short Story: Montaigne's Brevity." *Yale French Studies* 64 (1983): 24–50.

Cotgrave, Randle. *A Dictionarie of the French and English Tongues* (London, 1611). Available at http://www.pbm.com/~lindahl/cotgrave/.

Cottrell, Robert D. *Sexuality / Textuality.* Columbus: The Ohio State University Press, 1981.

Dacos, Nicole. *La découverte de la Domus Aurea et la formation des grotesques à la Renaissance.* London: The Warburg Institute, 1969.

Delègue, Yves. "*De l'art de conferer* (III, 8) ou de la 'sottise.'" *Bulletin de la Société des Amis de Montaigne* 8: 29–30 (January–June 2003): 29–42.

———. *Montaigne et la mauvaise foi: L'écriture de la vérité.* Paris: Honoré Champion, 1998.

Desan, Philippe. *Montaigne dans tous ses états.* Fasano, Italy: Schena editore, 2001.

Dictionnaire de Michel de Montaigne. Edited by Philippe Desan. Paris: Honoré Champion, 2007.

Douglas, Mary. *Thinking in Circles: An Essay on Ring Composition.* New Haven: Yale University Press, 2007.

Duval, Edwin M. *The Design of Rabelais's* Quart Livre de Pantagruel. Geneva: Droz, 1998.

———. *The Design of Rabelais's* Tiers Livre de Pantagruel. Geneva: Droz, 1997.

———. "Le début des 'Essais' et la fin d'un livre." *Revue d'Histoire Littéraire de la France* 99. 5 (1988): 896–907.

———. "Lessons of the New World: Design and Meaning in Montaigne's 'Des Cannibales' (1: 31) and 'Des coches' (III: 6)." *Yale French Studies* 64 (1983): 95–112.

Étienne de La Boétie: Sage révolutionnaire et poète perigourdin. Actes du Colloque International, Duke University 1999. Paris: Honoré Champion, 2004.

Fenoaltea, Doranne. *Du palais au jardin: L'architecture des Odes de Ronsard*. Geneva: Droz, 1990.

Filho, Celso Martins Azar Filho. "Le premier chapitre des *Essais*." *Bulletin de la Société des Amis de Montaigne* 8. 37–38 (January–June 2005): 15–30.

Friedrich, Hugo. *Montaigne*. Translated by Dawn Eng. Berkeley: University of California Press, 1991.

Garavini, Fausta. "Le Fantasme de la mort muette (à propos de I, 2, 'De la tristesse')." *Bulletin de la Société des Amis de Montaigne* 7.13–16 (July–December 1988 / January–June 1989): 127–39.

———. *Monstres et chimères: Montaigne, le texte et le fantasme*. Translated by Isabel Picon. Paris: Honoré Champion, 1993.

Gendre, André. "Les 29 sonnets d'Estienne de La Boétie publiés dans les *Essais* de Montaigne." *Montaigne Studies* 6.1–2 (October 1999): 45–60.

Glauser, Alfred. *Montaigne paradoxal*. Paris: Nizet, 1972.

Gray, Floyd. "Montaigne's Friends." *French Studies* 15.3 (July 1961): 203–12.

Hampton, Timothy. *Fictions of Embassy: Literature and Diplomacy in Early Modern Europe*. Ithaca: Cornell University Press, 2009.

Hardie, Philip, ed. *Virgil: Critical Assessments of Classical Authors, volume 1: General Articles and the Eclogues*. New York: Routledge, 1999.

Harpham, Geoffrey. *On the Grotesque: Strategies of Contradiction in Art and Literature*. Princeton: Princeton University Press, 1982.

Henry, Patrick. "Ces vers se voient ailleurs." *Bulletin de la Société des Amis de Montaigne* 3–4 (1980): 77–80.

———. "Reading Montaigne Contextually: 'De l'incommodité de la grandeur' (III, 7)." *The French Review* 61.6 (May 1988): 859–65.

Herodotus. *Herodotus*. Translated by A. D. Godley. Cambridge: Harvard University Press / Loeb Library), 1981.

Hoffmann, George. *Montaigne's Career*. Oxford: Clarendon Press, 1998.

Jakobson, Roman. *Language in Literature*. Cambridge: Harvard University Press, 1987.

Jakobson, Roman, and Krystyna Pomorska. *Dialogues*. Cambridge: MIT Press, 1988.

Jeanneret, Michel. *Perpetual Motion: Transforming Shapes in the Renaissance from da Vinci to Montaigne*. Translated by Nidra Poller. Baltimore: Johns Hopkins University Press, 2001.

Kritzman, Lawrence. *Destruction/Découverte: Le Fonctionnement de la Rhétorique dans les "Essais" de Montaigne*. Lexington, KY: French Forum Publishers, 1980.

———. *The Fabulous Imagination: On Montaigne's Essais*. New York: Columbia University Press, 2009.

La Boétie, Étienne de. *Montaigne's Essay on Friendship, and XXIX Sonnets by Estienne de La Boétie*. Translated by Louis How. Boston: Houghton Mifflin, 1915.

———. *Oeuvres complètes d'Estienne de La Boétie*. 2 vols. Edited by Louis Desgraves. Bordeaux: William Blake, 1991.

———. "Translation of *The Twenty-nine Sonnets*" by Randolph Paul Runyon. In *Freedom over Servitude: Montaigne, La Boétie, and On Voluntary Servitude*, edited by David Lewis Schaefer, 223–35. Westport, CT: Greenwood Press, 1998.

La Charité, Raymond C. "The Coherence of Montaigne's First Book." *L'Esprit Créateur* 20.1 (Spring 1980): 36–45.

Leake, Roy E. *Concordance des Essais de Montaigne*. Geneva: Droz, 1981.
Legros, Alain. *Essais sur poutres: Peintures et inscriptions chez Montaigne*. Paris: Klincksieck, 2000.
Littré, Émile. *Dictionnaire de la langue française*. Paris: 1877. Available at http://francois.gannaz.free.fr/Littre/accueil.php .
Logan, J. L. "The Poet's Central Numbers." *MLN* 86 (1971): 95–98.
Maclean, Ian. "Montaigne, Cardano: The Reading of Subtlety/The Subtlety of Reading." *French Studies* 37.2 (1983): 143–56.
Macphail, Eric. "Mémoire." In *Dictionnaire de Montaigne*, 748–50.
Magnien, Michel. "De l'hyperbole à l'ellipse: Montaigne face aux sonnets de La Boétie." *Montaigne Studies* 2.1 (September 1990): 7–25.
Martial. *Epigrams. Book 2. Bohn's Classical Library* (1897) at http://www.tertullian.org/fathers/martial_epigrams_book02.htm.
Mathieu-Castellani, Gisèle. *Montaigne: L'écriture de l'essai*. Paris: Presses Universitaires de France, 1988.
———. *Montaigne ou la vérité du mensonge*. Geneva: Droz, 2000.
McKinley, Mary. *Words in a Corner: Studies in Montaigne's Latin Quotations*. Lexington, KY: French Forum Publishers, 1981.
Mehlman, Jeffrey. "La Boétie's Montaigne." *Oxford Literary Review* 4 (1979): 45–61.
Meijer, Marianne S. "Guesswork or Facts: Connections between Montaigne's Last Three Chapters (III: 11, 12, and 13)." *Yale French Studies* 64 (1983): 167–79.
———. "L'ordre des «Essais» dans les deux premiers volumes." In *Montaigne et les Essais: 1580–1980*, edited by Pierre Michel, 17–27. Paris: Honoré Champion, 1983.
———. "'Des postes' et 'Des pouces': Plaisanteries ou points de repère?" In *Columbia Montaigne Conference Papers*, edited by Donald M. Frame and Mary B. McKinley, 105–18. Lexington, KY: French Forum Publishers, 1981.
Montaigne, Michel de. *Essais. Reproduction photographique de l'édition originale de 1580*. 2 vols. Edited by Daniel Martin. Geneva: Slatkine, 1976.
———. *Essais. Reproduction photographique du livre troisième de l'édition originale de 1588*. Edited by Daniel Martin. Geneva: Slatkine, 1988.
———. *Essais. Reproduction photographique de la deuxième édition (Bordeaux 1582)*. Paris: Société des Textes Français Modernes, 2005.
———. *Essais de Michel seigneur de Montaigne (Cinquiesme édition augmentée d'un troisiesme livre et de six cens additions aux deux premiers)*. Paris: L'Angelier, 1588. Available at http://gallica.bnf.fr/ .
———. *Les Essais*. Edited by Pierre Villey. Paris: Presses Universitaires de France, 1965.
———. *Essais de Michel de Montaigne, Livre I*. Edited by André Tournon. Paris: Imprimerie Nationale, 1998.
———. *Les Essais*. Edited by Jean Balsamo, Michel Magnien, and Catherine Magnien-Simonin. Paris: Gallimard / Pléiade, 2007.
———. *Oeuvres complètes*. Edited by Albert Thibaudet and Maurice Rat. Paris: Gallimard / Pléiade, 1962.
———. *The Complete Essays of Montaigne*. Translated by Donald M. Frame. Stanford: Stanford University Press, 1965.
———. Montaigne, *Essais de Michel de Montaigne*. 3 vols. Edited by Emmanuel Naya, Delphine Reguig-Naya, and Alexandre Tarrête. Paris: Gallimard / Folio Classique, 2009.
———. *The Essays of Michel de Montaigne*. Translated by M. A. Screech. New York: Penguin Books, 1991.

———. *The Essayes of Montaigne*. Translated by John Florio. London, 1611. Available at www.luminarium.org/renascence-editions/montaigne/.
Morales, Helen. "Endtext." In Helen Morales and Alison Sharrock, eds., *Intratextuality: Greek and Roman Textual Relations*, 325–29.
Morales, Helen and Alison Sharrock, eds. *Intratextuality: Greek and Roman Textual Relations*. Oxford: Oxford University Press, 2000.
Most, Glenn W. "The Structure and Function of Odysseus' Apologoi." *Transactions of the American Philological Association* 119 (1989): 15–30.
Nakam, Géralde. *Le Dernier Montaigne*. Paris: Honoré Champion, 2002.
———. *Montaigne: La Manière et la matière*. Paris: Honoré Champion, 2006.
New Larousse Encyclopedia of Mythology. Translated by Richard Aldington and Delano Ames. New York: Hamlyn, 1959.
Pérouse, Gabriel-André. "Montaigne, son lecteur et les Vingt-neuf sonnets d'Étienne de La Boétie." *Montaigne Studies* 11.1–2 (1999): 77–86.
Peytavin, Sylvie. "L'exceptionnelle amnésie de Montaigne. Constat ou signe?" *Nouveau Bulletin de la Société Internationale des Amis de Montaigne* 50 (July–December 2009): 91–107.
Plato. *The Collected Dialogues of Plato*. Edited by Edith Hamilton and Huntington Cairns. Princeton: Princeton University Press, 1961.
Plutarch. "Comment il faut que les jeunes gens lisent les poètes" [How young men should read the poets]. Translated by Jacques Amyot. Available at http://www.chass.utoronto.ca/~wulfric/rentexte/amyot/am_txt.htm.
———. "On talkativeness" (De garrulitate). In *Moralia* vol. 6, 429–31. Cambridge: Harvard University Press / Loeb Library, 1939.
Poètes du XVIe siècle. Edited by Albert-Marie Schmidt. Paris: Gallimard / Pléiade, 1953.
Pouilloux, Jean-Yves. *Lire les « essais » de Montaigne*. Paris: Maspero, 1969.
Quint, David. *Montaigne and the Quality of Mercy: Ethical and Political Themes in the Essais*. Princeton: Princeton University Press, 1998.
Reeser, Todd W. *Moderating Masculinity in Early Modern Culture*. Chapel Hill: North Carolina Studies in the Romance Languages and Literatures, 2006.
Regosin, Richard. *The Matter of My Book: Montaigne's* Essais *as the Book of the Self*. Berkeley: University of California Press, 1977.
———. *Montaigne's Unruly Brood: Textual Engendering and the Challenge to Paternal Authority*. Berkeley: University of California Press, 1996.
Rendall, Steven. *Distinguo: Reading Montaigne Differently*. Oxford: Clarendon Press, 1992.
Rigolot, François. *Les métamorphoses de Montaigne*. Paris: Presses Universitaires de France, 1988.
———. "Montaigne's Purloined Letters." *Yale French Studies* 64: 145–66.
Rudd, Niall. "Architecture. Theories about Virgil's *Eclogues*." In Hardie, ed., *Virgil: Critical Assessments of Classical Authors*: 91–115.
Runyon, Randolph Paul. *The Art of the Persian Letters: Unlocking Montesquieu's "Secret Chain."* Newark: University of Delaware Press, 2005.
———. *The Braided Dream: Robert Penn Warren's Late Poetry*. Lexington: University Press of Kentucky, 1990.
———. *The Complete Tales in Verse of Jean de la Fontaine: An Illustrated and Annotated Translation*. Jefferson, NC: McFarland, 2009.
———. "'continuelz discors': The Silent Discourse of *Délie*'s Emblems." *L'Esprit Créateur* 28.2 (1988): 58–67.

———. "The Double Discourse of I:21–25 and I:37–33." In *Montaigne and the Gods: The Mythological Key to the "Essays,"* edited by Daniel Martin. Amherst, MA: Hestia Press, 1993: 131–54.

———. *Ghostly Parallels: Robert Penn Warren and the Lyric Poetic Sequence.* Knoxville: University of Tennessee Press, 2006.

———. *In La Fontaine's Labyrinth: A Thread through the Fables.* Charlottesville, VA: Rookwood Press, 2000.

———. "Montaigne bis." In *Renaissance et Nouvelle Critique,* edited by Raymond Ortali. Valencia, Spain: 1978: 117–34.

———. "Montaigne's Larceny: Book III's Symmetrical Intertexts." In *The Order of Montaigne's "Essays,"* edited by Daniel Martin. Amherst, MA: Hestia Press, 1989: 58–76.

———. "The 'Oblique Gaze': Some Evidence of Symmetry in Montaigne's *Essais* (I: 1–6, 57–52)." In *Essays in European Literature for Walter A. Strauss,* edited by Alice N. Benston and Marshall C. Olds. Manhattan, KS: Studies in Twentieth Century Literature, 1990: 13–26.

———. *Reading Raymond Carver.* Syracuse: Syracuse University Press, 1992.

———. *Intratextual Baudelaire: The Sequential Fabric of the* Fleurs du mal *and* Spleen de Paris. Columbus: The Ohio State University Press, 2010.

———. "La parole gênée: Genèse et palinodie." *Change* 16/17 (1973): 248–64.

———. "La séquence et la symétrie comme principes d'organisation chez Montesquieu, La Fontaine et Montaigne." In *Le Recueil littéraire: Pratiques et théorie d'une forme,* edited by Irène Langlet. Rennes: Presses Universitaires de Rennes, 2003: 177–86.

———. "The Vanishing Center." In *Freedom Over Servitude: Montaigne, La Boétie, and "On Voluntary Servitude,"* edited by David Lewis Schaefer. Westport: Greenwood Press, 1998: 87–113.

Santirocco, Matthew S. *Unity and Design in Horace's Odes.* Chapel Hill: University of North Carolina Press, 1986.

Sayce, R. A. *The Essays of Montaigne: A Critical Exploration.* London: Weidenfeld and Nicolson, 1972.

———. "L'ordre des *Essais* de Montaigne." *Bibliothèque d'Humanisme et de Renaissance* 18 (1956): 7–22.

Schaefer, David Lewis. *The Political Philosophy of Montaigne.* Ithaca: Cornell University Press, 1990.

Scholar, Richard. *Montaigne and the Art of Free-Thinking.* Oxford: Peter Lang, 2010.

Segal, Charles. "*Tamen Cantabitis, Arcades*—Exile and Arcadia in *Eclogues* 1 and 9." In Hardie, ed., *Virgil: Critical Assessments of Classical Authors:* 172–202.

Seneca. *Ad Lucilium Epistulae Morales.* Translated by Richard M. Gummere. Cambridge: Harvard University Press / Loeb Library, 1920.

Sève, Bernard. "Les 'vaines subtilitez': Montaigne et le renversement du pour au contre." *Montaigne Studies* 16.1–2 (March 2004): 185–96.

Singleton, Charles S. "The Poet's Number at the Center." *MLN* 80 (1965): 1–10.

Skutsch, Otto. "Symmetry and Sense in the *Eclogues.*" *Harvard Studies in Classical Philology* 73 (1969): 153–69.

Starobinski, Jean. *Montaigne en mouvement.* Paris: Gallimard, 1982.

Tetel, Marcel. *Montaigne: Updated Edition.* Boston: G. K. Hall / Twayne's World Authors Series, 1990.

Tournon, André. "Du bon usage de l'édition posthume des *Essais.*" *Bulletin de la Société des Amis de Montaigne* 7.29–30 (January–June 2003): 77–91.

———. *La Glose et l'essai.* Lyon: Presses Universitaires de Lyon, 1983.
———. *Route par ailleurs: Le « nouveau langage » des* Essais. Paris: Honoré Champion, 2006.
———. "La segmentation du texte: usages et singularités." In Claude Blum and André Tournon, eds., *Éditer les* Essais *de Montaigne:* 173–96.
Villey, Pierre. *Les sources et l'évolution des "Essais" de Montaigne.* 2 vols. Paris: Hachette, 1908.
Wheeler, Kip. "Literary Terms and Definitions." At http://web.cn.edu/kwheeler/lit_terms_I.html.
Whitman, Cedric W. *Homer and the Homeric Tradition.* Cambridge: Harvard University Press, 1958.
Wright, James R. G. "Virgil's Pastoral Programme: Theocritus, Callimachus and *Eclogue* 1." In Hardie, ed., *Virgil: Critical Assessments of Classical Authors:* 116–71.

INDEX OF NAMES

Aristotle, 11

Balsamo, Jean, 21, 66n35, 134, 172, 227, 228n4
Baudelaire, Charles, 22–23, 24
Beaujour, Michel, 24
Beck, William J., 117n
Blake, William, 23
Blakewell, Sarah, 227n2
Blum, Claude, 21
Bowen, Barbara, 44n, 119
Brahami, Frédéric, 11–12
Brody, Jules, 24, 198–99, 203, 221–24
Brooks, Cleanth, 23–24
Brown, Frieda S., 27, 52–53
Butor, Michel, 4–8, 41, 45, 247

Catullus, 15–17, 22–23
Cave, Terence, 251n
Charpentier, Françoise, 117, 235
Chaucer, Geoffrey, 23
Claes, Paul, 15–17
Compagnon, Antoine, 14
Corbeill, Anthony, 164n

Coste, Pierre, 21–22
Cottrell Robert D., 117n

Dacos, Nicole, 7
Delègue, Yves, 8, 222n11, 226–27, 253
Desan, Philippe, 228–29
Douglas, Mary 18–19
Duval, Edwin, 18, 19, 27, 45n, 218–20

Fenoaltea, Doranne, 18
Filho, Celso Martins Azar, 26
Frame, Donald, 2n2, 228, 242n
Friedrich, Hugo, 27

Garavini, Fausta, 32n13, 160
Gendre, André, 228n5
Glauser, Alfred, 10
Gournay, Marie de, 20–21, 228
Gray, Floyd, 117n

Hampton, Timothy, 83n
Harpham, Geoffrey, 3
Henry, Patrick, 1n, 9n15, 228n5
Herodotus, 58

Hoffmann, George, 52
Homer, 14–15
Horace, 4, 16–17, 23

Jakobson, Roman, 19–20
Jean d'Udine, 7n10
Jeanneret, Michel, 254

Kritzman, Lawrence D., 26, 240n

La Boétie, Étienne de, 2, 30n, 186–87.
    See also I: 28; I: 29.
La Charité, Raymond C., 115n
La Fontaine, Jean de, 22–23
Leake, Roy E., 4
Legros, Alain, 4n6
Logan, J. L., 252n

Maclean, Ian, 49n
Macphail, Eric, 214n
Magnien, Michel, 228n5
Martin, Daniel, 2n2
Mathieu-Castellani, Gisèle, 12–13, 145n, 247n
Maury, Paul, 15, 16n29
McKinley, Mary, 166
Mehlman, Jeffrey, 228n5
Meijer, Marianne, 24, 179n23, 216, 256
Milton, John, 23–24
Montesquieu, 22–23
Morales, Helen, 22
Most, Glenn W., 14

Nakam, Géralde, 7n11, 8n13
Naya, Emmanuel, 2, 3, 246–47
Nero, 2–3
Nicoletto da Modena, 6–7

Ovid, 128, 166, 255

Pérouse, Gabriel-André, 115, 228n5
Peytavin, Sylvie, 214n
Pinturicchio, 7n10

Plato, 233–34
Plutarch, 30n, 127–28, 130–31, 205–6.
    See also II: 32.
Pouilloux, Jean-Yves, 10n16

Quint, David, 27

Rabelais, François, 18, 19
Raphael, 7n10
Reeser, Todd W., 117n
Regosin, Richard, 166n, 226
Rendall, Steven, 27n6
Rigolot, François, 227, 254–55
Ronsard, Pierre de, 18, 21
Rudd, Niall, 16n29

Santirocco, Matthew S., 16–17
Sayce, R. A., 11, 24, 256
Scève, Maurice, 18
Schaefer, David Lewis, 117n
Scholar, Richard, 60–61
Screech, M. A., 52n26, 135, 228
Segal, Charles, 16n28
Sève, Bernard, 43n
Singleton, Charles S., 252n
Skutsch, Otto, 15–16
Starobinski, Jean, 90n39

Tarrête, Alexandre, 52, 53
Tetel, Marcel, 30n
Theocritus, 16
Tournon, André, 1n, 5–8, 10–11, 13, 19, 20–21, 52–53, 62n, 120n, 125n, 216–17, 242, 254

Villey, Pierre, 2n2, 13, 26, 155n, 228
Virgil, 15–16, 23
Vitruvius, 3

Wheeler, Kip, 23
Whitman, Cedric W., 14–15
Wright, James R. G., 16

INDEX TO THE *ESSAYS*

Principal references are in **boldface**.

Au lecteur, 47, 61
I: 1, 10, **26–31**, 78
I: 2, 10, 17, **31–36**
I: 3, **36–40**
I: 4, 5, **41–49**, 76
I: 5, **49–51**, **52–53**
I: 6, **52–55**
I: 7, **55–58**
I: 8, 12–13, **58–62**, 119–20, 238–39
I: 9, 5, **63–66**, 69, 70, 255
I: 10, 9, **66–70**, 251–52
I: 11, 5, **70–72**
I: 12, 5, **72–74**
I: 13, **74–75**
I: 14, 21, **75–78**, 252
I: 15, **78–80**
I: 16, **80–82**, 83
I: 17, **82–84**
I: 18, **84–88**
I: 19, 45, **88–90**
I: 20, 5, **90–92**
I: 21, 5, 34n14, **92–95**

I: 22, 5, **95–96**
I: 23, **96–98**
I: 24, 5, 17, 86, **98–102**, 253–54, 255
I: 25, **102–5**, 162
I: 26, **106–9**, 162, 233n9, 255, 256
I: 27, 5, **109–12**
I: 28, 1–8, 25, **112–18**, 121, 144–45, 219–20, 225–27, 232, 233n9, 234, 236, 240
I: 29, 4–8, 30n, 45, 46, 48, **112–18**, 219, **225–52**, 256
I: 30, 5, **112–18**, 218, 228–29
I: 31, **109–12**, 164, 228–29, 237–38
I: 32, 5, 7, **106–9**, 255, 256
I: 33, 5, **102–5**
I: 34, 5, **98–102**, 254, 255
I: 35, **96–98**
I: 36, 5, **95–96**, 218
I: 37, 5, **92–95**
I: 38, **90–92**
I: 39, 45, 52n27, **88–90**
I: 40, 18–19, 20–21, 52n27, **84–88**, 125
I: 41, 20–21, **82–84**

I: 42, **80–82**, 83, 242
I: 43, **78–80**
I: 44, 5, **75–78**, 154
I: 45, **74–75**
I: 46, **72–74**
I: 47, 5, **70–72**
I: 48, **66–70**
I: 49, **63–66**, 70, 255
I: 50, 13, **58–62**, 120
I: 51, 5, **55–58**
I: 52, **52–55**
I: 53, 5, **49–51**
I: 54, **41–49**, 76
I: 55, **36–40**, 52n24
I: 56, 10, 17, **31–36**
I: 57, 10, **26–31**

II: 1, 8–9, 12, **119–21**, 254
II: 2, **121–25**, 164
II: 3, **125–30**
II: 4, **130–32**, 256
II: 5, **132–36**
II: 6, **136–41**
II: 7, **141–43**
II: 8, 11, **143–48**, 166, 255
II: 9, **149–51**
II: 10, 10, 11, **151–55**, 251–52
II: 11, 5, 7–8, 125, **155–59**
II: 12, 44, 64n, **159–67**, 255
II: 13, **167–72**, 173, 255
II: 14, **172–76**
II: 15, 10, **176–79**
II: 16, **179–82**
II: 17, 9–10, 21, **182–87**, 233n9
II: 18, 12–13, **187–89**, 255

II: 19, 4, 45, 48, 116n, **240–49**
II: 20, **187–89**, 255
II: 21, **182–87**, 242
II: 22, **179–82**
II: 23, 10, **176–79**
II: 24, **172–76**
II: 25, **167–72**, 173, 255
II: 26, **159–67**, 255
II: 27, 5, 7–8, 125, **155–59**
II: 28, **143–48**
II: 29, 5, **149–51**, 238
II: 30, 13, **143–48**, 254, 255
II: 31, **141–43**
II: 32, **136–41**
II: 33, **132–36**
II: 34, **130–32**, 256
II: 35, **125–30**
II: 36, 30n9, **121–25**
II: 37, 12, **119–21**, 128

III: 1, **190–97**, 208
III: 2, 8, 9, **197–203**, 221, 255
III: 3, **203–9**
III: 4, **209–13**
III: 5, 11, 179n23, 196, 208, **213–17**
III: 6, **217–24**, 255
III: 7, 4, 45, 48, 116n, 240, **244–49**
III: 8, 11, 162, **217–24**, 255
III: 9, 10–12, 14, 43–44, 161n, 162, 199, **213–17**, 235
III: 10, **209–13**
III: 11, **203–9**, 233n9
III: 12, 186–87, **197–203**, 221, 233n9, 251, 255, 256
III: 13, 140–41, **190–97**